JOHN LAHR is a theater critic, novelist, biographer and editor. He is the author of two novels, HOT TO TROT and THE AUTOGRAPH HOUND, and two books of essays on theater, UP AGAINST THE FOURTH WALL and ASTONISH ME. His bestselling biography, NOTES ON A COWARDLY LION, chronicles the life and work of his father, American actor and burlesque comic, Bert Lahr, and represents the beginning of his continued inquiry into the nature of comedy. John Lahr is the youngest recipient of the George Jean Nathan Award for Dramatic Criticism.

PRICK UP
YOUR EARS

The Biography of Joe Orton

JOHN LAHR

 A DISCUS BOOK/PUBLISHED BY AVON BOOKS

Selections from *Entertaining Mr. Sloane, Loot, The Good and Faithful Servant, The Ruffian on the Stair, The Erpingham Camp, Funeral Games* and *What the Butler Saw* are reprinted from *Joe Orton, The Complete Plays*, published by Grove Press, Inc., New York, New York, 1977, with permission of the publisher.

AVON BOOKS
A division of
The Hearst Corporation
959 Eighth Avenue
New York, New York 10019

First Discus Printing, February, 1980

DISCUS TRADEMARK REG. U.S. PAT. OFF. AND IN
OTHER COUNTRIES, MARCA REGISTRADA, HECHO EN
U.S.A.

Printed in the U.S.A.

To ANTHEA
&
CHRISTOPHER
Gravity's angels

CONTENTS

ILLUSTRATIONS

Illustrations

ACKNOWLEDGMENTS

"LIFE BEING WHAT IT IS, one seeks revenge," wrote Paul Gauguin. The comedian gets even with laughter: a hostile sharpshooter using his wit to kill the past and defend himself from the present. Joe Orton was the only other person to make me laugh in the theatre the way my father did. In their unique ways, both men created the purest of theatrical experiences: joy. In *Notes on a Cowardly Lion*, I had the good fortune to chronicle at first hand the life and laughter of Bert Lahr. *Prick Up Your Ears* is an extension of my inquiry into the nature of comedy. I consider Joe Orton to be as great a comic playwright as Bert Lahr was a comic actor. They shared, as all comic spirits must, the capacity for being at once mischievous, irreverent, truthful, outrageous, infantile, vulgar, and brilliant. Comedy challenges romantic formulations about creativity, making something beautiful and positive out of a variety of murky emotions. For those unfamiliar with Orton's special brand of humor, a paperback volume of his collected plays is published in England by Eyre Methuen and in America by Grove Press.

Prick Up Your Ears has taken a long time to write—some would say too long. In the biography of Bert Lahr, I had a career of over fifty years with which to deal and access to the beloved grouch himself. With Orton, things were different. Killed in his prime, Orton barely had time to establish himself in public life. His sexual life was anonymous; and his social life was just beginning to be studded with the familiar names in the aristocracy of British show-biz success of which he was a new and glittering member. No one knew him well, or for long. The biography became a mosaic, pieced painstakingly together with his own words and the observations of those whose paths he crossed.

In search of the man and a sympathetic interpretation of his work, the biographer throws a wide net. He relies on the wisdom of friends and the kindness of strangers. Fred Jordan, then of Grove Press, first told me of Orton's diaries in 1970. Peggy Ramsay, who as Orton's agent had suggested he keep a diary as early as 1965, gave me the run of her office and a great deal of time and initial encouragement. She provided me with Orton's diaries (two covering the last six months of his life and an adolescent diary), his clipping books, the various drafts of his plays, and the unpublished novels. She also gave me entrée to London's theatre world and Orton's family. James Price, then head of Allen Lane, commissioned the book but left before I delivered it. Kenneth Williams talked with illuminating candor and affection about both Halliwell and Orton. He trusted my biographical approach, giving me a great deal of his time and allowing me to quote from his diaries. Bob Gottlieb of Knopf and Paul Sidey of Penguin Books have been superb editors of the biography, giving it many careful readings and offering editorial suggestions which have, I hope, rid it of prolixity.

The early period of both Orton's and Halliwell's life required a lot of sleuthing. Orton was then known as John Orton, and few people I interviewed connected him at first with Joe Orton the playwright. Halliwell, like Orton, kept to himself. Finally, a network of informants from Leicester and the Wirral emerged. The Orton family was crucial to my research. William Orton, Douglas Orton, Marilyn Orton Lock, and especially Leonie Orton Barnett with her perceptive and affectionate regard for Joe were a great help. As were Mrs. C. A. Bish, David Bowers and Joyce Holmes Bowers, David Campton, Bruce Cleave, Mrs. Sheila Cook, Mr. and Mrs. S. Coppack, Dorothy Dalby, J. P. Howarth, Mr. and Mrs. Noel Lacey, L. Moore-Tucker, Roy Mothersole, Millicent Overon, John Pooley, Dorothy Root, Ada Rothery, Edna and Harold Rowson, Joanne Runswick, Sylvia Sargeant, Michael Steele, Eric Swift, B. H. T. Taylor, Bernard Widdowson, and Trevor Williams.

For information about Orton's and Halliwell's theatrical and literary life prior to Orton's success I am grateful to Gene Baro, Richard Brain, Maxwell Burten-Shaw, Hugh Cruttwell, C. A. Elliott, Lawrence Griffin, June Clark Howarth, Rosalind Knight, Keith Lyon, John Moffat, Charles Monteith, Richard O'Donoghue, Jack Payne, Mary Phillips, Sidney Porrett, Barbara Rowlands, Diana Scougall, Claire Tompkins, and Margaret Whiting.

Orton's success was meteoric. While he rarely had a nice word to say about anybody, his producers have been as loyal to the memory of his talent as they were to his work. Michael Codron let me snoop through his production files of *Entertaining Mr. Sloane* and *Loot* in Harrods cavernous storage rooms. Oscar Lewenstein, who produced the successful versions of *Loot* and *What the Butler Saw*, and later in 1975 as artistic director of the Royal Court mounted revivals of Joe Orton's three full-length plays, was a great source of information. In building up a picture of Orton's professional and private life during this period,

I would like to thank Lindsay Anderson, Sheila Ballantine, Michael Bates, Stanley Baxter, Miss D. I. Boynes, Coral Browne, Robert Chetwyn, Mr. and Mrs. W. E. Corden, Adrienne Corri, Kenneth Cranham, Martin Drew, Patrick Dromgoole, Martin Esslin, Crispin Evans, James Fox, Peter Gill, Penelope Gilliatt, Sheila Hancock, Barry Hanson, Julian Holloway, Dr. Douglas Ismay, Colin Jeavons, Nigel Logan, Glenn Loney, Frank Marcus, Charles Marowitz, Geraldine McEwan, David Mercer, Lee Montague, Braham Murray, Timothy O'Brien, James Ormerod, Harold Pinter, Sir Terence Rattigan, Peter Reeves, Karel Reisz, Madge Ryan, Mr. and Mrs. Aldo Salvoni, Alan Schneider, Dudley Sutton, John Tydeman, Simon Ward, Michael White, Peter Willes, David William, and Peter Wood.

And for various services rendered—either stimulating discussion, advice, enthusiastic support, or technical assistance—the biography cannot go to press without acknowledging the generosity of Ann Adelman, Paul Barker, Alan Bennett, Georges and Anne Borchardt, John Connell, Tish Dace, Tom Erhardt, Sir John Foster, Stephen Frears, Ray Gosling, Peter Grose, Vaughn Grylls, John Hirsch, Neal T. Jones, Martha Kaplan, Robert J. Lifton, Kit Lukas, Raymond Mander and Joe Micheson, Martin Paisner, Richard Seaver, Geoffrey Strachan, Annette Taylor, Christopher Tugendhat, and E. Willats.

In this book, as in all my writings, Anthea Lahr has been my intimate collaborator. Her editorial acumen, her sound judgment, and her insight into the neurotic patterns of Orton and Halliwell are present on every page. She has blue-pencilled my excesses, answered my endless questions, and with typical patience and generosity listened as I read her each day's writing. The debt that authors always acknowledge to their wives has become a publishing cliché. In my case, reader, believe it. Without Anthea, this book and my writing career would not exist.

London
May 1978

Cleanse my heart, give me the ability to rage correctly.
—Joe Orton, *Head to Toe*

. . . Edna Welthorpe writes "The people here leave a lot to be desired and flaunt their preferences for what they cryptically call 'bits of the other' at every café. I might have been assaulted through the ears on many occasions—by words only," she adds.
—Joe Orton to Kenneth Williams
in a letter from Morocco

1

JOKERS ARE WILD

Murder is negative creation, and every murderer is therefore the rebel who claims the right to be omnipotent. His pathos is his refusal to suffer. . . . —W. H. Auden, *The Dyer's Hand*

MISS PRISM. *The good ended happily, and the bad unhappily. That is what Fiction means.*
—Oscar Wilde, *The Importance of Being Earnest*

J OE ORTON and Kenneth Halliwell were friends. For fifteen years, they lived and often wrote together. They wore each other's clothes. Their wills each named the other as sole beneficiary. They shared everything except success. But on August 9, 1967, murder made them equal again.

The note was found on top of the red-grained leather binder that held Orton's diary. The words, fastidiously written, had none of the horror of the actual scene:

> If you read his diary all will be explained.
> K. H.
>
> P.S. Especially the latter part

Halliwell lay nude on his back in the centre of the room, three feet from Orton's writing desk. The backs of his hands, the top of his chest, and his bald head were splattered with blood. Except for his arms, rigor mortis had set in. His gory pajama top was draped over the desk chair. On the linoleum floor near him was a glass and a can of grapefruit juice, which had speeded the twenty-two Nembutals into his blood, killing him within thirty seconds. Halliwell had died sooner than Orton, whose sheets were still warm when the police discovered him in bed, his head cratered like a burnt candle.

At forty-one, Halliwell was no stranger to horrific death. When he was eleven, his doting mother had been stung in the mouth by a wasp and within minutes choked to death before his eyes. As a young man of twenty-three, he came downstairs for breakfast to discover his father with his head in the oven, dead from asphyxiation. Halliwell was haunted by his father's death. While studying at RADA (the Royal Academy of Dramatic Art) in 1953, he told an actress who had tried to rally him out of one of his frequent depressions, "I'll end up just like my father and commit suicide," and he had, in 1962, attempted it. Halliwell had no reason to trust life.

"God laughs and snaps his fingers," he and Orton wrote in an unpublished novel, *The Boy Hairdresser* (1960). "The only thing for man to do is to imitate God and snap his fingers too." Halliwell's final fillip was nine hammer blows to Orton's head, a last crazy gesture of omnipotence in a life which from the time of his parents' deaths had been out of control. The hammer lay on top of the bedcover over Orton's chest. Halliwell, who had once taken Marlowe as his stage name, had dispatched Orton with the frenzied brutality typical of that Elizabethan playwright's blood-lust. He had walloped Orton's head so furiously that the vault of his skull had been bashed open and several lacerations on the scalp held the shape of the hammer. The brain had been splattered on wall and ceiling.

It was Orton's mind—the gorgeous, wicked fun it poked at the world—that made him irresistible and obsessed Halliwell. He had known that brain before it had been tutored by him in literature. He had nurtured it, enjoyed it, provoked it to defy convention, edited its excesses. "Marriage excuses no one the freaks' roll call"—Halliwell and Orton both shared a trickster's suspicion of normality, but only Orton could give the anarchic instinct memorable shape in a sentence. A curious chemistry of anger, optimism, and erudition blessed him with a comic style unique to his era. The mind that was meant to be Halliwell's cultivated and constant companion had acquired an independent life and vision. Often during the last months of their lives, Orton tried to reason Halliwell into a life of his own. The diary describes many such scenes:

> When we got home we talked about ourselves and our relationship. I think it's bad that we live in each other's pockets twenty-four hours a day three hundred and sixty-five days a year. When I'm away Kenneth does nothing, meets nobody. What's to be done? He's now taking tranquillizers to calm his nerves. "I need an affair with someone," he says. He says I'm no good. I'm only interested in physical sex, not love. "Your attitude to sensitive people is Vic-

torian," he said. "Basically, it's Dr. Arnold's 'get on the playing fields. You won't be so sensitive then.' All you need is a field of interest outside me. Where you can meet people away from me. . . ."

[April 30, 1967]

Halliwell's threats in the last year were always attempts to maneuver Orton back into the cosy family unit he had outgrown:

Kenneth H had a long talk about our relationship. He threatens, or keeps saying, he will commit suicide. He says, "You'll learn then, won't you?" and "What will you be like without me?" We talked and talked until I was exhausted. . . .   [May 1, 1967]

Had Halliwell killed Orton and himself four years earlier, their deaths would have been just another short item in the local newspaper. Instead, they made headlines. Between 1963, when his first play was accepted, and 1967, when he died, Joe Orton became a playwright of international reputation. His oeuvre was small but his impact was large. By 1967, the term "Ortonesque" had worked its way into the English vocabulary, a shorthand adjective for scenes of macabre outrageousness. Orton wrote three first-class full-length plays: *Entertaining Mr. Sloane, Loot,* and the posthumously produced *What the Butler Saw,* as well as four one-act plays. Two films were made from his plays, and *Loot* was voted the *Evening Standard*'s Best Play of 1966. Orton's plays had often scandalized audiences, but his wit made the outrage scintillating. Orton's laughter bore out Nietzsche's dictum that "He who writes in blood and aphorisms does not want to be read, he wants to be learned by heart." Orton brought the epigram back to the contemporary stage to illuminate a violent world. "It's life that defeats the Christian Church, she's always been well-equipped to deal with death" (*The Erpingham Camp*). "All classes are criminal today. We live in an age of equality" (*Funeral Games*). Orton's laughter created a "panic." His stage gargoyles tried to frighten their audience into new life.

Orton's death—laced as it was with the irony of his own fascination with the grotesque—had special public interest. No playwright in living memory had met a more gruesome end. The news was reported on the front page of *The Times* and in all the major English papers. *The Times* obituary (written by its drama critic, Irving Wardle) called Orton "one of the sharpest stylists of the British new wave . . . a consummate dialogue artist, and a natural anarch." It was a better review than he ever earned from *The Times* in life. Almost instantly, Orton's death became more famous than his work. Many interpreted his death as retribution for the unrelenting anarchy of his laughter.[1] But Orton was not hounded by society into a self-conscious martyrdom. He was

not a victim of the gospel of ecstasy that burned out the lives of so
many pop stars of the sixties. A voluptuary of fiasco, Orton died rather
from his short-sighted and indecisive loyalty to a friend.

IN 1959 Halliwell had purchased the second-floor bed-sitting room at
25 Noel Road, Islington, in North London, so that he and Orton could
have some security while they tried to write. But it was finally Orton
who persevered, sitting at their glossy white desk and writing while
Halliwell looked on. Even the financial balance that had given Halliwell so much power over Orton in the early years had shifted dramatically. It was now Orton who had the big bank balance of £20,222, and
Halliwell whose inheritance had dwindled in support of them to £5,817.
"Joe has everything, doesn't he?" Halliwell complained to Miss Boynes,
the elderly lady who lived beneath them and to whom he came for
scraps of conversation during the long days when Orton was absent
from the flat. Halliwell, who longed to be an artist, had played midwife
to his friend's talent. This creative gesture was the source of his sadness
and undoing. There was no visible sign of his contribution; and
Halliwell, pathetically, was forced to substantiate his claims in speech,
as if syntax could somehow bind him permanently to Orton's success.
He employed the royal "we" when speaking of Orton, and referred to
his talent as "a genius like us."

At 11:40 a.m. on August 9, 1967, a chauffeur arrived at 25 Noel
Road to take Orton to Twickenham Studios, where he and his producer, Oscar Lewenstein, were meeting with Richard Lester to talk
about Orton's film script *Up Against It.* The chauffeur trudged up the
bleak staircase with its linoleum steps smelling of wax and the grey-
striped wallpaper stained with damp and peeling. He knocked at Flat 4
on the top floor. There was no answer. He checked back with the
Lewenstein office, who told him to try again. Orton's agent, Peggy
Ramsay, had tried to reach him at 8:30 that morning to confirm a date
for lunch, and she too had received no reply. She was worried. The
chauffeur tried twice again and on the third reconnoiter squinted
through the letterbox to make sure nobody was home. "This time,"
he told the coroner, "I noticed the light was on in the hall. I thought
this was unusual. I could see the top of a man's head. He appeared to
be lying on the floor. I could see his face from the nose upwards. His
eyes were closed. I knew this was not Mr. Orton because this man
appeared to be bald-headed. I knew Mr. Orton because I had driven
him in the firm's car to different destinations."

Two stools, two chairs, two single divan beds, and now, so the police discovered, two bodies. The only identifying mark on Orton's body was a blue swallow tattooed over his appendix scar. Orton was planning to refurbish the design; he wanted a flock of swallows on the wing arching across his stomach like porcelain ducks over a mantelpiece. The joke imprinted on his body and the ghoulish spectacle of his bludgeoning made a contrast that matched the weird surroundings. Orton and Halliwell's bedsitter had seemed to visitors like some extraordinary tomb. There was no sense of comfort to the austere room—venetian blinds, electric heater, scrubbed lineoleum floor. The ceiling was painted in a checkerboard of pink and yellow, and the colors weighed down on the small space. The walls were covered with an elaborate collage, which stretched up to the ceiling and in which recognizable shapes merged with mythical beasts, Renaissance art, and tabloid headlines. "The room was very arid," Penelope Gilliatt recalls. "It made me want to put my elbows out and stretch the walls."

Above Orton's bed and overlooking his battered body was a Renaissance crucifix pasted on top of a Union Jack. On another wall near Halliwell's corpse was a map of Australia transformed into a tutu. At the bottom of the map was a pair of crossed horse's legs; on top was an ape's body, with hands dangling down onto the "skirt." A Cro-Magnon head had been mounted on this torso—and blood had been spliced into the image.

The room was Halliwell's theatre and a mosaic of his mind. Its humor was a testament to his fear and loathing. Halliwell's design—in its startling and aggressive flatness—was a collage of fractured images, a series of haunting notions where the past, the present, and the surreal co-existed but never coalesced to make a coherent whole. The warped images signalled an imagination in retreat:

> Which is worse [asks Donelly, the failed artist and Halliwell's fictional alter ego in *The Boy Hairdresser,* just before he attempts murder], fruitless running or aimless drifting? Evil to look back on, nothing to look forward to, and pain in the present. The faces passing seemed to him pale, with hunger not physical, a mixture of brute and human, devouring and defiling: long claws and bird mouths, fat hips and loins.

This description was an accurate account of the panic which plagued and distorted Halliwell's every encounter with the world and which he made explicit in his anarchic wall collages. They were more powerful, precise, and disturbing than his writing. Halliwell came to look upon his murals as his art form. He even wrote to Peggy Ramsay asking for her professional opinion of them:

> Must make it plain this invite is not from J or anything to do with him or his Works. I should like your opinion of my collage murals. Does my real talent if any lie in this direction, etc. I know how unspeakably more than busy you are so quite understand if you can't spare time for even a cuppa any time. For instance the woman who came to interview J for the *Evening Standard* this afternoon spent her time admiring my murals and saying did they cost a terrific lot of money and how professional they were, etc. This has happened before with all sorts of people. However.   [October 3, 1966]

Lost to himself, Halliwell lacked the self-regard to state any demand directly. He hadn't the courage to put forward and promote his own art. The hope of glory and the fear of rejection were a paralyzing combination. Trying to give Halliwell some interest outside himself, Orton encouraged his work on the murals and in 1967 arranged for an exhibition of fifteen pictures in a Chelsea antique store. A few pictures were sold to Orton's business associates, but the public showed little interest. It was a familiar pattern.

Halliwell had always yearned to be visible. "Applaud me," says Donelly in *The Boy Hairdresser*, "but no one applauded. Instead, in the distance, a child screamed." Halliwell had worked hard to win the world's attention. He had trained at RADA as an actor but swiftly abandoned the profession as a bad bet. He had labored at writing for a decade, then given it up. Six novels and one stage adaptation were stashed in the drawer under his bed; they suffered from the same posturing and self-consciousness that he did. As late as 1966, Halliwell had sent his stage adaptation, *The Facts of Life*, to Peggy Ramsay, London's most powerful play agent, whose literary instincts are as sharp as her tongue. "I haven't really got through your adaptation," she wrote him. "The first scene sent me into such a well of boredom that I had to struggle to continue which I did in a kind of abstract anguish!!!"[2]

Having educated Orton to be his intellectual equal, Halliwell was now drawn into inevitable and unequal competition with him. Orton radiated a sexuality and warmth that attracted people. He spoke with an appealing Leicester accent, his lazy upper lip slurring consonants and making the delivery funny. "He thought he was really beautiful, Joe did," says Kenneth Cranham, one of Orton's favorite actors and closest acquaintances. "The buzz was him himself. When he'd leave a room he would stand in front of a mirror—very upright—and look at himself like he thought he was very butch. If you saw him, it was quite exciting. You knew he was a promising person. You knew he'd say something funny." Buttocks clenched, pelvis thrust out, Army bag slung over his shoulder—Orton strutted through a world he found "profoundly bad and irrisistibly funny."[3]

Halliwell was more daunting. Seven years older than Orton and totally bald from an early age, Halliwell had always been conscious that youthfulness eluded him. When he applied to RADA in 1950, he confessed to the registrar, "I'm already twenty-three and, God knows, look thirty."[4] Without his wig, Halliwell was a grave and menacing presence whom people remembered as larger than Orton (although in fact at 5 feet 8 inches Halliwell was 2 inches shorter). Orton bought Halliwell his first wig in 1964 with the first profits from *Entertaining Mr. Sloane*. It was ungraded, and perched ceremoniously on Halliwell's head like a tea cosy. "Kenneth improved when he began wearing the wig," Peggy Ramsay says. "He was very ashamed of his baldness and he kept his hat on everywhere, including the theatre. I think that looking in the mirror with it actually altered his personality. He became rather charming and sincere, so that I quite forgot my first alarmed reaction to his personality."

Halliwell vacillated between extraordinary aggressiveness and timidity—a characteristic their good friend the comedian Kenneth Williams found ludicrous. "Halliwell never seemed to me ever to establish himself," Williams says. "He always seemed to melt into the background and simper, 'I'm not wanted,' 'I'm not spoken to,' 'I'm only here because Joe's here.' The only time he seemed to be bold and resolute was in contradicting Joe's apparent errors." Halliwell was too defensive about himself to put others at ease. He tried fiercely to hide his sadness, which only made him sadder and more isolated. "It was quite hard to see Joe because you always risked incurring Kenneth's wrath," Cranham recalls. "Joe gave me an old coat of his, and Kenneth got very uptight. He saw me as a threat. One night they were backstage and Kenneth said, 'I thought you were all beautiful.' He turned to me. 'Which is very surprising for you because you're ugly, really.' "

Halliwell's pride made it hard for him to command respect, and he did not welcome sympathy. Always on guard, he lacked any spontaneity. Even his voice had a pedantic, prissy tone that was offputting. In *The Boy Hairdresser* they'd analyzed the difference in their personalities. Donelly wistfully considers the charming truculence of his roommate Peterson who, like Orton, was able to generate easy affection:

> There are many kinds of crucifixion: not all involving the use of wood and nails. Long before Donelly saw Peterson, he heard his

voice and then his laugh. He experienced a feeling of nausea, knowing each careless phrase, each lie meant to win friendship. . . .

Ten minutes on his own and Peterson had picked up somebody;
he had found an audience: it was an enviable habit.

Since childhood, Halliwell's life had been one long adjustment to
anxiety. The pain of failure, the waste of talent, the isolation, and the
sense of betrayal an orphan feels toward those who have "left" him, all
bred in Halliwell a festering and terrifying hostility toward the world.
He could love literature but never life or himself. He tried to examine
his battle to contain this rage in *The Boy Hairdresser*. There Donelly
contemplates suicide and the death of his friend; he dreams of punishing society for its "stupidity." Unable to win love from the world,
Donelly settles for its hate, going berserk and shooting grapeshot at an
indifferent public to make it take notice: "His vision was now clear:
people ran, hiding in doorways, away from him, out of control." The
spirit of revenge—to impose on others the emptiness one feels in oneself
—was something that both Orton and Halliwell understood. Only
Orton, however, could displace this anger creatively in laughter.
Halliwell's instincts lacked Orton's resilient wonder and detachment.
" 'Life was a joke,' Donelly said. 'Beauty, culture, civilization—death.
Spring, the universe, God.—Christ!—who laughs?' "

Joking takes confidence, and Halliwell had lost that strength. He
could instruct but not please. He had hoped and worked for the miracle
of fame to eradicate the weight of his past, yet it was Orton who was
being reborn before his eyes. To Halliwell, the situation was typical of
his life: a hateful joke that couldn't be revenged in laughter. Obsessed
with his anger, he had to use all his energy to control it. His fiction
could not convey the overwhelming sense of suffocation and terror that
haunted him and that enervated Orton during the last abusive months.
Halliwell contained so many "murdered selves," and they emerged in
fits of violent self-loathing during these wrangles. Halliwell hated the
lingering pain; but in order to appease these destructive forces and
salvage some identity, he became their ally against himself:

Suddenly I realized that Kenneth was looking tight-lipped and
white-faced. We were in the middle of talks of suicide and "you'll
have to face up to the world one day." And "I'm disgusted by all
this immorality." He began to rail savagely at Tom and Clive [two
new homosexual acquaintances] and after a particularly sharp outburst, alarmed me by saying "Homosexuals disgust me!" I didn't
attempt to fathom this one out. He said he wasn't going to come
away to Morocco. He was going to kill himself. "I've led a dreadful,

unhappy life. I'm pathetic. I can't go on suffering like this." After talking until about eight he suddenly shouted out and hammered on the wall, "They treated me like shit! I won't be treated like this."

[May 1, 1967]

Numb to himself and the world around him, Halliwell defended his shrinking ego in those last months by shrinking the circumference of the "dead" world around him. He stayed at home, venturing out only to shop or accompany Orton:

Dreary day, Kenneth in an ugly mood. Moaning. I said, "You look like a zombie." He replied, heavily, "So I should. I lead the life of a zombie."   [April 23, 1967]

There was truth in Halliwell's observation. Even the room where their emotional and artistic life had taken place for eight years was tainted. To Halliwell, the room was a fortress. His personality, so easily dismissed by the outside world, was the pervading presence, pasted on every inch of wall. He fussed and cleaned and decorated. But Orton had begun to hate the place. "I really do think I'll have to get something larger soon," he told the *Evening News* on June 9, 1967, while Halliwell was in Morocco and he had returned to London briefly for the opening of *Crimes of Passion.* "Just to have a room to work in. I work better when there's someone else wandering around but it's not fair to the other person. They can't read and if they want to type anything the place sounds like a typing pool." In private, Orton was more scathing. "Joe wanted to get the hell out of there," the actress Adrienne Corri recalls. "He felt confined. He used to talk a lot about how he hated it. Ken didn't want to change. He did most of the housekeeping and it would have changed Ken's whole way of living if they'd left the room."

But Orton was changing; and the room only reinforced his fear of coming to an emotional and creative standstill. He stayed away often for long periods of the day. Halliwell was painfully aware of the meaning of these absences. In April—perhaps sensing the threat to their relationship—Halliwell had suggested moving to Brighton and keeping the London flat as a *pied à terre.* The move would mean a return to the comfy isolation of their earlier years. Orton saw the house outside London as a means of setting up a home for his friend in much the same way as Halliwell, fifteen years before, had used his inheritance to make a home for Orton. Orton confided the plan to Kenneth Williams. "I'll pop down on weekends," he said. Williams was dubious: "Weekends? That's not much of a life." Orton didn't reply. He was searching for ways to extricate himself honorably from Halliwell's yapping misery. The Brighton house never materialized, although he and Halliwell spent a day looking at properties. Halliwell continued to push for a new home, wanting to keep Orton to himself; but Orton had other ideas:

> "I hate this time of the year," Kenneth says. He's been looking through a property paper and has found a "marvellous" house in East Croydon. He's sulking at the moment because I've said quite firmly that I won't go and live in East Croydon. "You're so unadventurous," he said. We went for a walk. . . . Kenneth began to carp about the weather and lead by degrees into a tirade against London and a eulogy of the life in the country. I remained unimpressed because although I don't mind moving out of London, I'm not going to be buried in some God-forsaken hole in the wilds. Kenneth sulked a lot more. In the end I said, "You're getting to be a fucking Mater Dolorosa, aren't you?"   [April 22, 1967]

The complaints, the tears, the diatribes, the threats were distress signals that Orton, with a new sense of his worth, could not allow himself to interpret. In their writing Orton and Halliwell had imagined everything about their relationship except success. Now success had put Orton out of touch with his friend's suffering. "You're turning into a real bully, do you know that?" Halliwell shouted at Orton. "You'd better be careful. You'll get your deserts."[5] The balance of their relationship had been tipped irrevocably in Orton's favor. Halliwell was trapped, a prisoner of his neurotic dependency. His life was in Orton's hands, but Orton would not take responsibility for it. Without Orton, Halliwell knew he had nothing; and death would be a welcome release from his punishing sense of failure. Like Donelly contemplating Peterson's death ("his beauty smashed forever"), Halliwell had an appetite for the death he finally sought:

> He wanted to die. To get back to a dim memory of a better place. In his heart each man carries some lost paradise, a ruined world of submerged continents. He wished to return.

The preview of their end did not occur only in their writing. Six weeks earlier, during their holiday in Morocco, Halliwell attacked Orton.

THE DAY Halliwell and Orton left for Morocco, Halliwell wrote to Peggy Ramsay urging her to visit them in their large Tangier apartment on the Rue Pizarro, with its "superb rather Noel Coward rep set salon." Halliwell dated his high-spirited letter, "hectic last day in hell." But it was not simply a crowded, dusty city that was torture. He signed himself: "Kenneth Halliwell, Secretary to JOE ORTON."[6] He was now—for tax, visa, and banking purposes—a "Personal Assistant," and not even his bravado could deflate the lingering hurt of being officially an appendage. The anxiety was bound to breed disagreement, even in their "Eden."

They were occupying the flat in which Tennessee Williams had written *Suddenly Last Summer*. It was an overpowering apartment, decorated in fustian Second Empire style with antiques, gilded chandeliers, and ornate mirrors. The apartment's main attraction was the terrace that protected them from the "hellish Tangier wind" that blew sand into Halliwell's wig and kept them from sunbathing. They were not at ease in the chic spaciousness. On the second day of their holiday, Orton wrote:

> We locked the main salon of the flat which is enormous and gives an impression of millionaire elegance. We'll just pretend that the flat consists of the kitchen, bathroom, and two bedrooms. Kenneth worried. "It's so dangerous," he says. "Look," I've said, perhaps rashly, "if there's real nastiness we can just sling him out. We're never having more than one in at a time, our money is locked away and up to date, I've *never* had any trouble with a boy." "There's always a first time," Kenneth said darkly, with which I can't argue.
>
> [May 9, 1967]

Orton eyed the prospect of Moroccan boys like Pinocchio at the fair. But sexual abundance was more threatening for Halliwell, who was no longer pretty or sure of the affections of his friend. Whereas Halliwell was sexually timid, Orton was brazenly promiscuous. Halliwell had to accept Orton's "trolling"; but he never condoned it. In moments of anxiety, his own fear of abandonment and inferiority tried to disguise itself as worry about their well-being. The danger in rough trade, the lack of intimacy in "tea-room" sex, was not what Halliwell craved. He wanted what J. R. Ackerley called "that sad little wish—to be loved."[7] Despite the Librium and Valium that Halliwell handed around at meal times, he was unnerved by the first few days in Tangier, which were spoiled by the hysterical performances that had begun to constrict and annoy Orton:

> I went back and faced Kenneth in such a rage at the Windmill [Orton wrote after an expedition to buy hashish]. "Where've you

been? You have been gone an hour and a half. I was nearly out of my mind with worry." With that, on the terrace of the Windmill, he burst into tears, to my own embarrassment. "My nerves can't stand you going off without my knowing where you are." After a great scene he said that Mohammed el Khomsi with the gold tooth, a boy of about eighteen, had been looking for me. "I've arranged for him to come to the flat tomorrow," he said. I was rather choked by this as it ties me down. "Well, you said you wanted to fuck him," Kenneth said peevishly, "and he's going to Gibraltar in a fortnight to work as a page boy in a hotel." He then began complaining about my liking Mohammed (the first one) and how he was a nasty bit of work. "And you're so mad to go along the beach with him. Absolutely mad." He then began saying I would get into trouble. "That boy of yours looks like a nutter to me." In the end, fed up to the back teeth with nagging, I said, "Every boy in town is no good except the marvellous one you attach yourself to. . . ."

[May 12, 1967]

Halliwell did not adjust easily to shifts of locale. His dread of going nowhere and being nobody made it hard for him to relax into the idle rootlessness of a vacation. In the first few days in Tangier, Halliwell jockeyed nervously for Orton's affection and esteem. He needed to feel equal to Orton's sexual enterprise, which inevitably led to sad, fatuous moments of abrasion:

We were hailed with "Hallo" from a very beautiful 16 year old boy whom I knew (but had never had) from last year. Kenneth wanted him. We talked for about five minutes and finally I said, "Come to our apartment for tea this afternoon." He was very eager. We arranged that he should meet us at the Windmill beach place. As we left the boy Kenneth said, "Wasn't I good at arranging things?" This astounded me. "I arranged it," I said. "You would have been standing talking about the weather for ever." K. didn't reply. . . .

[May 9, 1967]

Halliwell feared being excluded from Orton's orbit. Whenever possible he tried to pander to Orton's enthusiasms. Orton didn't like it:

We had tea and Ken and Lhabi went into the bedroom. . . . When Ken came back they had had sex. "I've arranged for you to have him tomorrow," Kenneth said in a confidential tone when the boy was out of the room. "I've already arranged to have Mohammed tomorrow," I said. "I really wish you wouldn't play the procuress quite so much. I'm quite capable of managing my own sex!!"

[May 10, 1967]

Gradually, the bickering abated; and by May 17, Orton could report in his diary, "Kenneth in his element and holding forth. I'm glad he's happy for a change." As for Orton, "My life beginning to run to a time table no member of the Royal Family would tolerate. Life is perfect," he wrote to Kenneth Williams on May 27, "and the pleasures of the senses never pall and never have been better."

The combination of sex, hashish, and sun fulfilled the Dionysian intention that lies behind Orton's comedies. They celebrate instinct and gratification, and Orton aspired to corrupt his audience with pleasure:

> I always say to myself that the theatre is the Temple of Dionysus, and not Apollo. You do the Dionysus thing on your typewriter, and then you allow a little Apollo in, just a little to shape and guide it along certain lines you may want to go along. But you can't allow Apollo in completely.[8]

Orton was obsessed with the Dionysian theme. In early June of 1967, the Royal Court premiered *The Erpingham Camp*, his reworking of *The Bacchae*. Along with a new version of his first play, *The Ruffian on the Stair* (1963), it was presented under the title *Crimes of Passion*. And it was passion—the thrilling, punishing battle between license and control—that gave a hard edge to Orton's life and his plays.[9] *What the Butler Saw*, which lay in a drawer beneath his bed in Islington awaiting a final draft, planned comic revenge on Pentheus, the persecutor of Dionysus who is at the same time doomed to suffer from Dionysian passion. At the finale, the figure of control—Sergeant Match—climbs down through the skylight on a rope ladder. With a wink at Euripides, Orton has Match wearing a leopard-skin dress.[10] Instead of condemning the spectacle, he joins the participants and ascends toward a new light. "Providing one spends the time drugged and drunk, the world is a fine place," Orton wrote on June 3. A month later, in rewriting the finale of *What the Butler Saw*, he worked this observation into the final stage direction. "They pick up their clothes and weary, bleeding, drugged and drunk, climb the rope ladder into the blazing light." Orton's vision of suffering had finally merged with his dream of survival.

Like the votaries of Dionysus, Orton was hounded by his passion. In his plays, he faced his rage and exorcised it by his lethal wit. The visits to Morocco slaked the tension that was always erupting in Orton's life between his emotional needs and the society's sexual and social taboos:

Here and there were numbers of nearly naked young boys [Orton
wrote later, after walking with Halliwell along Brighton pier]. This
made me unhappy. After passing a fifteen year old youth lying face-
downward wearing red bathing drawers, I said in a rage, "England
is intolerable. I'd be able to fuck that in an Arab country. I could
take him home and stick my cock up him!" "This is verbal exhibi-
tionism!" Kenneth said, glancing at a number of evil-faced old
women in a shelter. "Look at them—crouching like Norns or the
spirit of fucking British civilization," I said. "I hate this tight-assed
civilization."   [July 28, 1967]

Orton tried to practice the sexual ethic he preached. "You must do
whatever you like as long as you enjoy it and don't hurt anybody else.
That's all that matters," he told a homosexual friend who felt guilty
about his activity. "You shouldn't feel guilty. Get yourself fucked if
you want to. Get yourself anything you like. Reject all the values of
the society. And enjoy sex. When you're dead, you'll regret not having
fun with your genital organs."[11] But the battle against society was
difficult, the social controls impossible to overlook. In England, the
strain could create a painful, confusing rage:

I saw a young boy, blond and very healthy-looking filling a bucket
with water on the promenade. As he turned the tap off, he looked
up. Our eyes met. A great spasm of rage overtook me. I find lust
an emotion indistinguishable from anger. Or at least anger pre-
dominates when I see something I can't have. I feel I may run mad
one day and commit rape.   [July 29, 1967]

The startling aggressiveness with which Orton's plays toppled conventional morality helped him to get even for his private pain. It gave
his comedies their urgency and power. In Morocco, Orton dedicated
all his energies to passion and pleasure. Fame seemed a comic memory:

So we had sex, or at least I lay and allowed him to fuck me and
thought as his prick shot in and he kissed my neck, back and
shoulders, that it was a most unappetising position for an inter-
nationally known playwright to be in.   [May 19, 1967]

Even ambition became insignificant. The lukewarm reception of
Crimes of Passion in London could not upset the delicious sexual
serenity of his days and nights:

We showered and I gave him five dirham. . . . He went off perfectly
satisfied, and not for the first time I reflected that having had a boy

of his age in England I'd spend the rest of my life in terror of his parents or the police. At one moment with my cock in his arse, the image was, and as I write still is, overpoweringly erotic, and I reflected that whatever the Sunday papers have said about *Crimes of Passion* was of little importance compared to this.   [June 11, 1967]

Orton was a modern Lord of Misrule whose plays are a holiday from the established order. He had realized early in his writing career that for there to be a rebirth in society, there had to be a killing. "Without cruelty," says Nietzsche, "no feast."[12] Comedy could kill and renew. Orton wanted his words "to vibrate the structure." "To be destructive, words had to be irrefutable," he wrote in his posthumously published novel *Head to Toe* (1961):

> And then the book might not be read. He was aware that words and sentences often buried themselves in the reader's mind before exploding and then went off harmlessly. Print was less effective than the spoken word because the blast was greater; eyes could ignore, slide past, dangerous verbs or nouns. But if you could lock the enemy into a room somewhere and fire the sentence at them you would get a sort of seismic disturbance. . . .[13]

The "enemy" rarely showed its face in the Casbah; but when it did, Orton would deploy outrage to parry the smug judgments of the straight world. At a sidewalk café, a "rather stuffy American tourist and his disapproving wife" sat next to Orton and a group of friends:

> They listened to our conversation and I, realizing this, began to exaggerate the content. "He took it up the arse," I said. "And afterwards he thanked me for giving him such a good fucking. They're a most polite people." The American and his wife hardly moved a muscle. "We've got a leopard skin rug in the flat and he wanted me to fuck him on that," I said in an undertone which was perfectly audible to the next table, "only I'm afraid of the spunk, you see, it might adversely affect the spots on the leopard." Nigel said quietly, "Those tourists can hear what you're saying." He looked alarmed. "I mean them to hear," I said, "they have no right to be occupying chairs reserved for decent sex perverts," and then with excitement I said, "He might bite a hole in the rug, and I can't ask him to control his excitement. It wouldn't be natural when you're six inches up the bum, would it?" The American couple frigidly paid for their coffee and moved away. "You shouldn't drive people like that away," Nigel said. "The town needs tourists." "Not that kind, it doesn't," I said. "This is *our* country, *our* town, *our*

civilization. I want nothing to do with the civilization they made. Fuck them! They'll sit and listen to buggers talk from me and drink their coffee and piss off." "It seems rather a strange joke," Frank said with an old school teacher's smile. "It isn't a joke," I said. "There's no such thing as a joke."

Nigel who was drinking some strange brandy got very excited by a girl who passed. She looked like a boy. She was German. . . . "Who wants a girl to look like a boy?" I said. "Or a boy to look like a girl? It's not natural." "I really think, Joe," Nigel said, "that you shouldn't bring Nature into your conversation quite so often, you who have done more than anyone I know to outrage her." "I've never outraged Nature," I said. "I've always listened to her advice and followed it wherever it went."   [May 25, 1967]

The American tourists momentarily revived the anxiety of sexual stigma which Orton's laughter kept at bay and which he could forget in Tangier. His diary otherwise is suffused with moments of strange and surprising contentment. May 21, he wrote, was "a day so perfect that sex really seemed irrelevant." On May 22, he found himself standing on a terrace at twilight looking over the city and the bay, the purple glow of the sunset matched by the inner glow of hashish and Scotch:

The world became even more wonderful, my limbs felt as if they were made of rubber and catching sight of myself in the mirror I gazed, without self-consciousness, for perhaps five minutes, or so it seemed, into my own eyes. . . . I felt elated and danced a wild dance around the hall positively spinning round the urns and hubble-bubbles, like a teetotum. The others came down the stairs talking in mellow English tones, and upon seeing me, Nigel remarked, "Is this his farewell performance?"

Halliwell reminded Orton of the high price Dionysus paid for ecstasy. Orton knew his friend was right. Neither of them had had much experience of happiness—and they distrusted it. Over tea and hashish cakes in the first month of their vacation, they contemplated their pleasure:

Kenneth and I sat talking of how happy we both felt. We'd have to pay for it. Or we'd be struck down from afar by disaster because we were, perhaps, too happy. To be young, good-looking, healthy, famous, comparatively rich *and* happy is surely going against nature, and when to the above list one adds that daily I have the company of little boys who find (for a small fee) fucking with me a delightful sensation, no man can want for more. "*Crimes of Passion* will be a disaster," Kenneth said. "That will be the scapegoat. We must sacrifice *Crimes of Passion* in order that we may be spared disaster more intolerable." I slept all night soundly and woke up at seven feeling as though the whole of creation was conspiring to make me happy. I hope no doom strikes.   [May 25, 1967]

But it was Orton himself, not his play, who would be sacrificed for his glorious talent. The first hint of Halliwell's rough justice came three days before they planned to return to London. "Although the last two months have been very enjoyable and a great success neither Kenneth nor I will be sorry to leave on Friday," Orton wrote on June 25. "I feel the need for something fresh. Not work—though undoubtedly I shall finish *What the Butler Saw*—just a change of scene. Even sex with a teenage boy becomes monotonous. Ecstasy is as liable to bore as boredom. I need the atmosphere of London for a month or two in order to stir me from the lethargy in which I am in danger of falling." Orton was returning to the rewrite of his last and most accomplished farce. His film script, *Up Against It*, was being actively shopped to directors, and his first full-length play, *Entertaining Mr. Sloane*, as well as his newest one-act, *Funeral Games*, were both scheduled to be aired on television later in the year. *Loot* was still running in the West End.

Halliwell was returning with no prospects. The anticipation of the old oppression made him brittle and quarrelsome. Every disagreement was magnified into a threat to his identity. Orton's disenchantment with Halliwell was too close to the surface of their fights to make it easy for Halliwell to express his anger. Orton's success made him invulnerable to Halliwell's abuse, which only reinforced Halliwell's sense of impotence. But when his anger did erupt, as on June 27, Halliwell struck out in unexpected fury. "Kenneth became violently angry shortly after this and attacked me, hitting me about the head and knocking my pen from my hand," Orton reported in his diary.

Overnight, Halliwell's haughty fearfulness had returned. "In a growing rage," Halliwell locked out their cleaning woman, who had disappeared from work leaving her yashmak and slippers in their house. Halliwell and Orton went out to lunch with friends; and Halliwell, trying to assert his will, built up the skirmish into a major victory:

Kenneth in a very loud voice said, "I've taught our Fatima a lesson." He then told the whole story and ended saying, "Joe

wanted to ignore her, but she's got to be made to realise." Nigel
said, "How right you are, dear, it takes a woman to deal with a
woman." "If I'd said that," I said aside to Kenneth, "you'd be on a
charter flight back to London by now."   [June 28, 1967]

Predictably, Halliwell showed his defensiveness by becoming argu-
mentative and loud:

Kenneth began an argument. "He's *awful*," he said in loud irritat-
ing tones [of a blond fourteen-year-old boy who passed their table].
"If he takes it and he's 14," I said, "I can see perfectly why the
Moroccans are interested and I would be too . . ." There was a
licking of lips all round. "Well," Kenneth said in a tight voice, "all
I'd like to do to that creature is whip him." "You're simply substituting violence for sex," I said. "Your psychological slip is showing.
A whip is a phallic symbol. You're doing on a symbolic level
exactly what I do in reality."   [June 28, 1967]

Orton and Halliwell hoped to return to Tangier in October. As
their plane touched down at Heathrow on June 30, Orton said to
Halliwell, "The party's over." But it was clear from the mail that
awaited Orton that there was still the fiesta of Orton's new fame. "A
great many letters," he wrote. "And press cuttings. Invitations to
parties I shall not accept. And an invitation to a private viewing at
the Drian Galleries of some sculpture. I shall go to this because it
might be good for Kenneth's collages." The routine had started again,
and with it, for Halliwell, the same sense of suffocation. "How dead
everyone looks," he'd remarked to Orton, as they stood on Gloucester
Road waiting for a taxi to take them from the bus terminal to the
home that had become for both a kind of purgatory.

THE FIRST WEEKS of July were hot and unusually muggy. London
wilted in the unfamiliar heat. Pavements emptied; the city's pace
faltered; everything seemed to lose the will to live. And with its dusty,
treeless sidestreets and gnarled thoroughfares choked by exhaust fumes,
Islington was particularly unpleasant. Orton was immediately dis-
tracted from the stifling weather by the excitement of his rewrites.
"Today I read *What the Butler Saw* and was pleased with it," he
wrote on July 2. "There are sections that have to be rewritten and
others to be clarified. Not a lot of hard graft, though. I shall enjoy
this part of the work. It's a final polish." While Orton made steady

progress on his most ambitious and best play, Halliwell was immobilized with a bad attack of hay fever. "I wish I'd stayed in Morocco," he moaned. "Oh, this terrible city." But he could not bear to be away from Orton, especially during the final revision of a work, when his own critical ability was needed. Orton's success gave Halliwell acute anxiety; but his role as Orton's literary editor was one of the few accomplishments and legitimate sources of pride he had.

"Telephone off," Orton noted in his diary on July 8 about a fault on their line. "So no one could contact me. . . . Did nothing at all except type *What the Butler Saw*." All the calls were for Orton, while Halliwell's only distraction from the heat and hay fever was his friend. In the first two weeks of July, they visited Kenneth Williams, checked up on the cast and production of *Loot* at the Criterion Theatre, and with two actors from the *Loot* company spent one delightful afternoon at the Palace Theatre discreetly giggling at the dialogue of *Desert Song*. ("Kenneth Halliwell said that a lot of it reminded him of my writing," Orton wrote in his diary. "Not surprising really since my writing is a deliberate satire on bad theatre. The plot gave me the idea for my next play."[14])

On July 10, Halliwell read *What the Butler Saw:*

Kenneth read the script and was enthusiastic. He made several important suggestions which I'm carrying out. He was impressed by the way in which, using the context of a farce, I'd managed to produce a "Golden Bough" subtext—even (he pointed out) the castration of Sir Winston Churchill (the father-figure) and the descent of the god at the end—Sergeant Match, drugged and dressed in a woman's gown. It was only to be expected that Kenneth would get these references to classical literature. Whether anyone else will spot them is another matter. "You must get a director who, while making it funny, brings out the subtext," Kenneth said. He suggests that the dress Match wears should be of something suggestive of leopard-skin—this would make it funny when Nick wears it and get the right "image" for the Euripidean ending when Match wears it.

Halliwell's casting suggestions were as trenchant as his criticism. "Kenneth says that Alastair Sim would be ideal for Dr. Rance. Agree with him. And Arthur Lowe as Dr. Prentice," Orton wrote in his diary on July 12. "Kenneth also says that we should offer Mrs. Prentice to Coral Browne. She'd be rather good—though I doubt whether she'd accept it." By July 16, working through the sweltering summer days, Orton had finished typing the final draft of the play. Halliwell was "ill with Hay Fever," while Orton was invigorated by his accomplishment:

> I finished typing *What the Butler Saw*. I added very little on this
> version (just incorporated Kenneth's suggestions which were excellent). . . . Great relief to have finished *Butler*. I can now give my
> mind full rein for the historical farce set on the eve of Edward VII's
> coronation in 1902 and called (at the moment) *Prick Up Your Ears*.
> I hope I can write a play worthy of one of Kenneth Halliwell's
> most brilliant titles. I've already got a quotation from *The Critic*
> for the play, "Where history gives you a good heroic outline for a
> play, you may fill up with a little love at your own discretion: in
> doing which, nine times out of ten, you only make up a deficiency
> in the private history of the times."

On July 17, Orton took *What the Butler Saw* to Peggy Ramsay.
Halliwell, who could see the play's excellence and knew that his own
suggestions had given it added brilliance, chose this day to quarrel with
Orton—their first fight since returning from Morocco. The cycle of
Orton's success was sure to begin again, and, as surely, Halliwell's
nagging anxiety about his worthlessness would be reactivated.

> Kenneth very irritating today. Weather hot again. Blue skies.
> Kenneth's nerves are on edge. Hay Fever. He had a row this morning. Trembling with rage. About my nastiness when I said, "Are
> you going to stand in front of the mirror all day?" He said, "I've
> been washing your fucking underpants!" That's why I've been at
> the sink!" He shouted it out loudly and I said, "Please, don't let
> the whole neighbourhood know you're a queen." "You know I have
> hay fever and you deliberately get on my nerves," he said. "I'm
> going out," I said. "I can't stand much more of it." "Go out then,"
> he said. "I don't want you in here."

Halliwell had been masculine and assertive when they'd first met in
1951. But in the three years since the success of *Entertaining Mr. Sloane*
in 1964, Orton had witnessed his gradual and disquieting transformation from partner to sidekick. Orton hated what he called "the pinafore
number" that Halliwell adopted as his new role. "The virtue of
homosexuality, Joe said, was in liking men not girls," Kenneth Williams
recalls. "So why imitate girls?" Orton's threat to Halliwell was as real
as it was intimidating. Halliwell's "household," like his housewifely
role, had become a farce. And Orton, who hated fakery of any kind,
knew it. The antidote to *angst* is action—a comic remedy Orton found

easier to manage on stage than in life. In *What the Butler Saw,* Dr. Rance offers a two-sentence homily on mental health: "Reject all paranormal phenomena. It's the only way to remain sane." Orton couldn't completely follow these words of advice: his friendship with Halliwell forced him to keep on pretending. Yet he despised this hypocritical domesticity, and instinctively endangered it, deliberately stalking rough trade:

> Took a walk. Nobody around to pick up. Only a lot of disgusting old men. I shall be a disgusting old man myself one day, I thought, mournfully. Only I have high hopes of dying in my prime.
>
> [July 14, 1967]

WHILE HE WAITED for the first reactions to *What the Butler Saw,* Orton busied himself with being famous. Within the confines of their flat, Halliwell's abusive frustration continually cast Orton as the heavy; but in the outside world, Orton was greeted as a luminous, affable good guy:

> I went on to a house in Aubrey Walk W.8 to be photographed for *Queen* Magazine. It was all very bright. A lot of clever and attractive young people. A young man said, "We're doing the 'goodies' today." "What do you mean?" I said. He showed me a photograph to be included in the same issue as ours. It was a group of about eight people—including Nicholas Tomalin and Cathy McGowan. "They're the baddies," he said. "That'll be on the opposite page to yours." They're going to contrast various sets of people. The rest of my group were soon assembled—Tom Courtenay, Lucy Fleming, Susannah York, Twiggy, and a Chinese girl and a young man wearing a gold coat and a male mini-skirt. "Do you go around in that all the time," I said. "No," he said, "I changed upstairs."
>
> [July 18, 1967]

On July 22, Orton and Halliwell were scheduled to attend a swank party at the home of Peter Willes, the head of drama for Yorkshire Television, who had played an important part in Orton's career. Orton showed his gratitude by dedicating *Crimes of Passion* to him. "He telephoned every day either about his work or mine," Willes wrote in an introduction to a posthumous collection of Orton's television plays. "His complete originality . . . is what I miss most of all."[15] Willes's interest in Orton did not extend to Halliwell, whom he found "gentle, cloying, and wildly dated. He behaved very much like a camp

young man of the thirties. He was an oddity, an irritant." Orton moved
more easily than Halliwell through the lords, ladies, and theatrical
celebrities at Willes's parties. "The class of my characters has gone up
over the years," Orton quipped, and Willes was in large part responsible
for widening his social horizons.

Willes was aware how strained the relationship between Orton
and Halliwell had become. In April, at Orton's request, Willes had
contacted his own private GP, Dr. Douglas Ismay, so that Halliwell
could talk to someone about his psychological problems. "Willes suggested that Halliwell come to see me because Orton complained that
Halliwell was really getting on his back. It was a method of syphoning
off," Dr. Ismay recalls. Halliwell never suspected that he'd been fobbed
off; but his own possessiveness of Orton and the threat of Willes's
indifference to him made attending such affairs difficult. For the
July party, Halliwell armed himself with an Eton tie, an emblem of his
disdain for Willes's chic milieu, and something, besides Orton's success,
to talk about. The attention he got was more than he'd expected:

Went to Peter Willes for dinner. When we got there [a TV pro-
ducer] stared at Kenneth in horror. "That's an old Etonian tie!" he
screeched. "Yes," Kenneth said, "it's a joke." [The producer] looked
staggered and wrinkled up his face in an evil sort of way. "Well, I'm
afraid it's a joke against you then. People will imagine you're
passing yourself off as an old Etonian. They'll laugh at you." "I'm
sending up Eton," Kenneth said. "Oh, no!" [the producer] cackled
with a sort of eldritch shriek. "You're just pathetic! I mean it's dis-
graceful wearing that tie." "It's a joke!" Kenneth said, looking tight-
lipped, a little embarrassed and angry. "People will know." "Not
the people I meet," Kenneth said, "they'll think it's funny." "You're
making people angry," [the producer] said. "I don't care," Kenneth
said, laughing a little too readily. "I want to make them angry."
"But why?" [the producer] said, as we sat down. "People dislike you
enough already. Why make them more angry? I mean—it's per-
missible, although silly as a foible of youth, but you—a middle-aged
nonentity—it's sad and pathetic!" I could see that the conversation
had become impossible and that unless something were done the
evening would begin in ruins. "Now stop this both of you!" I said,
in a commanding voice. "It's ridiculous to carry on in this way over
a wretched tie." . . . The conversation drifted on in a desultory way,
meandering through insults and bubbling over recrimination until
Kenneth exploded, "All you people that are mad on Joe really have
no idea what he's like." [The producer] paled. "I'm not mad on
Joe! Whatever do you mean?" Fortunately before Kenneth could
answer this question (and rend our relationship with [the producer]

to shreds) the doorbell rang. . . . We went out to dinner later. . . . Lady Glasgow and Peter Willes discussing the merits or demerits of Kenneth's joke against Eton. "I always say that my son goes to Slough Grammar School," Lady G. said. I'd taken two Librium tablets. Lady G. gave two more to me. Producing them gayly from her handbag. "I have to take tranquillisers when my husband is driving," she said. "I simply cannot stand the nervous strain of having him behind the wheel. And prayers are of no avail. It's medical science that calms me down." . . . We went back to Willes's flat. After a short discussion on customs of the English gentry towards the end of the 19th century apropos of Willes producing *Lady Windermere's Fan* for television, Kenneth and I trooped off. "If only my old aunt were alive," Wanda, Lady Glasgow said, with a shake of her head, "she could really have told us whether or not the footmen would've worn gloves." . . . Outside on the pavement, [Kenneth] was still smarting from the "middle-aged nonentity" line. And quite right too. Kenneth has more talent, although it's hidden, than [the producer] can flash if he had the reflector from Mount Palomar to do it with.   [July 22, 1967]

The party episode confirmed what Halliwell feared was the world's low opinion of himself. It left him stunned and dejected. His ability was not only hidden from the world by his abrasive defensiveness; it was twisted and weakened by it. And by Orton's brilliant success, which blinded anyone in their company to Halliwell's presence. This incident was the deepest of Halliwell's public rejections, but not the first time he'd felt diminished by Orton's celebrity. In May, after an evening with two friends, Halliwell had erupted in a bitter tirade against Orton and the inequality of their social encounters, pounding the walls and screaming:

"They treated me like shit! I won't be treated like this. . . . You had tea, they had tea; you had jam tarts, they had jam tarts. And those photographs of Mustapha—he was so unattractive and because you'd had him they said 'what a dish.' " "Surely you expected this?" I said. "I expected to be treated with a little more respect." He began to cry. . . . "He's a tuft hunter. . . . I saw through it. You saw through it. If I'd been taken in by it then there would have been cause for rage. As it is, it looks like 'Hell Hath No Fury.' " . . . "When I'm not here you won't be able to write in this flip way," Kenneth said. The inference that I don't know how cruel, despicable and senseless life is hurt me. "I won't have you monopolizing the agony market," I shouted at last in a fury. For the best part of a day the to-ing and fro-ing went on. At last, the threats of suicide abated until the last was "If you have both of them you can say goodbye to me!" And with that we began to pick up the pieces.

[May 2, 1967]

Soon afterwards, they departed for Morocco, where Orton's fame was of no importance and victories could be purchased for a few dirham. Momentarily at least, Halliwell could feel equal to his friend.

But now, back in London, there was no way to sustain the illusion. Orton was the centre of attention and Halliwell was pushed to the periphery. On the same day the producer confronted Halliwell with being a middle-aged nonentity, Orton received his first delighted feedback about *What the Butler Saw.* "People must've thought I was mad," Peggy Ramsay cooed over the phone, calling him early in the morning. "I simply had hysterics. It's the very best thing you've done so far. And technically in advance of *Loot.*" The next day, July 23, Oscar Lewenstein rang to invite Orton and Halliwell for a weekend at his home in Brighton to discuss production plans; and that afternoon, as Halliwell brooded over the insult at Willes's party, Willes called to gush to Orton about his new play.

"Oh," he said, "it's so exciting. It's like a Palais Royale farce. It's simply splendid. And it must be done exquisitely." "He only likes it because I said he wouldn't," Kenneth said, bitterly. . . .

[July 23, 1967]

The cycle had begun again. Orton's heady success was in the foreground of everybody's mind, while Halliwell's leaden sense of failure kept him immobilized. The calls, the meetings, the plans, the letters were for Orton. Soon the interviews would start again, with Halliwell making himself absent while Orton explained his own bedsitter life. "I'm very conscious of what's come before," he had told an interviewer earlier that year. "I like Lucian and the classical writers, and I suppose that's what gives my writing a difference, an old fashion classical education! Which I never received, but I gave myself one, reading them all in English, for I have so little Latin and less Greek."[16] In private, Orton always acknowledged Halliwell's contribution; but in public, he never admitted to either a teacher or a friend. The press releases said merely that he had been married and divorced. This was insufficient for Halliwell who, under this pressure, was forced to make unrealistic claims for himself.

Halliwell wanted a family; Orton wanted freedom—a difference painfully apparent in their attitudes toward sex. On the afternoon of

July 23, they were visited by Kenneth Williams, who recorded the meeting in his diary:

> Went up to see Joe Orton and Kenneth. Both were so kind. We talked a lot about homosexuality and the effect the new clause would have (the Humphry Berkeley Bill not Leo Abse.*) We all agreed it would accomplish very little, that it was the climate of opinion that really counted more.
>
> Joe walked me all the way to King's Cross. I remonstrated with him, "No, it's not fair. You must go back to Ken. He's on his own." He said it didn't matter. Then he said, "I'll never leave him."
>
> We talked about his inability to love and his horror of involvement. He said, "I need to be utterly free." In the flat K. Halliwell had disagreed with this saying that love was involvement and you cannot live without love.

Williams remembers that when Orton said, "I'll never leave him," he stopped on the pavement and looked him in the eye to emphasize his sincerity. "I hadn't said, 'leave him.' Joe was answering his own question, what was in his mind or what other people said."

Evidently, Orton was toying with the idea of leaving Halliwell. At one of Adrienne Corri's parties he had been attracted to a novelist whose accomplishment, university education, and poise were the fulfillment of Halliwell's wasted potential, and he was flirting with the idea of living with him. In his sickness, Halliwell, who needed love and said so, became increasingly unlovable. His panic to make people draw closer only pushed them away, and he broadcast his pleas for attention in his complaints about Orton's "trolling," his demands on Orton's allegiance, and his psychosomatic illnesses. Orton's sexual rapacity was a threatening reminder of Halliwell's emotional dependence. He wanted Orton to share some of his newly won success and public life, but Orton could not do so.

Kenneth Williams sensed Orton's feisty independence. "I kept saying, 'You'd better go back Joe.' Halliwell had asked how long he'd be because he was making a meal. It was just like a wife asking the husband what time he'll be home for dinner. It irked Joe. He kept saying, 'Let's go on walking.' He wanted to get away. He was buoyant.

---

* The Bill, identical to Lord Arran's in the House of Lords, sought to make sex in private between two consenting adults no longer an illegal offense and to fix the age of adulthood at twenty-one. The Bill had its Second Reading in Parliament on February 11, 1966. Soon afterwards, Berkeley lost his seat in a General Election. A similar bill sponsored by Leo Abse finally became law on July 27, 1967.

He'd become somebody in his own right. It was no longer 'we,' but 'I'—'I'll find the house.' 'I'll never leave him.' Increasingly, it was the sense that I am important."

Orton had sought the advice of Adrienne Corri and Penelope Gilliatt, two women who had survived marital turmoil and could talk intelligently about it. "I think he was going to leave Halliwell," Miss Corri says. "We talked about the ramifications of leaving someone and sorting oneself out. He said that the terrible thing was he didn't know what Ken would do without him." Miss Gilliatt, who had written about the problem in *Sunday, Bloody Sunday*, had a similar hunch: "I had the feeling he wanted to leave Halliwell if he could handle things and introduce some balance into the situation. He wanted always to find out whether it was cataclysmic to leave someone or whether it could be done without such violence as would eventually happen. He was talking mainly about how dependent Halliwell was on him. He wanted advice about how he could lift the weight of this dependence from his shoulders and put it elsewhere."

They argued at length about promiscuity, which Halliwell found upsetting but Orton claimed stimulated his view of the world. "He felt very strongly that the energy of making a piece of art came out of the energy of chaos," Miss Gilliatt says. "I don't agree with that. We had long arguments about it. He was probably trying to rationalize his own way of life. He was fighting for his life. He was a born writer and he lived in chaotic emotional conditions. He needed time to write. Sometimes he arrived for drinks absolutely worn out from these fights with Halliwell." The more ferociously Halliwell clung to Orton, the more Orton felt the need to put distance between them. He could not easily face Halliwell with the facts. Orton even asked Miss Gilliatt to plead the case of promiscuity for him; she refused. Orton sought release in rough trade and Halliwell reassurance in involvement.

"Halliwell's argument was that continual immersion of yourself in an anonymous sexual set-up, going with strangers into rooms or alleyways was going to lead to a wastage of aims," Kenneth Williams recalls. "Halliwell was not a fool. He had a very good mind. 'Don't you see,' he said, 'that these sexual experiments can only lead to a dead end?' My immediate response was to agree; but as an actor, I could not help but respond every time Joe told me these anecdotes about his adventures because they were terribly funny and always illuminating."

Orton exploded at Halliwell. "Look, I've got to do it. I've got to be the fly on the wall!" He'd been equally adamant in talking to Penelope Gilliatt. As she describes it, "He wanted to know whether I thought it could work in any set-up. He talked about the damage it did; and at the same time he wanted to kick the sides of society apart. He asked if he should deceive Halliwell about it or give it up. And then he said furiously, 'No, I can't give up promiscuity! I won't give it up!' "

Orton had a clown's appetite for political anarchy; but for him this was impossible without sexual anarchy. The lavatories were a sordid setting for sexual adventure, and these encounters confirmed his sense of human suffering and outrageousness. They were dangerous and pathetic. Orton knew this and was drawn tò them. "When I meet people casually," he told Kenneth Williams, "I always call myself a packer. I make things up. I call myself a packer, a metalworker, a lithographer, a hairdresser's assistant. That way I put people off guard. Their dialogue is natural. It's also better for sex." No matter how successful he became, the lavatories confirmed Orton's destiny as an outsider. The encounters also stoked his anger against a society whose taboos forced adults into hidden corners to take their furtive pleasure. As the "fly on the wall," he paid attention to the detail of character and the stilted language that negotiated these anonymous gropings:

> After walking for a while I found a gents lavatory on a patch of grass near a church. I went in. It was very dark. There was a man there. Tall, grand and smiling. In the gloom he looked aristocratic. When the lights were turned on (after about five minutes) I could see that he was stupid, smiling and bank-clerkish. He showed his cock. I let him feel mine. "Ooh!" he gasped . . . "Oo!" I asked if he had anywhere to go back to? "No," he said, "I don't have the choice of my neighbours, you see. They're down on me and I couldn't take the risk." He nodded to a dwarf skulking in the corner of the lavatory. "He'll suck you off, though. I've seen him do it." He made a motion to the dwarfish creature rather as someone would call a taxi ànd then, I suppose, went back to his neighbours refreshed. [July 30, 1967]

Like the obsessive adulterers in Restoration comedy, which Orton studied with admiration, the spectre of death lurked behind his own pursuit of pleasure. It was impossible to celebrate one without accepting the other. Promiscuity was a submersion in chaos, a flirtation with death, a ritual wasting with its "magical" corollary of renewed fertility. Orton felt compelled to explore the taboos surrounding life and death. His trips into forbidden territory were the only alternative he saw to the quiet, cosy suffocation of conventional British living that he satirized so brilliantly in his plays, where people ask little of life and receive

little in return. Orton had the detachment and brazenness of the dis-
possessed; he had nothing to lose.

In his laughter Orton could admit the perverse and demystify it by
making it delightful. The rewritten opening lines of *The Ruffian on
the Stair* (1967) capture a lifetime of impoverishment in the jolt of one
exchange:

> JOYCE. Have you an appointment today?
> MIKE. Yes, I'm to be at King's Cross station at eleven. I'm meeting
> a man in the toilet.
> JOYCE. You always go to such interesting places.

ON JULY 27, Orton and Halliwell set off with Oscar Lewenstein to his
home in Brighton for a long weekend. It was a wet, tense time. They
had little in common with Lewenstein besides an enthusiasm for
Orton's work. By the time the train pulled into Brighton Station,
production plans had been mapped out—which left four days of
desultory conversation and random reading ahead of them. It was an
enervating prospect from which, as usual, only Orton would benefit.

They had been on a Brighton weekend once before, with Sir
Terence Rattigan after the success of *Entertaining Mr. Sloane* in 1964.
Even then Halliwell had dismayed rather than impressed. "He was a
bit round the bend," Sir Terence recalls, noting that Halliwell wore a
little "slap" (rouge). "He seemed quite determined that Joe should
never speak at all. He was desperately trying to give the impression
that he wrote all Joe's plays. Joe wasn't denying it. Joe had very
good natural manners. He let Halliwell go on and on. But it was
perfectly clear that the man who was overtalking wasn't the man who'd
written the plays. It was perfectly plain to me—and this isn't being
clever after the event—that Halliwell was wildly jealous of Joe's sexual
escapades. He resented Joe's success in that sphere as well. It was one
part of Joe's life he couldn't collaborate in." On the second night of
their strained stay, Sir Terence, who had a standing emergency arrangement with his neighbors the Oliviers, called on them to help weather
the boredom of Halliwell's performance. "Larry and Joan came over,"
Sir Terence says. "You saw the royal pants being bored off Larry.
Halliwell lectured him. It was a very depressing evening. Joe didn't
seem to mind. He was quite sensitive enough to know what kind of
appalling impression Halliwell was making. And also the appalling
impression he was giving of Joe. Obviously Joe was going to have to
leave this man. He couldn't have lived with him much longer and kept
his sanity."

The Lewenstein weekend was another setpiece for Orton, while Halliwell felt increasingly incidental. Closeted in the company of strangers, obedient to an alien routine, they quickly grew depressed.

"On the way back we tried to avoid looking at the boys and talking about Tangier," Orton wrote of one of their frequent walks. " 'We must get back there as soon as possible,' Kenneth said. 'We could be there now. Instead of this wilderness. . . .' "[17] They were, as Orton wrote, "numbed" by the weekend. When they got back to London on July 31, Halliwell's gloom had not lifted. "We went to bed early," Orton noted. "Kenneth was looking wan."

The next morning, August 1, Orton set off to visit his family in Leicester, where the local theatre was mounting *Entertaining Mr. Sloane,* the first of his plays to be staged in his hometown:

> Said goodbye to Kenneth this morning. He seemed odd. On the spur of the moment I asked if he wanted to come home to Leicester with me. He looked surprised and said, "No."

Halliwell had never visited Orton's family. Orton's offer, though well meaning, was misguided. He couldn't read the signs of Halliwell's depression. Having just left one "wilderness," Halliwell had no appetite to languish without family or function in another alien territory. Orton had roots and sweet public revenge awaiting him in Leicester. If Halliwell tagged along, he would be a prop in another Orton production. Life was empty without Orton and insufficient with him. On August 3, after two days alone, Halliwell's emptiness and fury overwhelmed him. He felt suicidal.

"The number of humiliating admissions I've made. You'd think it would draw me closer to somebody. But it doesn't." Orton's startling lines in *The Ruffian on the Stair* pinpointed Halliwell's predicament. No one was really listening or willing to hear. As with his first wig, nobody took much notice. He therefore had to shout louder, which made people listen even less. Halliwell went first to the Samaritans, who couldn't deal with him immediately. He was too desperate to wait, and went instead to Dr. Ismay. But even Ismay was unsympathetic: "I thought he was a bit of a pain in the neck, a bit of a burden. You felt you couldn't get rid of him. It was the holding on relationship . . . a depressed, deprived person who wants more and more of the doctor or the interviewer." Halliwell arrived without an appointment, but Ismay agreed to see him. "He told me that following the long holiday, the relationship between him and Orton was not good. He was very depressed about it. He talked about leaving Orton and at the same time committing suicide." Ismay prescribed an anti-depressant and a small quantity of amphetamines for Halliwell, who made an appointment to see him again the next day.

After visiting the doctor, Halliwell made his way to the one community that remained for him: the cast of *Loot*. Sheila Ballantine, who played Fay in the London production, found Halliwell sitting on the stage-door steps of the Criterion when she arrived at seven o'clock for the performance. He had been there since six, making conversation with the ninety-year-old stage doorman. Halliwell was carrying a book and the manuscript copy of *What the Butler Saw*. "I brought you the book," he said, handing her Malcolm Muggeridge's *The Thirties*.

"We'd never discussed Muggeridge," Miss Ballantine recalls. "I thought to myself: 'I never said anything about this.' But I thought he wanted to talk. So we went into my dressing room while I made up. It had taken me ages to realize that one hardly ever asked Kenneth what he'd been doing. Kenneth was always the one standing alone, listening. People would always be asking Joe things, and he was the one who monopolized conversation. It must have been like that with everybody." While Halliwell was talking to Sheila Ballantine, Kenneth Cranham came in. Halliwell started to tell them how ill he was, how he was going to have a nervous breakdown. Cranham remembers that "Halliwell was very upset about [the producer's] middle-aged nonentity dig. He kept saying, 'It was me who thought up the title for *Loot*. It was me who got Joe to write.'" Neither actor had ever seen Halliwell by himself, but even alone his conversation returned obsessively to Orton. After the show they took him for a drink. He told them about *What the Butler Saw*, making it seem he was letting them in on a secret. "He was rather suggesting how important he was in the decisions Joe made. He was making a lot of that. It was a bit sad," Miss Ballantine recalls. "I knew he was disturbed. I said, 'Do come and stay with me tonight.' 'No,' he said, 'I'll be perfectly all right because Joe's coming back tomorrow.'"

Halliwell saw Dr. Ismay again on August 4. His anxiety had not decreased and he wasn't sleeping well, even though Orton had returned. Dr. Ismay gave him a small quantity of Elixir Chloral. Halliwell reiterated his complaints of Orton's rejection and promiscuity, as he would do repeatedly during the last three weeks of his life. "I never took it too seriously," Dr. Ismay says. Halliwell told him that "Orton depended on him in phrasing and that he helped him in a very basic way. He wanted to be acknowledged and be included in the glamour and exaltation Joe was receiving with success." It was an impossible demand.

Since *Entertaining Mr. Sloane,* in which he'd been a major influence, Halliwell had become more a sounding board than an inspiration. Even Orton, according to Peggy Ramsay, referred to *Entertaining Mr. Sloane* as "our play." "The first time Joe came to see me, he didn't produce Kenneth," she recalls. "But the second time he came, he said, 'Can I bring a friend?' Afterwards he always brought Kenneth with him, and Kenneth always attended rehearsals." But this procedure had stopped after *Entertaining Mr. Sloane.* Like the influence of any partner in a marriage, Halliwell's contribution to Orton's work and his life had been rich and varied. But Orton did the writing. There was no way to deny him that—except to kill him.

Orton and Halliwell appeared together backstage at the Criterion on August 5. Orton was effervescent, Halliwell morose. "Kenneth was very much stranger," Sheila Ballantine recalls. "He had a weird, shut-off presence. Joe was being hilarious, describing Kath in the Leicester production and how she had overdone her sexual advances to Sloane. I was being the boy and Joe was being Kath. He was groping me in front of Kenneth. I thought to myself, 'He obviously doesn't know how ill Kenneth is or he wouldn't be mucking about with me in front of him.' Right in the middle of this, Kenneth started talking about himself: 'And I went to the Samaritans. And I . . .' 'Yes I know,' I said. Joe said, 'Oh, you told her that, did you?' Then he went on with his description. And I thought, 'My God, he can't see! He hasn't noticed!' "

Simon Ward, who played Dennis in the *Loot* production, was also puzzled by Orton's indifference to Halliwell's pain. "Maybe Joe wanted out. It looked as though he were trying for out. No one could be as insensitive as that if you really cared about the person. Ken was looking really bad."

Halliwell had already attempted suicide once in 1962. Now Orton was worried about his increasing dependence on anti-depressants and barbiturates, which he mixed together into one large jar. But as he confided to Adrienne Corri, he didn't think Halliwell would kill himself. On August 6, Orton came backstage without Halliwell during *Loot's* intermission. "He was a bit skittish. Bright-eyed," Sheila Ballantine says. " 'I've got somebody with me,' he said. I thought to myself, 'I must tell him how ill Kenneth is.' I didn't. I decided not to interfere."

On August 8, the day before he left on vacation, Dr. Ismay received an urgent call from Halliwell. He saw him at 5:00 p.m. "He wasn't functioning when he came to see me. He seemed anxious that I was going on holiday. It was serious enough to consider admission to a hospital." He told Halliwell he should see a consulting psychiatrist and that he would make the proper arrangements. He changed Halliwell's prescription to more powerful anti-depressants. While waiting for Ismay's newest prescriptions to be filled, Halliwell made his way to Peter Willes's nearby flat to pass the time. "I'd never been alone with Halliwell," Willes remembers of Halliwell's rambling, distraught conversation. "He said, 'Of course, Joe would miss me more than I'd miss Joe. I've got money. I've got £5,000.' I never realized Halliwell had money. I thought he lived off Joe. He said, 'You should see Joe, he's much different when you're not there and I'm with him. If I say I'm going to leave, he staggers about saying, "You can't destroy me! You can't leave me! I can't bear it!" ' I didn't believe any of this, but Halliwell obviously did. When he left, I phoned Joe immediately. I knew Kenneth was very ill." (Earlier in the week, Willes had arranged a party for Orton with Dorothy Dickson, the music-comedy star of the twenties, so that Orton could meet some of his theatrical admirers—Vivien Leigh, Emlyn Williams, Harold Pinter. Halliwell was not to be invited. Orton had consented. It was, Willes recalls, the first time he'd been disloyal to Halliwell.) Now Willes rang up Orton to advise him to be careful. "I said, 'Joe, you mustn't leave him for a moment.' " Orton agreed to stay at home and watch Halliwell closely.

Orton and Halliwell were last seen together returning from shopping that evening. Halliwell was dressed in a safari jacket, hiding the bags beneath his eyes under sunglasses. Over the last few weeks, their neighbors—the Salvonis—had noticed that Halliwell, even on the greyest days, rarely was without the sunglasses. He seemed withdrawn. He'd stopped greeting people in the street. That night when Aldo Salvoni stopped and asked them in for a beer, Orton was, as always, boyish and friendly. Halliwell was quiet. They declined the invitation. Orton explained about the meeting with Richard Lester and the plans to make a movie of *Up Against It*.

Kenneth Cranham called Orton to ask if he and Halliwell would like to go to a late-night screening of Yoko Ono's film *Bottoms*. Orton said he'd like to come, but he didn't think Halliwell was feeling well. There was a pause while Orton asked Halliwell, then Orton said, "No, Kenneth doesn't want to come." Orton's words to his friend gave no indication of how serious Halliwell's condition was.

That night most of the calls were for Halliwell. Dr. Ismay called three times. There is always a high incidence of suicide between arranging hospitalization and a patient's actual admission, and Ismay was worried. In the first call, he informed Halliwell that a psychiatrist had been found and that he would call at Noel Road in the morning. But

Halliwell told Dr. Ismay that he was "taking the matter far too seriously
and he would make arrangements to see the psychiatrist at a more convenient time." Dr. Ismay then made an appointment for Halliwell on
August 10; and by the last call, Halliwell reported, "I've started taking
the new tablets. I feel much better. Thank you for the trouble you've
taken." Perhaps the drugs, which Halliwell could only have acquired
three hours before, were beginning to have a soporific effect. Or perhaps the rapid change in Halliwell's temperament which Dr. Ismay
noticed over the phone was due to the knowledge that neither life nor
Orton would punish him much longer.

ORTON WAS KILLED between two and four in the morning. The
Salvonis, whose bedroom was adjacent and who were awake, heard no
struggle or argument. Ordinarily even the clatter of Orton's typewriter
or Halliwell's sudden bursts into song were audible. The police
described Orton's bludgeoning as "a deliberate form of frenzy."[18]
Halliwell's death note guided them to the diary of the oppressive farce
that their life together had become:

> Exhausting wrangles over trivia. Kenneth, laying in bed, suddenly
> shouted "I hope I die of heart disease! I'd like to see you manage
> then." He talks a lot of *The Dance of Death*. "We're living it," he
> suddenly said. "This is Strindberg!" Soothed down the situation
> only to have it break out later. "You're quite a different person,
> you know, since you had your success."   [March 18, 1967]

Halliwell had read and re-read the diary. In it, bruising sentences
hinted at the retreat of Orton's affection: "Arguments continue
sporadically, breaking out like sudden flames on a dying fire" (April
4). Orton's pages preserved scenes of aching frustration and failure that
Halliwell wanted to forget but that Orton's presence only exacerbated:

> When I got back home Kenneth H was in such a rage that he'd
> written in large letters on the wall "JOE ORTON IS A SPINELESS
> TWAT." He sulked for a while and then came around. He'd been to
> the doctors and got 400 Valium tablets. Later we took two each and
> had an amazing sexual session. . . . But it didn't work out. "I'm not
> sure what the block is," I said. "I can fuck other people perfectly
> well. But up to now, I can't fuck you." This is something quite
> strange.   [May 5, 1967]

The diary read like a fever chart of Halliwell's depression and a catalogue of the excruciating emptiness of his life. In it, Halliwell could see himself playing an increasingly minor role in the eventful drama of Orton's life. The diary made Halliwell's sense of failure a sideshow; the homicide made it the main attraction. Through murder, Halliwell achieved the public association with Joe Orton's career that he had been denied in life. The diary, which ended as Exhibit A at their inquest, was entitled "Diary of a Somebody."[19]

2

SOMEBODY FROM NOWHERE

GERALDINE. *I lived in a normal family. I had no love for my father.*
—*What the Butler Saw*

JOE ORTON always wanted to shine. He polished the wit of his plays with the same delighted concentration that he rubbed baby lotion on his face to make it gleam. The result, in both cases, was dazzling. Orton looked on his ascent to wealth and celebrity with amusement, as the title of his diary shows. "I have often seen reminiscences of people I have never heard of," says Charles Pooter, the prim, social-climbing diarist of George and Weeden Grossmith's *Diary of a Nobody*. "I fail to see why—because I am not a Somebody—my diary should not be interesting." Pooter's humorless egotism makes his diary a ludicrous chronicle of suburban misadventures whose situations sometimes paralleled those in Orton's life:

> I have received an invitation to a banquet given by the Lord Mayor of London—just like Pooter Kenneth says. . . . It's really absurd, though. The letter says that the banquet is being held "in honour of those eminent in the arts, sciences, and learning." "It's just because of the £100,000," I said to Peter Willes. "They've realized that I'm as rich as they are and now they invite me to their rubbishy dinner." P. Willes looked shocked. "I really don't think you should talk about the Lord Mayor's banquet like that," he said. "I believe they have excellent turtle soup. . . ."   [March 14, 1967]

Pooter was a Victorian Malvolio lost in the fantasy of his own perfection, and Orton was a modern Feste, a realist who was compelled to speak the unspeakable. Like his laughter, Orton's triumph never forgot his past:

We parted having agreed to make a list of possibilities [for casting the Broadway production of *Loot*]. "Like a nice afternoon, gents," a tout outside a strip club said as we passed. "Naked ladies. All alive." "You look very pretty in that fur coat you're wearing," Oscar Lewenstein said, as we stood on the corner before going our separate ways. I said, "Peggy Ramsay bought it me. It was thirteen pounds fifteen." "Very cheap," Michael White said. "Yes, I've discovered I look better in cheap clothes." "I wonder what the significance of that is?" Oscar said. "I'm from the gutter," I said. "And don't you ever forget it because I won't."   [January 9, 1967]

The "gutter" to which Orton referred was the Saffron Lane Estates, in Leicester, where he grew up. These were one of the sprawling city council developments built on the unfertile boulder clay of Leicester's south side between 1920 and 1925 in order to accommodate the city's growing work force. Leicester's problem during the twenties and thirties was one of growth, not depression. The town's unusual prosperity was due to the nature of its major industries. Women like Elsie Orton could find work easily in the hosiery factories, Leicester's oldest and largest industry.[1] Elsie was a machinist. From eight in the morning until six at night she stitched underwear, trousers, vests, blouses. Her "villa" was close enough to the factory for her to cook lunch for her children in the lunch break. Men like William Orton could get work in the footwear business. With both men and women absorbed by light industry, Leicester's city fathers could point with self-congratulation to statistics that showed Leicester with the highest per capita income of any city in Britain. Even more astounding, there had been no major labor disputes in the city since 1918.

The Saffron Lane Estates were another sign of Leicester's progress and prosperity. Orton's "gutter" was not the brutal and bustling industrial landscape of the North, but the drab monotony of a comfortable city whose council housing reflected its unimaginative mediocrity. The bleak adequacy of the Saffron Lane Estates had a deceptive violence. Fayhurst Road, where Orton lived, and the narrow streets around it seemed to have been vaccinated against life, corroborating a recent city history that claims: "The dramatic has no place at all in the streets of Leicester."[2] With its tuft of grass for a front lawn and its maple tree planted ten feet from the next, each house was solid, quiet, and tidy. The sameness of the architecture and expectation had its special oppressiveness. Cramped, cold, and dark, the rows of sooty pebble-granite homes were to Orton a grey backdrop of impoverishment: set-pieces for a lifetime of making do. "I remember as a kid feeling there was no escape," says Leonie Barnett, Orton's youngest sister, and the one member of his family with whom he remained friendly. "Fayhurst Road where we all grew up hasn't changed. It's still as mucky as ever. I always thought, 'This is it, mate. Either you swim or drown.'"

Orton's plays dug angrily at this numbed acceptance. An epigraph to *The Good and Faithful Servant* (1964) is taken from the *Concise Oxford Dictionary*: "Faith, n. Reliance, trust, *in;* belief founded on authority." Like Buchanan, the play's central figure, who has given a lifetime and an amputated limb in loyal service to the company, Orton's parents had only wounds and paltry dividends to show for their faith in industry. Elsie Orton had lost a lung from an early battle with tuberculosis. After decades at the knitting machine, her eyesight failed badly. She was forced to leave and become a charwoman. Seeking financial security, William Orton had taken a job as a gardener for the Leicester Council in 1929, and lost a finger pruning the trees of a public park. He was not compensated. His security was as "durable" as the toaster and alarm clock Buchanan receives on retirement from the firm. "Now, you see when I should be having a good life, I'm almost blind," explains William Orton, retired, bewildered, and alone. "I worked hard for that pension. I had to give it to the blind to keep me."

Orton's laughter was an enemy of work, not only interrupting it but casting doubt on its seriousness. In play Orton took his revenge on the devouring work routine that had robbed his family and the society of so much of its humanity:

RAY. I don't work.
BUCHANAN. Not work!? (*He stares, open-mouthed.*) What do you do then?
RAY. I enjoy myself.
BUCHANAN. That's a terrible thing to do. I'm bowled over by this, I can tell you. It's my turn to be shocked now. You ought to have a steady job.
EDITH. Two perhaps.

But in the days before he found the right language to satirize the work ethic, the young John Orton's diaries recorded the boredom of routine and the banality of his surroundings. Orton called his early diaries, kept between sixteen and eighteen, "conversations with myself." In his private and often misspelled thoughts, the need to make money is already at odds with his resentment at unstimulating toil:

January 9, 1949
Very quiet day. Listened to Gilbert and Sullivan on the wireless. Went to bed feeling ill at the thought of work tomorrow.

January 10
Work again. I felt "so tired" when I got up. Fed up. . . .

January 14
Thank god it's Friday again. I wish I belonged to one of the idle
rich and didn't have to work. . . .

January 24
Work, how I hate it in the morning when Dad says, "It's ten to
seven."

With their neat gardens and peaceful tree-lined streets, the Saffron
Lane Estates kept the suburban fantasy of leisure and the good life in
the foreground. But Leicester's industrial landscape was always in the
background, as ugly and unheroic as the jobs the workers held. From the
front door of the Orton house, a barren horizon loomed up over the
maple trees. A clutter of electricity pylons were strung like scarecrows
against a skyline dominated by BRITISH MADE emblazoned on a
behemoth smokestack. Over the years, the canal two blocks from Fayhurst Road where Orton liked to walk and swim became fouled with
industrial debris. Garages and houses pushed up to one side of the
waterway; on the other, storage barns from the gasworks swelled up
out of the marshes like ugly sores. "Who conceived the idea of building
a house in the midst of a rubbish dump?" Sloane asks the old father,
Kemp, in *Entertaining Mr. Sloane.* Orton, who saw himself as the
physical prototype for Sloane, and whose father like Kemp was almost
blind and called "Dadda," always felt the desolation outside the cosy
home his mother tried to make. If 9 Fayhurst Road wasn't the model
for the wasteland Orton examined in *Entertaining Mr. Sloane,* it was
symptomatic of the sad bargain so many Englishmen made with their
society and the scraps of life they settled for. Orton couldn't stand it.
"I was sacked from all the jobs I had between sixteen and eighteen
because I was never interested in any of them. I resented having to go
to work in the morning and very often I didn't bother—I just looked
in shop windows, or if it was a nice sunny morning I'd sit in the Town
Hall Square and have an ice-cream."[3] Orton put both Leicester and
his family behind him at eighteen; but Leicester had left its mark. In
his early writing, he dreamed of doing damage to authority and its
smug indifference:

Words were more effective than actions; in the right hands verbs
and nouns could create panic. . . . The blast of a long sentence was
curiously local, and a lot of shorter sentences seemed better. And

then there was the problem of gathering enough of the enemy together in order that they might listen. He started wondering where
and how he could hit the enemy most. He started calculating and
found some sentences were puny against large targets. Then perhaps
a new type of sentence. . . . His figures showed that when a particularly dangerous collection of words exploded the shock waves
were capable of killing centuries afterwards.   [*Head to Toe*, 1961]

The vigor of Leicester's indifference was stifling. Even the authorized history of the county maintained proudly that Leicester was
marked "by the absence of any extreme or distinctive movements in
politics, religion, or culture."[4] Orton spent over half of his life there.
His plays wanted to rattle the underpinnings of society with a rage
spawned by a city whose essence was in its motto: SEMPER EADEM—
Always the Same.

WILLIAM ORTON first met his wife in her favorite Leicester habitat, the
pub. "Elsie used to do a few turns—singing—in the pubs. All over
Leicester more or less. Very good mezzo-soprano, she was. She sang
classic operas." Three years later, in 1931, they were married. He
was twenty-six, she was twenty-seven. They thought themselves lucky to
be allocated the corner house at Fayhurst Road in 1935. As with everything else in their life, they'd had to wait for it. They were in lodgings
when John Kingsley Orton was born on January 1, 1933. He was their
first child. They had three more children at Fayhurst Road: Douglas
(1937), Marilyn (1939), and Leonie (1944).

The house the Ortons had looked forward to occupying was never a
happy home. Low-ceilinged and drab, the main room was in the front:
a dingy square with two small sash windows looking out onto the wood-
shed and neighboring laundry lines. Above the fireplace was the room's
only picture—a print of Highland cattle. On the wooden sideboard
were William Orton's mementos from six years' duty in the medical
corps in World War II: a Nazi dagger with the swastika sawn off, and
a beer stein, in which Elsie kept flowers cut from William's private
backyard garden. Between the fireplace and the window was a piano—
an incongruous extravagance in the spare, uncomfortable room. Elsie
Orton had purchased it so John, whom she favored as the most gifted
child, could learn to play. He didn't, and the only tune she could bang
out on the keys was "Don't Fence Me In."

"Everybody seemed to be happy but us," Leonie Barnett remembers. "We always seemed to be bickering." The house caged them. The

thin walls were covered with sombre flowered wallpaper that stank with the odor of fried food and damp. The kitchen was painted dark green, the hall was grey, and the front door chocolate brown. The bleakness had its effect on Orton, whose acute asthma as a child kept him at home much more than the others. He painted his bedroom a glossy white and decorated it with the mysterious hieroglyphics of Pitman's Shorthand. "Maybe we'd have been more of a family if we'd had a car and had money," Leonie thinks now. But there was no privacy and no peace. The house was as threadbare as their lives. "I had a hard life," William says. "It was just a means of existing." His house embodied this sad, makeshift destiny.

Aspects of William Orton's frail, cowed presence reappear in many Orton characters: the myopic Kemp in *Entertaining Mr. Sloane;* the flower-loving and woebegone husband, McLeavy, in *Loot;* the lost and crumpled commissionaire Buchanan in *The Good and Faithful Servant,* whom out of uniform Orton describes as "smaller, shrunken and insignificant." A country boy, William had tried his hand at the boot and shoe trade in Leicester. He was a "puller-over," stretching the tip of the shoe over the sole while a machine tapped in the nails. It was piecework, and William found it hard to compete with others. He was not a fighter. He left to become a gardener for the city. He earned £2.10 a week; by the time he retired thirty-five years later, he was up to £14. It was a meagre sum, but he was happy in the outdoors. Each morning at seven, after he'd brought Elsie her tea and roused the children, he'd mount his old black bike and peddle fifteen miles to Stoneygate on the rich north side of Leicester. "I had nicer flowers to plant." On Sunday, he would often bike out to his greenhouse and light the heaters. There, he had his tea and his flowers and his quiet. He was a simple man, and the flowers could not talk back. "Gardening kept you busy. You always looked forward to something coming up, you see. It was exciting to see if they came up and see how they were doing every year. I liked the area. It was the richest place in Leicester. There were a lot of trees. A lot of grass. More space."

Sometimes William brought his children with him. The boys were indifferent and went out of a sense of duty. But the girls loved it. They could ride the bikes left at the nearby University during the vacation. But if William let them share his world, he could not share theirs. "Dad was always an old man," Douglas Orton remembers. William never played with his children or bought them presents or even ate dinner with the family. He rarely went on vacations with them; and, in later years, when he and Elsie took a holiday, Elsie would bring one of her friends along for company. From William the children inherited their angular, lean faces, the sharp beady eyes, and fair complexion. But there was little else they would be able to acknowledge. A sense of anger at this absence sneaks into Orton's exaggeration of McLeavy's gardening obsession in *Loot*. Hal, McLeavy's bisexual son, has Orton's detached wit as well as his surface appearance. He renders the verdict on his father:

HAL. Do you know what his only comment was on my mother's death?

FAY. Something suitable, I'm sure.

HAL. He said he was glad she'd died at the right season for roses. He's been up half the night cataloging the varieties on the crosses. You should've seen him when that harp arrived. Sniffing the petals, checking, arguing with the man who brought it. They almost came to blows over the pronunciation. If she'd played her cards right, my mother could've cited the Rose Growers' Annual as co-respondent.

FAY. The Vatican would never grant an annulment. Not unless he'd produced a hybrid.

Hal's attitude toward McLeavy has the same aggressive disdain Orton held for his father. Even as an adolescent, he bought birthday presents for Elsie but never anything for William. When Leonie called him in 1966 to say that their father had been hit by a car and fractured his skull, Orton replied, "That won't make any difference to his brain." Indifference had been an integer in the family equation from the beginning; and mockery was one way of filling the void. William had been at the centre of the problem. Unwilling and unable to control his family, he never earned its respect. Elsie rarely treated him like a husband. "I'm mother and father to this family!" she would scream. "I've raised four kids on one lung!" No one, least of all William, could deny her claim. William was a stranger to his wife, his family, and himself.

Elsie claimed later that she'd married William on the rebound. She confided the fact to her children and never stopped reminding her husband. "I should've married him," she'd say, reminiscing out loud about her first engagement. "It was only pride. This fellah's mother was an alcoholic. I thought he'd turn out the same way." Elsie had such high expectations from life that almost everything was a letdown. Certainly, William was. Her thin, handsome, passive husband was a will-o'-the-wisp she could never crush with her disappointment. The children were always within earshot of their parents' many one-sided brouhahas.

They remember Elsie throwing William's money back at him and yelling, "I want more than this!" When he protested that the gardening job would give him security after he retired, Elsie would counter, "I don't want the money *then*. I want it now!" They remember the taunting scenes in which Elsie, taller and heavier than her 112-pound husband, ridiculed him for his size. "You look like a mouse! You eat like a bloody mouse!"

Elsie was never satisfied with William. The same theme was broadcast in many different stories. "In all the years I was married to your father, I had the chance to have affairs. But I never went off with another man. I was always true to *my* children." The point was not lost on them: it was to the children, not William, that she was loyal. In retrospect, William agrees with his daughter Marilyn that what Elsie wanted was some six-footer to give her "a bloody good hiding." "Then she'd have thought all the more of me, wouldn't she?" But William never gave her a "backhander" or an argument. "You ever lay your bloody hands on me, it's the last bloody thing you'll do," Elsie crowed at William, while he stared up from his newspaper. "She wanted him to fight back," Leonie says. "So she could hit him." But William never responded to her hectoring. He disappeared behind the Leicester *Mercury* or escaped into his garden or went down to the Saffron Lane Working Men's Club for a drink and a game of skittles. Besides gardening, skittles was William's only pleasure. He was good at it. He played in club tournaments. Often after a competition, he'd bring home a small silver-plate trophy with his name inscribed on it. These were the one sign of victory in his life. But Elsie commandeered the trophies as egg cups. They were always stained with egg; after a while, they turned brown.

"Dad was everything John didn't want to be," Douglas Orton says. "You could push Dad around. He was domineered. If you said sit there, Dad would sit. He'd never tell John what to do. He could do whatever he wanted. He never showed any affection." The emotional starvation took on the outrageous dimensions of one of Orton's plays. None of the children can remember their parents displaying any public affection. "I never saw Mum and Dad kiss—not once, not in all my life," Marilyn says. And until Elsie died and William started visiting his children's homes, they never kissed him. After Leonie was born, Elsie banished William to another room, giving William's incessant coughing as an excuse. Elsie slept in a double bed with her younger daughter. "I had four accidents," she'd explain. "A fifth would be a tragedy." After 1945, William never again had sex with his wife. "Mum hated sex," Marilyn says. "She told me she hated it. She said to me,

'How I ever got four children I don't know.' She hated it. She meant it."

Orton's life and his laughter were hell-bent on making sexual connection. Kath in *Entertaining Mr. Sloane,* Joyce in *The Ruffian on the Stair,* Mrs. Prentice in *What the Butler Saw* are all in some way punished by their sad hunger:

> MRS. PRENTICE *(quietly).* I hardly ever have sexual intercourse.
> PRENTICE. You were born with your legs apart. They'll send you to the grave in a Y-shaped coffin.
> MRS. PRENTICE *(with a brittle laugh).* My trouble stems from your inadequacy as a lover! . . .
> PRENTICE. How dare you say that! Your book on the climax in the female is largely autobiographical. *(Pause. He stares.)* Or have you been masquerading as a sexually responsive woman?
> MRS. PRENTICE. My uterine contractions have been bogus for some time!

In the world of *What the Butler Saw,* husband and wife make a sexual adjustment and are able to love again. Orton's mother and father never did. Sex was dirty, and so was the body. "I never saw her body," Leonie says. "I only saw her head, her hands, and her legs." Elsie's prudery was laughable. Elsie Orton, who kept her children in the dark about sex, was as nervous on the subject as Kath in *Entertaining Mr. Sloane,* who claims that "until I was fifteen I was more familiar with Africa than my own body." Elsie never knew that John had been molested at the same movie house they attended each Monday after work where she would caution her children not to look at the couples kissing around them. Orton had more mischievous memories of those family entertainment outings:

> Watched an old film on television called *My Favourite Blonde* with Bob Hope. This had sentimental overtones for me. It was at the companion picture, *My Favourite Brunette* (also with Bob Hope) sometime in the early forties that I was interfered with. A man took me into the lavatory of the Odeon and gave me a wank. I relived those happy moments as I sat watching the picture today. I remember coming down his mac. I must've been about fourteen.
> [February 19, 1967]

At the pub, Elsie had a vivacious come-on: "How you fixed for a giddy barmaid?" She kept to her own pub and her own friends. Away from William, she put on a jolly, rambunctious face for the world with the same broad garishness that characterized her clothes. Still, she was shocked and disgusted by the men who—not surprisingly—tried to pick her up. Once, when Marilyn was with her at the pub, a man approached and offered her a chocolate. "Yes, please," said Elsie, picking one from the tray. The man leaned over to her: "Come outside and I'll let you have the whole box." Elsie's face flushed. "I wouldn't come outside with you for a box of Cadbury's Black Magic!"

The animality of sex offended the alabaster image Elsie had of herself and her children. She could not abide jokes about sex, and she didn't like language that admitted physical contact. "I remember when I was courting a fellow," Leonie recalls, "and I said to Mum, 'I'm gonna give him up.' She says, 'Why?' I says, 'He's dead randy.' Her eyes were like organ stops." Elsie never discussed sex with her children. "Feel your own way through life, you did," Leonie says. "Sex was dirty. It bloody was. She wouldn't have anything to do with it." The taboos about the body were felt by Orton, whose adolescent diary switches to shorthand when describing anything to do with his body or sexual practice. In later years, when Leonie suggested that John was "queer," Elsie sternly invoked her familiar censorship: "Don't say that!" After Orton had invited Elsie to see *Entertaining Mr. Sloane*—a play that put so many of her eccentricities bitterly on stage—he pretended to be out of town and sent Kenneth Halliwell with her instead. Elsie praised the play to friends, but sidestepped the central issue of sex in her demure way by confessing, "It were awful in parts."

Orton was always shocking his mother. When he paraded downstairs as a teenager, swathed in a bath towel and flexing new muscles from his body-building exercises, Elsie would shoo him back upstairs. "Look at you—you're disgusting walking around like Sabu!" In 1955, after Douglas's wedding party, Orton snuck a bridesmaid upstairs to his mother's bedroom. Elsie caught them in bed, and her caterwauling reached such a hysterical pitch that Leonie—then ten—started to cry. "Get that whore out of my house!" Elsie shrieked. "What do you think this is, a bleeding brothel?"

Elsie's preposterous propriety would always haunt Orton. A month before his death, he visited Kenneth Williams for tea and met Williams's mother, "Louis." He was astonished by their camaraderie. Williams traded stories with his mother, who had a delivery as salty as her son's. "She was staring so rudely I very nearly said, 'Wait a minute, I'll get a basin for your eyes.'" Williams also remembers his mother saying, "Posh? Spit in her eye and it wouldn't choke her." Orton loved the performance and listened carefully. "J.O. liked Louis very much,"

Williams wrote in his diary on July 5, 1967. " 'You come out with everything in front of her. Very different from my mother. I could never talk like that to her.' "

Elsie's advice to her children was the same in theme, if not diction, as Mrs. Vealfoy's advice to Raymond, the young hedonist in *The Good and Faithful Servant* who puts his girlfriend in the family way:

> MRS. VEALFOY. . . . There is no finer sight than two married people making love.

The double meaning of Mrs. Vealfoy's words escapes her. So it was with Elsie Orton, who never realized how clearly her children saw beneath the web of words and memories she spun around herself to disguise her false pride. Fantasy renovated every sad corner of her life. The cheap pink Woolworth glass dish which she fussed about and kept under lock and key in the sideboard was, she maintained, a Jacobean heirloom. The £40 beaver coat she paraded in the middle of summer at the pub as a token of William's affection after twenty-five years of marriage had been purchased by Elsie herself on the correct assumption that William would not remember their anniversary. "She would never admit she was poor," Douglas recalls. Elsie envied the wealthy, and dreamed of what she'd do with the money if she won on the pools. "She was going to buy us all a house," Marilyn recalls. "She was going to buy her own house. Send some money to 'our John.' She never mentioned Dad."

Between them, she and William never earned more than £23 a week; and for many years, while the children were growing up, their income was much less. They had no phone, no car, no appliances, and, so Elsie thought, no life. "She lived in Cloud Cuckoo-land," Douglas says. "She wanted to live like a queen but she couldn't afford it." If there was a choice, Elsie would plump for the best: Players cigarettes instead of Woodbine, ham instead of Spam, classic opera instead of Gilbert and Sullivan. Elsie was always in debt while pretending to friends that the family was well off. She was forever juggling her bills and dodging court actions, paying off her extravagances in 5- and 10-shilling installments. Creditors often came to the door collecting for food and clothes. "John used to say, 'Mum won't pay him this week, 'cause it's not his turn,' " Douglas remembers. "She hadn't got the money. She'd buy the things, and worry about paying later. But me Dad wasn't like that. He wouldn't have anything he couldn't pay for. She thought he was a skinflint; but he just hadn't got the cash."

Elsie's desire to impress even extended to her dentures. She preserved her life-of-the-party smile not with conventional cleanser, but by keeping her teeth in bleach. Later Orton would delight in sending up Elsie's eccentric pretensions. "My teeth," says Kath, in *Entertaining Mr. Sloane,* "since you mentioned the subject, Mr. Sloane, are in the kitchen in Stergene. Usually I allow a good soak overnight. But what with one thing and another I forgot. Otherwise I would never be in such a state. *(Pause.)* I hate people who are careless with their dentures." Kath, of course, loses her dentures in the play's tensest moment; and this "carelessness" is taken still further in *Loot* when Hal, having dumped his dead mother out of her coffin, uses her teeth as castanets.

Elsie had always dreamed that her voice, not just her teeth, would be on stage. She once considered a career in show business, and took singing lessons, as a teenager, in the hopes of strengthening her lungs. "If I'd had the money when I was a child," she confided, "I'd have been in Covent Garden today." Elsie was liable to break into song anyplace —not hackneyed pub ballads (although she enjoyed belting these out) but arias from *Tosca, Madama Butterfly,* and *Rigoletto.* Her soprano could sometimes be heard trilling an aria on the local bus. "She made a spectacle of herself," Leonie says. "I used to say, 'Stop it!' And she'd say, 'Oh shut up, you! I'm enjoying myself!' I used to be that ashamed. But everybody liked it. It was only us kids that didn't."

Elsie loved a party, and her singing—whether at the pub or a coach outing—always put her at the centre of it. Her children never brought dates home to meet the family because Elsie could not be trusted not to sing at them. "Just for Awhile," "You Are My Heart's Delight," "It's Only a Shanty in Old Shanty Town" were the highlights of her repertoire. If the world wouldn't treat her voice as special, at least she did. "Vera Lynn was a club turn to her," says Leonie, laughing. Often, when Elsie returned home sozzled after an outing, she'd act posh, and swan outrageously around her living room.

Nothing in the Orton family life had the elegance, class, or promise that Elsie so vainly tried to conjure. Her refusal to admit the ordinariness of her life had its corollary in an obsession with living up to the expectation of others. This hypocrisy was a major source of family unhappiness—and her children never forgot it. "She wanted us to look nice, but only so people would look at us and say, 'What lovely children,'" Leonie remembers. "She did everything for what other people thought. Not what we wanted, but what she wanted." Orton's dialogue, which playwright John Mortimer has called "South Ruislip

Mandarin,"[5] revelled in this fatuous slavery to appearance. And his plots would be a bitter revenge on the norms and mediocre tastes to which his mother gave such unstinting lip service.

Elsie always felt that her first child was special. For seventeen years, Orton tried to live up to her dream of him. He inherited her belief in himself. He read books, so it was deduced he was "gifted." He was also handsome and well groomed. Elsie used to hold up John as a model to the rest of her brood. "John was always the goody-goody," Douglas explains. "He could never be in trouble. He could never do anything wrong. I was the tearaway. . . ." Elsie's ambitions were stalled, but her dreams of success were to live again in John. When John failed the eleven-plus examination that would qualify him for grammar school, because of the recurring asthma attacks that kept him away from school for long periods of time, Elsie was stunned. She would not allow him to attend the local secondary modern school. Her children must have the best. No other family in the Saffron Lane Estates of 1,500 homes sent their child to private school, but Elsie enrolled John in Clark's College. Elsie liked to drop the word "college" at the pub (just as "my son at RADA" and "my son the playwright" would follow). She also liked the stylishness of the maroon Clark's College blazer and grey slacks that set him apart. Sadly, Elsie paid for a private education without realizing that Clark's College was the wrong kind of school for her son, with a commercial rather than an academic curriculum. According to Orton's teacher at the college, which he attended between 1945 and 1947, "John was semi-literate. He couldn't spell. He couldn't string a sentence together. He couldn't express himself. He used to start a sentence and then get all het up. He had no vocabulary. It was ridiculous sending him to Clark's College, because he couldn't get the right kind of tuition. He was really the secondary modern type." But the thought seems not to have daunted Elsie. She offered Douglas the same opportunity but he refused to attend such a "lah-de-dah school." As it was, she had to pawn her wedding ring to pay the school fees. She told her cronies that she'd lost the ring while hanging the laundry in the garden. She never got it back.

"JOHN, I look back on my life and wonder where I have slipped up," Elsie wrote Orton in one of her rare letters, in 1963. "I have always tried to be a good mother and shield all of you where as it got me, by the way don't think I feel sorry for myself I don't I'm getting passed it. . . ." Her memory of her accomplishments as a mother was as erratic as her spelling. Always quick to defend the family name, Elsie was often indifferent to the family. In Orton's adolescent diaries, his mother makes infrequent appearances, none of them affectionate. She scouts for jobs in the Leicester *Mercury* and sends Orton off to interviews. She is the censor from whom at seventeen Orton must hide the fact that he has smoked a cigarette. "Mustn't let Mum know, though." She is the worrying presence whose apprehension is as much a threat as an assurance of love. When Orton spits blood after an asthma attack, he ponders, "Don't know whether to tell Mum I spit up tonight. I don't want to worry her." She is the drain on his carefully accumulated spending money. With some weariness, Orton notes how much money Elsie has asked to borrow:

> I think dry rot must have set in on this holiday. Mum asked if she could borrow £2. Of course there was an argument, and Mum suddenly flung her coat on and said she was off home. So we went to Rhyll for the afternoon and of course when we came back Mum was there in a furious temper.   [September 7, 1950]

Elsie always hoped that, after her son's literary success, John would give her an allowance and let her indulge herself. He didn't. In fact, he frowned on her extravagance. He hated the waste and the mediocrity that stimulated Elsie's consumer zeal. He was as dutiful a son as she was a mother. He brought her little presents when he arrived for his two-week visit each summer; he wrote her letters which she rarely answered; he even bailed her out of debt when she was hospitalized and worried about her finances. But he made no provisions for his family in his will.

The ambivalence toward family that Orton would dramatize was also something his brother and sisters felt. "Since my mother's death in 1966, I've never missed her, never wished her back," Leonie says. A family that never received love had little to give. Orton never got on with his brother; neither sister liked the other; and the running battle between Elsie and William was the numbing backdrop of daily life. "Nobody discussed anything with anybody," Leonie remembers. "We lived in our own little environments." The family's mutual indifference was interrupted only by Elsie's sudden rages.

Although, in company, Elsie would talk posh and reprimand her children for using rude words, in private, she swore like a soldier. Her most infamous curses were about money. When William turned over his odd-job money to her, Elsie accepted it with a ferocious "It's neither arse-hole nor watercress!" And when Leonie gave Elsie the first

£2 she'd ever earned at the hosiery factory, Elsie scowled. "What am I supposed to do with this? Do wonders and shit miracles?"

Elsie's brutality and frustration were not only verbal. "She was a cruel bitch," Leonie says. Listening to this summary of his dead wife, William says, "Yes, she was." Very few of the children's memories of Elsie are benign. Once, when Marilyn refused to get dressed and Elsie was rushing to work, she grabbed her daughter by the hair and swung her around. Then, clutching the copper poker by the fireplace, she started to beat her. "She got me in a corner with this stick and she just wouldn't stop hitting me. I had welts across my back. I thought I'd broken my thumb. I went to my teacher, and she sent me to the clinic. I told the nurse that me Mum hit me with a copper poker. She was horrified. When I told Mum what the nurse had said (I can remember this as clear as yesterday), she said, 'Don't say that, Marilyn. You'll get me had up.' "

Elsie could not abide her children laughing at her authority. Another time, in a fury, she knocked Marilyn unconscious against an iron mangle. Elsie thought she'd killed her. Leonie also got a taste of the violent side of Elsie's temper when she wouldn't eat her breakfast. Elsie shoved her head into the cereal bowl. "It quite knocked me out," Leonie says. The penalties for disobeying Elsie's orders were harsh, Leonie remembers. "Marilyn and me used to go down to the gasworks where they make coke fire fuel. When Mum didn't have money to buy coal, me and Marilyn used to take an old pram and get a bag of coke. I remember once I wouldn't go. 'Right,' she says. 'You won't sit by the bloody fire.' She made me sit in the bloody lav."

Nobody felt close to the family, and Orton always put quotations around the word in his adolescent diary. William, who never kept a family photograph, admits: "There was a time I thought of leaving her. Now and again. I don't know why I didn't. I think it was the children." He is equally blunt when asked if there were times when the family got on well together. "Yes," he says. "Several." Trying to squeeze some smidgeon of enjoyment from her leisure time, Elsie often neglected her children. Sometimes they had to wait outside the pub— The City Arms—and call for her to come home. Elsie would stick her head out the front door: "What do you want!" "We wanted to go home, we wanted to eat," Leonie says. "She never worried where we were. She let me stay out to midnight. When I was only sixteen, I stayed out all night. When I was six, I was miles away from home and she never cared where I was." Elsie never "called in" her children around eight at night the way the other mothers on the Saffron Lane Estates did. "Deep down, I really hated it," Leonie says. "I wanted to be called in, and looked after like the others. I wanted my mother to get me into the bath and get me into bed."

When Orton met Kenneth Halliwell in 1951, he found a surrogate father with whom he would form the only family he ever acknowledged. Halliwell by then was a genuine orphan. His letter requesting scholarship support from RADA played on this theme: ". . . I am an orphan with no relatives keen enough on my going on the stage to sponge on. . . ."[6] Symbolically, Orton felt himself an orphan too. He had found neither support nor friends within his own family. At first he was merely "different"; later, with success, he would become a kind of freak. "John must have been a throwback," Marilyn says. "Where did it come from? We're ordinary people doing our little bit. Doing ordinary living, and earning ordinary wages."

Orton's resentment at the emotional wasteland of his family first expressed itself in adopting a sexual bond that offended and denied the bourgeois sense of "family," and a lifestyle that mocked the sermons about work that William and Elsie tried to give their children: "You've got to graft bloody hard for your money. And then when you've grafted, you have your enjoyment. . . ." Later, Orton's anger found its creative form in comedy that made pleasure irresistible. Ray (*The Good and Faithful Servant*), Sloane (*Entertaining Mr. Sloane*), Wilson (*The Ruffian on the Stairs*), and Nick (*What the Butler Saw*) all share two attributes. They are young and have, so they say, no family. To have lost the family or never to have known it are conditions that Orton presents without a tinge of sentiment.

Orton's last glimpse of his family merely confirmed the vision of them he'd carried throughout his life. When Elsie died on December 26, 1966—slumped in a chair downstairs where she slept because of her bad heart—Douglas lifted her onto her bed. According to Orton, William, who was recuperating at Leonie's home after his car accident, returned to the house to sleep with the corpse.

Orton's first reaction to the news was ambivalent. "I'll have to send a telegram to find out details of my mother's funeral," he wrote in his diary. "I can't go home if there's nowhere to sleep. And I don't fancy spending the night in the house with the corpse. A little too near the Freudian bone for comfort."[7] The shift in the Orton family structure had all the familiar pathetic and farcical touches that Orton re-created in his plays:

December 28, 1966
Leonie rang about six. . . . She said that Dad had gone back home. Sleeps in my mother's bed downstairs with the corpse. After his

accident he can't piss straight and floods the lavatory with it whenever he goes. She said, "Well, I'm shocked by our Marilyn, you
know." I said, "Why, what's she done?" Leonie said, "Oh, you
know, she behaves very ignorantly all around. And when I told her
Mum was dead all she said was—'I'm not surprised.' Well, you
know, what kind of remark is that?" Dougie was upset. Remarkable
how those without hearts when young suddenly develop them in
later life. . . .

I promised to go home tomorrow. Leonie and George will come
around in the evening. As the corpse is downstairs in the main
living room it means going out or watching television with death
at one's elbow. My father, fumbling out of bed in the middle of the
night bumped into the coffin and almost had the corpse on the
floor. . . .

THE JOE ORTON who returned to bury his mother in December 1966
had changed dramatically from the John Orton who, sixteen years
earlier almost to the day, was trying to coax himself into a model of
conventional behavior:

January 1, 1950
During 1950, writing must be improved. . . . Tennis must be taken
up seriously this year not half-heartedly like in the past. . . . Gramophone must be paid for this year and an effort made to save.

Orton's special courage as a comic writer lay in facing and
chronicling the intense and ambivalent emotions he had learned to
accept in himself. Elsie's funeral brought together all the complexities
of his past and his present:

December 29, 1966
I arrived in Leicester at four thirty. I had a bit of quick sex in a
derelict house with a labourer I picked up. He wore a navy blue
coat with leather across the shoulders. He carried a sort of satchel.
Some kind of roadmender, I thought. The house was large. Windy
because the doors were off. We went into the hall. He took his pants
down. He wouldn't let me fuck him. I put it between his legs. He
sucked my cock after I'd come. He didn't come himself. It was
pissing with rain when we left the house. Mud all over the place.

I got home at five thirty. Nobody in the house. My father was
across the road with friends. He can't see now. The accident has
affected his walking. He trembles all the time. . . . Later on George

and Leonie came round. We went to see mum's body. It isn't at home as I'd supposed. It's laid out in a Chapel of Rest. . . .

We all went to the Chapel of Rest. It's a room, bare, white-washed. Muted organ music from a speaker in the corner. The coffin lid propped up against the wall. It said "Elsie Mary Orton aged 62 years." Betty [Douglas's wife] said, "They've got her age wrong, see. Your mum was 63. You should tell them about that. Put in a complaint." I said, "Why? It doesn't matter now." "Well," said Betty, "you want it done right, don't you. It's what you pay for." . . .

Mum quite unrecognisable without her glasses. And they scraped her hair back from her forehead. She looked fat, old and dead. They made up her face. When I asked about this the mortician said, "Would you say it wasn't discreet then, sir?" I said, "No, it seems all right to me." "We try to give a lifelike impression," he said. Which seems to be a contradiction in terms somehow. I've never seen a corpse before. How cold they are. I felt mum's hand. Like marble. One hand was pink, the other white.

Great argument as we left. The undertaker gave Marilyn a small parcel containing the nightgown mum was wearing when she died. Nobody wanted it. So the undertaker kept it. Not for himself. "We pass it on to the old folks," he said. "Many are grateful, you know."

Didn't sleep much. Awful bed. Damp. And cold. House without mum seems to have died.

December 30

I got up at eight o'clock. I went downstairs to the kitchen. My father appeared in the doorway of the living room dressed only in a shirt. He looks thin and old. Hardly more than a skeleton. He weighs six stone four. I said, "Hallo." He peered blindly for a second and said, "Hallo." After a pause he said, "Who are you?" "Joe," I said. He couldn't remember I'd come last night. Then he said, "D'you know where my slippers are?" I said, "What do you mean—where your slippers are?" He got down on his knees and began feeling around. "I can't find my slippers," he said. "They're on your feet," I said. And they were. He'd been wearing them all the time.

I made a cup of tea and shaved. Then I went out to try and buy some flowers. I had no intention of getting a wreath. Putting money in some ignorant florist's pocket. I couldn't get flowers. The shop said they didn't deliver until ten thirty. The funeral is at ten. So I didn't give mum any flowers. Actually when I read the dreadful, sickening wording on the other wreaths, "To a dear Mum. At peace at last with little Tony [her grandson]," from Marilyn and Pete I was glad not to be involved.

When I got back home Leonie and George had arrived. Also

Dougie and Betty. My father was in such a state that he had to be dressed. I took him to the bathroom and shaved him. At ten the undertaker arrived. "What about the flowers?" he said. I said I'd no idea what to do with the flowers. "Where's father's tribute?" he said. "I think just father's tribute on the coffin." He found my father's wreath and put it on the coffin. Then we all got into the cars. My aunt Lucy was upset because strict protocol wasn't observed. "They're all walking wrong," she said. "They shouldn't be with husbands and wives. Just immediate circle should be in the first car." Several women were at their garden gates as the cortège passed. I noticed two old women weeping on each other's shoulders.

At the chapel in the cemetery they held a brief burial service. They didn't carry the coffin into the chapel. They wheeled it in on a trolley. The vicar, very young and hearty, read the service in a droning voice. And then the coffin was wheeled out and to the graveside. It was a cold, bright morning. My mother's grave was a new one. Her last wish was to be buried with Tony, my nephew who was drowned aged six, eighteen months ago, but Pete and Marilyn refused to have the grave re-opened and so my mother's last wish was ignored. . . .

The coffin was lowered. The vicar said his piece. The earth was sprinkled over the coffin. My father began to cry. And we walked back to the waiting cars. Immediately the mourners left the graveside a flock of old women descended on the grave, picking over the wreaths and shaking their heads.

We got back home at half-past ten. Sandwiches and tea had been prepared by a neighbour. The party got rather jolly later. . . . My father sat through the party looking very woebegone. The only person who seemed to be at a funeral. Mrs. Riley, mum's lifelong friend, was crying quietly in a corner and drinking endless cups of tea. "I don't expect I'll see you again," she said as she left. "Your mother was very dear to me. I shan't come up here now she's gone. Goodbye," she said, kissing my cheek. "I hope you have a happier life than your mum did."

Leonie and I spent part of the afternoon throwing out cupboardsful of junk collected over the years: magazines, photographs, Christmas cards. I found a cup containing a pair of false teeth and threw it in the dustbin. Then I discovered they belonged to my father. I had to rescue them. I found my mother's teeth in a drawer. I kept them. To amaze the cast of *Loot*. . . .

After I left Leonie, I picked up an Irishman. Pretty baggy. I wasn't going to bother but he had a place so I said "O.K." It was an empty house. Not derelict. Just unoccupied. He had a room on the ground floor of a large house. The place was damp, not lived in.

A smell of dust. He didn't live there. He rented it for sex. There was a table covered in grime. Bits of furniture. A huge mantelpiece with broken glass ornaments on it. All dusty. There was a double bed with greyish sheets. A torn eiderdown. He pulled the curtain which seemed unnecessary because the windows were so dirty.

He had a white body. Not in good condition. Going to fat. Very good sex, though, surprisingly. The bed had springs which creaked. First time I've experienced that. He sucked my cock. Afterwards I fucked him. It was difficult to get in. He had a very tight arse. A Catholic upbringing, I expect. . . .

January 2 [Back in London]
. . . In the evening P. Willes rang. . . . I told him about the funeral. And the frenzied way my family behave. He seemed shocked. But then he thinks my plays are fantasies. He suddenly caught a glimpse of the fact that I write the truth.

When Orton himself died, his father heard the news not from the other members of the family, who were notified immediately by police, but from television. For him, shut away in an old-people's home, life was even more remote than in the park greenhouse. His existence was reduced to small memories and idle chat with old men and women who sat like cadavers in the red straight-backed chairs of the Smoking Room. For a time, there was a woman with whom William could be seen holding hands. She had proposed both sex and marriage, but William was unfit for either. He had never impressed himself on life ("I never seemed to get anywhere. I was always a failure"), and now he was fading slowly out of life with the tepid, brutal anonymity his son had chronicled so movingly in *The Good and Faithful Servant*. "You have philosophy then?" Buchanan, who is about to be retired, asks Edith. "Are you resigned to anything in particular?" "No," Edith says. "Life in general. Isn't that enough?"

Orton never saw his father's new home. But its details—a traffic sign (CAUTION: BLIND PEOPLE CROSSING), the aviary and goldfish ponds, the polished entrance hall with white canes for the blind crammed like golf clubs into a box—evoke just such a life of perpetual loss as Orton's laughter captured and tried to control. William, who died in January 1978, kept a photograph of "his John" on the Formica bureau of his antiseptic room overlooking the car park. The picture was of John aged eighteen, taken just after he went to RADA: a suave smile is contradicted by the boyish, olive-smooth complexion and the shock of straight black hair curling like a comma across his unlined forehead. The photograph, the family agreed, made John look like a young Dirk

Bogarde. William kept no other family picture near him. "His John" flowered by some bewildering accident like none of the others, only to be cut down in full bloom. It was typical of William's life and luck. He had loved his son but never connected with him. Even the plants he cared for never seemed to flourish. "I didn't think I was a good gardener. It upset me. I didn't tell anybody. Always kept it to myself." William wanted only one thing in life: a greenhouse. He never got it. His son was much more ruthless in pursuit of his desires. He would not defer pleasure, but actively seek it. He would not accept the fatality of working-class life. From the beginning, Orton exhibited a trickster's appetite for transformation and triumph.

THE COLORFUL Pitman's Shorthand characters with which the young Orton decorated his bedroom walls were symptomatic of his desire to paint over the banality of Leicester life. Orton hankered for the extraordinary. The books he cherished were *Alice in Wonderland, Peter Pan,* Bulfinch's *Mythology;* the roles he longed to play were Ariel and Puck. These characters appealed to his mischievous desire to change shape and turn invisibility into a lethal asset. "Hope that I am allowed to let my imagination run riot," he wrote in the diary in 1950, contemplating a production of *The Tempest* in which he would play a mariner and a spirit. "Have notion of putting red sequins on my eye lids and having carmine for eye shadow. This would give the impression—I hope—of eyes of flame—ah-la-Jabberwocky."[8]

When Orton discovered the theatre, he found a focus for his energy and an answer to his needs. "I was never able to imagine myself as ordinary all my life,"[9] he said at the height of his success; but, as a youth, theatre was the only thing that elevated life "out of the ordinary." Besides, it was a friendlier, better educated community than his home, where Orton could invent possibilities for himself and indulge an imagination that was of no use in the workaday world and of no interest to his parents or teachers. "He wasn't terribly bright, but he had ideas," recalls Mrs. C. A. Bish, who taught him at Clark's College. "He came to me one day and said, 'I'm very interested in the theatre and the only thing I want to do is go on the stage.' I dismissed it."

The only person not to dismiss Orton's hopes was Orton himself. At sixteen, his future seemed cast in the dreary routine of office factotum. Theatre and the promise of productions were the sole antidote to his stalled life. His fantasy of theatrical success was as desperate

and unfounded as the rest of his aspirations. Even before he had spoken
his first three lines on the stage, he had dedicated his life to it:

> It's nearly 12 noon. I am writing this on paper at work. I know
> I am slacking but I don't feel like work. I am longing for dinner
> time to come because then the time whizzes by and its soon 6–30.
> I will work really hard this afternoon and forget the theatre for a
> while at least. Last night sitting in the empty theatre watching the
> electricians flashing lights on and off, the empty stage waiting for
> rehearsal to begin, I suddenly knew that my ambition is and has
> always been to act and act. To be connected with the stage in some
> way, with the magic of the Theatre and everything it means. I know
> now I shall *always* want to act and I can no more sit in an office
> all my life than fly. I know this sounds sentimental and sloppy but
> it is all perfectly true.   [April 13, 1949]

Orton's diaries at this time were filled with peevish asides about
the grinding tedium of work. "This week has gone by like a century";
"Nothing much happened as usual"; "Nothing to do"; or—a familiar
entry scrawled and underlined beside many days—"QUIET DAY. WORSE
LUCK." Excitement was one commodity Leicester didn't manufacture.
Orton had to create his own events. Even before he discovered amateur
dramatics, he was resourceful at keeping busy. There were classical
records, books, films, and plays to devour and then comment on in the
front of his diary. ("January 9, 1950—*Last of the Redskins*. Story about
war with redskins. Very poor film, came out before end.") In his anxious-
ness to coax any response from the world, Orton kept up a constant
correspondence: letters for job interviews, letters for pen pals, letters for
body-building courses, including the Charles Atlas chest-expander. The
prospect of a reply gave his life a sense of expectation:

> . . . Came home at dinner time browned off. Mum said there was
> no letter from Bolton and B. I felt as though I'd like to lay down
> and die. Anyway, I had dinner and went into the hall and in the
> box was a letter. I had got the job, but I've got another interview
> tomorrow. Feel extremely happy tonight.   [June 9, 1949]

The "urge" to join the Leicester Dramatic Society had seized Orton
on January 13, 1949. "I have written the Manager asking him for a
subscription. Will send the letter tomorrow. Query: Hope I don't
forget." Orton had already joined the Leicester Dramatic Society, the
city's oldest and most prestigious amateur group, two years earlier,

and then let his membership lapse. The LDS boasted Richard Attenborough as its most famous alumnus, and it had the advantage of having the Little Theatre, the best-equipped amateur stage in Leicester.
But, as Orton learned, it had its own self-perpetuating aristocracy,
which made it difficult for ambitious newcomers to get decent roles.
Orton auditioned for *Richard III* on March 1 and waited impatiently
to see if he'd been selected. On March 19, he had his answer:

> Feel thrilled to death. Had a TELEGRAM from the Little Theatre
> saying that rehearsal is tomorrow at 6:30. Boy oh boy! I'm in at last.

Immediately, the drab days were overshadowed by the aura of adventure theatre gave to his evenings:

> No need to say what tonight has been like. Wonderful. I play two
> very small parts, still I don't mind. I am Dorset, the son of some
> Queen (Elizabeth, I think) and a messenger. Am just a little worried
> as I have never had to speak Shakespeare before. . . .
>
> [March 20, 1949]

Orton's nervousness about speaking Shakespeare was symptomatic
of his uneasiness with language in general. "He couldn't express himself," Mrs. Bish, his teacher, recalls. "He'd get so far in talking with
you and then, if you didn't understand immediately, he'd become
impatient. He would close up, move away, go back into his world. I
think he was afraid of being made fun of. . . ." Orton had difficulty
making people pay attention to his dreams and the disregard maddened
him. But the text of a play was a poetic blueprint for language that
made it possible to master words and make people listen.

A boy without society's credentials, Orton struggled to build up his
mind and body from their skimpy, undernourished beginnings. "He
read and copied styles," Mrs. Bish remembers. Like his books and his
body building ("I shall be the most perfectly developed of modern
playwrights if nothing else,"[10] he wrote to Peggy Ramsay in 1966, still
doing his exercises), theatre was an extension of Orton's passion for
self-improvement. Theatre consolidated his fascinations—literature,
music, and make-believe—and made them legitimate labor. On stage
the actor, isolated by light, by costume, and by role, could lose himself and his past. Identities could be exchanged; time and destiny
momentarily mastered. In the theatre he could be visible, the centre of
attention instead of on society's periphery. Orton's identity was always

fluid. "I'm not committed in politics or sex or life,"[11] he said in 1964.
This detachment was present even in adolescence; it was the mischievous quality that gave acting its special appeal. Bernard Widdowson, a close amateur acting friend of those years, with whom Orton
walked the streets of Leicester after rehearsals talking passionately
about his stage dreams, recalls a chameleon quality—"The physical
image of Orton always remained the same: he always looked terribly
thin and cold. Winter or summer. He wore the same riding mac and
lovat corduroys. But this was the only thing about him that remained
static. His ideas would change from day to day. You could never feel
certain he'd be exactly the same."

At work, Orton found himself "yearning for rehearsal," and on
days when there was no theatre in his routine the whole amperage of
his life seemed to sink, making him feel "so low." He could hardly contain himself at the prospect of an upcoming rehearsal:

> . . . I had a bath. Must look "all right" for tomorrow's rehearsal.
> Have sorted out a nice box for my make-up box. Oh please god let
> me have another part before the season ends. Or I shall be so dis-
> appointed. Query: What *are* the numbers of the make-up I use. Silly
> of me but all I can remember is cleansing cream.   [March 26, 1949]

Orton's moments on stage in *Richard III* were drastically reduced
when the producer explained that he was too young to play Dorset.
"The producer said that historically I was supposed to be 23. Well, I
don't look or sound 23. So I am a messenger with one line to say and a
soldier with nothing to say." Even with these meagre roles, Orton
luxuriated in fantasies of conquest. Sitting in the Little Theatre two
weeks before *Richard III*'s April opening, he was ravished by the
thought of fame. "Found myself thinking what I would say when asked
to take part in a broadcast called 'How I became an Actor.' Probably
start 'I think I have always had a sort of yearning . . . etc, etc.' Pulled
myself together quickly."[12] Orton stood careful guard over his emotions. His dreams were too brittle, his emotions too raw to withstand
scrutiny. Around older people, he erected a persona of shy detachment
and worked hard to keep envy and self-doubt from upsetting the
surface:

> Must check growing tendency to think
> a) Nigel Pochin (he plays Rivers, Norfolk, and Largest Messenger)
> got his part through influence (his dad's assistant stage manager).

b) That because quite often I sit and read on my own (I hardly
know anyone) people think how lonely I must be (which is ridiculous).   [April 3, 1949]

In fact, Orton was too busy with plans for himself to be lonely.
Adolescent self-consciousness dictated every gesture, with a sense that
the whole world would be watching. Two days before the opening, he
locked himself into the bathroom and made up:

I did this partly because I wanted to see if I know how and partly
because I don't want the greasepaint to have that "never-used-
before" look.   [April 10, 1949]

Behind Orton's fussing about his appearance was the fear that he
wouldn't be noticed. After the photo call at the final dress rehearsal, he
wrote: "I am in two [photos]. Don't know whether I'll be seen." But
these worries were swept aside by the exciting anticipation of an
audience.

When the first night arrived, Orton's only comment was "felt a
little nervous but not really." He was resigned about the reviews
("Quite good on the whole except for elephantine efforts of scene
shifters. Of course I wasn't mentioned as I only had three lines") but
by the end of the week was already complaining of "a strange feeling
of flatness." There were only three more performances of *Richard III*.
Completely stage-struck, Orton was now overwhelmed by a new
ambition:

Feel a mixture of feelings after ten days of speaking three lines a
night and trying to look intelligent; but this is drowned by the fun
I've got out of it. I shall be very sorry when it's over. Have heard
that Derek Crouch who plays Clarence is at RADA. He once said
he was "a gentleman of leisure," but I thought he was a student or
something. I do envy him. But thinking on it, he's older than me
and must have been in the same position as me at 16. Am wondering if, if I saved at least 5 shillings a week I could go to RADA in
the remote future. Of course I have no idea what the fees are, etc.
. . . In the course of conversation last night I found that the fees
for RADA are 20 guineas per term. But I am determined to keep
on saving. . . .   [April 26, 1949]

Sentiment was rare in the Orton family, but on the night of the
last performance Orton was quite overwhelmed: "Feel an awful touch

of nostalgia tonight [April 27, 1949] when the costumes were all packed
in their boxes and the dressing room was bare. When shall I be in
another play at the Little Theatre?"

A year and a half later, the question would be answered by Orton
himself in a letter of resignation to the Leicester Dramatic Society:

> I have been a member for two years now and during that time you
> have presented 22 plays. In April 1949 I was asked to play a small
> part in *Richard III*. Since then I have heard nothing from the
> society. . . . I don't expect a part every month but 17 is more than
> I'm prepared to stand.[13]

Orton was not the hot acting property he hoped to be. His bravado
backfired. "LDS acknowledged my letter with a very cold note," he
entered in the diary on September 13, 1950. "Not (as I hoped) with a
part."

In the intervening months, however, Orton had not been idle.
Following his performance in *Richard III* with the Leicester Dramatic
Society in 1949, he joined two other drama clubs, the Bats Players and
the Vaughan Players, an amateur group associated with Vaughan College. "At night I belonged to an amateur society—in fact I belonged
to so many it got ridiculous—the rehearsals for the shows clashed,"[14]
Orton said. His passion for the stage seemed to increase as his enthusiasm for girls decreased:

> My opinion of women is going down. At present it is zero. Dot
> [Dorothy Crashley] never turned up at all [for a date to see *The
> Mikado*]. Am completely fed up with girls in general. Bought two
> sticks of greasepaint.   [April 2, 1949]

On stage, Orton's vulnerable ego could be reinforced and protected.
Socially he was, by his own admission, "a bad loser though I try not to
show it." Theatre could be counted on to yield pleasure. Girls, on the
other hand, never seemed to pay him the right kind of attention. They
confounded and often rejected him, a familiar adolescent obstacle that
was made more daunting by the deep distrust of women Elsie Orton's
volatile behavior had bred in her son. "I'm fed up with girls" was a
phrase he wrote often in his 1949 diary, as they systematically intruded
on his fantasy of perfection: "I'm really mad tonight. Penny said she
would come to dancing school tonight and was to meet me outside the
library. I turned up, but did she. NO she didn't, and I waited like a

fool in the howling wind and pouring rain . . ." [February 9, 1949]. "This is really the last straw. D.L. and I went to the theatre and we saw Penny with Dickie B., George B and some other boy, 14 I think. Well, if she prefers their company to mine, she's welcome to it. I have finished with her completely" [March 12, 1949].

Much later, in describing Eddie, the bisexual brother of Kath who also fancies Mr. Sloane, Orton said: "He's quite potent or could be potent again but he just sort of got fed up messing around with women and all the things one has to put up with in a woman."[15] This was his attitude toward his own sexuality and heterosexual courtship. As an adolescent, Orton was as much a stranger to sexuality as Kath claims she was in *Entertaining Mr. Sloane.* The transformation of his feelings for women from ambivalence to anger is chronicled in his allegorical novel, *Head to Toe:*

> They closed in: he heard their voices now only as myriad and interminable insects . . . when he was younger, a boy, a youth, he had loved the sight of female flesh and the sound of women's voices, of walking and sitting alone with them under trees. He never knew the danger. Then the pavement, the stones, became actual, savage, filled with, evocative of, the claws of birds, maddening, terrifying sounds. He was afraid.

With success and the social confidence it brought, Orton lost his angry edge, but not his ambivalence toward women. There were moments in adulthood when he found himself savoring fantasies of physical contact he'd long ago abandoned:

> Went to the Windmill and because the beautiful German (or Danish) Vipsil wished to buy some souvenirs I walked her into the Casbah. How slow women walk. She talked all the way about how Islam women were "Treated so bad, you know." How she couldn't walk down the street without "the bad things being said to me, you know." And I thought what a beautiful cow and how right the Arabs were about women. I enjoyed the looks of envy as I walked along with her. In a shop a shopkeeper lifted a silver chain and offered it to her. "Where does it go?" she said. He was just about to put it around her waist. He completely accepted the reason for my taking the waistband from him, accepting also that she, whilst in my company, was my possession. And so, in fact, for a morning's walk around the town, I possessed the most beautiful and desirable girl in town. I was curiously excited by the fact.   [May 19, 1967]

But the only conquests Orton made in 1949 were stage-managed. He lived in a daydream of theatrical success. Orton's public recollections of his early fascination with the stage miss the sense of urgency and obsession he invested in it. Time was measured by the hiatus between productions. As 1949 drew to a close, Orton assessed his "career" sadly:

> Nothing much has happened since I last wrote in this dairy. I have played Tyltyl in the Vaughan Players Production of *The Bluebird* from 12th–17th December. Also Robert in the Bats Production of *Without the Prince*. Now I am back where I was last April. No player at nothing and no chance of being in one for at least a couple of months. Vaughan are doing *Murder in the Cathedral* in February but I am not in it and don't think I shall be in any of the LDS productions. The Bats only do two productions a year and they did *W.T.P.* in November and there will be a break of two months at least.   [December 24, 1949]

Orton had made a particular splash in Maurice Maeterlinck's *The Blue Bird*. As the boy Tyltyl who, with his sister, sets out on an odyssey to discover the blue bird of happiness, Orton had a substantial part. Tyltyl is supposed to be ten. The combination of Orton's innocent vulnerability and playful imagination made him credible in the role. Previously, he had read for another Vaughan College production and made a poor showing. "I had a bit of a chest bout that night and the reading . . . didn't go down too well, in fact it was bloody awful." But Tyltyl was a character he could immediately identify with and love. When Orton heard that he had got the role, he was overjoyed. "I learned three acts all at once, but then cooled down a bit because I didn't know what scenes were going to be cut." He brought to Tyltyl his own aura of wonder and willpower, which were right for the part. "It's a play that calls for a boy who has visions and ideals, and that's what John gave it," says Joanne Runswick, who directed the production. "Offstage he didn't laugh much, he was ever so serious. When he did laugh, he laughed in the play. He was living in a world of his own in the play. It was uncanny. He was always going on about how he was going to be a great actor. He was so tense about it—about becoming somebody. He spoke like a man of twenty. He lived in a fantasy world . . . I had the feeling there was something wrong. He seemed like a child who'd missed a lot of love. I used to want to draw him to me because he used to 'go away' . . . always apart. He was so apart."

The Leicester *Mercury* praised Orton for "great confidence"; but enthusiasm and theatricality don't shine through the cast's picture in the paper. Orton sits forlornly in the front row, his hands self-consciously hiding his bony knees from the camera. He stares blankly into space, lost in thought.

Orton's notoriety in *The Blue Bird* made his dreams of being an actor more luscious. He had jumped from a three-line walk-on in his first play to "star" billing in his second. His new-found talent seemed confirmed. The buzz of excitement and visible proof of his accomplishment from the audience had made him, according to Joanne Runswick, "a bit cocky; he really thought a lot of himself by the end of the show."

ON NEW YEAR'S DAY, 1950, Orton turned seventeen. The new decade heralded in the papers as an era of abundance and progress held no promise for him. "I feel so fed up, fed up with girls, my work, and life in general. I'll be damn glad if I do have to go into the Army. At least, it'll be a change." There were no theatrical productions on the horizon, so he retreated into his theatrical fantasies. He mounted the programs from the previous productions on his brightly painted walls and designed a lighting plan for *Richard III*. To fill time while he waited to hear about parts, he took up drawing and designed "marvellous sets for *Blue Bird, The Palace of Happiness* and *Land of Memory*." The only theatrical area in which he made some progress was the dance floor. Grace, Charm, Poise—the entire tinsel production of would-be elegance that ballroom dancing staged—appealed to Orton long before he understood and satirized the sweet conformity of its fantasy. In *The Erpingham Camp*, Erpingham's voice announces the ballroom dancing competition winners: "Our disability bonus was won by Mr. Laurie Russel of Market Harborough. Both Laurie's legs were certified 'absolutely useless' by our Resident Medical Officer. Yet he performed the Twist and the Bossa Nova to the tune specified on the entrance form." In his youth Orton knew the compulsion to look good. He was a high-stepper and proud of it: "Can now dance the Quickstep, Waltz, Barn Dance, Military Twostep, and St. Bernard's Waltz. Well, well, well."

With RADA as a vague goal, Orton needed steady work. As a junior clerk earning £3 a week, he lived to please and had to please to live. Later, when he surfaced as the successful author of *Entertaining Mr. Sloane,* Orton would try to refashion the dogsbody's terror of necessity into something suitably heroic. "When I'd go to the Labour Exchange to ask for work—a question of necessity—they always seemed to offer me a labouring job."[16] Asthmatic and frail, Orton never held a labour-

ing job in Leicester. But by February 1950, he was struggling tena-
ciously to keep the job he had. The trouble began on January 27 when
he arrived at work groggy from a Leicester Dramatic Society party the
previous night. He reported happily in his diary, "I was pleased when
someone said, 'Well, if it isn't Johnny Orton.' . . . Was quite surprised
how many people I knew." But the office jolted him back into the
familiar status of marginal man:

> Work today, oh how tired I felt. I didn't get in till 12.30 and I had
> to be up at 8. Felt dizzy all day and am sure some people thought
> I was drunk. (Hope they did.) Saw in my stamp book "Leicester
> Mercury and reply" 5d. Do hope they are not advertising for a
> "Junior Clerk" as I'm out if they are. . . .   [January 27, 1950]

Orton searched the accounting department letter files the next day
for a memo about the ad. He found nothing. Finally, sneaking a look
at the secretary's notebook, he decoded her shorthand and discovered
the order for the ad. Panicked, he devised a scheme to come to work
early and intercept the mail: "If it's alright and has nothing to do with
me getting the sack, I shall take it out and repost it. If it encloses anything about me, it will be burnt." Despite his "morning vigils," Orton
was fired at the weekend.

Out of work, Orton flung himself onto the merry-go-round of job
hunting. Although he wanted nothing to do with his parents' world,
Orton's life—like theirs—was shaping up into one long forced march
to the cadence called by interviewers and employers. His days had a
familiar, inevitable repetitiveness:

> Lying in bed this morning half awake, Mum barges in with two
> letters. 1. Freers, Bauskell and Co., like the sound of this one and
> 2. British Railways—don't like this so much but I'll go see. FB's
> tomorrow at 11, so I can lounge about today doing nothing which
> is pleasant.   [February 13, 1950]

Still without a job in late February, Orton wrote adamantly in his
diary: "Rehearsal the only thing I want to do."[17]

All through the cold and dismal winter, Orton had warmed himself
on his hothouse dreams of the stage. In the last week of January, he was
back at the task he longed to make his real work:

> Playreading tonight. Three plays were read. No. 1 was *Before You
> Cook Your Beef*, a Spanish play in which I read Francisco, a very
> jealous husband. No. 2 *The Foeman* about border feuds in the 17th

Century. I read Davie. And No. 3 in which I didn't read was *The Sword Is Double-Edged* about a Greek artist who calls upon the gods to bring life to his beautiful statue. This was very funny. Wish I could play this. But imagine to my surprise and joy when, upon picking characters Mr. Atkinson said, "I think we'll have this young man to play Davie." I'm in a play—oh joy, oh joy. Must put all my thoughts of the Greek play out of my mind. I'm lying down in my bed now and am going to mark my part. Query: Did they wear kilts in the 17th Century?   [January 23, 1950]

The promise of a production gave life immediate direction. "I have a great passion for energy," he wrote that year. And theatre for Orton was exactly that: a scintillating exchange of energy. The diary is cluttered with reports of rehearsals for *Foeman* and the sweet anticipation of parts from other play readings. "Glad when Sunday comes for the casting reading [for the Vaughan Players' productions of *Aria da Capo* and *The Golden Fisherman*]. Do hope I get in one or the other of the plays. But I am not desperate because I am in one already." At the end of February, with a handful of rejection letters from local businesses, theatre gave him his only taste of success:

> "Joy of joys" as I lay in leaden slumber this morning Mum's angel sweet voice?? floated through the air telling me there was a p.c. for me. Dressed hurriedly hoping all the time for details of a play and telling myself that it could only be from the library. Got down and it was from Vaughan. It said that a meeting to discuss the production of *Aria da Capo* would be held on Friday. Rehearsals would be held on Tuesday, Wed., Frid. and Sun. . . .   [March 2, 1950]

The sudden buzz of stage activity bolstered Orton's determination to make a life of the theatre. In his eagerness, he took the advice of anyone who cared to give it. He was inventing himself, and every suggestion helped fill in the shadowy outline. The first indication of his seriousness is on March 4:

> Long discussion with our insurance man last night about me taking up the stage. He advised me to get some elocution lessons, so I am going to. Then when I come out of the Army—I shall try and get into repertory.

He did not act immediately on his new plan, but in the month that followed, his rehearsals earned him enough praise to confirm his unabashed confidence in himself. Both *Aria da Capo* and *The Foeman*

were entries in the National Festival of Community Drama. Orton took
his playing seriously, and his enthusiasm was applauded:

> Rehearsal of *Aria da Capo*. We did the piece with the shepherds
> [Thyrsis and Corydon]. Feel rather pleased with myself as the pro-
> ducer was obviously pleased with me. I couldn't say the same for
> the person who is playing Thyrsis. He is very wooden indeed.
>
> [March 7, 1950]

Orton was equally critical of *The Foeman*. To his annoyance,
rehearsals never began on time, and the atmosphere seemed to him
"unprofessional." He didn't like the play. "Must find some way of getting more life into an uninspiring part."[18] Since he lived for his moments in front of an audience, Orton had to invent the kind of detail
that made his precious performances count. His studiousness paid off.
The Foeman won third place in the festival competition.

By April 1 the excitement of both productions was over. Life, Orton
reported in his diary, "is very flat indeed. For the next few weeks I
know (until I am in another play) I shall keep looking at the calendar
and thinking THIS TIME WEEKS AGO I WAS MAKING UP FOR *Aria da Capo*,
ETC."[19]

On April 5, he wrote to the Leicester Information Bureau about
RADA and two days later, on a whim, sent letters to two regional theatres
—"Wrote to the Birmingham Rep and Peterborough Players. Don't
really know what I expect to get out of them. But you never know your
luck." Even a ripple of response was better than the present still-water.
In later years, the spark of Orton's malicious wit, the jokey outrageousness he tried to cram into every line, would betray a similar restlessness:
an imagination in isolation trying to keep itself amused. In 1950, Orton
knew the boredom, but not the furious alienation that would give his
style its belligerent extravagance.

Not only did theatre allow him to invent and inhabit worlds more
interesting than his surroundings; it transformed his sense of well-being.
On April 10, with his letters to professional theatres still unanswered,
he was asked to play in *And No Birds Sing*. "Oh boy, oh boy. I have a
deliciously warm feeling inside me." The next morning, despite a cold,
he reported: "Delicious feeling still with me." After a month of
fatiguing anticipation, things suddenly began to fall into place. No
sooner did he have a new part than answers from the repertory companies arrived. "Both advised me to get some training at RADA. Information Bureau sent me the names of some people to get in touch with

regarding RADA." A newspaper article by Laurence Olivier on April 15 raised his hopes still higher: "He says there are scholarships one can win to the RADA. And for exceptionally talented there are maintenance grants as well. Hope one of those elocution teachers I wrote to answer my letter. Failing this, I'll write RADA itself. I know the address is Gower Street. But I must get an evening job somehow. . . ."

The brazenness of Orton's enterprise sometimes deluded him into equating the size of his ambition with his ability. When the Vaughan Players announced a casting reading for *The Tempest,* Orton had written in his diary: "In the letter it said, 'largely a male cast but some singing goddesses and attendant spirits and Miranda.' Not a mention of Ariel. So perhaps they are having Ariel played (as it should be) by a male, if so I do hope I get the part."[20] Two weeks later, at the next reading, Orton's daydream took a pratfall: "Not very profitable as far as I'm concerned because I didn't even read Ariel, so I can't possibly play it. I read Trimalchio quite a lot, although whether I've a chance of playing it, I don't know." When Orton hadn't heard from the director a week later, he was scheming of other ways to get a part: "Am going to take my costumes for *Aria* back (to Vaughan College) tonight. This is only an excuse to show myself at *The Tempest* rehearsal as I am only hoping the producer will give me a part. Query: Is this a vain hope? Answer: 'Fraid so" [April 28, 1950].

The adult amateur players lacked Orton's estimation of his talent; he got a part playing a lowly spirit. "Of course I am very lucky to be in it at all, but after playing quite big parts for the Vaughan, it is rather a blow to one's pride to be lumped together with somebody who has about as much acting ability as a flea: namely—Widdowson, Burchell and quite a few *new* people."[21] But if the role in *The Tempest* was unchallenging, the disappointment was balanced by the prospect of elocution lessons. Voice is the first signal of class distinction. Orton's East Midlands accent drawled vowel sounds that turned "duck" to "dook" and made a sloppy indistinct blur of aspirates that changed "he has" to "e az." This pigeon-holed Orton into a class, with a whole series of attendant expectations. Orton's upper lip protruded over the line of his mouth, which impeded clarity and gave his delivery a casual, slightly slack-jawed look. The sound he produced was monotonous, the inflection faltering. The effect, even to him, was unimpressive: "I found myself listening to my voice and my acting and thinking how awful I sounded" [May 3, 1950].

In later years, Orton would often slip into a working-class accent which, like his dark blue labourer's overcoat, added spice to his sexual capers. But in 1950, he wanted to lose every vestige of his past. His sudden awareness of serious limitations in his voice had been sparked by the elocution lessons he began in late April.

To eradicate his Leicester accent he chose a handsome lady who called herself "Madame" Rothery. She came recommended by the Leicester Information Bureau and his former Clark's College teacher, Mrs. Bish. "I don't know why they called her 'Madame,'" Orton recalled in an interview in 1967: "there was nothing Madamish about her at all. She was just an ordinary pompous middle-class lady."[22] But at their first meeting, Orton's eyes were on his goal, not her condescension:

> I went to see Madame Rothery at her house. We had a long talk about the scholarship, etc. She said that I could get a maintenance grant from the Education Committee to go to RADA. Then she said she would give me private lessons (fees 4 guineas per 10 lessons). I got £1 toward it and with my ten shillings spending money at the end of the week makes 30 shillings. But honestly don't know how I'm going to get the rest. I'm not going to ask Mum for anything at all because she can't afford it. Wrote a letter to the library about a job this evening.   [April 17, 1950]

The young man had not impressed Madame Rothery. "He was just an ordinary, unsophisticated boy. I was quite staggered he wanted to go on the stage. His people were ordinary working-class people. There was no culture, no education. I felt sorry for him. Here's a boy that wants to do something. He's not got much talent, but I was out to help him."

Whether Madame Rothery told Orton to his face that he had no talent (as she claimed) is unconfirmed in his diary. Perhaps an insult of that magnitude was too painful to include in those hopeful pages. His single-mindedness seems to have brushed aside her dismissive attitude while still harboring resentment about it. As Orton would tell it in later years, Madame Rothery left him with a painful impression of his own inadequacy:

> She didn't think much of me, just a yob, I could tell that. She offered coffee and I said yes, and she asked me did I take sugar and I said yes; and she went away and came back with the coffee with sugar, but it wasn't sugar, it was saccharine in the bottom of the cup and so I thought, "Oh yes, she's a right bitch," and she had these biscuits in a biscuit barrel, you know, these awful cheap biscuits. Oh, she didn't think much of me. She thought more of a pompous

middle-class young man who was going to her because she thought he was going to be God's gift to the English stage. I was very glad to notice that he turned out to be a disaster. She had no taste.[23]

Madame Rothery was the only architect of his hope. He needed to believe in her: "Polished up my Ariel speech from *The Tempest* and although the way Madame wants it isn't my way, it's coming on famously" [May 17, 1950]. The modesty of Orton's effort conflicts with his later memories of Madame Rothery's dismissal of his dreams: "She'd always say, 'You'll have to try some other school like the Guildhall,' and then she went even lower naming schools I don't think exist now."[24] But the diary is only enthusiastic about Madame Rothery's suggestions: "Elocution lesson. Madame asked me if I would like to take the Guildhall exam or RADA. I prompted for RADA. Do hope I get it as it would show everybody that I can do something" [September 21, 1950]. "Madame Rothery says I have improved considerably and would like to see me revise Ariel's speech (I did this for my very earliest elocution classes) to see if it has improved" [June 23, 1950].

The first tangible measure of improvement was a stage technical exam in July. Orton was "rehearsing like anything for it."[25] He had chosen two pieces that indulged his appetite for fantasy and theatrical excess: one from J. M. Barrie's *Peter Pan* and one from A. A. Milne's *The Ivory Door*. He was uncharacteristically apprehensive. His fears were compounded when he watched another classmate rehearse her scenes from *Vanity Fair* and *Children in Uniform*. "The reading really impressed me, if that is the competition I am up against, I don't think I shall go far."[26] The exam tested not only Orton's ability, but the credibility of his dream:

> Exam. Did feel scared. Felt just as if I was going to the dentist and was counting how many people had to go before me. Then came my turn. I told the girl in charge where to put the chair for *The Ivory Door* and then (with heart quaking) I went in and announced that I was doing a scene from *The Ivory Door* by A. A. Milne. The adjudicator said, 'Thank you.' I did it without a blemish and went on with *Peter Pan*. Got through that. And imagine my surprise when the adjudicator said I'd got 70 marks out of 80. Wonderous.   [July 8, 1950]

Slowly he was getting closer to his goal:

> Feel very elated as Madame Rothery suggested I should do my RADA entrance for January. Of course I've got a lot to do before that,

but, oh boy, at least it's been mentioned. But before then I'm going to try for the Nottingham Festival of Music and Drama. Do hope that I get a chance to go on the stage. [July 14, 1950]

Orton won third place at the Nottingham Festival, teaming with another of Madame Rothery's pupils to do the Oberon-Titania quarrel scene from *A Midsummer Night's Dream*. They repeated the performance later in the year when Madame Rothery held an evening show to display her students not only to their parents but to the educational authorities. Emboldened by his success at Nottingham, Orton seized his opportunity:

I had a marvellous idea. I thought I'd play Oberon green, so I bought a lot of green distemper from the local shop. I'd no idea about stage make-up and put on a pair of bathing trunks and just covered myself from head to foot in green, including my hair, surprisingly I didn't get skin rash. Then, I got a green bedspread from my mother's and father's bed and wrapped that round me and appeared on stage in this fantastic outfit, the bedspread was covered with green distemper while the girl wore a conventional muslin ballet dress as Titania. Anyway, it was very successful because Madame introduced me afterwards to this man who was in charge of giving away grants. I had a long talk with him. He thought the performance was very interesting.[27]

The educational officer also conveyed his enthusiasm to Mrs. Orton. "John is absolutely wasted in an office," he told her. Elsie quickly countered: "Well, I can't afford to send him anywhere." He explained about local grants. (In fact, the Leicester Educational Committee later contributed a generous £310 a year toward Orton's education at RADA. It was the second acting grant ever awarded from Leicester.)

Orton applied to RADA on November 6, 1950. Besides his stage technique exam, the only thing he could list under Special Distinctions or Examinations Passed was Pitman's Shorthand 100 w.p.m. and Typewriting 40 w.p.m. On his eighteenth birthday—January 1, 1951—Orton packed a small bag, took the train to London, and did two auditions for RADA, one for entrance, the other for a scholarship. Once again he brazened his way to attention. "I did a piece from *Peter Pan* between Captain Hook and Smee, both at the same time, a kind of schizophrenic act."[28] Like Hook, Orton felt himself handicapped; but he also had an innocence and sense of fun that fought against it. The Hook-Smee exchange contained the frenzy that always fired his imagination. "It was quite alarming," Orton recalled. "It impressed the judges."[29]

RADA accepted him. He went immediately to tell Madame Rothery. "When I took the letter round to Madame she could hardly conceal her rage that I'd gotten in. She continued to be bitchy, because when I went to RADA I was supposed to have had eight lessons, actually I'd had seven, and she kept writing saying I hadn't paid her for the last lesson."[30] Even in retrospect Madame Rothery disdains Orton's "surprising" result. "Fate was with us. It was just after the war and men were extremely scarce; so they would have taken practically anything that could stand up."

Orton's success was dampened almost immediately by an appendicitis attack that made it impossible to begin at RADA the next term. He would have to wait until the summer. But no sooner had he left the hospital than the prospect of attending RADA's summer session was jeopardized. The Army called Orton for his physical examination. Only a year before he had welcomed the idea of a National Service stint as a relief from the tedium of his job ("Goodbye Fire Services, Army here I come!"[31]). Now he plotted frantically. Leonie remembers: "As the scabs from his appendix operation fell off the stitches, John was sticking them back on so the scar looked worse. He never smoked in his life, but he puffed cigarettes to try to bring on an asthma attack. When he went for the medical, he wanted it to seem as though he were dying." The asthma, combined with his appendix and a fictitious hearing complaint improvised on the spot in front of the Army doctor, convinced them that he was not military material. "If the doctor could have seen me racing down the street after the exam," Orton told his mother, "he'd have fetched me back and passed me A-1."

WHEN ORTON LEFT Leicester for RADA in May 1951, he closed the door on his past. Elsie Orton cried for a few days after he'd gone. She confided to Leonie: "I know I've lost him. I've lost my boy. He'll never, ever, come home again." But Orton had never, ever, really been with the family. They loomed in his mind as vague and incidental intrusions—like extras in an epic. His absence was felt, but he felt no absence. "Whenever John looked distant and offhand, it was in relation to his family," his Leicester friend Bernard Widdowson says. "He used to dry up every time the family was mentioned." The lengthy walks they took together along the High Street toward the Clock Tower and then to Victoria Park, ended at the junction of the Saffron Lane Estates. "Orton made it fairly obvious that this was as far as it went."

Orton left a photograph of himself with the family. Elsie quickly framed it and locked it in the china cabinet, where a few years later she

would enshrine his RADA diploma. The picture commemorated the new
John Orton—composed, seasoned, too staunch and sleek to fail. The
image suited the pedestal on which Elsie placed him. The rest of the
family carried with them warmer, happier images. Douglas remembers
the fastidious John, the one his mother bragged was so well kept and
well mannered that somebody had asked to adopt him. Douglas pictures
him folding his clothes neatly on the bank of the canal before diving
in. He sees him kneeling on the bank beside Leonie with a jam jar and
a net snaring fish he'd later try to keep alive in the bathtub. This is
"The Cut" which Elsie shouted to the kids to keep away from and
where Orton escaped for long walks. His brother threw their rust-red
mongrel—Ronick—into the narrow, muddy canal to watch it swim.
This was their playground and, later, when Marilyn's six-year-old son
Tony drowned there, a landmark of the quiet harshness of their lives.
Douglas recalls John dressing him up as a bear and making him parade
in his living-room Christmas pageant. John was always doing something
"strange," "different," provoking this unhappy family into gaiety.

Marilyn has memories of John's "lovely speech." She recollects
him on the bus coming home from Clark's College, his head bent over
a book while the other boys giggled and joked around him. "Nobody
left an impression the way he did. You always wanted to live up to him
after he'd left." Leonie recalls his dry laugh. How his head would jerk
back, then the sudden flash of teeth, and finally he'd register his amusement with a sound as sharp and short as the clap of a hand. It was John
who filled her Christmas stocking. "Whenever he bought you anything, it was good. He bought me *Alice in Wonderland*. It was a blue
leatherbound." She pictures John with her in tow stealing a copy of
Black Beauty from the Bishop's Street Library, where he spent so much
of his time and where she almost gave him away. He read her Greek
mythology and Oscar Wilde's *The Importance of Being Earnest*. She
can still see him looking up from the play with an eyebrow arched in
mock astonishment to exclaim in fluting voice: "A handbag!"

Home was not where Orton's heart was. He had no sentimentality
about family matters. When Marilyn's son died in 1965, he wrote her:

> There's nothing I can write that will make any difference. I know
> how you must be feeling. Do understand that I would've come home
> if I'd known, and if there was anything I could've done. . . . I
> haven't been told when the funeral is and I suppose it's over.
> I wouldn't send a wreath. I don't begrudge the money, but it seems
> a lot of show. Nothing can bring the kid back.   [March 31, 1965]

Orton's aloofness was something the family understood and accepted. He wrote home frequently, but the family rarely answered. In 1962, Leonie started a correspondence. "He used to write me mother and me mother never used to write back. He kept writing and nobody answered." Orton's annual visits for a fortnight each summer were happy occasions, especially for Elsie. But they had the hurried, strained inadequacy of a conversation with a friend who is anxious to depart. When he was back with his family, Orton got up to his familiar pranks. He enjoyed turning off the television sound and laughing at the people on screen mouthing words like puppets on an invisible string. He took Elsie's women's magazines and got Leonie to read the questions on the problems page. Orton invented irreverent answers. He liked to outrage them with his loud clothes and his brash claims. "He reminded me of Cassius Clay," Leonie says. "He did actually say, 'I'm the greatest.' So I says, 'What about Shakespeare, then?' And John said, 'I hope I never write first plays as bad as his!' "

Orton's excuse for cutting short his family holiday was always Kenneth. He declined every Christmas invitation because Kenneth would be alone. Elsie often suggested he return to live in Leicester. "What's the attraction down there?" she would ask. Orton smiled and said nothing. His first mentions of the mysterious "Kenneth" were interpreted by Elsie as another of her John's practical jokes. When Orton sent a picture of Halliwell, she was shocked by his baldness. "What do you want to live with a bald man for?" she asked. Orton just laughed.

Kenneth Halliwell was Orton's emotional home, and that relationship began almost as soon as Orton found digs in London.

"DARLING," Orton wrote to Joyce Holmes, an aspiring Leicester actress on whom he had a crush, three weeks after beginning RADA in May. "What do you think of 'free love,' I think it's cute. Some of the types in this place, seven-eighths of them look at you as if it's an insult to be a virgin (I'm still pure, but only just)." Joyce Holmes's "virginal qualities" had appealed to Orton ever since he had first met her at a Vaughan Players' rehearsal in 1949. He found her accessible, intelligent, and irresistible. Bernard Widdowson, who often stood with him outside the second-floor window where she lived above her father's sweet shop, says, "Orton had an almost unhealthy preoccupation with her. She'd gone, he mistakenly thought, to a convent school. That seemed to excite John more than anything." They shared a love of theatre—and families that thought their interest "daft." Now Orton

was swept up in the delight and excitement of the big city, and his
gossip was filled with a timid lover's oblique affection. He wanted to
encourage her to come to RADA. He'd already seen Alec Guinness in
Hamlet and Orson Welles's *Macbeth*. The letter bubbles with gaiety:

> Wilfred Pickles and Mabel (Mabel Pickles sounds like something
> you have with cheese) came into the room last week as we were
> doing a queer class called movement, which consists of flopping
> about in the most obscure positions. The teacher, I am quite con-
> vinced, invented some even more "obscure positions" just for Mr.
> Pickles' benefit, they so damaged the bone structure of the class that
> six of them are in hospital and having their necks re-twisted and
> I have my left leg permanently round my right ear. . . . On Mon-
> days, we have a sort of gym class. The teacher shows his legs and
> wears body make-up, he also makes obscene suggestions in a polite
> way. We have in the class something called "free running," not to be
> confused with "F.L." [Free Love].

Orton's romantic interest glowed through the bravado—"I'm just longing to come home and see you, your company is so refreshing. I know
you don't believe me, but then I'm always 'misunderstood.' " He asked
for her photograph "to keep the cats away," and signed off with "Yours
until I have a better offer." The offer came soon enough.

Orton had acquired two student roommates: Lawrence Griffin, and
James Hilbern—an American. They had basement digs at 31 Gower
Street, two blocks from RADA. Orton also quickly acquired a new style.
He sent a photo of himself back to Leicester, a dramatically revised
fantasy of the sophisticated actor John Orton. He was certainly Dirk
Bogarde in this one: white shirt open "naughtily" to the third button,
tousled hair, mouth turned up in a tentative, new flirtatiousness. This
was the first picture with a hint of sexuality, but the family saw only
the smiling, smooth face.

In July, during the summer vacation from RADA, Orton took part
in a Vaughan Players' production of *Measure for Measure* in which
he was praised for his "odious, fantastical Lucio." He also kissed Joyce
Holmes in the lighting booth—a curiously unsexual embrace that left
her thinking, "He's just a boy." By then Orton had found a lover more
eager for his affection. His RADA diary tells the story in a style as teasing
as his new photo. The last entries before he became famous fifteen
years later read:

May 15, 1951
Started at RADA O bliss!

May 16
Met Florentic G. A sister. You are she.

May 17
An actor's life for me.

May 18
Digs in Gower Street. Such fun.

May 19
Oh the larks.
Memo

Someone in the other class keeps looking at me.

May 20
Did nothing.

May 21
Mr. Constable's special movement. Was eyed.

May 22
Florrie ate all the biscuits.

May 23
Florrie ate all the cheese.

May 24
Florrie ate all the eggs.

May 25
Met Ken and John at Charing Cross Road.
Memo

I don't quite understand Ken.

May 27
Did nothing.

May 28
Mr. Constable's movement.

May 29
Florrie ate all the nuts.

May 30
Florrie ate all the bacon.

June 1
Met Ken and John again. This time with Rex Butler.

June 2
Flo rang Ken.
Memo

Am beginning to understand Ken.

June 3
Did nothing.

June 4
Mr. Constable's movement. Well!

June 5
Florrie ate all the cheese.

June 6
Florrie ate all the cake.

June 7
Fuck Florrie.

June 8
Met Ken. He invites us to live with him.

June 9
Went to the pictures.
Memo

I am puzzled.

June 10
Did nothing.

June 11
Must leave our digs.

June 12
Ken offers to share flat again.

June 13
I say No.

June 14
Ken offers again.

June 15
We accept because we must.

June 16
Move into Ken's flat.

June 17
Well!

June 18
Well!!

June 19
Well!!!

June 20
The rest is silence.

3

UNNATURAL PRACTICES

The solitary, in his own way a combatant, feels the need to populate his solitude with enemies, whether real or imagined.
—E. M. Cioran, *The Temptation to Exist*

The citizens boo loudly, wave their banners. McTurk and Low turn and walk away. The gap between the citizens and the two boys widens.
—Stage direction, *Up Against It*

THE ENGLISH PUBLIC first learned of Orton and Halliwell eleven years later, in 1962. It was not exactly the debut they had dreamed of. On May 15, the *Daily Mirror* devoted a banner headline to a story about a mischievous form of literary vandalism. Books from the Islington and Hampstead libraries were appearing on the shelves with photographs and book jackets humorously altered. The *Mirror* story was headed GORILLA IN THE ROSES, referring to a monkey's head pasted in the middle of a rose on the cover of the *Collins Guide to Roses*. In Leicester, the Orton family had skimmed the *Mirror* and all except William had gone to bed. He settled himself in front of the television. During the commercials he picked up the paper again and perused GORILLA IN THE ROSES expecting to find some gardening tips. When he read the small print, he rushed upstairs to tell Elsie. "Our John's been nicked," he announced. Elsie wouldn't believe it. She called the paper to confirm the story.

Orton, aged twenty-nine and described as a "lens cleaner," had been arraigned with Kenneth Halliwell, aged thirty-five and a "cleaner," at Old Street Magistrate's Court for stealing seventy-two library books and "wilfully" (the word was carefully typed over "unlawfully" in the court's citation) damaging a number of books, which included the removal of 1,653 plates from art books. Total damage was estimated at £450. They had been sentenced to six months in jail.

The story made funny copy (reprinted by the *Reader's Digest* and featured in other national English newspapers), but the scope of Orton's antics never got into print. The notorious "gorilla" was a gibbon grimacing in wide-eyed terror. Its small pear-shaped head was in exact proportion to the rose stem, and the yellow petals curved snugly around its face like a bleached-blond bouffant. The juxtaposition was startling and disturbing. "One of the greatest things at the trial, the greatest outrage, the one for which I think I was sent to prison, was that I had stuck a monkey's face in the middle of a rose," Orton said years later. "It was a very beautiful rose. . . . What I had done was held up as the depth of iniquity for which I should probably have been birched. They won't ever do that, so they just sent me to prison for six months,"[1]

Orton's jacket designs didn't stop at gardening books. In a critical study of the poet, a pot-bellied old man tattooed from head to toe and clothed only in a skimpy swim suit stood stiffly beside the name JOHN BETJEMAN. The first volume of Emlyn Williams's collected plays had a curious repertoire of *Knickers Must Fall, Up the Front, Up the Back, Olivia Prude, He Was Born Grey, Mr. Winifred,* and *Fucked by Monty.* Instead of displaying their photograph, a biography of the Lunts had tacky Christmas figurines, including a stuffed snowman, red and white reindeer, and two red and white does called Jill and Judy. In Alec Clunes's biography his face was replaced by a skull with a hole in the cranium. *Glok,* an American novel by Richard G. Stern, had its author as Hedda Hopper in one of her preposterous feathered *chapeaux.*

Orton remembered others. "I did things like pasting a picture of a female nude on a book of etiquette, over the picture of the author who, I think, was Lady Lewisham. I did other things, very strange things. There was the business when I got the biography of Sir Bernard Spilsbury and there was an illustration, which said: 'The remains discovered in the cellar at number 23 Rosedown Road.' I pasted over the illustration, which was a very dreary one of a lot of earth, David's picture of Marat dead in his bath. It was in black and white. I left the original caption underneath. This picture of the corpse in the bath had quite an effect on people who opened the book."[2] Orton's most successful paste-up illustration was of Dame Sybil Thorndike locked up in a cell as Nurse Edith Cavell. A man peeks surreptitiously through a window at her. But what he sees is Dame Sybil staring at the mammoth genitalia of a superimposed Greek torso. The caption reads: "During the Second World War I was working from dawn to dusk to serve the many thousands of sailors, soldiers and airmen. American G.I.s came in shoals to my surgery and some had very peculiar orders for me."

"I used to write false blurbs on the inside of Gollancz books," Orton remembered. "Because I discovered that Gollancz books had blank yellow flaps and I used to type false blurbs on the inside." Halliwell told the police: "I saw Orton typing on the covers of books. I read what he typed, and I considered it a criticism of what the books contained."[3] The target for most of this mischief was Dorothy Sayers's Lord Peter Wimsey whodunits:

> When little Betty Macdree says that she has been interfered with, her mother at first laughs [Orton wrote on the flap for *Clouds of Witness*]. It is only something that kiddy has picked up off television. But when sorting through the laundry, Mrs. Macdree discovers that a new pair of knickers are missing she thinks again. On being questioned, Betty bursts into tears. Mrs. Macdree takes her to the police station and to everyone's surprise the little girl identifies P. C. Brenda Coolidge as her attacker. Brenda, a new recruit, denies the charge. A search is made of the Women's Police Barracks. What is found there is a seven inch phallus and a pair of knickers of the kind used by Betty. All looks black for kindly P.C. Coolidge. . . . What can she do? This is one of the most enthralling stories ever written by Miss Sayers.
> It is the only one in which the murder weapon is concealed, not for reasons of fear but for reasons of decency!
> READ THIS BEHIND CLOSED DOORS. And have a good shit while you are reading!

"My blurbs were mildly obscene," Orton admitted. "Even at the trial they said they were only mildly obscene. When I put the plastic covers back over the jackets you couldn't tell that the blurbs weren't printed. I used to stand in corners after I'd smuggled the doctored books back into the library and then watch the people read them. It was very funny, very interesting."[4]

Although Orton never admitted to it publicly—choosing to emphasize his satire on pulp literature—he and Halliwell also jazzed up many of the drab designs for the outstanding Arden editions of Shakespeare with tactful collages from the art books they'd stolen. Their cover for *Titus Andronicus* combines an opulent Renaissance banquet in the foreground with two superimposed images of Goya's "Saturn Devouring Her Children" in the background. The visual effect is shocking and strong. When tampering with Shakespeare, they respectfully retained the name of the editor as well as the play on the cover. It was their disrespectful images that scandalized the court. Birds' heads pasted over the faces of eminent figures of Tudor history; monkeys adorning a book of exotic caged birds; a cartoon cat's head featured as

OH, WHAT A LOVELY WAR, film adaptation of Joan Littlewood's theater workshop production. Screenplay by Len Deighton. Paramount Studios. 134 mins.

"Oh, What a Lovely War!," the hit British musical that was successfully transplanted to Broadway a few seasons back, is now a film. In its new format the World War I story generates wry smiles at the outset and steady discomfort as the film progresses. Despite the songs and dances, this is no gentle satire of society's idiosyncracies, but an exposé of the psychology of war, which perpetuates itself from generation to generation.

World War I, which began and concluded in genteel palace settings, is "fondly" recalled—the songs and dress of the era, the bands, the innocence of proud women and callow men who march merrily to the War Carnival. Generals plan for victory, women and children yearn and

F 70 :

Control and Disarmament Agency. They will face their Soviet counterparts.

The format of the convocation is consistent with many statements about the Fund made by Joseph P. Lyford, the former Berkeley professor who became the organization's first full-time president last October. "The Fund," he says, "does not see the problems of peace in traditional terms. It seeks to establish connections between war systems and such problems as those concerning the environment, overpopulation, racism and poverty." None of these problems, he said, can be solved in isolation from the others, and none can be solved so long as some 75 per cent of public resources go into military expenditures.

During 1969, the Fund underwrote peace fellowships and research projects at Columbia University's School of International Affairs, Duke University's Rule of Law Research Center, Howard University dance for it, ministers pray for it, while soldiers in trenches, too miserable to enjoy the rhetoric of war, literally dig in to endure the harsh reality of the fight.

One scene is particularly devastating: on Christmas Eve the German and English soldiers sing carols across the trenches. Timidly, the antagonists lay down their arms and meet each other in no man's land. The soldiers exchange their names and their whisky, and, in the ultimate irony, shake hands. Bursting shells send the group scampering, and a moment later the arbitrary hostility between men is re-established.

As time elapses, as fatalities increase, participants in the War Carnival may vaguely doubt the worth of the endeavor, but such ignoble thoughts are quickly brushed aside. Why else do men die in war if not for the Good?

"Peace" is finally established and the actors go home, their numbers greatly diminished, with only the faintest inkling of what has happened to them. The audience, on the other hand, leaves the Carnival quite certain of what has taken place, and with the added understanding that the Carnival will come to town periodically. The oldsters will romanticize the past for the youngsters, never fear, and sooner or later the band will start playing and on it will go . . . until the people are somehow struck wise enough to say NO MORE!

JANET DILLEHAY

doxical Theses

nity are immoral and criminal in-
ld.

China and the American right
n interest.

t really fighting each other; they
selves.

merica is really an agent of mili-

ism is one of the gravest threats

berrant tactic of radical national-

motivates all men and underlies
ish.

Hegel has immense relevance for
ems and their solutions.

surpassed by a higher form of life.

icy must be actively supported in

ernment is the worst possible.

est way an American student can
conflict once and for all.

**es and heretical ideas are pro-
blished by *The International-
r periodical which considers
relate to the problems of war
ary world. Sound interesting?**

one of the schizoid personalities in *The Three Faces of Eve*—these typical grotesqueries, as well as the photographs of the collage murals in the bedsitter at Noel Road, led the prosecuting counsel to maintain to the magistrate: "In some thirty years of experience I have never seen anything of this nature before."[5] Most perturbing to the court was not the abuse of private property but the care and intelligence with which Orton and Halliwell tampered with the books. "For some reason which seems not to be clear," the prosecuting counsel said, "the two men had not only stolen the books but had caused the most extraordinary damage to them."[6]

Orton and Halliwell never admitted their rationale for this prank to the court. The senior probation officer mentioned that "in a sense both defendants were frustrated authors."[7] Rejected by the literary world, they made a spectacle of published books and the public that evaded them. They turned the library into a little theatre, where they watched people reacting to their productions. It was one way of getting into print and making their statement. There was sorrow in their anger, but also hilarity. In its ruthlessness, the caper displayed both the solitary's groping to connect and the prankster's wish to turn the world into his playground. In later years, forgetting the debt he owed to the Leicester libraries, Orton used "good taste" as his explanation for defacing the books:

> The thing that really put me in a rage about librarians was that I went to quite a big library in Islington and asked for Gibbon's *Decline and Fall of the Roman Empire*. They told me they hadn't got a copy of it. They could get it for me, but they hadn't one on their shelves. This didn't start it off, but it was symptomatic of the whole thing. I was enraged that there were so many rubbishy novels and rubbishy books. It reminded me of the Bible: "Of the making of books, there is no end," because there isn't. Libraries might as well not exist; they've got endless shelves of rubbish and hardly any space for good books. . . . You can obviously say when some things are rubbish and some things aren't. I can obviously say Gibbon isn't. He said a very funny thing about books: when the Arabs took Alexandria they used the contents of the library to provide fuel for the baths and Gibbon thought the books were doing more good being so used than they were being read. . . .[8]

Halliwell smuggled the books in and out of the libraries in a service gasmask case. Orton used a satchel. "Ken would be with me on most occasions," Orton told the police. "I wouldn't know what he was doing, but when we got home, I'd show him what I'd stolen and he'd show me what he'd stolen." When the police asked Orton why he'd done it, he replied: "I wanted these books but haven't been able to afford them. That's why I took them."[9] But, besides the art books, most of the stolen titles were frivolous. The actual anarchic intention was spelled out in Orton and Halliwell's autobiographical novel, *The Boy Hairdresser* (1960), when Donelly and Peterson confess to a female visitor that they steal books:

> "I think it's terrible," she said.
> "We're public benefactors in a way. We steal—the shops order more—the publishers are pleased—and everybody is happy. We finance literature. We are a sort of Maecenas."
> He kept his malice under control.
> "You wouldn't even begin to understand the real reason why we do these things."
> "Do you understand yourself?"
> She wandered around the room, touching things, wrinkling her nose in disapproval.
> "Do you know what subreption is?" said Donelly.
> "No."
> "To obtain something by misrepresentation. That is what our civilization does—it holds carrots in the air to make donkeys work. Do you know what it wants in exchange for a house, a car, a larger house, two cars, a television in every room?"
> "No."
> "It wants our lives."

Orton and Halliwell began stealing books in 1959. As they boasted in *The Boy Hairdresser*, they never expected to be caught. But the library had been quietly on the lookout for them for eighteen months. In January 1962 a branch librarian became suspicious of two men who always visited the library together and who shared the same address. At the suggestion of the police, assistants from other library departments who were not known to be staff were posted as browsing readers at the time when Orton and Halliwell changed their books. According to the *Library Association Record*, in an article about their prosecution, "It was hoped that they would be caught red-handed illicitly replacing 'doctored' books on the shelves. After several weeks of unproductive observation, we contrived to obtain a sample of typewritten matter done on a machine belonging to one of the two men."[10] The responsibility for outfoxing Orton and Halliwell fell to the Islington Borough Council's legal clerk, Sidney Porrett. "I had to catch these two monkeys. I didn't want the case. I had to get results," says Porrett.

"I played them a slightly dirty trick. I thought 'OK, I'll let my ethics slip a little bit.' I wanted to get them aggravated. They were a couple of darlings, make no mistake." Porrett's letter was written in the bureaucratic jargon which Orton and Halliwell hated.

15 Feb. 1962

Dear Sir,

Standard Vanguard—KYR. 450

The above numbered vehicle appears to be abandoned in Noel Road, and I have been given to understand that you may be the owner thereof. As you are aware, my council has recently been given power to remove abandoned vehicles which obstruct the highway. But before looking into the question of enforcing its remedies in the matter, I give you the opportunity of taking the necessary steps to cause the vehicle to be removed from the highway. I attach a notice addressed to yourself in this matter.

Porrett's cagey letter flushed out a salvo from Halliwell:

17 February 1962

Dear Sir,

I should like to know who provided you with this mysterious information?

Whoever they are, they must be a liar or a moron: probably both.

I have never possessed a car of any make whatsoever and never wish to.

I can only presume that somebody is staging a leg-pull with you or me or both.

I would suggest that in the future you obtain your information from some more reliable source before pestering people with inexplicable letters.

Halliwell signed his letter "Yours contemptuously"—but the letter's typeface matched the blurbs of the defaced books. The police had sufficient evidence to make an arrest. At 9:00 a.m. on April 28, 1962, Detective Sergeant Henry Hermitage and Detective Constable Gray knocked at Flat 4, 25 Noel Road. Halliwell opened the door. As Detective Sergeant Hermitage explained in his police statement: "I said to him, 'We are police officers and I have a warrant to search your flat as I have reason to believe you have a number of stolen library books.' He said, 'Oh dear.' "[11]

"We think it was very naughty of you to send us that letter," Orton told Porrett, to which Porrett replied: "I fetched myself down to your level. I'm quite happy to let you think I'm a fool, but I'm one step ahead of you all the time." He goes on: "It was just my psychological attempt to get on top of them. They realized they'd met somebody as cute as them. When I saw them standing there, I thought Orton was the overgrown schoolboy who was trying to draw attention to himself; Halliwell was the older, and, I would have said, the dangerous type. Deep-thinking. Surly. He couldn't look straight at you when he spoke. Both looked like a couple of silly boys lost."

Orton was never abused by the police, but he felt threatened. "I wasn't actually beaten up," he said. "But they hovered around. . . . I found that the best thing was to be as nice as possible and as utterly vulnerable as possible because it was no use standing on your rights once they've got you in their power."[12] Privately, he contended that their severe sentence was "because we were queers."[13]

Orton did most of the talking about prison afterwards in public; but it was Halliwell, dominating the relationship at the time, who spoke for them in court. They pleaded guilty to five counts of theft and malicious damage. Halliwell disputed the court's assessment of the damage of their prank. He also explained that, if each defendant was forced to pay £200 from their Post Office banking account, the mortgage on their £2,000 flat would be jeopardized.

But the presiding magistrate—Harold Sturge—rebuked them sternly from the bench: "What I am anxious to see is that the decision of this court should make it abundantly clear to those who may be clever enough to write criticisms of other people's books—public library books—or to deface them or ruin them in this way are made to understand very clearly that it is disastrous. . . . I am most concerned about the malice shown by both of you in what you did—sheer malice towards fellow users of this library who, until these books are replaced, will be denied what they might reasonably have expected to enjoy. . . ."[14]

"Magistrate" would become a term of abuse in Orton's vocabulary: a word that epitomized everything quietly violent, sterile, and inflexible in the English middle class. "The kind of people that walk out of *Loot* in a rage are the kind of people that are magistrates," he said years later. "Now they can't do anything to me as the author of *Loot* but if I was up before them and I was the prisoner and they were the judge, they would be able to do something against me. I was exactly the same, though I hadn't written *Loot* and *Sloane*, and I was in the clutches of people who walked out of *Loot*. I mean, it was absolutely unforgivable. I'm not excusing myself, I'm just unrepentant."[15]

The trial festered in Orton's imagination. In *Loot*, he would dramatize the terror of being hamstrung by authority:

Door chimes.

FAY. Would you excuse me, Inspector?

TRUSCOTT (*wiping his brow*). You're at liberty to answer your own doorbell, miss. That is how we tell whether or not we live in a free country.

FAY *goes off left.*

(*Standing over* HAL.) Where's the money?

HAL. In church.

TRUSCOTT *kicks* HAL *violently.* HAL *cries out in terror and pain.*

TRUSCOTT. Don't lie to me!

HAL. I'm not lying! It's in church!

TRUSCOTT (*shouting, knocking* HAL *to the floor*). Under any other political system I'd have you on the floor in tears!

HAL (*crying*). You've got me on the floor in tears.

Orton and Halliwell were taken first to Wormwood Scrubbs and then sent to separate open prisons: Orton to H.M. Prison Eastchurch at Sheerness in Kent; Halliwell to H.M. Prison Ford at Arundel in Sussex. While at the Scrubbs, both men were interviewed by the resident psychiatrist. Halliwell told the truth; Orton did not. "I didn't trust the psychiatrist because I knew anything I told him would be reported to the authorities." Always a good actor, Orton charmed the psychiatrist. As he told it later, the psychiatrist confided to him, "I think your friend is homosexual." "You don't say," Orton replied, wrinkling his forehead in amazement.

The moment was a rare flash of humor in an otherwise dismal situation. At the time, both Halliwell and Orton were mortified by their imprisonment. Orton would not allow his family to visit him; and Halliwell, writing to the caretakers of their building—the Cordens—confided, "We have been utter fools and hope there will not be too much bad feeling about it when we return to Noel Road. . . . What a mess!"[16] Orton adapted to the situation more easily than Halliwell. "I was locked in my cell for twenty-three hours a day. I used to have a half an hour's exercise in the morning and half an hour in the afternoon. Now this didn't worry me so much, but it worried a lot of the other people. I used to read a lot. I didn't read the Bible which we were supposed to read. I read strange things like [A. J. Cronin's] *Hatter's Castle*, the sort of thing I wouldn't normally dream of reading, cheap novels and capers. . . ."[17]

Halliwell was repentant. Orton was not. "I'm afraid my tendency to get into hot water will never be entirely squashed," he wrote to the

Cordens. "However, I am treading very carefully here: I want to get out on September 14—only forty-five more days."[18] Characteristically, Halliwell was more tentative about the future. Disappointment had dogged his life too closely and too long for him to put complete faith in any expectation. "Look forward to seeing you all for a more protracted period," he wrote the Cordens. "Though, of course, one never knows. . . . We are not quite out of the woods yet, though John may decide we are. . . ."[19]

Both men tried to laugh away their incarceration, but the laughter was strained. "Glad to hear of Miss Boynes's holiday," Orton wrote about the tenant below them at 25 Noel Road. "I hope she had better weather than we're having here. I'm sorry I booked for so long. I definitely shan't come again next year."[20] Halliwell struck the same jocular tone: "As you will see from the address, John and I are at present guests of her Majesty."[21] To the Cordens, Halliwell worried about the security of their flat ("Even convicts, I presume, have their property under the protection of the law"), the electricity bills, the house provisions. Orton was not interested in the minutiae of domestic life. Instead, his letters reveal a bumptious energy and an anger at the maneuverings of the authorities that his public statements about life in prison never admitted. When the Borough Council tried to get money from Orton and Halliwell's savings accounts, Orton was up in arms. He wrote urgently to the Cordens:

. . . This is, of course, the Islington Borough Council trying to pull a fast one. Now I have NO intention of signing away any of my money. I would be very surprised if Ken did either. You know he thinks I'm a bit of an idiot. So will you write to him, tell him about the letter. . . . The thing to impress on Ken is I'm not signing anything! Of course I don't need to tell you not to let my bank book out of your grasp. Guard it with your life. It's all the money I have in the world. . . .

I hate to burden you with all this, but I really feel so *angry*. Admittedly what I did is not to be defended, but I'm paying for it here. They want me to come out of prison literally penniless. Also they must imagine I'm a mental case indeed if they think that kind of tactic is going to succeed with me. Or Ken either, unless prison has altered him for the worse.

Anyway, once again, do write to him and let him know that I'm too old, and after all this, too wise, to be caught that easily.

My mother said she read of the case in the *Daily Mirror*? Did you also? You must have read such a garbled account of it. I don't know what the *Daily Mirror* said. I would probably be extremely

embarrassed if I did. I do hope it wasn't too sickening. I know what
they make of the simplest case.

Once again, my apologies for not being amusing. . . .[22]

Orton and Halliwell were scheduled for release on September 14,
1962. While still in prison, they received a summons to appear at the
Clerkenwell County Court on September 17. The Council had reduced
the estimated damage of the books to £262; and they would have to
pay it. Orton could hardly contain himself: "I had hoped to get out on
the 14th and try to pick up the pieces and forget what had happened—
however that is not now possible. . . . Talk about the Hounds of
Vengeance!"[23]

When they returned to the flat on the fourteenth, they found it
stocked to order with their familiar and minimal necessities: a half
dozen eggs, a pound of sugar, cheese, a large sliced loaf. Mrs. Corden
had even washed and pressed their sheets—symbolic, so she wrote, of
the fresh start she hoped they would make. "The future if not rosy, at
least will be bright." (Mrs. Corden decorated her language as absurdly
as her flat. "My vagina has come up the size of a football," she told
Orton, who visited her in hospital after a spilt cup of tea had scalded
her in the lap. "The Matron of the hospital said to me that in all her
years of medical experience she'd never seen anything like it. But I've
no complaints. I've been given top-class penicillin."[24])

At the court hearing, Orton and Halliwell agreed to pay £200
from their Post Office account immediately for damages. They went on
the dole—and did not come off the £3 a week allowance until 1964,
when *Entertaining Mr. Sloane* became an established commercial success. But Porrett wasn't finished with them yet. He had, as he says,
"another trick up his sleeve" to ensure he got the remaining £62 in
damages. He threatened them with a charging order that gave him
power of sale over their mortgaged flat to meet the unsettled debt.
"I wanted to let them know that I was still the governor in this
matter. I was still that much on top." From January 1, 1963, Orton
and Halliwell agreed to pay £6 a month. "They paid up like little
darlings," Porrett says, smiling. "I left them financially pretty rocky."
In his final letter to Porrett on December 4, 1962, Halliwell indicated
the effects of this bureaucratic vindictiveness:

I should like to point out that (as the employment situation looks
at the moment) we shall be paying [the £6 a month] out of our
National Assistance it will thus entail an element of real hardship.
For what was (surely?) a comparatively mild crime, we have thus:

a) lost our jobs and been thrown on the barest subsistence level of National Assistance.

b) done six months prison sentence.

c) paid practically all our pathetically small bank accounts.

Justice has certainly been done. Some people might think, perhaps, even a little bit *more* than justice.

Prison proved more of a turning point in their lives than either Orton or Halliwell at first admitted. Orton found a focus for his anger and a new detachment in his writing. For Halliwell, prison was more humiliating—a symbol of the larger pattern of defeat in his life. It made mockery of his dreams for himself, dreams that Orton had adopted in 1953. Within the year Halliwell would try to slit his wrists. Having once savored the role of literary renegades, they now had bona fide criminal credentials. Their decade of disappointments had its consummation in their prison record. The failure was complete—both were now resolutely at the bottom rung of their society. Orton persevered because he expected nothing from life and was now strangely free of society's values. But Halliwell was stymied because, no matter how hard he tried, he could not forget how much he had been led to expect and how dramatically these expectations had receded. As Donelly, Halliwell's surrogate in *The Boy Hairdresser,* taunted himself:

> *And so the gods distinction drew,*
> *Good luck to art, a sod to you.*

CHARLES HALLIWELL, Kenneth's father, was a man of few words and much responsibility. A chartered accountant, he was chief cashier at Cammell Laird and Co., one of Liverpool's biggest shipbuilding companies. His neat semi-detached house at 286 Heath Road, Bebington, was as tidy and sombre as he was. The furniture was heavy oak; the rooms were dark green. Kenneth Halliwell was brought up there. When, at twenty-three, he took over the house, his next-door neighbors recall that he immediately painted the furniture and the walls bright colors. The bedroom became light pink; the dining room was papered with murals composed of art book reproductions; the lawn was revamped to include a sunken garden. But no matter what hopeful veneer he gave to the house, there was no way of pasting over the past.

Halliwell had been a shy child. "Kenneth tended to keep to himself. He was keen on dressing up and acting. He was a great reader," remembers J. P. Howarth, who lodged with the Halliwells between

Kenneth's seventh and eleventh years, from 1933 to 1937. "Kenneth was very much a mother's boy. He tended to cling to his mother. If she came into the room, he'd come in with her and stay by her the whole time." Daisy Halliwell was a stout, tall woman with a vibrant personality. "She was a very cheerful and charming lady, while Kenneth's father was a quiet, unassuming man with very little conversation. 'I have to talk for both of us,' she would say." Daisy had wanted other children; but the Caesarian operation that brought Kenneth into the world on June 23, 1926, made it dangerous for her to have more. She pampered Kenneth and was ambitious for him. "They talk of the silver cord between mother and son," Mr. Howarth says. "Well, it would never have been severed between them." It was broken off traumatically in September 1937, the month in which Kenneth started at the Wirral Grammar School. Daisy's gruesome, sudden death from a wasp sting was a profound shock to Halliwell and his father. "Kenneth became very introspective and difficult to talk to," Mr. Howarth says. "Obviously after his mother died, conversation between Halliwell and his father would have been very limited—just the essentials." The next year Halliwell ran away from home, the first of many dramatic exits. He left a rose and a note. Mr. Howarth and Mr. Halliwell found him sitting in a local restaurant where Kenneth and his father often had lunch together.

Halliwell's drastic measures could not earn his father's attention or love. Halliwell's mother had pampered him; his father ignored him. They inhabited the same semi-detached house at Bebington in the Wirral, but they shared nothing. "Mr. Halliwell was a man I never saw smile," Mr. Howarth remembers. "He had no warmth. He could never hold a conversation." Typical of his habitual reticence, Mr. Halliwell left no note for his son when he committed suicide in 1949. Halliwell could not love someone with whom he'd had only the meagre relationship. When he discovered his father in the kitchen, Halliwell stepped over the body, turned off the oven, and put on the kettle. After his morning tea and shave, he reported the suicide to the next-door neighbors.

"Kenneth never seemed young." This is how Halliwell's neighbors, Mr. and Mrs. Noel Lacey, remember him. They watched him grow up, would later house him briefly after his father's suicide, and acted with him in amateur dramatic productions. Halliwell was often cast in older roles (at sixteen he played Count Orsino in *Twelfth Night* for the Carlton Players). He impressed people with his intelligence and precocity. He had been sobered by study and pain, and recast his sense of separation in a more heroic artistic mold. He excelled at school, but stubbornly refused to continue his education at university. "His classics master said that Kenneth was a born classical scholar," says J. P. Howarth, who also taught at the Wirral Grammar School. "And that he'd have no trouble getting into Oxford or Cambridge." Halliwell was being groomed for conventional English middle-class success, and he had the ability to achieve it.[25] Much was expected of him. His father wanted him to become a teacher; his mother had talked of her young son one day being a doctor.

Halliwell decided on an acting career. To his father and relatives, who aspired to respectability, the idea was preposterous. But, convinced of his intellectual gift, Halliwell wanted to display it in a spectacular way. "What wretched creatures we actors are," he observed in his first play, *The Protagonist* (written in his early twenties about Edmund Kean). "Our art has no existence until it is recognized. What was the use of my power when I could only display it before yokels? This is the end to which my being has been directed: the acclamation of the world and nothing less."

After leaving the Wirral Grammar School in 1943, Halliwell enrolled at the Liverpool Playhouse. He craved attention. His life had been touched early by grief, and he opted for glory to even the score. "I have always challenged Fate," Kean says in *The Protagonist*. "I shall always challenge it." Halliwell had a well-trained mind and an untutored heart. His fear of confronting the world was transformed into the heroic isolation of creative make-believe. He yearned for so much from life that only the imagination could satisfy the scope of his craving. Here, too, Kean speaks for him:

> I dreamed of a life of simplicity. But it was a sham. The only world for me is the world of make-believe. And to it I will return. Where else can I find anything that fulfills its promise? In my imagination only. In glorious make-believe.

Unlike Orton, who elbowed his way into minor parts, Halliwell was warmly welcomed into the Carlton Players. Male actors were at a premium in wartime. Between 1942, when he joined at the age of sixteen, and 1951, when he left for RADA, Halliwell would take prominent roles in twenty productions. He had been discovered by Roy Mothersole, a member of the theatre group, who had been teaching a class on verse drama at the Wirral Grammar School. Halliwell and a friend were the only two boys who showed talent. "They were

active homosexuals even then," Mothersole recalls. "They told me
about the number of schoolboys they'd 'had.' Halliwell's friend was
very handsome and blond. He was the extrovert. Halliwell was quiet.
Even when he talked animatedly, he was detached and remote." There
was nothing effeminate in Halliwell's manner. When he talked, he
craned his neck so that his head tilted back and his chin jutted out. It
was a familiar posture and it gave him a haughty look. Halliwell spoke
with authority (and even then could be bitchy), but he impressed the
people around him as a gentle, mild person.

The Carlton Players rehearsed four nights a week; and when not
performing, actors were put to use backstage. Halliwell was always
around. He had found his calling and a real home. He helped build the
Little Theatre, a three-hundred-seat house converted from an old
church, which was to house the group after 1950. Halliwell fastened
onto the leaders of the Players, Edna and Harold Rowson, who appreciated his intelligence. "Kenneth had a terrific sense of humor," Mrs.
Rowson recalls. "He always found the most unusual angles on his part.
He had a terrific sense of the ridiculous. He was an exceptionally good
actor by any standard. He used to get right into the heart of a character. He was wonderful to act with. He gave so much." Their faith was
rewarded with loyalty. "He was always very sympathetic if you were
troubled or upset, or if anything went wrong," Mrs. Rowson says. When
Mrs. Rowson broke her foot during rehearsals of *Road to Rome* in
1943, Halliwell arrived at her home every night with his bicycle to
wheel her to the theatre and back.

On leaving school Halliwell had become eligible for the Army but
declared himself a conscientious objector. In 1944 he became a "Bevan
boy," and was sent to work in the coal mines at Wigan, Lancashire. He
hated it. On his first day in the pits he adopted the Lancashire accent
in an effort to be accepted by the miners; he could not drop the mas-
querade and was trapped in a permanent Lancashire performance.
"Kenneth came back once to see us while he was in the mines," recalls
Mrs. Rowson. "It had a terrible effect on him. He couldn't bear the
darkness and the claustrophobia. He was suicidal."

Halliwell ran away from Lancashire to Scotland, the first of a long
list of retreats from his ideals. He had a hunger for victory but not the
stamina for battle. He acted with the Perth Repertory Company for a
few months, then took a more permanent job with the Dundee Rep.

Halliwell returned to his home in Bebington in 1946. His hair had
receded dramatically, giving him an austere, adult, and jowly presence.
The hardships of a wartime economy and the routine slog of repertory

had given him an appetite for leisure and luxury. After his father died in 1949, he could afford to indulge himself. His father had left him £4,321. As a man of independent means, Halliwell started to enjoy himself. He hired a housekeeper (he could never keep one long), dressed himself in expensive clothes—including a camel-hair overcoat with sash belt, which he draped over his shoulders at rehearsal—and settled down to become a writer. "He gave the impression he didn't need to work," Mrs. Rowson says. "We felt this was a pity. If he hadn't had so much money and had to earn a living, he might have stuck at acting and made more of a success of his career. When he came home after the war, he said to us, 'I'm fed up with theatre. I'm getting down to writing.' He was terribly dedicated." Occasionally, he would tell friends he was writing an article for *Reader's Digest* or that Heinemann's was interested in a novel. But nothing came of it, and none of his acquaintances ever saw the work. The only writing he did show them was *The Protagonist*. It was the first play ever written for the Carlton Players, but it was never put on. The script strained and sank beneath the ponderous weight of its pretensions.

On stage Halliwell could connect with people, where in life he kept his distance. "There was something bottled up in Kenneth that prevented him from fully expressing himself like other people do. He would go so far and then the shutters would come down," Mrs. Rowson says. "There was a barrier between Kenneth and the world, something you couldn't penetrate. A separation from people." Theatre was the bridge not only to people but to emotions. As a stage character, Halliwell could "lose himself"; and this unleashed a powerful, disturbing passion that he kept otherwise well guarded. Halliwell defended himself against betrayals. Offstage he was "retiring"; on stage he was outgoing and capable of terrifying displays of aggression. In *Judgment Day*, a courtroom drama by Elmer Rice, Halliwell was cast as the lawyer for the prosecution, a role in which his suppressed anger had a field day. "I played opposite him and I didn't have to act. He scared the living daylights out of me," remembers Sylvia Sargeant. "Halliwell had the ability to draw fear out of anyone." The production was voted the best of the year (1950) by the local press, and Halliwell received special attention:

> I doubt if Kenneth Halliwell has ever done better than he did in this fiery role . . . of the prosecuting counsel. Here was a part that called for an actor who could dominate the stage. Here was an actor who could do it.   —Birkenhead *Adventurer*

Earlier Halliwell had had two other theatrical successes. He was amusing as Shipuchin in Chekhov's *The Anniversary* and terrifying as the sinister escaped criminal in Clemence Dane's *Granite*. Bolstered by this achievement, Halliwell shelved his literary aspirations and applied to RADA in August 1950, hoping to win a scholarship for the autumn term. It was an impulsive decision, and Halliwell's application was far too late to be considered. He had to reapply for an audition in January. He did not need a scholarship but he promoted the myth of himself as an impecunious orphan. "If I am not good enough to win an outstanding scholarship with maintenance to live in London," he wrote to RADA, with a familiar hint of arrogance, "I could not consider going to the Academy."[26] What he wanted was some tangible confirmation of his talent from the most prestigious of English drama schools. Everyone who acted with Halliwell anticipated his success. He auditioned in January—the same tryout in which Orton won a place. Halliwell did a scene from *Pygmalion*, but he did not impress the judges. The rejection flummoxed him. He wrote to RADA asking for explanations, a plaintive insecurity beneath his questioning—"I wished to enter for the Scholarship test and then to be given as good a Scholarship as they thought me worth. Or did they not think me worth any scholarship of any degree?" And he went on to flap at the registrar: "I should like to know whether my age is against me. Because if so, it will be little use my going in for it again in April when I will be three months older."[27]

Next, he "discovered" an aunt in Clapton whose hospitality in London, he claimed, would allow him to apply for a scholarship without maintenance. By the April 1951 audition, he had dropped the pretension to a scholarship completely.

Meanwhile he had moved to London and bought himself a flat at 161 West End Lane, West Hampstead. "Who Pays the Fee to RADA?" the questionnaire asked its new students. "Self," Halliwell wrote on May 15, the first day of term. His achievement was somewhat dampened in his eyes by his fee-paying status. But he had still made his exit from Cheshire as dramatic and portentous as possible. Abandoning his first directing assignment, he left the Rowsons a note of resignation and farewell:

> I have been accepted at RADA, and I am going.
> I am terribly sorry for letting you down.
> I cannot tell it to your face.

At first, Halliwell's letters to the Rowsons from RADA were posted on the Green Room bulletin board and read by the company. He was

the first and last of their eager group to reach RADA. In one letter he
said, "I shall never return to that muddy little town beside the Mersey."
He kept his promise. Halliwell never saw the Rowsons or Bebington
again.

RADA WAS NOT a happy time for Halliwell. His theatrical experience
had been primarily with adults. Now he found himself surrounded by
less tolerant and more talented teenagers. "Halliwell was an old man to
us," remembers June Clark Howarth, who acted opposite him in *Wild
Decembers*. "Most of the girls and boys were seventeen or eighteen. I
thought Halliwell was much older than twenty-five. He looked easily
between thirty and thirty-five. He was very bald and very dark; only one
other actor in the school was bald. I suppose we were a little afraid of
him." Halliwell was victimized by the moods that aggravated his reputation for ominousness, and by his isolation. There was no warmth or
simplicity in his personality. When one young actress—Diana Scougall—
teased him before a rehearsal and pulled his tie, Halliwell slapped her.
In an acting class, he shocked both the students and the teacher with
the anger behind his improvisation. "Halliwell acted a scene with an
imaginary cat. He began by loving the cat. He was nice to the cat.
A plaything," recalls his teacher, Mary Phillips. "Then his expression
changed, and he strangled it. Everyone was horrified. It was so unexpected. There was a laugh from him." Halliwell's displays of anger
were memorable. "He would color up," says June Clark Howarth.
"You could see him grow gradually pink, working its way from his neck
to the shiny part of his dome. All the muscles around his mouth would
tighten. Then he'd go red. It would highlight his five o'clock shadow."
The students kept their distance.

Halliwell affected a sinister superiority. His suits were invariably
grey or black pin-stripe worn with black tie, black beret, and gaberdine
raincoat. The shaved head, the padded shoulders, and the lifts built
into the black crepe soles of his shoes were calculated to make him look
imposing. But Halliwell's personality was completely at odds with his
presentation. "He was perpetually wiping the palms of his hands with
a handkerchief," Margaret Whiting, another student, remembers. "He
was always sweating. Clammy hands. His handshake was weak, absolutely desperate. He never stood still when you spoke to him. Very
nervous. Never looked you straight in the eye. Very unrelaxed. He did
anything to make himself appear bigger." The same deadly insecurity
showed in his conversation. He saw himself as a wit and a great actor.

"He gave the impression that he was better than anyone else at RADA," says Lawrence Griffin, who together with Orton and Maxwell Burten-Shaw moved into Halliwell's West Hampstead flat in 1951. "He used to criticize the other actors who got parts that he thought he could do better. Halliwell had the idea that he'd win the Bancroft Medal for the outstanding performer."

It was Margaret Whiting (who had acted opposite Halliwell in *The Brontës*) who won the prize in Halliwell and Orton's year. "In *The Brontës* Halliwell was so self-conscious he could hardly bear to do mime," she says. "He always surprised me with that. Ken, who thought he was such a wit, who sent up other people unmercifully at their expense, wouldn't come out of his extraordinary shell. When it came to being really inventive from within, to exposing himself, he just couldn't do it. After listening to his palaver, the incessant talk of ambition, ambition, ambition, when he got up to perform you were looking at a shy, very inhibited, self-conscious little man." Halliwell was too defensive to "give himself away," and the various postures he adopted only made his emotional impoverishment more blatant. "His voice was dreadful," Margaret Whiting says. "The quality of his sound was terrible. It happens with a lot of actors. They get nasal strangulation. Tension. I remember in *The Brontës* Ken couldn't get his elbows away from his body. You see a lot of bad actors do this. They imprison themselves. He was terrified to let go." Wrapped in a fantasy world, Halliwell dreamed of glory and talked for victory. But his tantrums were a signal of an undisciplined and uncreative imagination. "You don't behave like that if you have any kind of ability," says Margaret Whiting. "If you've got ability, you're too busy working on it."

Orton was also having a difficult time adjusting to RADA. "I completely lost my confidence and my virginity," was Orton's summary of his first term. "I was lost. I didn't have a very good time because I found that in the very first term that I wasn't learning anything."[28] A provincial boy, whom his classmates saw as a mere "lad," Orton was learning more about life and literature from his surly new adult acquaintance. They were a curious combination. "Orton was the bubble," June Clark Howarth recalls. "Halliwell was the drag."

The greatest impression Orton and Halliwell made at RADA was on each other. Neither had previously been able to sustain a close relationship. Both were disgruntled and lonely. Each filled an absence in the other's life. Halliwell found in Orton a surrogate brother, a companion who looked up to him, who needed him, who had faith in his intelligence and his aspirations. Orton was good company: a buoyant, in-

quisitive chatterbox, who was also a good listener. Boyish and handsome, aspects of his features matched with astonishing coincidence the
idealized beauty Halliwell had imagined in Edmund Kean: "he is pale,
with untidy black hair, and large, smouldering black eyes."

In Halliwell, Orton for his part discovered someone who could be
both father and friend: an authoritarian figure older and wiser in the
ways of the world, who shared his interests and was prepared to engage
in an unequal but enthusiastic dialogue. Halliwell offered knowledge
and stimulation, and Orton gave attention and good spirits. Orton
would come to understand very clearly the sibling overtones in their
relationship. In the stage version of *The Ruffian on the Stair* (1967),
he made it explicit by having Wilson, the grieving friend, talk about
his "brother" in a very moving autobiographical fragment of dialogue:

> MIKE. It's the Assistance Board. . . . They say my circumstances have
>   altered. I haven't any circumstances to alter. They should know
>   that. I've filled in a form to the effect that I'm a derelict.
> WILSON. Yes. My brother and me had the same trouble. . . . We lived
>   in Shepherd's Bush. We had a little room. And our life was made
>   quite comfortable by the N.A.B. [National Assistance Board] for
>   almost a year. We had a lot of friends. All creeds and colours.
>   But no circumstances at all. We were happy, though. We were
>   young. I was seventeen. He was twenty-three. You can't do better
>   for yourself than that, can you? (*He shrugs.*) We were bosom
>   friends. I've never told anyone that before. I hope I haven't
>   shocked you.
> MIKE. As close as that?
> WILSON. We had separate beds—he was a stickler for convention,
>   but that's as far as it went. We spent every night in each other's
>   company. It was the reason we never got any work done.

Halliwell was seven years older than Orton. Despite the gap in
sophistication and accomplishment, it was Orton, not Halliwell, who
was chosen to perform in the Public Show at the Phoenix Theatre at
the end of their two-year course. Halliwell—"the stickler"—was well
intentioned, earnest, hardworking, and wooden on stage. He had not
stunned RADA; rather, he had been stunned by it. A sense of umbrage
seeps through the right-mindedness of a letter to the registrar explaining
why he will not attend the final fortnight of his RADA training:

> . . . As I am not in the public show, I intend to get on with the
> serious business of getting a job. . . . I remain convinced that there
> is nothing further to be gained in the next ten days, and that I am
> therefore "doing the right thing." . . . [29]

Halliwell's teachers at RADA were never convinced of his ability.
Actors are technicians of the spirit—and from the beginning, Halliwell
was inaccessible to himself. The RADA reports charted his physical and
imaginative limitations, characteristics of a personality that could never
free itself from emotional impoverishment. His voice was marked by
monotony and heaviness. "A good natural voice, plenty of power," said
his voice coach in the first term. "He must acquire more lightness of
touch, variety of pace." He could analyze a character but never successfully breathe life into it. "Seems to be unconvinced that acting is the
expression of emotions," observed one acting coach in Halliwell's last
year. "The result is that his approach is all mental—giving a tight,
almost prim aspect to his work. I should like to see a more *generous*
attitude of mind developing with this student in relation to his ideas of
acting. A good student with a keen sense of wit—if not real humor.
Must not be *afraid* of acting." On leaving, he received the Certificate
of Merit, which was given to students who had passed the course but
fell below the RADA standard as actors.

In awarding Orton his Diploma, Sir Kenneth Barnes—the principal
of RADA—was enthusiastic about Orton's ability. "He has talent,"
he said emphatically. From Orton's first term, his teachers reacted to
him with enthusiasm. "This boy has vitality and imagination"; "His
performance as the Ancient Trajanos was very attractive. A promising
student." Orton's boyish playfulness earned him the role of Feste in
Twelfth Night in the first year. He had a clown's gift of impersonation
and was a good mimic. "Good sense of character," wrote the director.
"But the work lacks strength. There is a sad note to your personality
which must be held in check." (Orton's sense of isolation and his
urgency to recoup his life from its barren beginnings would linger
beneath the hilarity in all his plays.) His teachers remarked on his
diligence, describing him as "extremely keen," "very hard working,"
"quick to learn." There was something unshaped, amorphous, in his
personality that was conveyed on stage. "A fluid, flexible youth who
might turn into anything." Orton was both inventive and uneven in
his work; but according to the director who worked with him as
Richard in *Ah! Wilderness* in his fifth term, he was "at all times interesting to watch—either in rehearsal or performance." One other
trait, mentioned in his last term at RADA, contrasted dramatically with
Halliwell's reports: "Can be very funny."

Language, at first Orton's bogey, became his obsession, and finally
his triumph. "At present," wrote an instructor in his last term at RADA,
"he has little knowledge or control of variety of speech—range of tone—
timing . . . etc." Part of the vindictive gusto of his comedy would lie

in his strutting mastery over the mother tongue. At RADA, a "general
tendency toward flatness and monotony" was the consistent complaint
of his voice teachers. Orton's frustration took the form of mockery.
"By the fifth term at RADA I'd got very cynical," he recalled in 1967.
"I remember doing a diction test. It was the Buckingham speech from
Henry VIII. Well, I thought it was silly being sincere about a thing
like that, so I just did it on a purely technical basis, booming in a
parody of the RADA manner. I won the diction test, and I got congratu-
lated, all the teachers coming up to me and saying it was 'marvellous.'
This was terrible because I knew it wasn't. It was a fool of a thing
to do. I went on like this for the next term, doing absurd caricatures
of the RADA voice and the RADA manner. This was of course before the
new style at RADA, and I got into the public show. I played Bates in
Venus Observed. Did absurd things. Wore absurd costumes which were
quite wrong. I looked like a sort of gay girl out of a 1920 revue."[30]

Orton took his acting career more seriously than he recounted it in
hindsight. Immediately after graduating from RADA in April 1953, he
joined the Ipswich Rep as an Assistant Stage Manager, billing himself
John K. Orton. Halliwell had to settle for a less reputable summer
season in a resort town on the Welsh coast. He had taken the name
Kenneth Marlowe. "I am doing quite nicely here," he wrote to the
RADA registrar from the Grand Theatre, Llandudno, explaining his
absence from RADA's prize-giving. "We only do 6 performances a week—
at 8 p.m. And am this week playing the juvenile lead in *Quiet Wedding*.
But I shall not be staying here very long as the future list of plays to
be done is quite beyond the pale. And at this stage in one's career the
experience of acting in tolerably good plays is of primary importance."[31]
The idea of Halliwell in a juvenile lead was as misguided as his visions
of theatrical stardom; he would get no more stage work after the
summer.

Orton's experience was also disheartening. "Repertory is terrible,"
he said, recollecting his four months at Ipswich between April and
July. "It so lacks ideas. Most people have bad ideas, but at least they're
their own. The people in rep have just none at all. . . ."[32] "I did a lot
of moaning."[33] For an aspiring and impatient actor, the lot of Assistant
Stage Manager was not a happy one. "We spent most of our time
trudging the streets of Ipswich looking for props," recalls Rosalind
Knight, who shared ASM chores with Orton and went on to an acting
career. She remembers Orton as sallow, spotty, and sniffling from a
perpetual cold. "John wasn't very good at getting the props or doing
the work. He never got cross. He was just lackadaisical." In later years

Orton quipped that the only thing the Ipswich Rep taught him was "not to write in too much business about drinks or telephones in a play because it is so awfully hard on the assistant stage managers to have to fix all that sort of thing."[34]

After each show, Orton would come back to his boarding house with the Stage Manager, Jack Payne, and read Shakespeare into Payne's tape recorder—a novelty in 1953. "The particular parts that delighted Orton and which he never tired of repeating were Puck and Ariel," says Payne. "We also had great fun doing the Bottom scenes from *A Midsummer Night's Dream*, in which we did all the voices between us, imitating the dreadful accents. Orton would roar with delight at the playbacks." Orton spent a lot of his free time in long conversations with Payne. The talk was frank and barbed. Orton made no attempt to hide his homosexuality but he was not camp. Payne, who was much older than Orton, was a great source of theatre lore and gossip. "Orton would always urge me to tell him more—whether about the history, the technique, or the current theatrical scene," Payne says. "He was only twenty, but I was still impressed by his knowledge of subjects unusual for a boy his age. His knowledge of Greek gods and goddesses took me by surprise." Orton was the youngest occupant of their boarding house, and the landlady fussed over him. He was always polite and well mannered around her. She loved it and responded by overfeeding him. "I remember once Joe couldn't finish his plate of food and scraped it under a bush in the garden," Payne recalls. "The landlady discovered the food the next day and collared the four tenants for an explanation. Joe just grinned quirkishly. Nobody squealed."

Too young and inadequate an actor to get major roles, Orton was also too ambitious and full of fun for the arid grind he discovered was the regimen of the rep actor. His contract at Ipswich was not renewed. "I was bored," he explained later. "I left the theatre and got married." Orton was never married except in his imagination. ("I was too young," he told reporters. "We just drifted apart."[35]) He was twenty; and his "bride" was now twenty-seven and totally bald.

ORTON HAD ORIGINALLY moved into Kenneth Halliwell's flat in West Hampstead with Lawrence Griffin and Maxwell Burten-Shaw, another RADA student from their class and a former ballet dancer. It was a comfortable arrangement and a great improvement over Orton's previous cramped cold basement digs. Halliwell's home reflected his age and his urbane image. To Orton, it was impressive. Halliwell owned what most

people in Orton's life had had to borrow: his house, his books, his
records. Instead of the usual cooking ring, Halliwell had a kitchen set
apart from the living room by louvered doors. He knew about wines;
and he cooked for his roommates, not the meat and mussel pudding
that Orton was used to, but continental dishes. Halliwell charged 30
shillings a week, a pittance compared to the £2.50 Orton had agreed to
pay the landlord of his first flat, thinking it was the entire rent instead
of the price per man. Griffin and Burten-Shaw slept on sofas in the
living room; Orton shared Halliwell's double bed. "In the beginning,"
Lawrence Griffin recalls, "most of the feeling came from Halliwell to
Orton, not from John to Ken. John just accepted it because it was nice
digs, a nice situation to be in. He must have liked Kenneth Halliwell.
He'd do anything Kenneth wanted him to." Burten-Shaw saw Halliwell
as the dominant force. "Ken was the much stronger personality, very
much *I* am and will be and you will one day work for me. John had
much more depth but was uncertain of himself and prepared to be
led."

In Orton, Halliwell sensed a perfect companion. He used to stroke
Orton's sleek head in front of Griffin and call him "my pussycat."
Halliwell played the man of the world, and Orton was impressed.
"Halliwell was like a Svengali to John," recalls Griffin. "He took John
over. It was as if he were playing God. When they went shopping, he'd
suggest that John buy certain colorful clothes. He showed John what
to wear, what to read, where to go." Halliwell spent his money as well
as his attention on Orton. Since Orton only had his £300 grant for
tuition and living allowance, Halliwell subsidized their frequent excursions to the theatre, concerts, and movies. (Anna Magnani, the flam-
boyant Italian actress, was one of their favorites; and Halliwell claimed
her as the major influence on his acting.) But this generosity was already
matched by fits of intense moodiness. "Orton put up with more than
I would," Griffin says. "Halliwell would arrange things and everyone
had to fit in with what he wanted. Even when we'd planned to go to
the movies, if Kenneth decided to stay in, Orton would stay with him.
He was very loyal to Kenneth."

Sometimes shouting matches flared up within earshot of the other
roommates. "They'd argue because they weren't having sex. Kenneth
wanted to, and John refused," explains Griffin. "Kenneth was a little
sadistic with him. He could be cruel. He could laugh at other people's
misfortune." But Orton wasn't put off. Always the flirt, he was flattered
by Halliwell's affection—the first person to pay him serious sexual
attention. They became constant companions, each buoying up the

other's fantasy of himself. "They looked upon themselves as being very special," says Griffin. "They had the idea they were going to be brilliant actors. Sometimes I used to feel the odd one out, they practically convinced me they were so good." Halliwell was unsure of Orton and very possessive. At the parties he gave in his flat and at The Rising Sun (the local RADA pub), Halliwell kept a careful eye on Orton and separated him from other men in whom he showed interest. Orton didn't bridle at this intrusion. "Halliwell was useful. He provided a base Orton could go back to," Griffin says.

Like most things at the beginning of their relationship, writing was Halliwell's idea. He was working on a novel when Orton moved in. Before long, Orton was seated at the living-room table contributing to Halliwell's effort the only literary skill he possessed: his typing. But as Orton transcribed Halliwell's novel, he would make suggestions. Halliwell found them helpful and incorporated them into his work. By including Orton in his literary ambitions, he was also binding him closer to his life. He was never threatened by the idea of a collaboration because there was never any doubt who the writer was. Halliwell was the man with the vocabulary, the tenacity, the sense of literary tradition. Orton had only his curiosity and enthusiasm. Following Halliwell's lead, Orton began to write material to perform at his RADA diction classes. "I never wanted to be a writer, I always wanted to be an actor," Orton recollected later. "But then I found that I had a talent for writing." His talent existed at first solely in the eyes of Kenneth Halliwell.

When their acting careers had sailed rapidly into still waters, Orton and Halliwell fell back on writing. For a few months after Orton returned from Ipswich in 1953, he and Halliwell took refuge from their repertory disappointments in the idea that they would work in the West End. Halliwell arranged auditions for them with H. M. Tennent, the producers who dominated London's commercial theatre (and who, in 1969, would be co-producers of the posthumous production of Orton's *What the Butler Saw*). They organized a portfolio of photographs and found themselves an agent whose homosexual connections, Halliwell assured Orton, were bound to get them work. But they got nowhere, and gradually their energy and their dreams shifted from the stage to the page.

They set about their collaboration with typical single-mindedness, Orton's coltish high spirits matching Halliwell's adamantine will. Orton's talent had never found its focus at RADA. "Is inclined to give the impression of being casual about his work," Sir Kenneth Barnes concluded in his final report. "He is young, and I think he will realize how essential it is—having talent, to do his best to make it evident to others by careful application and whole-personality concentration." Halliwell's partnership provided what Orton blatantly lacked: discipline. The business of reading and writing had a renegade appeal to two people so convinced that they were special. Orton had always hated the tedium and waste of the workaday world, and Halliwell's intellectual prodding and financial support bolstered his determination not to succumb to convention. "Men and women who work in shops, factories and offices are prostitutes slaving for a super pimp," says the shrill anarchist Donelly in *The Boy Hairdresser*, demolishing Peterson's vague yearnings for a more respectable life. Like the mates in *Loot* and the brothers in *The Ruffian on the Stair*, Orton and Halliwell set out together with "no prospects" and "no circumstances."

In order to save Halliwell's dwindling inheritance, they instituted an ascetic régime. They kept electricity to the minimum, choosing to rise with the first morning light and go to bed at dusk. They wrote in the morning. Their afternoons were spent reading, and, when the weather was good, sunbathing. Sometimes they'd borrow lengthy books from the library, like Gibbon or Lady Murasaki, and read to each other. They lived on £5 a week. Between 1957 and 1959 this routine was modified when both worked half of each year (earning £30 a week) at Cadbury's to buy a new flat. Orton loaded boxes of chocolates; Halliwell did clerical work. "Went back for a fortnight's work at Cadbury's," Halliwell wrote to a friend in 1959 from their new address in Noel Road, Islington. "Could not stand it. Don't know how one stuck it before. I shall go to the Labour Exchange in due course and register for 'clerical work.' I hope they can't give me any, and then they will have to pay us dole and National Assistance; but I fear they can probably always find one a job of some kind."[36]

Orton and Halliwell were dropouts before the Beat literature of the fifties filtered down through English society to make such behavior modish. They questioned the culture's values but absorbed its literary traditions. It was a hermetic existence, at once a pleasure and a necessity. Neither their identities nor their literary style were strong enough to venture into a society that threatened and angered them. Their solitude was a barometer of their vulnerability and suspicion. It also became a consolation for literary failure. "I don't know if you have any convictions about the way life is run: its inexorable rules and so on," Halliwell wrote to Charles Monteith, an editor at Faber & Faber, after the publishing house had rejected his novel *Priapus in the Shrubbery* (1959). "Personally, I am convinced that 'what you lose on the swings, you gain on the roundabouts' and vice versa. So it would, quite frankly, not be in the logic of things for John and I to have much success in any sphere. We live much too comfortably and pleasantly in our peculiar little way."[37]

ORTON started off with a comic spirit, but no tools for communicating it. With Halliwell's encouragement, he began by studying Ronald Firbank's clowning classicism. Firbank, who wrote nine baroque novels and one play, *The Princess Zoubaroff*, between 1905 and 1926, was, in Orton's estimation, "the only impressionist in the English novel." After reading Evelyn Waugh's *Black Mischief* and finding it "patchy," Orton wrote: "Waugh isn't up to Firbank: the source."[38] Firbank's convoluted rhythms and his characters' fluting voices hide murky passions beneath an elegant upper-class civility. (*Princess Zoubaroff:* "Claude's such an extremist, you know. They say when he kissed the Pope's slipper, he went on to do considerably more.") In Firbank's world, style becomes Fate. It was the manic maneuver of a solitary successfully killing time. Orton and Halliwell shared that solitude. Cut off from the world, they made a world of words. In maturity, Orton came to understand how the tempo of his life and his literary style were interrelated. "I've got the ability to write the kind of dialogue because of the life I've led in the past," he told the BBC in 1964. "I think that if you uprooted me and planted me in a different setting, a much more worldly setting, that I wouldn't be able to write as I do."[39]

Orton saw his study of language as "strategy." Gombold—the pilgrim-hero of his allegorical fantasy, *Head to Toe*—studies the destructive power of language so that lethal words can do battle with the enemy:

> Gombold bought a dictionary and began to study the construction of a sentence. . . . He started calculating and found some sentences puny against large targets. Then perhaps a new type of sentence. . . . He started to construct the perfect sentence. . . . He studied the chemistry and behaviour of words, phrase design, the forging, casting and milling, the theories of paraphrase, the fusing and the aiming. . . .

Like Gombold, Orton made lists of words, learning to spell them as well as to use them. He kept columns of neatly typed adverbs in a loose-leaf binder: "oxymoronically," "chrystalecently," "allergically." He free-associated with words: "prize price prig priapus primitive prism privacy

procreate procure promiscuous prison profane . . ." He experimented
with funny sounds and word combinations in lists of imaginary book
titles: *Strange Pedicure, The Painted Whip, Pigeon's Milk, Bugabooo,
Zoomorphe, A Stag for Nanny, The Decapitated Pansy, A Cow Called
Isis* . . .

He also composed pages of single sentences to build up his descriptive powers. Typing on the back of his first clumsy attempt at a novel,
Orton struggled to make language vivid.

> —Trees like twisted black arms against a red landscape.
> —White oxen moved over the plain.
> —On the tabletop stood a large anchor of peonies.
> —A cypress rose blackly out of a mist of olives.

Gombold studied "the propagation of idiom, the effect of adjectives
and found pages on the penetrating power of faulty grammar." So did
Orton. His feeling for words and idiom came out of a desire to get to
the meaning of them. His stage characters never listen to the implications of their idioms. Kenneth Williams says, "I remember Joe recounting to me a lady who said to him, 'I speak as I find.' And he answered,
'What have you found?' Another time someone said to him, '*Loot* is
unnecessarily filthy.' Joe examined the phrase. 'Isn't it funny?' he said.
'As though there was a *necessary* amount of filth.' " In his comic distortions of language, Orton at once celebrated and satirized the values and
vernacular of the English.

"The style isn't super-imposed," Orton maintained. "It's me. You
can't write stylized comedy in inverted commas, because the style must
ring of the man, and if you think in a certain way and you write true
to yourself, which I hope I do, then you will get a style, a style will
come out. You've only got to be sitting on a bus and you'll hear the
most stylized lines. . . . I don't like the discrimination against style that
some people have. Every serious writer has a style. I mean, Arnold
Wesker has a style, but people don't normally think of him as a stylist,
in the same way that they think of Wilde, Firbank, or Sheridan. Style
isn't camp or chi-chi. I write in a certain way because I can't express
in naturalistic terms. In the whole naturalistic movement of the '20's
and '30's you can't ultimately have anything except discussions of
Mavis's new hat. You can't have people. With the naturalistic style I
couldn't make any comment on the kind of policeman that Truscott
[in *Loot*] is, or on the laws of the Establishment. Oscar Wilde's style
is much more earthy and colloquial than most people notice. When we
look at Lady Bracknell, she's the most ordinary, common, direct woman;
she's not an affected woman at all. People are taken in by 'the glittering

style.' It's not glitter. Congreve is the same. It's real—a slice of life. It's just very brilliantly written, perfectly believable. Nothing at all incredible."[40]

But long before Orton's intuition about language found its expression in his own fluent comic style, he was analyzing and cataloguing the mannerisms of English speech. He made lists of the phrases that give English a formal and often comic sound:

> Are both, perhaps
> In the not
> not for not
> Thus, in you I
> not less than everything
> Towards the never
> Have has what
> I can only say how

He toyed with substituting new words into familiar metaphoric constructions: "the weakness of flesh," "the damnation of heaven," "the resolution of yet," "the enchantment of never." His notes show him balancing words and trying to make new equations with them: "release from release," "freedom from freedom," "x without x," "y without y."

Orton's earliest writing was a crude imitation of Ronald Firbank. He delighted in Firbank's zestful juggling of language. Firbank could whip up words into a soufflé of sound ("Head archly bent, her fine arms divined through darkling laces, the Duquessa stood, clasping closely a week-old police dog in the ripple of her gown"); Orton's concoctions inevitably fell flat. One early untitled novel (c. 1954) has a cast of typically swank Firbankian gargoyles, including Helen Hagg, Lord Emission of Semen, Lady Cucumber, Lady Melon, Olive de Pineapple. Helen Hagg has been unjustly accused of stealing her would-be mother-in-law's jewelry. But Olive de Pineapple is unmasked as the thief, paving the way for Helen's marriage into the aristocracy. " 'What you say is preposterous!' said Olive de Pineapple, pressing her hands together and casting down her pale-coloured, treacherous eyes. 'You force yourself into my room and bully me because you think I am a woman alone.' " In time, Orton would take Firbank's strutting mischievousness and bring it down to earth:

> —His Hellenism once captivated me. But the *Attic* to him means nothing now but servants' bedrooms.   *—The Princess Zoubaroff*

> —Have you taken up transvestism? I'd no idea our marriage teetered on the edge of fashion.   *—What the Butler Saw*

Orton's humor was always more robust and gregarious than Firbank's recherché fantasies. But he shared Firbank's obsessions and adapted many of his comic maneuvers to a much more popular dramatic form.

Orton first absorbed these comic stances through Halliwell, who was also imitating Firbank. In collaboration with Halliwell, Orton's writing was smoother and more defined than in his solo efforts. Halliwell's name was typed above Orton's on the title pages of their novels, and Halliwell's sensibility dominated them. Their fiction explored certain ideas that Orton later elaborated successfully in his plays: a delight in sexual ambiguity, a questioning of the perverse in experience; an appetite for anarchy and farcical situations, send-ups of figures of authority, a fascination with innocents at large in a violent, corrupt world. In later years, Orton would refer to the early failed manuscripts for dramatic ideas. *The Ruffian on the Stair* was a rewrite of their novel *The Boy Hairdresser*. *Up Against It*, Orton's film script for The Beatles, combined a plot idea from their first novel, *The Silver Bucket* (1953), with Orton's last novel, *The Vision of Gombold Proval* (1961), which was published posthumously as *Head to Toe*.

By 1955, Orton and Halliwell were submitting their manuscripts for publication. The first was a science-fiction spoof, *The Mechanical Womb*. "The reductio ad absurdum of the bug-eyed monster science fiction," wrote a reader for Faber & Faber, "complete with mutants, ailing robots and a lot of nonsense kept whirling around by sheer bewildering speed but without any claim to coherence or design." Charles Monteith confirmed the verdict. "Rather good, really," he scribbled on their submission letter. "But not good enough." (In 1966, Orton reread the novel with the idea of reworking it into a radio play for the BBC. "I'm afraid I can't let you read it," he wrote to the BBC producer. "It just isn't up to standard. I did write it ten years ago. It would need an enormous amount of work, and in fact, all I'd use would be the title.")

Their second effort in 1955 was *The Last Days of Sodom,* a caper that had a purpose behind its playfulness. It was their most brazen comic assault on the relativity of moral values. The theme percolated through their work. "The values of society?" mocks Donelly in *The Boy Hairdresser*. "What values? The things we take seriously will be laughed at in fifty years. Who doesn't laugh at nineteenth century attitudes and yet they imagined them to be the right ones." In *Head to Toe,* Gombold, like Orton, finds a teacher and "study took the place of liberty: absorbed in acquiring knowledge, days, months and years passed in rapid and instructive course." But when the teacher asks

Gombold what the abiding value is, Gombold answers: "truth." The teacher rebukes him: "The rulers of whatever country you choose will designate as 'true' that which is useful to them. Truth is relative, and always behind it stands some interest, furthering its own ends."

In *The Last Days of Sodom,* Orton and Halliwell attempted to make a farce of social conventions. They told the story of Sodom, treating it as a modern Western city, and recounting the lives led by male and female homosexuals before the city's destruction. The novel opens with Sodom seen in long shot from the window of a local psychiatrist:

> . . . There were towers in brick the colour of rose, cathedrals moulded in gold and bronze. The sea lay like a shield. In the stillness, the voices of fishermen called to each other across the water. . . .
>
> Abe Haranson sat back in the chair and surveyed his patient. "What did you dream next," he said.
>
> "It was horrible, doctor, I was being chased by a—"
>
> "Yes," he probed.
>
> The woman shuddered and hid her face. "By a man. Oh what does it mean, doctor, am I abnormal?"

The jokes turned the tables on manners and their morality. "He's terribly nice. But I hear he goes to one of those loose bars where men dance with women."

They submitted the novel to Charles Monteith of Faber & Faber, who liked it but felt it was too rarefied.[41] He passed it on to Richard Brain at Hamish Hamilton. "Plainly there was a literary quality here," remembers Brain. "The kind of jokes in the book were being told in the homosexual world of the early fifties. But the actual destruction of the city by fire and brimstone was a huge bit of purple patch writing. It was quite clear that from the point of view of subject matter—and to some extent of style—the novel wasn't good enough."

The two publishers then arranged to meet Orton and Halliwell. "They seemed as strange as their writing," Richard Brain recalls. "I quite soon got the impression that this was the oddest pair of people I'd met." Halliwell wore a beret to the rendezvous on January 4, 1956, at the Imperial Hotel in Russell Square. "They more or less intimated that they were at a loss. This was the first time they'd met strangers by arrangement," Charles Monteith remembers. "I had a very clear impression at the first meeting that Kenneth was the one that did the writing. Kenneth was the talker. He liked to turn words around and savor them. Kenneth's talk, his appearance, his age *vis à vis* Orton certainly gave the impression that Kenneth was the literary figure. I thought that John was quite simply his young, pretty, and rather vivacious boyfriend. It took me some time to see that John was more than an acolyte of Halliwell's."

On April 12, 1956, they sent Faber & Faber *The Boy Hairdresser*, a satire in blank verse that was quickly returned as an entertaining but uncommercial project. Undeterred, they continued to see Monteith and Brain. On August 1, Monteith took them to dinner with two other publishers. "They were quite fun," says Monteith. "They did make the point that they hadn't eaten in a restaurant for years." Three weeks later, Monteith and Brain understood their monastic existence when they visited Orton and Halliwell in West Hampstead. "I never thought human beings could live this way. It was extraordinary," Monteith says. "The flat was in a state of considerable decay and disrepair. The bedroom in particular had been attacked by rising damp. Kenneth had turned the damp patches into an abstract painting by outlining each patch in a different-colored broad stroke of paint. You felt like you were living inside an abstract painting of the New York School." But the most memorable event of the evening was Halliwell's cuisine, which was as eccentric as the surroundings. "We had a spartan and ghastly meal," recalls Monteith. Halliwell served them a first course of rice with sardines and a second course of rice with golden syrup. "On that occasion, John produced, I think, a very funny and penetrating piece of literary criticism," says Monteith. "I asked if they'd read Gibbon. To which John replied, 'What an old queen she is! Send up, send up, send up the whole time.'" Orton's vitality was more apparent at this meal; and both Monteith and Brain came away convinced that it was Orton who provided a great deal of the striking comicality in their writing.

Having befriended them, Monteith gave a party for them the next year, 1957, in May. "I realized that they had no friends whatsoever. The purpose of the party was to let them meet people who had influence in the literary world. It was a big party. They sat on the sofa the whole evening and didn't speak to anybody. Halliwell and Orton were hopeless socially. The party was a total flop." Halliwell laid the blame for their social awkwardness on their solitary life. "We are just no good at parties," he wrote to Monteith on May 22. "Personally, if there are more than six people in a room I just feel confused. There are prices one must pay for leading a hermit's existence, however happy." Throughout the letter Halliwell emphasized "I," but signed it "Believe us." This was typical. "They were two people with the same voice by then," says Richard Brain; "there was never any dissension or disagreement." The hermetic life was a united front against an untenable world. Orton and Halliwell lived and spoke as one.

However, it was Halliwell who still spoke for them when they resubmitted a revised version of *The Last Days of Sodom* together with the letter of May 22.

> Dear Charles,
>
> Here we are again. It looks as if we will never give up.
>
> With the spring, John's infectious enthusiasm drew me out of the T. E. Lawrence existence into which I had sunk during the winter. We gave in our notice at Cadbury's having saved enough money to live on until the autumn, and made a final gigantic attempt to *make* the Sodom novel publishable by sheer brute effort.
>
> If it is no good this time, well that is the end of the line, and after trying it on a few more publishers, and perhaps trying one or two on the other side of the Atlantic, it must be consigned to the limbo of forgotten genius.
>
> It has already been to Duckworths, and with their usual brilliant acumen they suggest turning it into a "short story"! . . .

The revision was a dud. "I'm afraid I thought—though I know you won't agree—that it isn't as good as the first version. It seemed to me to have lost some of its original subtlety," Monteith wrote. "Now there's only one point—which is being made at rather too great length and rather too obviously."[42] The rejection created a crisis in their collaboration. Six days later, Monteith received a diary novel, *Between Us Girls*. Both the manuscript and the note appended to it were from John Orton.

> Dear Charles,
>
> We were sorry to learn you thought so little of the Sodom novel. However . . .
>
> Kenneth and I have decided that there is very little to be gained by our collaboration and so we have split (for the purpose of writing). Here, for your approval, is a novel by me alone.[43]

Susan Hope is the naïve, frivolous diarist of *Between Us Girls* ("Laddered my stockings, broke two of my nails, and had Dubonnet spilled over my Madge Chard hat. Life is simply sickening sometimes"). Like her name, Miss Hope is a dotty figure of faith, whose earnest and unreflective enthusiasm glosses the seediness of her world. She is "in the theatre," but her stage is a strip club called the Rainier Revuebar. Ignorant of innuendo and experience, Susan Hope walks po-faced through triumph and tragedy. Like so many of Orton's stage characters, Susan Hope never hears what she is saying.

Between Us Girls was an experiment in tone. Orton had abandoned Halliwell's baroque for a more direct, concrete, and colloquial style. He was learning what he later allowed Gombold to articulate: that "the blast of a long sentence was curiously local, and a lot of shorter sentences seemed better." Orton had always been a good mimic, and the first-person narrative—no matter how aimless it appeared in *Between Us Girls*—gave an energy and impact to his writing that Halliwell's strained efforts lacked. Halliwell would continue in his fustian Firbankian mode, while Orton searched for new comic techniques. In 1959, when Halliwell submitted *Priapus in the Shrubbery* to Faber & Faber, his letter to Charles Monteith was as arch and insecure as his prose:

> Dear Mr. Monteith, sir,
>   I don't know whether you remember me, but about three years ago, you were I hope, I think, interested in the Firbankian novel I was writing in collaboration with John Orton. . . . I have been engaged in writing another novel, which will be finished in a few weeks time. I wondered whether you would be interested in seeing it on completion? I shall quite understand if you wouldn't. . . . It is still somewhat Firbankian but has its feet more firmly on the ground. I am not writing any more in collaboration. John is writing a play. . . .[44]

Halliwell signed his letter "Yours humbly"; but humility in laughter is as unwelcome as modesty in a prostitute. Orton was never hamstrung by that problem. In *Between Us Girls*, he had planned some irreverent surprises for Charles Monteith. The novel reworked the plot of *The Silver Bucket*. Susan Hope leaves the Rainier Revuebar for what she thinks is a three-year contract at an exotic Mexican club. But the "club" turns out to be a brothel ("most of us had to wear too much or not enough. Señora Josefa dressed me in something which I am not going to mention"). Susan Hope escapes to L.A. and movie stardom. The entrepreneur who signs her up and owns the chain of bordellos is mischievously named Liz Monteith. ("She was about as tall as a woman can be without having beans grow up her. . . . The hall Miss Monteith led us into was quite bare like her voice, polished, anaemic, scraped and clean.") The novel, submitted on June 2, 1957, was returned on June 5.

THE TRICKSTER'S FUNCTION, as Karl Kerenyi says, is "to add disorder to order, and so make a whole; within the fixed bounds of what's permitted, an experience of what is not permitted."[45] *Between Us Girls* contains neither venomous satire nor scurrilous outrage; but in it, the first tentative glimpse of Orton's trickster spirit—the mischief of the manipulated voice—begins to assert itself. The trickster is a protean figure, an outsider with the power to "become" anyone. *Between Us Girls* was Orton's first exercise in literary ventriloquism: speaking while yet not seeming to speak. The ventriloquist's accomplishment is in "throwing" his voice, projecting sound as if independent of the body. The act is reminiscent of the mythic trickster, who could crawl up his anus, detach his penis, and carry it in a box, or command one part of his body to fight another part. Orton's favorite literature was trickster tales: Greek mythology, children's fables. The protean mischief of the trickster—enemy of boundaries, spirit of disorder, agent of delight—was an important part of his infantile fantasies of omnipotence. In *Head to Toe,* Gombold crawls down the mouth of a giant and explores his massive body. He fights a war between the cleft in the giant's buttocks "for the independence of the body's parts." And in his plays, Orton exhibits a trickster's glee in making a ghoulish, malicious spectacle of the human anatomy, taking the body to pieces and letting its parts have their own dramatic life. The eyeball of the deceased Mrs. McLeavy rolls out of her coffin and under the bed in *Loot;* a severed hand is produced from a cookie tin in *Funeral Games.* The trickster's rapacious hijinks are expressed most profoundly in *What the Butler Saw,* when Sir Winston Churchill's "parts" are almost produced from a box at the conclusion of the play:

> RANCE *looks inside the box.*
>
> RANCE *(with admiration).* How much more inspiring if, in those dark days, we'd seen what we see now. Instead we had to be content with a cigar—the symbol falling far short, as we all realize, of the object itself.
>
> GERALDINE *looks inside the box.*
>
> GERALDINE. But it is a cigar!
> RANCE. Ah, the illusions of youth!

Orton originally wanted Churchill's penis to be displayed; but the Lord Chamberlain would not allow it. "It's only a statue," Orton complained to his producer Oscar Lewenstein, who had predicted the cut on the grounds of libel. "What am I saying about Churchill though?" Lewenstein replied, "You're saying he had a big prick." "That isn't libel, surely," Orton said. "I wouldn't sue anybody for saying I had a big prick. No man would. In fact I might pay them to do that."[46]

The trickster's emblem is the erect penis. Clowns, who embody the trickster's capricious and potent life force in their stage antics, often carried a vestigial phallus. The Elizabethan fool held a *baubel* or "plaything"; in contemporary comedy, the phallic anarchy is symbolized in Chaplin's cane, Harpo's horn, Groucho's cigar, Monsieur Hulot's umbrella.

Orton brought the clown's purest sexual impulse into dramatic literature. The phallus dominated his life and his laughter. "Noticed somebody had got a large and impressive book called *The English Organ*," he wrote in his diary. "It'd be nice to have the cover."[47] Writing to Kenneth Williams about the Arab-Israeli crisis while in Morocco, Orton said: "All the silly queens out here can talk about is 'this dreadful political situation.' They've transferred their allegiance entirely from the circumcized penis to the secretary general of the United Nations. Fickle in their emotions."[48] Even Gombold in *Head to Toe* swears an amazed and reverent oath to the awesome vista of the giant's gargantuan penis: "A world of its own; beautiful and menacing. A vast erection of the earth. Gombold caught his breath as he muttered 'Suspirum et decus puellarum et puerorum.' "

Orton was in touch with his sexuality, and all his plays chronicle sexual rapacity. He is unique among modern playwrights in finding a way to convey in stage terms the trickster's seething and often hilarious sexual itch, which the stage clown once incarnated. The phallus is sometimes playfully invoked in the titles of his work: *Up Against It, Prick Up Your Ears, Until She Screams*. On the cover of Orton's scrapbook for *Entertaining Mr. Sloane* he pasted the bulging blue-jeaned crotch of a muscular beach boy. But the real phallic power is always present in the teasing and unrelenting energy behind his laughter, which wants to "goose" the audience, and take it for a tumble:

> . . . Kenneth, who read the *Observer*, tells me of the latest way-out group in America—complete sexual license. "It's the only way to smash the wretched civilization," I said, making a mental note to hot-up *What the Butler Saw* when I came to re-write. "It's like the Albigensian heresy in the 11th Century," Kenneth said. Looked up the article in the Encyclopaedia Britannica. Most interesting. Yes. Sex is the only way to infuriate them. Much more fucking and they'll be screaming hysterics in next to no time.   [March 26, 1967]

Orton's first full-fledged trickster accomplishment was the creation of
Edna Welthorpe (Mrs.) in 1958. Watchdog of public morals and notorious letter writer, Edna was conceived in the spirit of fun, not literature.
Her fatuous suburban tones foreshadow the essential Orton. Edna was
a direct descendant of the fractious kill-joy Mrs. Grundy, "that amusing
old lady," as Oscar Wilde aptly observed, who "represents the only
original form of humour that the middle classes of this country have
been able to produce."[49] Under this *nom de plume* Orton carried
his clowning into public life, spoofing Edna's idiocy and goading institutions into betraying their own. These pranks had a refreshing ease
and brazenness that never found their way into Orton's early "serious"
writing.

2nd November 1958

Dear Sir,

Your name has kindly been given to me in connection with the
availability of the Heath Street Baptist Church Hall. If it is at all
possible, I would like to begin rehearsals there during the next
three weeks, and later to present for three performances, *The Pansy*,
a play which pleads for greater tolerance on the subject of homosexuality.

It is with the utmost hesitance that I approach a minister upon
so controversial a topic; but the attitude of enlightened Churchmen
seems to have undergone a favourable revolution during the past
decade. It is with this thought in mind that I decided to contact you.

I am told that you forbid dancing in your hall. This is a difficulty,
as there is a certain amount of dancing in several scenes. However,
if you too strongly object I could cut these as, at the request of
certain members of the cast, I have already expurgated the scenes
which were to have taken place in the Kilburn Branch Library in
Cotleigh Road.

Trusting to have your reply in due course, I am,

Yours faithfully,

Edna Welthorpe (Mrs.)

After a second, rude letter to the minister had produced only a
note scolding her for her "strictures," Orton declared Edna dead:

Dear Mr. S—

I am writing on behalf of my late niece, Edna. . . . I have taken
over from my niece the position of secretary to the Phallus Players,
and I am anxious to know what we are to do with regard to the
Hall.

Please let me say, sir, that I am not a party to the rude tone which
Edna adopted when crossed. I feel that I must give a definite answer
to the society, even though I myself do not altogether approve of
the play. . . . I did not want to put on this piece of near-pornog-
raphy. I have the strongest opinions as to what should and should
not be presented in a Church. . . .

This letter coaxed out the minister's piety. "I was shocked to learn that
your niece had died," he wrote back. "And I wish to say how sorry I
am and would offer you my sincerest condolences on this unfortunate
event. It is very sad to think that one's last contacts with anyone had
been on the level that mine were with her, but you, if I may say so,
have lifted the whole business onto a higher level."

Once invented, Edna busied herself over the years by throwing
spanners in a variety of works. She pestered the Home Shopping Service,
and then when they replied, denied her existence. She requested
seventy-eight tickets to the International Trade Fashion Fair, and
rounded on the publicity department when they were not forthcoming.
She badgered industry about their products:

30 April 1965

Dear Sir,
    I recently purchased a tin of Morton's blackcurrant pie filling. It
was delicious. Chock-full of rich fruit. Then wishing to try another
variety, I came upon Smedley's Raspberry pie filling. There wasn't
a raspberry in it. I was very disappointed after trying Morton's
blackcurrant.
    Please try to do better in the future. And what on earth is
"EDIBLE STARCH" and "LOCUST BEAN GUM"? If that is what you put
into your pie fillings I'm not surprised at the result.
    I shan't try any more of your pie fillings until the fruit content
is considerably higher. My stomach really turned at what I saw
when I opened the tin. . . .

The stage clown's appetite for vindictive triumph can be seen in his
language for success: he "kills the audience," "lays them in the aisles,"
"slaughters them," "knocks them dead." The Edna persona was part of
this lust for psychic annihilation—an attempt at comic domination in
keeping with the closed-off, hermetic life that defended Orton and
Halliwell against the world. With reproductions of great works of art
layered like bricks up to the ceiling, their room became a "wall of
culture" between them and the mediocre world outside. Edna was an

offensive weapon, a form of dissimulation in which Orton's personality could remain invulnerable to society's judgment while sniping at it. Edna's tone was not just a practical joke; it was an exploration of an idiom and attitude of mind.

Edna's scolding voice later often spoke out against Orton's own plays, adding vindictive insult to injury. "Today's young playwrights take it upon themselves to flaunt their contempt for ordinary decent people," she wrote to the *Daily Telegraph* in 1964, fanning the scandal of *Entertaining Mr. Sloane*. "I hope that the ordinary decent people will shortly strike *back!*"[50] The viciousness behind decency was a streak that Orton refined as his literary ability became more adroit. "If you really wanted to spot the nasty equivalent of fascism in England you have to read the letters to the *Radio Times* and the *TV Times*,"[51] he once said. Part of Edna reflected this. But Orton relished also the stupidity of her censoriousness. She even wrote to Kenneth Williams, "taking up cudgels" with him over remarks that "were quite uncalled for and tasteless in the extreme":

> Especially offensive to me as a nursing mother was your attack on infants and their ways. My own baby, born recently, cried throughout the programme. Which I feel more than proves my point.[52]

As did her author, Edna's milieu and feeling for the *mot juste* improved with age. In a letter to the manager of the Ritz Hotel, Orton showed how clear a bead he had on Edna's sublime egotism. She shared with all his farce characters an elegant incomprehension of herself and the world through which she bulldozed:

> Tuesday 14th February 1967
>
> Dear Sir,
>
> I'm writing to ask a question which, as a hotelier, I'm sure you'll be eager to answer. A month ago I visited the Ritz in company with Mrs. Sally Warren—a tall grey-haired lady. During our brief stay at your hotel I lost a brown Morocco handbag with the initials E. W. stamped on the flap. The contents of the bag weren't valuable —they consisted of a purse containing loose coins, a Boots folder with snapshots of members of my family and a pair of gloves made of some hairy material.
>
> I wonder if you, or any of your staff, have come across my handbag? If you can give me any assistance in its recovery I'd be most grateful. . . .
>
> And may I take this opportunity of saying that, in my opinion, the Ritz is unbeatable. I was staggered by the splendour of it all. . . .

Every comedian walks a tightrope between the sublime and the bestial; and his laughter marks this precarious balance. The trickster can be disgusting as well as delightful. Orton's impersonations also had a vulgar side:

                                                      [no date]
Postmaster: R. Ufick   North District Post Office

Dear Sir,

   For some time now the pillar boxes in this area have had two holes in them. I am sorry to tell you that a great many of these have been put to improper use. The unpleasant fact is that the slot marked "London" is being misused for the disposal of old French letters and other bric-à-brac, while the ones marked "Other Places" is being wanked-off into. . . . My object in writing is to ask you to make sure you post only "normal" letters and that you insert these in the right slot. It may be that you have already taken care to do this: if so, I would like to thank you. If not, I can only ask you to keep your great cock out of our boxes. . . .

The radio program "Mrs. Dale's Diary" was an early target—though not this time of Edna Welthorpe. Orton and Halliwell had questioned Mrs. Dale's virtue in *The Boy Hairdresser*. "I bet what she does in bed would shock her mother," says Donelly. "These conformists give me a pain in the arse. They look down on so many things—and yet they have vices."

Charles Monteith heard their version of "Mrs. Dale's Diary" in 1959. Orton and Halliwell had recorded the show's signature tune and then faded it out for their own version of a typical day in Mrs. Dale's life. Mrs. Dale's chatty kitchen was transformed into the scene of an orgy, in which she was the centrepiece. "It was funny and very, very dirty," Monteith says. "Every possible aperture was used by everybody and every object. I believe a broom handle had been lost. And just as the broom handle was being produced from an unsuitable place, Dr. Dale came in saying: 'Is there time for another cup of coffee?' "

Even as an established playwright, Orton still couldn't resist the idea of a romp for its own sake. "If I've time on my hands at the end of the year," he wrote in 1967, "I'd like to amuse myself by writing a bit of rubbish under an assumed name: in the nature of a joke play."[53] Orton's squandering of energy in pranks released a festive vulgarity which, when disciplined, found its way successfully into his plays. But when he indulged himself, his fun became frivolity, his outrage merely outrageousness. There was always a little boy in Orton—the Peter Pan part of him—that responded to Beatrix Potter and Daisy Ashford; who inflated prophylactics and dropped them into the caretaker's hollyhocks; who wrote obscene scenarios played against a backdrop of upper-class life. In *The Patient Dowager,* a pornographic sketch Orton wrote for Halliwell's amusement in 1960, the butler has a radioactive cock, and the sex-starved dowager billows smoke from beneath her dress after masturbating with a newspaper ("I always told you the *Daily Sketch* was highly inflammable"). The joke was to upstage elegance with obscenity. Orton and Halliwell acted the parts and taped them. Orton retitled the sketch *Until She Screams* when it was performed in Kenneth Tynan's erotic revue, *Oh! Calcutta!:*

> As I think that this revue is doomed from the start I wasn't going to put myself out. . . . Slightly altered some of the more deliberately pornographic element. . . . Kenneth Tynan apparently said the revue was to be straightforward, and no phoney "artistic" shit. Since the revue is called *Oh! Calcutta!,* it begins with an artistic title. Anyway, they can have the sketch. If they dare do it.
>
> [February 24, 1967]

ORTON'S PRANKS were the by-products of an imagination struggling with hostility. Anger obsessed him. In *Untitled Play* (1959) he first made the intellectual connection between laughter and revenge, fantasizing about a purifying laughter with the power to devastate and renew. Under the motto POX VOBISCUM, Dr. Petrie seeks converts to his faith in mockery. He finds them in Fred and Madge, a bored and aimless working-class couple who complain of the "fatigue of living" and their empty routines. Madge assesses her friends as zombies: "Nothing on their minds except the rates and no pleasures except the pools. . . . They're not even alive, at least not what anyone who was alive would call alive. They're dead. But you can't go around telling people they're dead without annoying them, can you?" Dr. Petrie does just that. An exhibition of his fulminating rage awakens "the dead," and galvanizes them with a new sense of mission. Anger is dramatized as a source of life—a connection to society which short-circuits boredom. "Is rage the prerogative of youth?" Dr. Petrie asks. "Must we cool with the years and die when our blood has chilled to the temperature of the society around us? . . . No! We must hurt the feelings of our enemies, infuriate those we dislike, and never cease to delight in bringing the hornets nest about our ears."

Orton saw that laughter could break down the solid state of society.

Behind Petrie's ranting is the comic's desire to reimagine the world. But *Untitled Play* was all talk and no destruction. Demolition was only an offstage sound effect: "With each laugh or series of laughs the sound of falling masonry and cracking glass increases. . . . The laughter grows more and more hysterical." Orton had grasped the importance of panic to laughter, even if the mishmash of borrowed styles in *Untitled Play* showed he was still at a loss about how to construct it. But he had stumbled onto his theme: to let laughter be lethal and irresistible.

The fury in Orton's laughter was both a mask and an admission of dangerous feelings that were slow to come into focus. Orton began defacing library books at about the same time that his writing became obsessed with laughter as revenge. *Untitled Play* had thrown a slack net around his anger, and he explored the idea of revenge more rigorously in *The Boy Hairdresser*, written with Halliwell between 1959 and 1960.* For the first time Orton's name was typed above Halliwell's in this manuscript, which would be their last collaboration. They condensed the characteristics of their personalities and the suffocating detail of their isolation into realistic, solemn prose. "We have always in the past been unsure of what we have written," Halliwell wrote to Charles Monteith, when they submitted the novel to Faber & Faber on June 20, 1960. "But this time we have written something both publishable and not lacking in brilliance. We have *tried*, successfully we hope, to write something much more realistic in style. . . . We, of course, think its brilliance is unbelievable. But are we going round the bend?"

The Boy Hairdresser was their most serious, passionate book. Too ungainly and oblique to be brilliant, it is important as a testament to their suffering. In Peterson and Donelly, they examined the tensions in their relationship. Looking at Peterson, Donelly thinks:

> What a charmer he looks, with the light falling onto his hair: tough yet in a way weak: in need of protection. . . . Peterson was as trapped as he was, and yet treated his cage as a playground, making the cage disappear, the bars melt.

Boredom is the enemy that shrinks and flattens Donelly's perception of the world. He can make no connections. Life is a barren parade of fragments. Actions and objections intrude on his solitude, and his mind records "the lifeless progression of detail":

---

* *The Boy Hairdresser* was first a verse satire, then a novel on which they collaborated, and finally a play loosely based on the incidents in the novel. For the play, Orton borrowed, really, only the title. In each case, while the title remained the same, the story that went with it was different.

Lying in the warm water, he hummed a tune, flicked soap over himself and stared at his navel. The house creaked, there was a patter of plaster, the gurgling of a pipe. One day he would shoot himself, he was living already in the future.

Both Orton and Halliwell were oppressed by a sense of cultural suffocation. Orton's laughter would triumph over his fears and afflictions. Halliwell had no such method of liberating his anger. *The Boy Hairdresser* dramatized the frustration of the imprisoned will, and its negative but "heroic" elevation into criminal revenge. Donelly, who "had proved to himself the pointlessness of so many things, so many virtues, so many vices, without purpose, leading nowhere," has no link to life except Peterson. "If Peterson were dead he could end it now," Donelly thinks at the beginning of the book. He and Peterson drift through the seedy backstreets of London, glimpsed in coffee bars, pubs, porno bookshops. People float like voices through a numbed, undifferentiated landscape. Wandering is the condition of their rootless, disintegrating world. Donelly coaxes Peterson into living with him, and then into the frivolous subversions of their pranks:

> They had been stealing for a year from bookshops. Peterson had a great enthusiasm for anarchy. The theft of toilet-rolls from public lavatories, pens from post-offices; the obscene telephone calls, the cards inserted in Praed Street windows giving the addresses of vicars' aunts and aldermen's widows. . . .

Donelly sees something more menacing in these petty rebellions. "They were rehearsals," he thinks. "One day he would show them." And he dreams of having the last vengeful laugh on society. He plans to make a spectacle of his death:

> When he went, he'd take others with him: five or six at least. Something for the Sunday papers to talk about. . . . The idea staggered. Why not cure the population problem by even so small an amount. It seemed as though he had cut himself free from everyone at that moment.

Despite its ferocious facade, revenge is an act of nostalgia—an attempt to force life back to an imagined earlier harmony. In its hatred, revenge registers a sense of loss and the yearning to put the moral universe in order. Donelly, echoing Orton and Halliwell's familiar lament, longs for society's sullied slate to be wiped clean:

God knows the sooner the Bomb fell the better. And one day, with a finality beyond the axe, docks and fools parsley, brambles and thick primeval green will cover the cathode ray tubes and traffic signs. Only the mice and beetles in the semi-detached villas will know the perfection of those Mod Cons.

But Donelly, who hates life and musters every tattered scrap of nihilist jargon to prove it, can't kill himself. He finds his suicidal excuse when Peterson is knocked down by a car and killed. "Suicide," Donelly says after Peterson's funeral, "is an insult to the body." It is a gesture that takes mockery to its extreme. Donelly hates himself as much as society for the pain; he wants to revenge it. So he starts to gun down people in the street, expecting to turn the gun on himself. But vengeance turns to farce. He loses consciousness, only to find himself waking up in a hospital.

"You did no harm to anyone but yourself," says his nurse, explaining that two of his fingers have been amputated. "I've ruined my life, nurse," Donelly says, contemplating the charges of attempted murder that the police will make against him. Later, as the nurse leans over to tuck in his blankets, Donelly grabs a vase of flowers and empties them on her head in a last unrepentant expression of his numbing frustration and isolation. "I hope you feel ashamed of yourself," the nurse says. "When I bring you lunch, I shall expect an apology." Her parting words demand capitulation to convention and manners. Mockery is always at odds with manners. To heal, mockery must break boundaries while manners must cling to established limits. Mockery is an act of no surrender. In the silence of his room, Donelly has a final elegiac vision of its heroism:

> It was like this for the Incas, the Aztecs, the pure-blooded Polynesians, for the golden bearded kings of Atlas and the legionary upon the wall. . . .
> They had ignorance and accepted custom in Alba Longa, Megiddo, and Illion: they had chicken-hearts and sleek ideals upon those topless towers. Youth had been betrayed and tears shed for its loss too often and too long for anyone, anymore, to feel anything.
> The endless spinning of the wheel; the perpetual closing of a circle.
> God laughs and snaps his fingers. . . . The only thing for man to do is to imitate God and snap his fingers too.

In Orton's last novel, *Head to Toe* (1961), the pilgrim-hero, Gombold, prays: "Cleanse my heart, give me the ability to rage correctly."

As a spokesman for Orton's quandary, Gombold observes: "But I want to get somewhere. I don't want to be lost in this wilderness forever." *Head to Toe* sported with problems of sexual guilt, isolation, and fulfillment which *The Boy Hairdresser* had debated in its overwritten meditation on suicide and revenge. Gombold is lost in an alien terrain that turns out to be the body of a giant. His identity is under continual siege as he wanders through the body, which inevitably becomes a metaphor of the body politic. Gombold is always being captured by hostile forces and imprisoned, then escaping, only to be captured again. His sole refuge from this pattern of painful retreat and enforced powerlessness is his imagination. "By use of images," he thinks, "it might be possible to extract from fantasy a kind of reality." Gombold's journey is a fantasy in which Orton's images tease out of him the sexual and social chaos that fed his obsession with comic revenge.

Orton's compulsive promiscuity, the aggression in his humor, showed a need to confirm his maleness. In *Head to Toe,* this sexual uncertainty is given playful shape. Gombold at first finds himself in a territory peopled only by women. He is seduced by the Amazonian chief of police, Connie Hogg. Fearing her wrath and the threat of engulfment, Gombold does as he's told. He is ordered to be a woman:

> The clothes she produced for him to wear had a curiously unfamiliar feel. . . . When he was dressed she watched as he minced before his image in the mirror.
> "Promise one thing," she said, standing over him, "never wear Daddy's clothes."

Gombold breaks the promise and dons Connie's men's clothes. His identity is so fluid that clothes have the power to change it.

Gombold was Orton's first attempt to explore what happens to human identity when the boundaries of the body become blurred. In his sexual confusion, Gombold admits: "I have difficulty in distinguishing a man and a youth from a woman." The confusion of man, woman, and youth is always the driving force behind Orton's farces, the sexual turmoil in his own life that works out in the equation of fun. *Head to Toe* never makes this psychic tug-of-war dramatic, but it elucidates Orton's predicament—from which his plays finally extricated him. When Gombold is trapped in prison and sees no way out, he writes poems in the shape of darts and throws them out of his cell, hoping they will bring about his escape. "It was the kind of writing he had never done before, indeed, he was convinced it was a type no one had ever attempted in any language. . . . After a second or two the dart was returned. His heart sank. There seemed no one here either to appreciate his writing or engineer his escape."

Orton's plays would be the darts that finally drew attention to him and freed him from his isolation. *Head to Toe*'s frantic playfulness was a search for the key to unlock the author's imagination. Here for the first time Orton toyed with the farcical, trying to mingle violence and laughter. Farce is an act of literary aggression. On stage, Orton made visual the visceral battle between ecstasy and fear, reason and irrationality that punished Gombold. *Head to Toe* made only crude flourishes in this comic direction. As a guerrilla assassin, Gombold dresses in drag and infiltrates a government cabinet meeting. The Prime Minister and the cabinet are women:

> "All right, dears, calm down [says Lillian, the Prime Minister]. The International Field . . . I've made a big decision. I'm going to the disarmament conference in a great flowing dress in white broderie anglaise with heavenly flounces. . . ."

Gombold—the victim turned victimizer—calmly assassinates the Prime Minister and escapes, only to be confronted later by a series of "unacceptable deaths." Gombold, like so many of Orton's comic characters, illustrates that when life is preposterous, so is death. Even in the plant kingdom the ability to inflict pain is the only defense against mankind. Gombold overhears a loganberry talking:

> "Oh, I prayed a bit, I admit. You couldn't stop me. But it wasn't prayers that saved me."
> "What then?"
> "It was my thorns. . . ."

Gombold's adventures are the faltering first steps toward making a situation dramatize an idea rather than, as in *The Boy Hairdresser*, allowing the ideas to swamp the situation.

On re-reading *Head to Toe* for script ideas for The Beatles' film in 1967, Orton was enthusiastic about it. "It had always been my intention some day to rewrite it," he noted, referring to his decision to use part of it as an "inspiration." "I found, to my surprise, that it was excellent. It had great faults as a novel, but as the basis for a film it was more than adequate."[54] *Head to Toe* dreamed out loud about theatrical impact, and many of the novel's scenes were salvaged from discarded plays. The passion and concerns of his later plays were in the work; but his language was too private and his imagery too confused for ideas to be clearly communicated. Publishers immediately responded to these problems. The editor from MacGibbon & Kee, to whom Orton first sent the book, explained: "The flight into fantasy is something I can't follow." Orton then submitted the novel to Charles Monteith at Faber on June 28, 1961. The tone of Orton's letter anticipated rejection: "I'm submitting this manuscript . . . in the hope that you'll find a certain amount of pleasure in reading it, and no guilt in refusing it." Monteith refused it, explaining, "Several degrees too odd." The criticism was apt; but the imagery and anarchic energy of the writing came closer to Orton's later comic revenges than anything he'd previously done.

Head to Toe's metaphor was very close to Orton's life. Gombold had searched for the perfect destructive sentence. The design of his sentences was defective. They needed to be tested and their effectiveness improved:

> Later he went into the city on his own to test another sentence: it was a failure. On the way back he saw an elderly woman in front of him. As she passed a group of children playing in the road, a small boy said something to her. The reaction was immediate. She turned a bright pink; cracks appeared across her face, patches of skin flaked and chipped. She crumbled before his eyes. Gombold questioned the boy and found the sentence he had used was quite simple in construction.

Orton then adopted Gombold's tactic and, together with his friend, offended the public directly. The book defacing was brash, simple, and often childishly rude. The library escapade set the stage for the literary impact that was lacking in Orton's fictions. Begun by Orton in August 1959, the project mushroomed obsessively with repeated literary rejection into a kind of art form by 1961. "I was really occupying myself with these library books which I'd borrowed and also stolen, and then I used to go back with them a couple of times a day."[55] The defaced books infiltrated the public and goaded it to respond. Orton was testing the destructive power of his laughter and watching for signs of shock. Gombold, the imaginary prisoner, presaged Orton's actual imprisonment in 1962.

THE LIBRARY PRANK was a misguided piece of theatre, but the work was very funny. The book jackets were concise, straightforward, irreverent, and vulgar: everything that his fiction was not. Orton had a strong

visual sense, and the distortions of his cut-up images played off against
language and made words more startling. By 1962, Orton had managed
to attract the attention of both the Royal Court Theatre and the BBC
with *The Visit* (1961), a short play about an old man who is dying in
a hospital ward, surrounded by the chatter of his daughter and the
nurses. The work had been praised, but rejected, by both institutions.
The Royal Court found the writing "excellent"; the BBC's verdict was
"excellent dialogue . . . the flaw is lack of dramatic shaping and
dramatic impact." The book jackets had none of these artistic faults.
The jackets were cunningly designed, and the prank carefully planned.
Orton displayed in public what he still lacked on the page: a revenger's
passion for plot.

After he became a famous playwright whose dramatic outrageousness had found its proper format, Orton enjoyed talking about prison
and the defaced books. But he always sidestepped the question of his
prank's success. His statement to the police stressed the craft he'd put
into the project. "Over the last twelve months," he told them on April
28, 1962, "we started to cut pieces out of these books and make false
book jackets. I tried to make them as effective as possible by making it
look like part of the book." Orton waited to see a reaction from the
public, but in fact got no satisfaction. "He couldn't understand why the
public wasn't getting stirred up," Sidney Porrett remembers. The work
did incite the public, but Orton couldn't gauge the reaction. When he
understood the elaborate lengths to which Islington had gone to catch
them, he realized just how disturbing the work had been. This pleased
him.

Celebrity has a way of turning stigma into asset, and Orton
glossed over his prison experience. "Prison did not make me bitter,
I enjoyed it very much,"[56] he told the *Daily Sketch,* echoing the tone
Kenneth Halliwell had taken with Sidney Porrett when, while still in
prison, he'd ended a letter, "Yours, having just had the best holiday
of my life . . ." To the *Evening Standard* Orton swaggered: "I didn't
suffer or anything the way Oscar Wilde suffered from being in prison—
but then Wilde was flabby and self-indulgent. There is this complete
myth about writers being sensitive plants. They're not. It's a silly nineteenth century idea, but I'm sure Aristophanes was not sensitive. I mean
there's absolutely no reason why a writer shouldn't be as tough as a
bricklayer."[57]

Orton liked to think of himself as tough, and prison hardened him.
Before prison, his anger displayed its wound and lost its aim. Afterwards sentiment and self-pity were banished by a show of wit, and his
laughter found its targets. "I tried writing before I went into the nick

. . . but it was no good," he told the Leicester *Mercury* in 1964. "Being in the nick brought detachment to my writing. I wasn't involved anymore. And it suddenly worked."

As Orton's rebellion came into focus, so did his style. Prison brought him "the revelation of what really lies underneath our industrialized society."[58] Laughter was the message sent back from his cultivated isolation. The boldness of Orton's distortions of reality, the brazenness of his macabre tone, demonstrated a new vivaciousness and innocent nihilism. After prison, Orton understood with his heart as well as his head that values do not exist and that the universe rolls on to no point or purpose. "Before prison, I had been vaguely conscious of something rotten somewhere: prison crystallized this," he said. "The old whore society really lifted up her skirts and the stench was pretty foul."[59]

Orton had passed beyond suffering. His laughter and style slowly assumed the cool and penetrating directness of a survivor. His manic playfulness dramatized laughter as a temporary consolation for an existence in which there was no relief. It hid pain from the world, if not from himself. On the empty back page of Orton's clipping book for *Loot* he pasted an anonymous quotation almost as a parenthesis to the critics' near-unanimous praise:

> I was not nearly so sure of myself as I should have liked, and this made me present a brassy face to the world and pretend to be more hard-boiled than I was. . . . I developed a mocking, cynical way of treating events because it prevented them from being too painful. . . .

4

MONSTROUS FUN

When you can assume that your audience holds the same beliefs as you do, you can relax a little and use more normal means of talking to it. When you have to assume that it does not, then you have to make your vision apparent by shock—to the hard of hearing you shout and for the almost blind you draw large and startling figures.
—Flannery O'Connor, *Mystery and Manners*

The nation's morals are like teeth: the more decayed they are the more it hurts to touch them.
—George Bernard Shaw,
Introduction to *The Shewing-up of Blanco Posnet*

ORTON'S PROFESSIONAL BREAKTHROUGH came in 1963, when the BBC Third Programme accepted *The Boy Hairdresser*—later retitled *The Ruffian on the Stair*. The BBC copyright form (dated August 21) lists Orton's payment as £65 for a forty-five-minute radio play. Orton was another happy example of the BBC's institutional kiss of life. In 1964, the year of *Ruffian*'s broadcast, there were 395 BBC radio dramas, and Orton was among 58 new writers.[1] The BBC had introduced the work of John Arden, Robert Bolt, Willis Hall, Henry Livings, John Mortimer, Bill Naughton, Alun Owen. It had sustained Harold Pinter after his first early stage failures. The acceptance of Orton's play came within a month of marking a decade of total literary failure.

The Ruffian on the Stair is the mirror image of *Entertaining Mr. Sloane*, which Orton wrote between September and December of 1963. It dramatizes the self-destructive bondage of people to their "loved-ones," and their inability to seize their freedom. The play's self-confessed revenger, Wilson, wants to engineer his own death out of grief for his brother's murder. Like Halliwell, Wilson has the courage neither to live nor die. His character displays the nihilistic, self-loathing aspect of anger that Sloane turns into a slick psychopathic style of survival.

With *The Ruffian on the Stair*, the BBC producers forced Orton to plot more carefully. He had to clarify his dramatic ideas and abandon his predilection for "arty" dialogue that lost the line of action. Wilson intrudes on the shabby isolation of Mike and Joyce, a petty thief and a former prostitute who are living together. While Mike is out, Wilson taunts and terrifies Joyce. Mike has run down Wilson's brother with his van, and Wilson finally goads Mike into killing him. "The death," Orton wrote to his producer John Tydeman, after the first of three rewrites, "brings Mike and Joyce together for only a short time; she wants him to stay with her; after he calls the police she will be alone again. This time perhaps forever."[2] The theatrical preoccupations of Orton's later work are present but unfocused in *The Ruffian on the Stair*—a fact reflected in Orton's inability either to title or satisfactorily conclude the play. "The title is difficult," Orton wrote Tydeman. "How about *The Wrong Door*? *The Victims*? *Die with the Dying*? I can't say I'm happy with any of them."[3] Neither was the BBC, who asked for more work. On December 6, the BBC finally accepted the play, but not until December 23 (four days after *Entertaining Mr. Sloane* was completed) did Orton furnish the right title. *The Ruffian on the Stair* was taken from a Victorian poem by W. E. Henley:

> *Madam Life's a piece in bloom*
> *Death goes dogging everywhere:*
> *She's the tenant of the room*
> *He's the ruffian on the stair.*

"It fits," Orton wrote his producer, who thought it "splendid." "And I don't think it's necessary to know the quotation for the title to be right."[4] There were two versions of *The Ruffian on the Stair*: the radio version based on the 1963 manuscript of *The Boy Hairdresser*, and the substantially revised stage version for the Royal Court's Sunday performance without decor (1966), later included in the double bill *Crimes of Passion* (1967). Between the drafting of these two scripts, Orton became a playwright.

"I FORBID the Royal Court to use the version of *The Ruffian on the Stair* printed in the BBC book of radio plays," Orton wrote to Peggy Ramsay in May 1966 from Morocco, instructing her to "burgle" his flat for a revised script. "I absolutely won't have that version performed anywhere!!"[5] He had reworked the play for television, only to have it temporarily shelved by ITV as unfit for family viewing. "It's much better, much funnier," Orton wrote to his agent. "And altogether a more 'Ortonish' play than the original the BBC published." By then Orton had developed his own unique theatrical style, and the radio play, erected on the scaffold of Pinter's plots for *The Room* and *The Birthday Party*, was embarrassingly derivative. Peggy Ramsay was told to locate the new version from the manuscript drawer underneath Orton's bed; the MS was identified by a note in Orton's handwriting: "Thanks for asking to read this. Sorry it had to be a carbon." The note was to Harold Pinter.

Orton could never quite get himself publicly to admit Pinter's influence. "I suppose he influenced me," he told a BBC interviewer in 1964. "I think there are other influences on my work far more important than Pinter, and of course you always have to remember that the things which influenced Pinter, which I believe are Hollywood movies in the forties, also influenced me."[6] Like Pinter, Orton wanted the seemingly artificial style of his plays to be seen as realistic. ("Had my hair cut at a new hairdressers in Knightsbridge," he wrote in his diary on March 6, 1967. "It appears to be quite natural whilst in fact being incredibly artificial. Which is a philosophy I approve of.") And, as Orton's production notes to the Royal Court for *Ruffian* imply, he also wanted to dissociate his mature style from Pinter's:

> . . . The play is clearly not written naturalistically, but it must be directed and acted with absolute *realism*. No "stylization," no "camp." No attempt in fact to match the author's extravagance of dialogue with extravagance of direction. REALISTIC PLAYING AND DIRECTING.
> Every one of the characters must be real. None of them is ever consciously funny. Every line should be played with desperate seriousness and complete lack of any suggestion of humour. Only in this way can a mixture of comedy and menace be achieved. There must never, from the actors, be the least hint of send-up. The most ludicrous lines—those at the end of the play for instance about the police and the goldfish—must be played quite sincerely. Unless it's real it won't be funny. Everything the characters say is *true*. Mike has murdered the boy's brother. Joyce is an ex-call girl. Wilson has an incestuous relationship with his brother. Wilson does provoke Mike into murdering him. The play mustn't be presented as an example of the now out-dated "mystery" school—*vide* early Pinter. Everything is as clear as the most reactionary *Telegraph* reader could wish. There is a beginning, a middle and an end. . . .

The play must be directed without long significant pauses. Any

pauses must be natural pauses. Pace, pace, pace, as well. Go for the
strong and natural climaxes. Everything else should be simple.

The note is already suspicious of the aura of poetic self-consciousness
that would infect Pinter's later work. Still, Pinter was the one living
English playwright Orton respected. "I've just finished filming a television play," Orton wrote to a friend in 1966 about *The Erpingham
Camp*, "which caused a sensation (among the technicians, actors, extras and canteen assistants including H. Pinter, who likes it. He's a
writer!)."[7] Orton was passionate about *The Homecoming*. "Very brilliant play. The best he's written," he noted, drawing a comparison
with *Entertaining Mr. Sloane*. "Sexual sharing takes place in that too.
A girl though. Makes it more wholesome, I suppose."[8] Orton saw himself as an influence on the play. *"The Homecoming* couldn't have been
written without *Sloane*," he said, remarking that his play was put on
two years before Pinter's. "And you know, in a way the second act—
although I admire it very much—isn't true. Harold, I'm sure would
never share anyone sexually. I would. And so *Sloane* springs from the
way I think. *The Homecoming* doesn't spring from the way Harold
thinks."[9]

"You're a bloody marvellous writer," Pinter wrote Orton after reading the rewrite of *The Ruffian on the Stair*, which he "loved."[10] Pinter,
who read a poem at Orton's funeral, found Orton's work "brilliant and
truly original. He has an instinctive grasp of construction."[11] And it
was Pinter, who so dominated English theatre during Orton's career,
whom Orton began by imitating and ended by parodying. "My name
is Caulfield. I've broken into your house," says the detective intruder
as he enters the room of the defrocked priest McCorquodale in
Funeral Games, lampooning Pinter's high serious pronouncements
about boundaries and "the room."[12]

Pinter invented images of entropy; Orton of action. In Pinter's
world, characters hide their needs and decoy the facts of their life. As
his production notes to the Royal Court show, Orton was in stylistic
rebellion against this obfuscation. "The whole trouble with Western
society today," Orton wrote in his diary, "is the lack of anything worth
concealing."[13] In Orton's world there is no uncertainty and no secrets.
Reality is outrageous enough without mystifying it. People say what
they mean—but the truth still does not help them.

"Melodrama," Eric Bentley writes, "depends for its power on the
degree of fear it can arouse, farce on the degree of aggression."[14] Pinter's
plays updated melodrama; and at first Orton stuck too close to Pinter's

formula for terror for his own aggressive comic spirit to flourish. Like
Wilson's revenge itself, the comic's murderous instinct is significantly
still turned inward. Orton began the radio play with Pinter's familiar
smokescreen of pause and patter as Joyce tries to coax some acknowledgment of her existence out of Mike over breakfast:

> JOYCE. Did you enjoy your breakfast?
> MIKE. What?
> JOYCE. Did you enjoy your breakfast? The egg was nice, wasn't it?
> The eggs are perfect now that I have the timer. Have you
> noticed? (*Pause.*) The marmalade was nice. Did it go down well?
> MIKE. The egg was nice. . . .

The scene is stolen from the opening of *The Birthday Party*. Orton
has changed the brand names, but little else:

> MEG. I've got your cornflakes ready. (*She disappears and reappears.*)
> Here's your cornflakes.
>
> *He rises and takes the plate from her, sits at the table, props up
> the paper and begins to eat. Meg enters by the kitchen door.*
>
> Are they nice?
> PETEY. Very nice.
> MEG. I thought they'd be nice. . . .

From *The Ruffian on the Stair*'s first beat, every theatrical move
seems to follow in Pinter's footsteps. Petey is hidden behind his morning
paper. Meg asks: "Will you tell me if there's something good?" Joyce's
life is equally eventless, and Orton reworks Pinter's line to prove it.
Joyce cajoles Mike into taking a walk in the park. "Go today," she says.
"It'll be something to tell me tonight." Wilson, himself a reversal of the
typical Pinter intruder, occasionally hits a note that foreshadows later
Orton characters: "The heart is situated . . . just below the badge on
my pullover. Don't miss, will you. I don't want to be injured. I want to
be dead." But most of Orton's choices stay close to Pinter's melodramatic
plan. *The Ruffian on the Stair* ends with the same unnerving rhetorical
coda as *The Birthday Party*. When Mike guns down Wilson in jealous
rage, Joyce thinks Wilson's death has brought them together:

> JOYCE. This is a happy ending we're having.
>
> *Pause.*
>
> Isn't it?

The Ruffian on the Stair was broadcast in August 1964. By that time, *Entertaining Mr. Sloane* was a success; *The Good and Faithful Servant* was completed; and *Loot*, subtitled "A Farce," was under way. Orton's theatrical gusto was increasing as rapidly as his reputation. The press dubbed him an *enfant terrible,* and Orton did his best to fit the image of literary hooligan. His first public statement, in the *Radio Times,* was meant to shiver the timbers of his audience and make a case for *The Ruffian on the Stair* as farce. His special pleading says more about the insolence of his emerging theatrical intentions than about actual accomplishment:

> If you weigh my play *The Ruffian on the Stair* in the balance of good taste you will find you have been short-measured. . . .
>
> Ten years ago this theme would have provided an addition to that moribund theatrical genre, Strong Drama. Since the mid-fifties, playwrights have forsaken the inshore fisheries for the ocean proper. Today it is farce.
>
> In a world run by fools the writer can only chronicle the doings of fools or their victims. And because the world is a cruel and heartless place, he will be accused of cruelty and heartlessness. If he thinks that the world is not only cruel and heartless but funny as well, he has given his critics an extra brickbat to fling and will be accused of not taking his subject seriously.
>
> But laughter is a serious business and comedy a weapon more dangerous than tragedy. Which is why tyrants treat it with caution. The actual material of tragedy is equally viable as comedy—unless you happen to be writing in English, when the question of taste occurs. The English are the most tasteless nation on earth, which is why they set such store by it.[15]

Orton protested too much. Under the headline STRONG MEAT ON THE AIR, *The Observer* began by discussing taste, only to pass *The Ruffian on the Stair* with flying colors. "Though not especially seamy," the paper said, "[it] was wild, harsh, and terrifying, an exercise in fear that roared along like an early Graham Greene."[16] *The Listener* pooh-poohed Orton's pronouncement in the *Radio Times* and flung an extra brickbat by proclaiming the play "rather a hit—if you don't take it too seriously."[17] Farce mixes wild fantasy with everyday reality; and it was clear in the extreme reactions to his play that Orton had not yet found the right comic chemistry for it. There was little aggression in his radio laughter and little laughter in the aggression. The sadness that once spoiled Orton's performing now muted the impact of his play. In the radio version, characters continually bleat their sense of loss and isolation. The day after Wilson's first threatening visit, Joyce hears another knock on her door. She contemplates praying. "I'd try maybe a prayer. But the Virgin would turn a deaf ear to a Protestant. . . . I can't be as alone as all that. Nobody ought to be. It's humiliating. (*Pause.*) God is so remote." For the stage version Orton would blue-pencil the excesses in Joyce's dialogue, realizing that a play must leave something for its audience to imagine. The explicitness robbed the first version of any genuine playfulness. Gaiety must emerge from apparent seriousness; sadness from apparent gaiety. There was no sprightliness in Wilson to play off against his morbid obsession. Self-pity sneaks into his character and diminishes him. His prose and his personality are lacklustre. Wilson came across as weak—a whiner. "I can see this is a failure like everything else," he says to Joyce, when his staged seduction doesn't lure Mike upstairs to kill him. Orton had misjudged his main character and the play's offensiveness. The "incestuous" relationship which Orton saw as shocking was too vague.

The stage version reversed this. Orton's rewrite of Wilson has comic sparkle and innuendo:

> I'm a Gents Hairdresser. Qualified. My dad has a business. Just a couple of chairs. I've clipped some notable heads in my time. Mostly professional men. Though we had an amateur street musician in a few weeks ago. We gave him satisfaction, I believe.

Wilson now talks with a hint of swaggering egotism that is the hallmark of all Orton's stage characters. In an exchange about his brother's death, Orton also establishes Wilson's kinkier side.

> WILSON. . . . He was a sportsman before his decease. He wore white shorts better than any man I've ever come in contact with. As a matter of fact, strictly off the record, I'm wearing a pair of his white shorts at this moment. They're inconvenient . . . because . . . (*He blurts it out.*)—there's no fly. (*Pause.*) He wore them two days before he was killed. . . .

"Orton never wrote another play with emotions of this kind," says Peter Gill, who directed the stage version of *The Ruffian on the Stair* in London. "It's the only play where he tried to write about genuine homosexual emotions. It's really very powerful and very upsetting because Orton hadn't completely found himself." Wilson's brother is his narcissistic ideal, his physical replica. "I don't take after him. Except in a physical sense," he says. Wilson proudly admits that they "spent every night in each other's company." Wilson has magically linked his identity to his brother's. When his brother dies, Wilson finds himself with no "heroic" aura to protect him from his own inadequacy and isolation:

> WILSON. . . . I expect he would have made good sooner or later. He was the go-ahead type. His mentality was fully developed. He used to read a lot about expansion. His death put a stop to that. . . .

"There is an atmosphere of total bleakness at that moment," says Peter Gill. "The landscape the actor is seeing is incredibly bleak." Success gave Orton a distance from his craft and his early life, and Wilson's revenge became, in the stage rewrite, Orton's partial revenge on his own past. He added his and Halliwell's biographical details to Wilson's—the bedsitter, the cosy life of "no circumstances" on the N.A.B., the twenty-four-hour companionship. "All our family seem to be some kind of idiot," Wilson says, in a bitter speech that echoes Orton's feelings. "If anybody so much as mentions the British Legion to my dad he goes into a trance. On armistice day he takes part in all the rituals. He eats poppies for a week beforehand. I haven't seen him since the funeral. I expect he's in a home by now."

"The English art of compromise is the thing," Orton said. "I see plays as a piece of meat which buries the hook of what the author has to say. Too many plays are just bare hooks that will never make anyone put it in their mouth."[18] *The Ruffian on the Stair*'s rewrite exemplifies Orton's search for a compromise between his sense of chaos and comedy. In the increasingly baroque rhythms with which he delivered his dark laughter, he evolved a balance between pleasure and pain, idealization and need. Language elevated man above the animal, and also hid the "beastliness" in man from himself. Orton found the juxtaposition of intentions hilarious:

> I read Genet's *Querelle of Brest*. An interesting book, but unformed. . . . Undoubtedly Jean Genet is the most perfect example of an unconscious humorist at work since Marie Corelli. I find a sentence like: "They (the homosexuals of Brest) are peace-loving citizens of irreproachable outward appearance, even though, the long day through, they may perhaps suffer from a rather timid itch for a bit of cock" irresistibly funny. A combination of elegance and crudity is always ridiculous. [January 23, 1967]

Orton wanted to make hilarity and terror co-exist as they do in farce. But with the earthbound characterization of the radio version, he couldn't accomplish the farce momentum to elevate the everyday into the extraordinary. By contrast, the stage version knows where it's going and how to get there. Situations now speak for themselves. Orton tells his story *with* character and action; not *about* character and action. Like Wilson, Mike is reconstructed larger than life, his personality and language inflated by bolder and broader theatrical strokes. No longer the beleaguered layabout of the radio play, he is quickly established as a criminal, and his dapper self-confidence never admits the sadness in the situation. Joyce doesn't want Wilson inside her house. But Mike takes no notice of her fear and invites him in:

> WILSON. I'm a Gents Hairdresser.
> MIKE. You wouldn't happen to be dabbling with birth-control devices? That's no way for a Catholic to carry on.
> WILSON. I don't handle that part of the trade. My old man does it. He has the free-thinking frame of mind. I can't approve, of course. It's the Latin temperament which has been the curse of our religion all along.
> MIKE. The Pope is Italian.
> WILSON. You have something there. I'd like to see a Liffey man on the throne of St. Peter myself. I'd be proud to hear the Lateran ring with the full-throated blasphemies of our native land.
> MIKE. What are you thinking of? The Vicar of Christ doesn't blaspheme.
> WILSON. He would if he was Irish and drank Guinness.

The strut and swagger of their first exchange move Mike and Wilson confidently toward the grotesque. In their distortion lies Orton's special perception of human caprice: the timid animal asserting its feeble powers, roaring at a dangerous world to keep life at a safe distance.

"I suppose I'm a believer in Original Sin," Orton said. "People are profoundly bad, but irresistibly funny."[19] Style—or attempts at it—was a stage-managed redemption. The bow-wow idiom of Mike and Wilson demonstrates their heroic posturing while spoofing the weakness it tries to hide.

Increasingly, Orton's characters would bolster themselves with stylized speech, dramatizing in every exchange the vital lie of human character, man's necessary dishonesty in defending himself against an awesome reality. "The morals of Nineveh were hardly so lax," bellows Mike, in a gradiloquent curse, which continues for a page and elevates Joyce's imagined adultery with Wilson to the size of Old Testament sins. Mike's revenger's "aria" was meant as a parody of Jacobean tragedy. Language is staged as a convincing self-hypnotic gesture of triumphant control in a life that denies it. Orton's words require a delivery of great self-possession, but the situation always betrays the tone. In *The Ruffian on the Stair* all the characters worry about possessing others; but they are never in possession of themselves.

The repertoire of experiences Mike and Joyce encounter includes incest, murder, rage, fear, frenzy, and loneliness. Yet they deny it all, demanding that a benign and dignified face be imposed on events. Orton's savage laughter refuses both his characters and the audience the comfort of their heroic illusions, while dramatizing why they are necessary. The rewritten *Ruffian on the Stair* makes a spectacle of this preposterous evasion, which was only a notion in the radio play. Wilson wants to be killed in the most heroic and authentic heterosexual circumstances. Just before he is shot, Wilson "unbuttons his shirt, pins a badge on his shirt above the heart and unzips his fly." When Mike bursts into the room, he fires two bullets. One shatters Joyce's goldfish bowl, the other hits Wilson in the chest. Wilson crumples to the floor, speaking his last words as "blood spurts from his mouth":

JOYCE. He's fainted.
MIKE *(laying the gun aside)*. He's dead.
JOYCE. But he can't be. You haven't killed him?
MIKE. Bring a sheet. Cover his body.
JOYCE. I've a bit of sacking somewhere.
MIKE. I said a sheet! Give him the best.

He goes into the bedroom and drags a sheet from the bed which he puts over WILSON's *body.*

Mike and Joyce then invoke "the best": their ideal sense of them selves—love, bravery, loyalty—to cover up their confusion:

JOYCE. What excuse was there to shoot him?
MIKE. He was misbehaving himself with my wife.
JOYCE. But I'm not your wife. And he wasn't.
MIKE. He called you Maddy.
JOYCE. Somebody must've told him about my past. You know what people are. *(Pause.)* Did you have anything to do with his brother's death?
MIKE. Yes.
JOYCE. This is what comes of having no regular job. *(Pause.)* Is the phone box working by the Nag's Head?
MIKE. Yes.
JOYCE. Go to the telephone box. Dial 999. I'll tell them I was assaulted.
MIKE *(horrified)*. It'll be in the papers.

JOYCE. Well, perhaps not assaulted. Not completely. You came in just in time.

MIKE. You'll stick by me, Joycie?

JOYCE. Of course, dear. (*She kisses him.*) I love you.

She sees the shattered goldfish bowl.

Oh, look Michael! (*Bursting into tears.*) My goldfish!

She picks up a fish.

MIKE. One of the bullets must've hit the bowl.

JOYCE. They're dead. Poor things. And I reared them so carefully. And while all this was going on they died.

She sobs. MIKE *puts his arms round her, and leads her to the settee. She sits.*

MIKE. Sit down. I'll fetch the police. This has been a crime of passion. They'll understand. They have wives and goldfish of their own.

JOYCE *is too heartbroken to answer. She buries her face in* MIKE'S *shoulder. He holds her close.*

CURTAIN.

The blunt and brutal comic ending was upsetting even to the director. "I felt my whole moral nature called into question," Gill says. This was the intention behind Orton's comedy. "I remember quoting Joe a line from T. S. Eliot: 'We must be forever rebuilding the temple,'" Kenneth Williams says. "And Joe said, 'That's it, exactly.' It wasn't shock for its own sake he was after. He wanted to force you to deliberately re-examine the structure—of language, of manners, of morals, of institutions. His instinct was always healthy."

The serious aim of Orton's humor was misguidedly dubbed "sick" by the press—a know-nothing word that overlooked both the moral anger and the generosity in Orton's comic performance.

"What is a healthy play? Just name me one," Orton said in 1966. "Every good play expresses something of the time in which it was written, and at the moment we're living in a very sick society. During the '50's, when people were still concerned with changing the world and finding useful political solutions, plays like Arnold Wesker's *Chicken Soup with Barley* were quite representative. But today there is a general sense of despair about politics because we know it can't provide any real solutions. Still, I would never claim that I was a pessimistic writer. I'm too amused by the way people carry on to give in to despair."[20]

"JUST BEFORE I wrote *Sloane*, there was a point at which I wavered, looking into the future and seeing nothing, when I thought—'I'm not going to be anything.' "[21] Orton knew the terror of psychic death: impotent, invisible, unfulfilled. He had imagined himself dead in fiction; and on TV he even played dead as the corpse of Erpingham, the panjandrum of a holiday camp. There was a ghostly disruptive ambition to his humor, haunting the society with the power acquired from forays between seen and subterranean worlds. Wilson, like Orton, wants to win the power of the dead by imitating the dead. Wilson is the first of many Orton characters to seek triumph over a sense of trapped energy. Orton's stage laughter signals his freedom, but his characters never laugh. There is something ghostlike about them. They are mischievous and often malicious. They haunt and terrorize people: externalizations of Orton's own struggle for imaginative freedom.[22]

Like his characters, Orton's life was filled with many tentative gestures of ghostlike mastery. "John Orton" the failed novelist and acolyte of Kenneth Halliwell returned as "Joe Orton" to distinguish himself from John Osborne in the public mind. Private failures were turned to public triumph. Wilson's friendship with his brother, like Halliwell's with Orton, was a neurotic solution to life; Wilson's desperate remedy to put things "right" was also Halliwell's constant threat to Orton. In working out the gloom of the past, Orton's laughter got even for the pain. Orton haunted not only his past but the public. "Edna Welthorpe" was a phantom delighting in her invisible power to provoke and confuse the community. Orton aspired to be the "fly on the wall"— his term for his nameless adventuring through London. He knew that eavesdropping was essential to his craft, and he guarded his anonymity:

. . . I heard a most fascinating conversation between an old man and a woman. "What a thing, though," the old woman said. "You'd hardly credit it."

"She's always made a fuss of the whole family, but never me," the old man said.

"Does she have a fire when the young people come to see her?"

"Fire? She won't get people seeing her without warmth. . . . I know why she's doing it. Don't think I don't," the old man said. "My sister she said to me, 'I wish I had your easy life.' Now that upset me. I was upset by the way she phrased herself. 'Don't talk to me like that,' I said, 'I've only got to get on the phone and ring a certain number,' I said, 'to have you stopped.' "

"Yes," the old woman said, "and you can, can't you?" "Were they

always the same?" she said, "when you was a child? Can you throw
yourself back? How was they years ago?"

"The same," the old man said.

"Wicked, isn't it," the old woman said. "Take care now," she
said as the old man left. He didn't say a word to her but got off the
bus looking disgruntled.   [March 7, 1967]

Even Orton's sexual encounters, as he recorded them in his diary,
have an eery anonymity. In every meeting Orton is both present and
absent, shadowing himself and his pickups: listening, judging, observ-
ing, absorbing the detail of each encounter but always outside the
experience:

In a lavatory I met a middle-aged man with a cropped haircut. Not
very attractive. He said he lived in a council flat. "I'm waiting to
go back to sea," he said. We walked for about a hundred yards and
he said, "You don't want it stuck up your arse, do you?" I said I
wasn't keen. "And you're not going to suck me off, are you?" he
said. "No," I said. "You just want to shoot your gun," he said, "like
me." He turned around. "We'd better go back," he said. "You can
pick up a queer in that toilet. They've got cars. And houses. The
best time is dinner time. They've got cars most of them. I've fucked
their arses in their rooms," he said, lighting a cigarette. "I expect
you have too." We went into the lavatory. Only one man there. I
stood next to him. The man with cropped hair went away. The
man I stood next to was a Greek Cypriot. He wasn't very young.
About thirty-five. Very stupid looking. "Come to the park," he said,
in an ice-cream seller's accent. "I'll shag you." I thought it was a
stupid idea. And when we got to the park it seemed as though I'd
met a maniac. "See over there," he said. "Two men. They shag.
And over there," he said, pointing to a clump of trees that were
perhaps three feet away from a well-lighted pavement. "Please let
me shag you," he said. "I'll be quick." "But we're in the light!"
I said. "We can be seen." "Naw," he said, "nobody notice." Up
against a tree I dropped my trousers and he fucked me. He was
quick. Afterwards he tossed me off. As we were walking away he
said, "I shag a boy last week. I pay him £2. You don't want money,
do you?" "No," I said, "I've plenty of money." He laughed at this
and said, "Me too. I've plenty of money. Too many people shag
here," he said, ambling off across the dark ground. "Maybe next
time we shag in a room. Maybe next time you shag me as well."
I said that it would be a pleasure and left him.   [July 13, 1967]

The detachment in *The Ruffian on the Stair*'s stage laughter
matched Orton's personal style. It gave him a curious tranquillity in

public. "Joe's vision was bleak," Peter Gill recalls, "but he was very stable in a funny sort of way. He had no worries. He had none of the neurotic panic of someone like myself who always thinks he's going to get killed in a sexual situation. Joe had a ruthless self-sufficiency." Peggy Ramsay was also impressed by Orton's "lovely detachment": "His detachment is what makes me feel he is better than practically every author we've looked after. I admired him for it more than anything else. It made him a consummate artist. . . . He wasn't prepared to sacrifice his ambition to life. The theatre is a mere reflection of life, dear; but it's life that's the important thing. The theatre throws it back, enhances it with a good play, makes life wonderful. Joe was never kidded that it was more than a reflection."

When *Crimes of Passion* opened at the Royal Court in June 1967, Orton returned from Morocco nervous and exhausted. "Took two of Kenneth's secret 'suicide pills.' Nembutal. Fell into a deep sleep." At the last dress rehearsal on June 5 he found *"Ruffian very slow. Erpingham* rather good though impossibly ragged and needed a lot of rehearsing. Peggy unenthusiastic. Think it isn't going to be a success. Had dinner with Bill Gaskill, Peggy and Oscar Lewenstein. 'It's quite an amusing evening,' Oscar said. Felt annoyed. *Erpingham* is the best (stage) play of mine performed so far. If only Arthur Lowe were playing Erpingham they'd all be raving. . . ." But he faced the opening night and the reviews with equanimity:

> The big day . . . Peter Gill spent most of the day tightening *Erpingham* especially scene changes in the blackouts. . . .
>
> I got to the Royal Court at 7. They were having difficulties with the programmes—only a few had arrived. I went to my seat and sat down. Saw Sheila Hancock sitting with Oscar. She smiled and blew a kiss. *Ruffian* began. It seemed slow at first. It was the best performance this cast has given of the play. The whole thing came over as a sad little play. Spoke to Sheila at the interval. She adored the play. "I liked the bits about loneliness," she said. "Loneliness in the theatre is usually so embarrassing." . . . The bell rang and we went back to the theatre for *Erpingham Camp*—the main part of the evening. It went extremely well. A great deal of enthusiasm from the audience. I was pleased that, within the limits and bearing in mind the difficulty, it went so well. I admired Peter's production. It had style. Too much enthusiasm afterwards though. I feared that when so many "pros" were raving in the dressing room after. "This should be transferred," someone said in a loud voice. "We must wait until tomorrow for the verdict," I said. "Oh fuck the critics," Peter Gill said. "They don't matter." This is bravado. Of course they matter. B. Gaskill seemed pleased and so did Oscar. Everybody

enthusiastic. Had a drink in the club of the Court. I left early as I wanted a bit of sex. Took two Valium tablets and waited for the no. 19 bus in Sloane Square. Got off at Piccadilly. Went to Holloway Road. Went to the Gents Lavatory. Nothing much in there. A man of about 30. Then another man came in in his twenties. He began to suck the first man off. The first man dropped his trousers and offered me his arse. I said it was too dangerous. This was immediately confirmed when three men came in and stood inside the doorway. The man doing the sucking left. I rather fancied him so I followed. "Who was that fellow?" he said in a little Irish accent. "I don't know," I said. "Have you got a place?" I said. "Yes, at Highbury," he said. He took me back to his furnished room. I took off my shirt. "You've a lovely body," he said, running his hands over, "and where did you get such a lovely tan?" "I went to Torremolinos." I chose this because it's quite a likely place for a working lad to go. The man dropped to his knees, undid my pants and pulled them down. I was going to get my cock out. Instead he nuzzled and sucked it through my underpants. After he'd done this for a bit I pulled him up and stuck my tongue down his throat and pulled him to the bed. He took his clothes off and I got on top of him. "Oh you've got a grand cock," he said stroking it. I realized how much of sex was missed in Morocco by not being able to talk the language. I lifted his legs in the air, spat on my hand, wiped my cock and got the end up his arse. "Oh no," he cried. "No, no!" I stopped and then realized that this was part of his personal kink. I gripped him hard. "I'm going to fuck you," I said, "keep quiet." I pinned him to the bed with his legs up in the air and shoved my cock right up him. He gave a cry, "Oh my God. Oh you're hurting me." I began to fuck him. It was a very good fuck. "Let me see," he said. "I want to see your cock going in and out." I had to lift myself up so that he could see my cock. He stroked my balls as I fucked him and I left my prick in after I'd come. "Oh I needed that," he said. "I needed a good fucking, you certainly know how to fuck." He then wanted me to lie on my belly. "Oh you've lovely muscles," he said stroking my back. "I'd love a threesome with you and some other chap," he said as a final shot. I got dressed after washing my cock and kissed him goodnight and went home. I had to walk all the way back. Outside a newsagent, I saw a placard announcing ISRAELIS KNOCKOUT ARABS. So I stole it. As a souvenir and a reminder that, whilst I was having a first night and fucking an Irishman (the second more satisfactory than the first) the third War would have been averted. Got in at 2 and slept until 7:30.

Wednesday June 7th

Went out at eight. Got all the papers. Read them. Not good reviews. All luke warm. Not a single review one could honestly say would do the box-office good. Rang Peggy. She'd read the *Times*, the *Financial Times* was very cool, *The Guardian* had reverted to its original position on *Sloane*. *The Mirror* hostile "Double bill that was almost a double bore." Oh well I did have a good fuck last night. I got something out of my return to London. Had an interview at 10 with a woman from the *Evening News*. A telephone chat with someone from the *Evening Standard* who had seen the plays at the dress rehearsal and liked them. . . . Went to the Court. Very downcast at the lack of enthusiasm for the plays. I had an interview for *Town and Around* in which they asked, rather aggressively I thought, "what the gimmick of having yourself drawn in the nude for the programme was." I said, "There are many people who might like a nude picture of me; I'm not unattractive you know." They said they wouldn't be using the interview today, perhaps sometime next week, which in polite terms I suppose means never. I was asked to be on "Late Night Line-Up" with John Mortimer. We had to watch and discuss *A Flea in Her Ear*, the National Theatre production which was televised earlier in the evening. I hated it as much as I had done on seeing it in the theatre. . . . It was directed and acted with great speed and no reality. I watched as I packed. . . . A taxi called at 9:20, took me to the studio at Shepherd's Bush. In a special viewing room the play was still going on. I watched and all the time I wondered how the second night of *Crimes of Passion* was going. Rang Peter. He said it was going v. well. Harold Pinter was in the front as well as all the weekly critics. Pinter, I'm sure, won't like the way *Erpingham* is directed or acted. He liked the much more naturalistic way it was done on telly. Said goodbye to Peter. Said I was sorry it hadn't been better received. He said that someone had said that Harold Hobson liked the evening—don't entirely believe this. He was supposed to have liked *Loot* but gave it a very small notice. No hope there I'm afraid. Did the "Late Night Line-Up." Expressed my views on *Flea* by saying that in Farce everything (the externals) must be believed. The actors were dressed as though they were period equivalent of Mick Jagger. Now it wouldn't be funny if Mick Jagger were caught in a brothel, but if Harold Wilson were caught in a brothel it would be extremely funny. . . . After the programme I was taken to the air terminal. . . . It was dawn by the time we took off. . . . Finally got in to Tangiers about tenish. Instead of a taxi I got the airport bus. . . . I sat next to a blond beatnik type. He said he'd seen me before. "Very likely," I said dryly, "there was a quarter page picture of me in the *Sunday Times* last week." "You're Joe Orton," he said. It's the first time I've been recognized. . . .   [June 7, 1967]

Back at play in Tangier, Orton brought critics and life into perspective with a saving laugh. "There have been a few 'incidents' of a political nature whilst I've been away," he wrote Peter Gill on June 10. "Yesterday I was out with some people, and in the street a boy made an ambiguous gesture in my direction. 'Was the boy spitting at me?' I asked. 'No,' someone said, 'he was blowing you a kiss.' So things are back to 'normal' here. (Notice the 'typical Orton use of the ironic word!!')."

"I'M AN ACQUIRED TASTE," Orton said in 1967. "That's a double en-tendre if there ever was one. The public will accept me. They've already given me a license, you see. What they'll do is say 'Joe Orton can do these things because he's a success.' But I'm a success because I've taken a hatchet to them and hacked my way in."[23] *The Ruffian on the Stair*, in retrospect a "sad little play" to Orton, was a flabby first jab at society. *Entertaining Mr. Sloane* was the corrosive successor to *The Ruffian on the Stair*, and Orton's first produced play. The acknowledgment of Orton's talent seemed to liberate it. *Entertaining Mr. Sloane* was a brazen fantasy of his new-found freedom. The play had a buoyant, self-confident control of language and structure that none of Orton's previous writing could muster. It stunned the British public and brought him immediate international attention.

Orton had finished the final BBC rewrites for *The Ruffian on the Stair* on November 30; on December 19, 1963, *Entertaining Mr. Sloane* was logged into the office of Margaret Ramsay. A former opera singer and actress, who had clowned in pantomime as well as sung at the Coliseum, Peggy Ramsay brought her special literary passions and eccentric energy to the English theatrical scene. Before becoming an agent, she had helped launch the Bristol Old Vic, as literary adviser and publicist; read plays for Peter Daubeny; and managed the Kew Theatre, choosing and casting fifty-two plays in a year. ("We gave most of the current leading directors of the British theatre their first chance. And they haven't improved, dear.") In 1959, with a loan of £1,000, she set up her own theatrical agency and her receptivity to new work soon earned her a reputation as imposing as her list of clients.[24]

Orton had been steered to Peggy Ramsay by his BBC producer, John Tydeman, who sent her a copy of *The Ruffian on the Stair*, touting the play as "fairly successful" and its author as a "genuinely interesting and original writer." Peggy Ramsay concurred. "What struck me about *Entertaining Mr. Sloane* was that it was luminous and spare, very spare and very sharp," she recalls. "What I didn't like about it was the con-venience of the end. I didn't like the shape of the play. I didn't think it was a great play, but I didn't hesitate when I read it. I read it in one night and the next morning, on December 30, I wrote Joe a letter. I was rather hard on him because he was talented. I said: 'I was very pleased to receive *Entertaining Mr. Sloane* which I think extremely fresh and interesting. I'm not absolutely sure it will hold a whole evening but I think it might.' I asked him to come and see me. I knew nothing about him when he walked in. He had considerable confidence and charm. He didn't mind me speaking about his play in rather harsh generalities—that's one of the reasons I liked him so much. He smiled and said, 'Yes, yes, I see.' And then he added, 'I'm glad you like my work. Next time I'll try and write you a better play.' And I said: 'Well, that would be gorgeous.' As he was getting up to go, I asked him what he lived on while he was writing. 'I'm living on National Assistance, £3.10 a week since I got out of jail.' I couldn't believe it. I took his address, and he left. I rang Michael Codron. 'I've just met a very promising writer, and he's living on £3.10 a week. Will you read his play immediately?' "

Michael Codron was then the artistic director of the New Arts Theatre. He was a serious and savvy impresario, who had been the first to produce Pinter (*The Birthday Party*, 1958), Henry Livings (*Nil Carborundum*, 1962), and David Rudkin (*'Afore Night Come*, 1962). "I told Michael if he took the Arts for a year, he'd make his reputation and lose his money," Peggy Ramsay recalls. Between 1962 and 1964, Codron certainly made his reputation, much of it by producing Ramsay's clients: Livings, Rudkin, James Saunders, Frank Marcus, Charles Wood, John Mortimer. "When I read *Sloane,* I felt it was unique stuff," Codron says. "I really did. Totally fresh. Having produced *The Birthday Party*, I never thought of Joe as Pinteresque. I had a theatre to run, or rather it was running me. I had to put on a new play every four weeks. I made a quick decision." The speed of the decision left even Peggy Ramsay incredulous. "I don't quite know how it came about but we have sold your play to go on at the Arts March/April," she wrote to Orton on January 20, 1964. "Michael Codron read it, loves it, Donald Albery says he will 'come in' with Michael and they will present it together. . . ."

"I have a strong hunch," Codron wrote to his investors about *Entertaining Mr. Sloane*, "that the new play I am doing (with Donald Albery) might turn out to have the most exciting commercial possibilities since *The Caretaker*." The play generated a kind of enthusiasm from management that dazzled the Ramsay agency. "It's very unusual for Managements to fall over themselves with eagerness to pay for an option on a play before the contract is signed," Peggy Ramsay wrote

Orton on February 5, herself investing £250 in the production unbeknownst to Orton. "But in this case it has happened. Wonders will never cease." And wonders continued. The next month, the producers doubled his advance to £100 (a sum that Orton never earned back in the Arts Theatre production, which was capitalized at £2,000).

"ONLY A SOCIETY in deep despair about itself," wrote *The Times* in a 1970 editorial, "would accept the hostility to meaning of some of the artists in the '60's."[25] By 1964 England was in a time of radical transition: from being top dog to becoming America's poodle; from a life built around the discipline of wartime scarcity to the ease of a new abundance; from thirteen years of Conservative rule to a Labour government. It was a time when the Lord Chamberlain still controlled the content of English theatre "to prevent public offence being given." It was the era of the discothèque and the twist, when the English were beginning to move to new rhythms and adopt new styles. "I saw no reason why childhood shouldn't last forever," Mary Quant told the press. "I wanted everyone to retain the grace of a child and not to have to become stilted, confined, ugly beings. So I created clothes that worked and moved and allowed people to run, to jump, to leap, to retain their precious freedom."[26] The Beatles, those "lads" who mixed Cardin chic with Liverpool cheek, epitomized the daydream of abundance and eternal youthfulness. Their success was as exciting as their songs. By late 1963, even if Britannia no longer ruled the waves, The Beatles dominated the airwaves. At the centre of the New Boy Network of renegade energy and "classless" attainment, their music and their popular saga gave British life the backbeat of promise.

Entertaining Mr. Sloane caught the abrasive and expansive mood of the time. "From what I remember [my family] was respected," Sloane tells Kath. "You know, H.P. [hire purchase] debts. Bridge. A little light gardening. The usual activities of a cultured community." Though spoiling for a fight, the original script pulled back from its deep-seated anarchic intentions. "The original ending," Orton said, "was quite different and much more complex, and it was wrong. Many writers I think compromise themselves with over-subtle endings—Tennessee Williams is an obvious example. The new ending to *Mr. Sloane* is very simple, but a natural outcome. This is how I always work: letting the situation emerge and develop gradually, without a preconceived plan— letting the characters take over."[27]

The first version of *Entertaining Mr. Sloane* ended abruptly with

Joe Orton, 1965: "I shall be the most perfectly developed of modern playwrights if nothing else."

Above: Orton's sister's wedding, 1964. George Barnett, Leonie Orton Barnett, Elsie Orton, and William Orton.

Left: William Orton in the old age home, 1970.

Top: Kenneth Halliwell with his parents, 1936.
Bottom left: Halliwell at age sixteen.
Bottom right: Orton's RADA "Dirk Bogarde" look, 1951.

Top: Orton, hands on knees, in cast
photo of *The Blue Bird*, 1949.

Bottom: Orton with chicken in Bats Players'
production of *And No Birds Sing*, 1950.

Commercial Studios, Ipswich

Top: Orton, right, as Lucio in
Measure for Measure, 1951.

Bottom: Orton as bellboy in *Born Yesterday*
at the Ipswich Repertory, 1953.

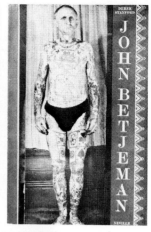

Above and opposite:
Book defacements for
which Orton was
sent to prison.

Right: Orton in the
bedsitter where he
and Halliwell lived
and wrote, 1966.

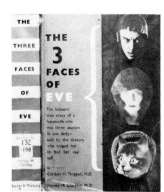

During the Second World War I was working from dawn to dusk to serve the many thousands of sailors, soldiers and airmen. American G.I.s came in shoals to my surgery and some had very peculiar orders for me. . . .

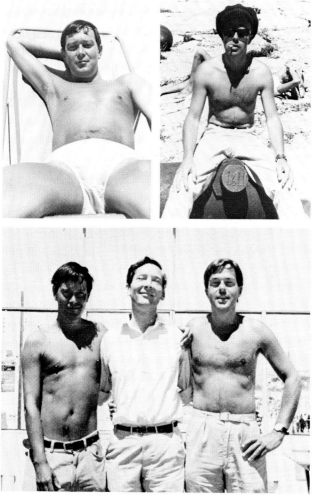

Top left: Orton in Morocco, 1967.

Top right: Halliwell in Tangier, 1967.
Orton sunbathes in background.

Bottom: Orton, Kenneth Williams,
and Halliwell in Morocco, 1965.

DRAWING OF JOE ORTON BY PATRICK PROCKTOR

Top: The first portrait of the
successful playwright, 1964.

Bottom: Drawing of Joe Orton by Patrick Procktor.

Opposite top: Beryl Reid as Kath and Malcolm McDowell as Sloane in the Royal Court revival of *Entertaining Mr. Sloane,* 1975.

Opposite bottom: "You should wear more clothes, Mr. Sloane. I believe you're as naked as me." Kath (Sheila Hancock) seduces Sloane (Dudley Sutton) in the Broadway production, 1965.

Above: Mrs. Vealfoy (Patricia Routledge) presents Buchanan (Donald Pleasence) with his retirement gift in the television production of *The Good and Faithful Servant,* 1967.

Above: Michael Bates as Truscott, right, sifts the evidence. Fay (Sheila Ballantine) and Hal (Kenneth Cranham) look on as McLeavy (Gerry Duggan) explains the funeral fiasco in *Loot*, 1966.

Opposite: Hal (Kenneth Cranham), the corpse of Mrs. McLeavy, and Dennis (Simon Ward) in the successful 1966 West End production of *Loot*.

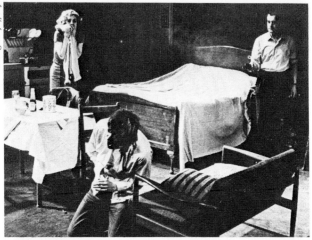

Top: The crime of passion. Mike
(Bernard Gallagher) shoots Wilson
(Michael Standing) as Joyce (Avril Elgar)
looks on in *The Ruffian on the Stair*, 1967.

Bottom: Holiday camp revels in the television
production of *The Erpingham Camp*, 1966.

Left: The defrocked priest McCorquodale (Bill Fraser) in the television production of *Funeral Games*, 1968.

Below: Winston Churchill's missing part is held aloft by Sergeant Match (Brian Glover) at the finale of Lindsay Anderson's Royal Court revival of *What the Butler Saw*, 1975. The phallus was cut from the original production.

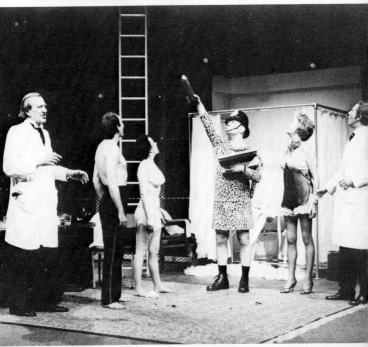

"Oh, this place is like a madhouse." Mrs. Prentice
(Betty Marsden) discovers Nick (Kevin Lloyd) in
Lindsay Anderson's revival of *What the Butler Saw*.

the murder of the father, a choice which didn't resolve the fascinating family relationships that revolve around him. The idea of sexual sharing was suggested to Orton by Peter Wood, who was supposed to direct *Entertaining Mr. Sloane* but was forced to withdraw because of other commitments. "Originally the play had more echoes of Pinter in it," explains Wood, who directed the first production of *The Birthday Party*. "The play started very well but Joe became naturally fascinated with the actual dialogue shapes and the structure became dislocated. The killing of the father at the end didn't seem to me to be what the play was about. The play seemed to me to be about the interaction between Sloane and the brother and sister. It wasn't ironic or amoral enough."

"I originally started with the Oedipus legend as a basis and threw it out half way through," Orton told the BBC in 1964. "It gave me the germ to start from. I got Eddie the brother and father relationship from *Oedipus at Colonus*—the old man won't speak to his son at all. There's no significance in the fact that I used the two Oedipuses at all, apart from the fact that it just gave me an idea and dramatists always need a plot. It doesn't really matter what you use as a plot on which to hang your dialogue and your ideas, but you must, I think, have a plot. . . ."[28] The original ending was a vestige from reworking the Oedipus legend; the new ending brought the play much closer to Orton himself. Sloane was polymorphous and definitely perverse. "I want a very young boy for Sloane," Orton later wrote about casting suggestions for TV. "Someone you'd like to fuck silly."[29] Sloane was lethal and charming, a combination of magical black leather meanness and boyish innocence—a sexy shadow of Orton's fantasy of himself. "I saw him as small and stocky," Orton said, describing Sloane in his own proportions. Orton dreamed of shattering taboos, and Sloane's shamelessness, which made taboos meaningless, was his revenge on society. "What many people have found difficult to understand about Sloane," Orton said, "is the combination of innocence and amorality. The English always tend to equate innocence with ignorance, which is nonsense."[30]

Sloane took his place among the theatrical rogues who characterized England in the sixties: Pinter's Mick (*The Caretaker*) and Lenny (*The Homecoming*); Osborne's Bill Maitland (*Inadmissible Evidence*); David Halliwell's Malcolm (*Little Malcolm and His Struggle Against the Eunuchs*). Sloane's nonchalant anarchy was a radical contrast to the shabby genteel setting that had been familiar on the British stage. He dramatized the psychopathic style that dominated the late sixties—that restless, ruthless, single-minded pursuit of satisfaction, transformed by drugs and rock music into myth. "There aren't any big, brave causes left," hectored John Osborne's Jimmy Porter in *Look Back in Anger* (1956). John Russell Taylor writes that in *Entertaining Mr. Sloane*, "Orton managed to write the first solid, well-managed commercial play which belonged, specifically and unmistakably, to the post-Osborne era."[31] Where Osborne's theatre and his characters by 1964 were stalemated by the impotent heroics of invective, Orton faced the loss of nerve in middle-class life and got beyond a sense of paralysis. Sloane's amorality was disillusionment in action. *Entertaining Mr. Sloane* made a myth of society's ugliness in order to expose it. Kath's house in *Entertaining Mr. Sloane* is in the middle of a rubbish dump. Everyone who enters it is tainted with a sense of waste. The characters live off the scraps of life and their conversation consists of vernacular throwaways. In a society without a heroic mission, surrounded literally by industrial rubbish, Sloane becomes his own most valuable project. He is a model of narcissistic noncommitment.

Orton wrote a revealing letter about Sloane to his American director, Alan Schneider:

> I don't know what you mean about the Eddie-Sloane relationship. Quite clear. Sloane knows Eddie wants him. He has absolutely no qualms about surrendering his body. None. He's done it many, many times. Sloane is no virgin. He's been in bed with men and women in the past. But he isn't going to give in until he has to. And while he can get away with . . . riding around in cars, just fucking Kath a couple of times a week, getting paid a good salary, why should he give up his trump card. Eddie, naturally, doesn't know how amoral Sloane is. He imagines that he has a virgin on his hands. He thinks he can get Sloane. Sure he can. But it may take a bit of time—cause Sloane is such a nice kid. Where's the problem? . . .

Orton described the plot: "It's about a young man, eighteen or nineteen, who wants a room and comes into this house. He's met the woman of the house in a public library. He comes to the house and she shows him around the house. Then within about eight pages, I suppose five minutes of being in the house, she attempts to seduce him. A bit later on, she actually has the trousers off him, and then her brother appears, and we see that her brother also would like to have the trousers off him. As the play goes on, one finds that Sloane has murdered a man in the past who was going to take pornographic pictures of him, it was just accidental. The man happened to be the boss of the woman's father, and the old man knows that Sloane murdered his boss. Sloane finally murders the old man, which gives the woman and her brother the opportunity of blackmailing Sloane into bed with them."[32] Orton's description emphasizes the characters' rapacious pragmatism.

"Sloane is dazed," observes Dudley Sutton, who originated the part. "This only comes out in the actual chemistry of performing the role." Sloane, as Orton says, "is the ambivalent figure"; but all the characters share some aspect of his numbed survival. The play's imagery refracted the sense of threat and cultural death of the revolts of the late sixties. The rubbish dump makes the visual point that death surrounds Kath's house. The spectre of the Dadda, the old man whom Orton conceived as "tottering at the edge of the grave," brings the threat of death inside the house. The characters fend off this death by not admitting it. "I'm going to die, Kath . . . I'm dying," says the Dadda (Kemp), panhandling for affection. Kath replies angrily: "You've been at that ham, haven't you? . . ." And so it goes, each character negotiating his own violent truce with reality.

Sloane adopts whatever identity suits the situation and serves his purpose. Uncommitted to anything but survival, he shifts his persona to keep his freedom intact. The similarities between Sloane and Joe Orton did not escape those around him. Patrick Dromgoole, who directed the original production of *Entertaining Mr. Sloane*, says: "Joe was a slippery bloke to talk to. A charmer. A manipulator. He could put on any face. To that extent he was very much like Sloane. He'd got the withdrawn, almost godly posture of the true ironist who genuinely finds most things funny. He wasn't really with you. He'd fit his statements about life to his assessment of your character. The first thing he told me when we started working together on the play was that he was living with a 'bird' and had to get back to her. He was very firm about it."

Orton himself could face up with disarming frankness to his tactics. Weighing the possibility of returning to London from Morocco for five days to see the last rehearsals and opening of *Crimes of Passion* in 1967, he confided to Peggy Ramsay, "That gives me plenty of time to see, and if possible, charm everyone."[33] Even Orton's jokes about himself hinted at his mercurial performance. "The other day I visited a small village about 50 miles from Tangier," he wrote to Peter Gill. "I went with a notorious one-eyed Welsh paederast. As we got out of the car, we were surrounded by boys. Several of them smiled at me and then spoke to the one-eyed paederast in French. 'What did they say?' I asked, when we were away from the boys. 'Oh,' he said, 'they wanted to know if you were English and did you do things!' I think that's my philosophy of life from now on: not to look English and not to look as though I do things."[34]

Sloane's innocent appearance disguises his predatory instincts. He molds himself into the expectations of others, transforming himself variously as son and lover to Kath; rude youngster and intruding lout to Kemp; and virginal, muscular Adonis to Eddie. He begins his changes as soon as he enters Kath's house. Sensing her need and the main chance, Sloane adapts with only a flicker of reluctance.

> KATH. Poor boy. Alone in the world. Like me.
> SLOANE. You're not alone.
> KATH. I am. (*Pause.*) Almost alone. (*Pause.*) If I'd been allowed to keep my boy I'd not be. (*Pause.*) You're almost the same age as he would be. You've got the same refinements.
> SLOANE (*slowly*). I need . . . understanding.
> KATH. You do, don't you? Here let me take your coat. (*Helps him off with his coat.*) You've got a delicate skin. (*Touches his neck. His cheek.*)
>
> *He shudders a little. Pause.*
>
> KATH. (*Kisses his cheek.*) Just a motherly kiss. A real mother's kiss. (*Silence. Lifts his arms and folds them about her.*) . . . You must treat me gently when I'm in one of my moods.

In Act 1, Orton emphasizes Sloane's role-playing by engineering the characters so Sloane is seen in bold relief with each of them. Sloane's initial passivity with Kath is replaced by tight-lipped aggression when he is left to chat with the feeble and squint-eyed Kemp. "Entertain Mr. Sloane now," Kath says to her father as she exits. "Give him the benefit of your experience. (*Pause.*) You want to learn manners. That's what you want." Sloane tests him, briefly trying on the posture of the courteous guest.

> SLOANE. . . . You don't resent my being in the house, do you?
> KEMP. Not at all.
> SLOANE. I thought you did. Just now.
> KEMP. No.
> SLOANE. This seems a nice place. Friendly atmosphere. . . .

Sloane's ironies ricochet off the old man, and this emboldens him. His put-ons become more blatant and malicious as his judgment of Kemp's stupidity increases. In his mockery there is a glimmering of his own genuine skepticism. He says of Kath's house: "A perfect skyline you've got here. Lord Snowdon would give you something for a shot of that. Stunning it is. Stunning. Was this house built as a speculation?" And in reaction to Kemp's admission of a twenty-year silence with his son, Eddie, after catching him "committing some kind of felony in the bedroom," having removed the lock from his door: "There are fascinating possibilities in this situation. I'd get it down on paper if I were you." Sloane's loathing of Kemp's Puritan oafishness bubbles up at the old man's mention of his boss's death. "Did he die for his country?" Sloane asks. And when the answer is an unsolved murder, Sloane's mockery goes over the top: "A murderer not brought to justice. That's a sobering thought." Sloane, gradually realizing that the old man hunched in front of the electric logs toasting his crumpet on a fork was a witness to his crime, starts to ask a few nervous questions. Kemp grabs hold of Sloane's arm and yanks him down to eye level. "I could still identify you," says Kemp, a death-dealer as well as a spectre of death. But the sudden crack in Sloane's well-guarded identity scares him. Sloane's tone gives way to gruff abuse: "Do lay-off, Pop. You couldn't identify a herring on a plate!" Sloane calls him a "superannuated old prat!", which earns him a jab in the leg with Kemp's toasting fork. Sloane then turns the incident into a melodramatic production that sends Kath scurrying into action with antiseptic spray and bandages, getting Sloane's pants quickly off him and the Dadda out of sight.

With Ed, Sloane adopts yet another course. Ed is visibly startled and pleased by Sloane's boyish good looks. His first words to Sloane pick up on the idea of Sloane's being an orphan while making it very clear where his own enthusiasms lie:

ED. . . . My sister was telling me about you being an orphan, Mr. Sloane.
SLOANE (*smiling*). Oh, yes?
ED. Must be a rotten life for a kid. You look well on it though.
SLOANE. Yes.
ED. I could never get used to sleeping in cubicles. Was it a mixed home?
SLOANE. Just boys.
ED. Ideal. . . . Well your childhood wasn't unhappy?

Ed presents himself as a hardworking businessman and a genial disciplinarian. ("I wouldn't want you to break your training," he tells Sloane. ". . . Drugs I abhor. You'll get to know all my habits.") He is already painting Sloane into his own "strict" military fantasy of domination when he asks: "You're interested in the army, eh? Soldiers, garrison towns, etc. Does that interest you?" Sloane understands Ed's kink and whets his appetite by repeating the word "orphanage" as he recounts his athletic ability:

> SLOANE. We had a nice little gym at the orphanage. Put me in all the teams they did. Relays . . .
>
> ED *looks interested.*
>
> . . . soccer . . .
>
> ED *nods.*
>
> . . . pole vault, . . . long distance . . .
>
> ED *opens his mouth.*
>
> . . . 100 yards, discus, putting the shot
>
> ED *rubs his hands together.*
>
> Yes, yes. I'm an all rounder. A great all rounder. In anything you care to mention. Even in life.

Puffing on cigarettes and stubbing them out as Sloane recounts his story, Ed is "burning" with excitement. Ed makes Sloane take an oath of allegiance to keep his hands off Kath but slyly angles it against the entire gender. "Women are like banks, boy, breaking and entering is a serious business. Give me your word you're not vaginalatrous." (Sloane, of course, gives his word without hesitation, although minutes after Ed's exit he will be rolling on top of Kath as the curtain comes down on Act 1.) Ed then promises security and Sloane plays the wide-eyed and grateful acolyte:

> ED. I might let you be my chauffeur.
>
> SLOANE. Would you?
>
> ED (*laughs*). We'll see . . . I could get you a uniform. Boots, pants, a guaranteed 100 per cent no imitation jacket . . . an . . . er . . . white brushed nylon T-shirt . . . with a little leather cap. (*Laughs.*) Like that?
>
> SLOANE *nods. Silence.*

Ed is decking out Sloane in the paraphernalia of sexual fantasy; Sloane, who can step into a new set of clothes as easily as a new identity, adjusts instantaneously. He has Ed firmly hooked. He will be Ed's "little matey," "the boy," in contrast to Kath's "baby." Ed and Kath even haggle about sharing these epithets for Sloane, verbal demarkations of their territorial rights to his body.

   ED [*to Sloane*]. That's a good boy.

   Pause.

KATH. Mr. Sloane.
SLOANE. What?
KATH. Can *I* call you Boy.
SLOANE. I don't think you'd better.
KATH. Why not?
ED. I'm his employer, see. He knows you're only his landlady.

   SLOANE *smiles*.

In the first round of sexual combat that ends Act 1, the victory belongs to Kath. From the moment she flounces into the living room proclaiming to Sloane, "This is my lounge," she swoops and flutters around him like a hawk disguised as a budgerigar. Like Ed, Kath is not subtle about disguising her needs. The joke on all the characters is that they think they're subtle. Kath's decorated vocabulary is as misguidedly elegant as the cheap bric-a-brac that clutters the room. "I married out of school," she confides to Sloane, obliquely describing her first pregnancy. "I surprised everyone by the suddenness of it." The pretension and precision of the line (Kath, of course, surprised no one) consolidated a special kind of cultural impoverishment in the new abundance of postwar English life. Kath's semi-literate badinage is peppered with the rhythms and phrases of the mass media. Her language aspires to refinement; but the plushness of her idiom, like her parlor, only betrays deeper emptiness. Sir Terence Rattigan, who provided England with some of its most popular theatre in the forties and fifties, heard in that line of Kath's the voice of the sixties: "What Orton had to say about England and society had never been said before. The first thing it showed was a society diminished by telly-technology. Everybody expresses themselves as if they were brought up on television."

With television, the public was capable of being touched by everything and moved by nothing; each newscast made the spectator an eyewitness to the pageant of human bestiality. Television inundated the community with superficial messages, undigested images, and a torrent of words. Orton's style was the first to embody this sensory overload, an eclectic brew of rhythms and idioms that captured and commented on the mutation of language.

The word Orton used to describe his distinctive literary style was "collage"—the same amalgam and juxtaposition of borrowed imagery he'd practiced for a decade with Halliwell on their walls. "It does have a collage quality," Orton told the BBC in 1964, speaking of *Entertaining Mr. Sloane*. "Shakespeare and the Elizabethans did the same thing. I mean you have absolute realism and then you get high poetry, it's just language. I think you should use the language of your age and every bit of it. They always go on about poetic drama and they think you have to sort of go off in some high-flown fantasy, but it isn't poetic drama, it's everything, it's the language in use at the time. I have to be very careful in the way that I write, not to let it become sort of a mannerism, it could very easily become a mannerism."[35] Orton's language assimilated the input of the popular culture. Advertising jargon (Kath: "You ought to see your oculist. See your oculist at once"). The stilted lusciousness of grade-B movies (Kath: "You have the air of lost wealth"). The boldface shorthand of tabloid journalism (Ed: "You're a source of amazement, a never ending tale of infamy").

Kath's language is funny, but there is panic and pathos in her craving. "All the characters are basically likeable and should be sympathetically portrayed," Orton said. "Much of the sympathy can be achieved through humour: the scene of Kath's seduction of Sloane is very funny and should also be very sexy. But sex doesn't just consist in undressing and wiggling as appropriate: sexiness can be just *there* without anyone moving a muscle. . . . Humour should make the sex more real. . . ." Kath's first attempt to establish a beachhead on Sloane's body comes after he's reclining, "wounded" and trouserless, on the sofa.

KATH (*confidentially*). I've been doing my washing today and I haven't a stitch on . . . except my shoes . . . I'm in the rude under this dress. I tell you because you're bound to have noticed. . . .

Orton made a spectacle of sexual appetite. Hunger and how people decoyed it amused him. "In Germany," he wrote to Alan Schneider, "Ed was the central pivot of the play. His stalking of the boy's arse was as funny and as wildly alarming as Kath's stalking of his cock. Unless this is so—you're in trouble."[36]

Orton wanted to shock the audience out of their lethargy, and "the only field still heavily unexplored is the sexual one."[37] *Entertaining Mr. Sloane* emerged six months after the Profumo scandal had reached its sad conclusion. "In the late spring of 1963," wrote Bernard Levin in his chronicle of Britain in the 1960s, *The Pendulum Years*, men and women all over Britain were telling, and others believing and embellishing and repeating, such stories as nine High Court judges had been engaging in sexual orgies, that a member of the Cabinet had served dinner at a private party while naked except for a mask, a small lace apron and a card round his neck reading "If my services don't please you, whip me," that another member of the Cabinet had been discovered by police beneath a bush in Richmond Park where he and a prostitute had been engaging in oral genital sex. . . .

In retrospect, the Profumo affair seems trivial. The overreaction of the British public was a barometer of the society's nervousness about the future of its ruling Establishment. Sexuality represented a threat to the old order. The Profumo case was one of the decade's watersheds. "If, in the Sixties the past was letting go of Britain, its grip was not to be prised loose without a struggle," wrote Levin. "And the Profumo affair can therefore be seen as the last struggle of the old, false standards (. . . some would say the old, true standards) before a new attitude emerged."[38]

Entertaining Mr. Sloane's mischievous wit was directed against the hypocrisy and intolerance of the well-bred and "right-thinking" middle class. Orton deflated the show of propriety in manners. Kath's "re-feened" gabble, like her actions, attempts to keep up appearances to hide her lust:

KATH. . . . Are you comfortable? Let me plump your cushion. (*Plumps a cushion behind his head. Laughs lightly.*) I really by rights should ask you to change places. This light is showing me up. (*Pause.*) I blame it on the manufacturers. They make garments so thin nowadays you'd think they intended to provoke rape. . . .

Ed, too, puts great store in his "principles." "One thing I wanted to give you—my principles," he tells Sloane in a moment of crisis. "Oh, I'm disillusioned. I feel I'm doing no good at all." Principles create the feeling of being good; they are man's boundaries, which prevent life from overwhelming him. The comic spirit is an enemy of boundaries. "What I wanted to do in *Sloane* was break down all the sexual compartments that people have," Orton said. "It didn't entirely succeed because it's very difficult to persuade directors and actors to do what you want. When *Sloane* was running for a while, it had got into compartments, so that Madge [Ryan] was the nympho, Peter [Vaughan] was the queer and Dudley [Sutton] was the psycho. Which wasn't what I intended at all, but people will put things into compartments. It's very bad in class, in sex, in everything." *Entertaining Mr. Sloane* had a carnival effect. The world and its values were turned topsy-turvy.

ACT 2 fleshes out Orton's fantasy of festival liberty. Kath is pregnant. ("Kath has to be pretty fat, brother," Orton wrote Schneider. "A belly you could loaf on. Six months gone. And none of this shit I got from Madge in London. This is the pregnant Mother-Goddess in her lair!") Ed is passionately pressing Sloane into his service. Sloane is enjoying the favors of both.

"In *Sloane*," Orton said in 1967, "I wrote a man who was interested in having sex with boys. I wanted him played as if he was the most ordinary man in the world, and not as if the moment you wanted sex with boys, you had to put on earrings and scent. This is very bad, and I hope that now that homosexuality is allowed, people aren't going to continue doing the conventional portraits there have been in the past. I think that the portrait of the queer in Peter Shaffer's *Black Comedy* is very funny, but it's an awfully conventional portrait. It's compart-mentalization again. Audiences love it, of course, because they're safe. But one shouldn't pander to audiences."[39]

In 1964, homosexuality was neither safe nor accepted. At the time of the Wolfenden Report of 1956, the maximum penalty for buggery was imprisonment for life. As late as 1963 there were still cases, like one between a twenty-two-year-old laborer and a twenty-four-year-old U.S. airman, both of whom were sentenced to three years' imprisonment for buggery and indecency, which bore out the contention that "throughout 1963 and 1964 homosexual offenders continued to be treated with considerable severity by the courts."[40]

On stage, the treatment of the homosexual was as violent and narrow-minded as the laws. In 1956, Terence Rattigan, explaining why he had transformed a homosexual incident into a heterosexual one as the basis for *Separate Tables,* said, "The Lord Chamberlain, our stage censor, bans any mention of that subject." By the early sixties the homo-sexual character had begun to appear sporadically on the British stage, dramatized primarily either as the limp-wristed queen, a toned-down maiden aunt of pantomime high camp (*Beyond the Fringe, Black Comedy,* Charles Dyer's *Staircase*), or the grave and often sentimental "problem" (Shelagh Delaney's *A Taste of Honey,* Christopher Hamp-ton's *When Did You Last See My Mother?*). The change in public attitude went "from ignorance and terror to familiarity and contempt," as E. M. Forster wrote in the afterword to his posthumously published novel about homosexuality, *Maurice.* "We had not realized that what the public really loathes in homosexuality is not the thing itself but having to think about it."

Orton's laughter disarmed an audience of its stereotypes while defying it to face sexuality's complicated and uncompromising demands. "Just as humour should make the sex more real, so too it should make Sloane's murder of Kemp more real," Orton said. "Put a murder on the stage with a straight face, and it's just a whodunit and nobody takes it seriously. Make it funny and you make people think about it."[41] The same was true of homosexuality.

In Eddie and Sloane, Orton aired the split in his own sexual nature—a struggle that the stage could resolve more elegantly than life. Act 2 raised the sexual stakes of the play as Eddie's fear of losing Sloane to women and the carefree life increased his demands on him. Orton always emphasized Eddie's sexuality as an act of rational choice. "Only a man who's had experience with women can dislike them. The adorers of women tend to be *impotent:* the priests of the mother goddess were always eunuchs. But Ed's hatred isn't violent or vitriolic, he's had the sense simply to see the obvious alternative."[42] Orton, who had no effeminate mannerisms, was quick to edit any signs of faggotry in the presentation of his characters. "I don't like the ring on Eddie's finger," he noted for Alan Schneider on September 14, 1965. "I don't think Eddie would wear a ring on his little finger. Queers have been doing that for years. Ed would know this and be self-consious enough not to wear one."

In *Entertaining Mr. Sloane,* Orton's emotional ambivalence was translated into a contest between man, boy, and woman—a crucial configuration in his own life. "Not a play about two women and a boy," Orton wrote to Schneider. "About a man, a woman, and a boy. Very, very important. Eddie is a great deal tougher than Sloane. Sloane is the ambiguous figure. Not Eddie." Sloane, after trying to manipulate Ed and Kath, ends up, in Orton's words, "the helpless victim of them both."[43] *Entertaining Mr. Sloane,* like *The Ruffian on the Stair,* acted out aspects of Orton's sexual dilemma and dummied up a destiny. Was he victim or survivor? The battle of possession by masculine and feminine forces is one of the themes worked out in his plays; in *What the Butler Saw,* confusion of genders would become the entire plot.

Entertaining Mr. Sloane is the most blatantly autobiographical of Orton's major plays. It is the unhappy son's daydream of the perfect family, in which he is never excluded and always needed. Kath and

Ed talk of Sloane as "boy," "kiddie," "baby," but they have no sexual connection to each other, only to him. Sloane not only had Orton's proportions, the same smooth skin, the same boyish look, but also his survivor's pragmatism. His sleek black leather outfit was Orton's style at the time. "It was almost as if he'd come to read the gas meter," remembers Peter Wood of his first meeting with Orton in 1964. "He was wearing boots, shapeless trousers, a little leather cap. His whole appearance was in total contrast to his reading and frame of reference. Quite fantastic. Totally intriguing."

Orton knew the impression he made; and he gave Sloane a charmer's confidence in his fatal fascination. Likewise, Kath is an amalgamation of many of Elsie Orton's mannerisms: the crooning of popular tunes, the obsessive neatness, the pining out loud for a lost lover, the domineering indifference to the frail, almost unnoticed man about the house. Kath's appreciation of her trashy bric-a-brac ("This shepherdess is a lovely piece of chinawork. She comes up like new when I give her a wash") was typical of his mother's pretensions about her trinkets. Her longing for the best in life, her panicky search for pleasure, were all part of the delusion and sadness Orton saw in his mother. "That's my mum!" Leonie Barnett said, laughing, as she watched Beryl Reid's brilliant interpretation of Kath in the 1975 Royal Court revival, wrapped in a fancy negligee to seduce Sloane. "That's her! It's like seeing a ghost. She was always overdressing. Once she got dressed in gold lamé and painted her shoes gold just to go to the pub. The paint cracked when she walked. There were gold flakes all the way to The City Arms." Even the plot of *Entertaining Mr. Sloane* was built around a family memory of Elsie Orton taking in a much-despised lodger. "His name was Jim," Leonie remembers. "We hated him. He was a lorry driver. Everything were done for Jim, know what I mean? I don't think Mum had an affair with him but she pandered to this lodger. The house had to be so clean. It was Dad that said he had to go."

In Act 2, it is the Dadda who wants the lodger out. Kemp breaks his vow of silence with his son to confide that Sloane has been hotrodding in Ed's car and has put his sister in the family way. He tells Ed that Sloane has been hitting him, a fact amusingly brushed aside by Ed when he confronts Sloane furiously with a list of his misdemeanors. Ed's lust is what stokes his disappointed rage. Orton conveys this nicely in the repetition of one word:

> ED. What a little whoreson you are you little whoreson. You are
> a little whoreson and make no mistake. I'm put out my boy.
> Choked. . . .

Ed can't understand why Sloane gave in to Kath. "I was worn out," Sloane lies. "I was overwrought. Nervous. On edge." Ed's rage has reached its crescendo, but Orton understands that anger is a heroic performance that must play itself out. Gradually, Ed slips from the role of wounded benefactor to tolerant savior. Ed's idealization of himself and the lecherous truth of his motive are neatly caught by Orton's double-entendres. Embellishing Sloane's hazy picture of his "confused" past, Ed suggests:

> ED. Never went to church? Correct me if I'm wrong.
> SLOANE. You got it, Ed. Know me better than I know myself.
> ED. Your youth pleads for leniency and, by God, I'm going to give it. You're pure as the Lamb. Purer.

Sloane coaxes Ed into forgiveness, playing into his priestly fantasy by acting the penitent. "Speak a few words of forgiveness," Sloane says. "Pity me." But it's Sloane who knows the right words to speak. He calls Ed "pal," "one of my mates" ("Am I?" Ed says, thrilled at the sound of the words. "How refreshing to hear you say it"). Ed launches into a familiar riff. "But do me a favour—avoid the birds in the future. That's what's been your trouble." Then he offers an impassioned piece of advice:

> ED. Why conform to the standards of the cowshed? (*Pause.*) It's a thing you grow out of. With me behind you, boy, you'll grow out of it.

The joke was on the censors as well as Ed. "The funny thing about the Lord Chamberlain," Orton said, "was that he cut all the heterosexual bits and kept in all the homosexual bits."[44] The Lord Chamberlain disallowed Sloane's pinching of Kath's breasts and warned that any simulation of intercourse when she rolled on top of him at the end of Act 1 would be interpreted as obscene. ("Must be a quick curtain to Act 1," Orton wrote to Schneider in a preview note. "Actually the Lord Chamberlain said there must be no attempt to simulate copulation. We'd be half way to the kid's conception at the speed of last night's curtain.") Homosexual passion could not be so explicit; and the play benefited from the necessity to be oblique.

Just after Sloane and Ed have firmed up their new alliance, Sloane tries to smooth things over with Kemp in what Orton called Sloane's "Messenger Speech." It is Sloane's only explanatory outburst. The speech establishes his sexual ambivalence moments before he is forced to take sexual sides:

SLOANE. . . . It's like this see. One day I leave the Home. . . . They'd
found me a likeable permanent situation. Canteen facilities.
Fortnight's paid holiday. Overtime? Time and a half after midnight. A staff dance each year. What more could one wish to
devote one's life to? I certainly loved that place. The air round
Twickenham was like wine. . . . I thumbs a lift from a geyser
who promises me a bed. . . . All you could wish he was, a photographer. He shows me one or two experimental studies. An experience for the retina and no mistake. He wanted to photo me.
For certain interesting features I had that he wanted the exclusive
right of preserving. You know how it is. I didn't like to refuse. . . .
But then I got to thinking. . . . And I gets up in the middle of the
night looking for the film see. . . . Well it appears that he gets
the wrong idea. Runs in. Gives a shout. And the long and the
short of it is I loses my head which is a thing I never ought to a
done with the worry of them photos an all. And I hits him.
I hits him. . . .

Kemp isn't assuaged by Sloane's story; he threatens to tell the police.
The terror and fury Sloane has described suddenly explode when he
again feels himself cornered. He knocks Kemp behind the sofa and
kicks him relentlessly. Orton relished the Grand Guignol horror of the
scene, letting Kemp's head bob above the sofa as he struggles to his
feet, then watching it sink slowly down behind the sofa again as he
collapses. Sloane prods Kemp with his boot. "Wakey, wakey," he says.
"Sloane doesn't immediately know what has happened," Orton reminded Schneider in a production note. "It takes him a second or two
to realize that the Old Man is ill. Let's see the change from anger during
the beating up to sheer panic. I'm not getting the thought between the
lines. He must think what has happened. And then the sheer panic of
the end of the act is clear and right. If Sloane doesn't think, it's messy."
Orton rewrote the scene's final image to emphasize Sloane's decision
about his sexuality being made for him by force of circumstance (as it
was for Orton with Halliwell). "Sloane goes to the door," Orton explained to Michael Codron in a letter accompanying his rewrite. "Calls
for Ed, Kath tries to push her way into the room, Sloane says 'Not you,'
she asks what's happened, and Sloane says, 'Where's Ed? I want Ed!'
Curtain. A good situation—Sloane rejecting her, calling for Ed when
he's in trouble, foreshadowing the end of the play. A good stage picture—the old man lying on the ground, Sloane trying to keep Kath
from entering the room."[45]
The moment is the play's turning point, illuminating the irony of

the title. Sloane, once entertained by Kath and Ed, will find himself their entertainment. Orton defended the Act 2 ending despite persuasive lobbying for change. "Take an old hack's advice," Sir Terence Rattigan told him. "Bring your second act curtain down when Kath says 'Dadda's dead' in the third act, instead of leaving the audience frozen by bringing the curtain down with the Dadda apparently being kicked to death. You'll find them going out to their gins and tonics in a much happier frame of mind." But Orton wouldn't listen to him. "I'm prepared to tell you that he'd probably have added three months to the run if he'd done it," says Rattigan.

"LET MR. SLOANE regain his composure, Ed," Kath says, at the beginning of Act 3, carpet-sweeping her living room and eager to brush away the memory of family friction. The Dadda lies dead upstairs. The men know it; Kath, for the moment, does not. "Sleeping off the excitement, is he?" she says. Kath is obsessed with sustaining a sense of order on the surface of life. She inflates every situation with her fantasy of perfection. "I cooked a lovely egg yesterday," she twitters to Sloane. A life-and-death struggle is going on in Kath's living room, yet she seems anesthetized to it. Orton dramatizes how much language contributes to her insensitivity. "Did he insult you?" she asks Sloane about the Dadda. "Was it a bad word? *(Pause.)* I don't expect you can tell me what it was. I'd blush." By censoring language, Kath can make life "safe."

> KATH. . . . How could you behave so bad. Accusing me of seducing you.
> SLOANE. But you did!
> KATH. That's neither here nor there. Using expressions like that. Making yourself cheap. . . .

Even when Kath discovers the Dadda's death, she can rationalize Sloane's violence. "The Dadda was rude. He said a rude word about me." And then in her profound superficiality, Kath worries about her appearance at the Dadda's funeral—"I shall never get in my black. I've put on weight since we buried mamma."

Sloane, however, is no longer willing to play up to the other characters' fantasies about him. His panic makes him talk straight for the first time: nor will he allow the others their illusions. Ed is the first to feel the jolt of Sloane's matter-of-factness. Sloane suggests that they fake the evidence and tell the police that the Dadda fell downstairs.

ED. . . . Now you ask me to help you evade Justice. Is that where
my liberal principles have brought me?

SLOANE. You have no principles.

ED. No principles? Oh, you really have upset me now. Why am I
interested in your welfare? Why did I give you a job? Why do
thinking men everywhere show young boys the strait and narrow? Flash cheque-books when delinquency is mentioned? Support the Scout-movement. Principles, boy, bleeding principles.
And don't you dare say otherwise or you'll land in serious
trouble.

Ed's rhetoric, like Kath's clichés, becomes a verbal cocoon that protects
him from accurately perceiving himself. Sloane cuts right through the
pretense.

ED. . . . You must accept responsibility for your actions.

SLOANE (*sits beside* ED. *Lays hand on his knee*). I accept responsibility.

ED. Do you?

SLOANE. Fully.

ED. Good. Remove that hand, will you?

Now Sloane asserts himself. He has made his decision and declared
his allegiance. He is equally abrupt and frank with Kath when Ed forces
a showdown. Sloane is packing his bag, Kath confused and protective.
She has agreed to lie to the police about Dadda's death, telling herself
that Sloane "did it out of love for me." She won't be disabused of her
dignity by Ed's brutal catalogue of her limitations. But she cannot
comprehend why Sloane would want to leave.

KATH. What are you going to give him?

ED. The world.

KATH (*comes round the case, looks in*). The state of this case. Mr.
Sloane, dear, you can't even pack. See how he needs me in the
smallest things? . . .

"Must pause after Ed's 'the world,' " Orton advised. "Kath has no
reply to what Ed has said, she doesn't understand what he means, so,
like any woman, she changes the subject rapidly to something else.
Must see that for a fraction of a second she's baffled."[46]

Orton contrives a double-barrelled demolition of Kath's fantasy. Ed
parades her in front of a mirror and asks her to look at herself. "What
have you to offer?" he asks. "You're fat and the crows-feet under your

eyes would make you an object of terror. Pack it in, I tell you. Sawdust up to the navel? You've nothing to lure a man." Kath is devastated. "Is that the truth?" she asks Sloane weakly. "More or less," he says. Ed tops the vicious spectacle of Kath's humiliation with one final rhetorical flourish: "You showed him the gate of Hell every night. He abandoned Hope when he entered there."

But Kath's revenge on Ed and Sloane is as delightful as it is cunning. She invokes morality. "I won't practise a falsehood," she says, refusing to support their alibi. When the air has cleared, Kath spells out her demands:

KATH. I was never subtle, Mr. Sloane . . . If you go with Eddie, I'll tell the police.
SLOANE. If I stay here he'll do the same.
ED. It's what is called a dilemma, boy. You are on the horns of it.

Silence.

There's a hint of triumph as Kath says, "You see how things are, Mr. Sloane?" Stalemated, Sloane lashes out. He slaps her. Orton plays off the righteousness in their language against the violence of their actions. Sloane starts to throttle Kath, with Ed mischievously incanting the kind of reactionary protest to Sloane's actions that Orton knew his audience would have to the play:

ED. Let her alone, boy.
SLOANE. Keep out of this! (ED *lays a hand on* SLOANE's *shoulder, tries to pull him away from* KATH. SLOANE *turns, shoves* ED *from him.*) Did you hear what I said? Keep out of it!
ED. Don't be violent. No violence at any cost. (SLOANE *gets* KATH *into a corner; struggles with her.*) What's this exhibition for? This is gratuitous violence. Give over, both of you!

The scene erupts, momentarily, into farce. By the end of the tussle, at the play's tensest moment, Kath is on her hands and knees groping for the false teeth Sloane has belted out of her mouth. But the hilarity never loses the serious purpose behind it. "I'll still forgive and forget," says Kath, gumming the words as she searches for her dentures. Each character is a past master at forgetting. In farce, the momentum of events has its own amnesiac quality, characters forgetting who and where they are as they scramble to set things right. Sloane helps Kath off the floor at her request. "See, Ed," she says, "he hasn't lost respect for me."

Orton's finale takes the English art of compromise to its logical conclusion. Kath and Ed will share Sloane six months of the year, with certain exceptions—like the birth of Kath's baby—to be mutually agreed upon. "It's all any reasonable child can expect," says Ed, the voice of conciliation, "if the dad is present at the conception." Orton spoofs the romantic conventions of the "happy ending" with his own more realistic version:

> SLOANE. Is it going to be O.K.?
> ED. Well . . . perhaps.
> SLOANE. I'll be grateful.
> ED. Will you?
> SLOANE. Eternally.
> ED. Not eternally, boy. Just a few years.

"Well, it's been a pleasant morning," Ed says, concluding the arrangement. He exits with the play's last line. The Dadda's death, Kath's battering, the rapacious stalking of Sloane, and his bondage are all forgotten; the past is obliterated by pleasantries. Evil, to Orton, was indifference to suffering, a moral stupor that extended to the corrupting power of language. *"Entertaining Mr. Sloane,"* Orton said, "is comedy in so far as the whole world and the whole human situation are comic and farcical."[47]

He had learned to make an audience laugh to make it listen.

ORTON GAVE Patrick Dromgoole an autographed copy of the published version of *Entertaining Mr. Sloane,* inscribed with one of Kath's lines: "I got over it though. You do, don't you." Orton had never liked Dromgoole's direction or his style. The word "Dromgoole" became an adjective of derision in his vocabulary. "Lots of bearded 'Dromgoole' types in the audience,"[48] he wrote to Peggy Ramsay, characterizing the middle-class audience at the Royal Court's notorious production of Edward Bond's *Saved,* which he thought a "remarkably cissy play." "Dromgoole" evoked for him the hearty, liberal bourgeois synonymous with the name of his first director. But during rehearsals at the New Arts before the premiere of *Sloane,* Orton was a model of tact. He sat quietly and intently behind Dromgoole in the eighth row, making notes and adjusting his rewrites. He carried his papers in the same gas-mask case Halliwell had used to smuggle books, and was dressed so casually that, in the first week, some of the stagehands mistook him for crew. The National Assistance boots, high-cuffed blue jeans, white T-shirt, and leather jacket became a part of his personality.

Halliwell often attended rehearsals with Orton, sporting his beret, which he never removed. Once, early in the rehearsal period, Orton invoked Halliwell's opinion in an argument with Dromgoole, and the director got furious. "It got such an explosive reaction from me that he stopped," Dromgoole remembers. "I said, 'I don't give a fuck who you talked with about it, least of all this goddam refugee from a second-hand clothes shop.' Halliwell was not allowed direct interference, but he'd try." The situation was smoothed over but not forgotten. "In doing *Entertaining Mr. Sloane*," Dromgoole says, "I had the usual blind certainty how to make it work. Inevitably with Orton as with others, this sets up conflicts. I don't think that they would have become in any way serious except for that little prick Halliwell. Things ended up extremely uncomfortable."

Entertaining Mr. Sloane was dedicated to Halliwell; and in the presence of the director and the cast, Halliwell (as well as Orton) referred to *Entertaining Mr. Sloane* as "our play." Halliwell's words thrust him into the centre of the enterprise, but in the theatre he was kept on the periphery. The stagehands dubbed him "Mrs. Orton." If he had no say in the production, Halliwell could make his own scenes. "He behaved very badly in the theatre," Dromgoole says. "I'd say to Joe, 'I want you to watch this scene,' and Halliwell would say, 'Oh dear, I suppose it's going to take another half hour.'" Dudley Sutton remembers Halliwell "always in a terrific state of agitation and jealousy. At the Arts, the management wanted us to take a cut in wages. We had a company meeting. Halliwell was storming around outside wanting to know why he hadn't been asked to it." Halliwell's insecurity and arrogance increased after the play's success. On the opening night of its West End run at the Wyndham's Theatre, Dromgoole was with Robin Maugham and Sir Terence Rattigan as they tried to chat with Halliwell. "Where do you go when you go out with Joe?" Rattigan asked politely. Halliwell answered: "I don't go out with Joe Orton. I go in."

"My main effort with Joe was trying to bring him down to something naturalistic," explains Dromgoole. "I recognized instantly that the value of Joe's comedy was that it went too far all the time. I didn't want to corrode that. But, for the sake of the audience, you need a feed for the comic, some safe place from which it can adventure. My influence on Joe was to bring him back from the fantastically exaggerated towards the reassuring. I directed each act as a different play because the play seemed to me to be written in three different styles. The first act is naturalistic. The second goes into high comedy. And the third finished virtually as farce."

While Dromgoole worried about how to present the play, Orton

fussed about how to present Orton. A small biography was required for
the Arts program, and Orton drafted two versions. The first, written on
April 15, was sixteen lines of fact and flim-flam. In it, Orton maintained
that he'd been "married and divorced," and listed among his odd jobs
"helping in the making of sex hormones." The posture of the joker
prevailed. "I was in prison for six months in 1962 for larceny (not
really as grand as it seems)." Orton, at least, gave his correct age: thirty-
one. The second version, the one printed in the program, was edited
down to eight lines of straightforward prose that only once hit a sardonic
note: "He has had various jobs and long periods of idleness." As a
second thought, Orton reduced his age to twenty-five, making him seem
even more promising.

ORTON'S FIRST PLAY—the cut-out letters were pasted together by Orton
in early May on the inside of his scrapbook like a headline. Within a
week, he would be glueing genuine headlines with his name in boldface
and his picture featured in quarter-page spreads: MR. ORTON ARRIVES
(*The People*); THEATRE'S NEW STAR SIGNS ON THE DOLE (*The Herald*).
Beneath Orton's collage of his name was pasted the stub of his fourth-
row opening-night seat for May 6, 1964 (E-10), and a copy of the
program. On the back of the program Orton taped the tepid *Evening
News* review ("Murder with a Flippant Touch") over a North Thames
Gas advertisement, leaving the first two lines of the ad visible as a playful epigraph to the critical waffle below it about Sloane's personality:
"Diplomacy, darling . . . that's all it was . . . I just let him. . . ."
Orton's scrapbook exudes a sense of fun and naïve delight at his sudden
celebrity. He enjoyed the hostility as much as the praise, bad reviews
featuring as prominently as raves. The most vitriolic attack on *Entertaining Mr. Sloane* came predictably from the conservative *Daily
Telegraph*. "Not for a long time have I disliked a play so much as I
disliked Joe Orton's *Entertaining Mr. Sloane*," W. A. Darlington
began his review, adding, "I feel as if snakes had been writhing round
my feet."[49] To Orton, this was sweet comic revenge, and he let Edna
Welthorpe fan the flames in the *Daily Telegraph*'s Letters to the
Editor column:

> As a playgoer of forty years may I sincerely agree with Peter Pinell
> [someone who had written a negative letter to the editor] in his
> condemnation of *Entertaining Mr. Sloane*.
>   I myself was nauseated by this endless parade of mental and

physical perversion. And to be told that such a disgusting piece of filth now passes for humour.

Today's young playwrights take it upon themselves to flaunt their contempt for ordinary decent people. I hope that the ordinary decent people will shortly strike *back!*

A few weeks later, Orton was in the *Telegraph*'s Letters column again, this time praising his play under the pseudonym of Donald H. Hartley:

I saw *Entertaining Mr. Sloane* twice at the New Arts. I shall see it again at the Wyndham's.

God knows the theatre is dreary enough at the present time. Any oasis in the wasteland is welcome. And *Entertaining Mr. Sloane* is not a mirage which disappears when the thirsty traveller approaches. The water is there, the exotic landscape is real. And if we find the customs of the country differ from our own—what else is foreign travel for?

There were other voices of disapproval and praise. The *Financial Times* bemoaned "a woeful lack of sophistication either in the way people act or in the way plays are constructed." The *Daily Mail* found the play "as mild and as tedious as soap flakes." Sean O'Casey wrote: "A play to make a man pull his trousers up." But the grumbling didn't muffle the chorus of excited discovery. "All good comes to him who stands and waits," wrote John Mortimer in the *Evening Standard.* "And after what now seems a long time waiting round the moth-eaten wings of the commercial theatre something really quite good has come to me at last." Alan Brien was even more outspoken in the *Sunday Telegraph:* "Mr. Orton is one of those rare dramatists who create their own world and their own idiom." Orton was described variously as "the Douanier Rousseau of the criminal suburbs" and "the Grandma Moses of the rubbish dump"; his play was "an unearthly marriage of Frank Norman and Muriel Spark" (*Evening Standard*) with "flashes of wit which at their best can match Oscar Wilde" (*The Observer*). But it was Harold Hobson's notice in *The Sunday Times* that took pride of place in his scrapbook:

I hope I shall not be misunderstood if I say that the English author of whom Joe Orton in *Entertaining Mr. Sloane* reminds me most vividly is Jane Austen. Miss Austen had a keen eye for the absurdities of the fashionable fiction of her day; and so has Mr.

Orton. His *Entertaining Mr. Sloane,* all proportions kept, is the *Northanger Abbey* of our contemporary stage. . . .

   Entertaining Mr. Sloane begins as a joke about moral horror; and as such a joke should it goes on to develop a horror of its own. It becomes a British counterpart of *Who's Afraid of Virginia Woolf?* and its third act does not succumb to the sentimentality that spoils Mr. Albee's play. It is a vision of total evil and it is possible to perceive its merits without approving it. It might be a coterie's success: a *Wrong Box,* a *South Wind,* a Beauvoir-Wences. I should not call it promising. It seems more like an end than a beginning.

"Hobson was the only critic who spotted what Sloane was," Orton told the critic Glenn Loney, an American friend. "This was absolutely amazing. I wrote him a letter saying that I've always admired Jane Austen's juvenilia which she rewrote later in her life. . . ."[50] When Loney sent Orton an article about his play, Orton replied: "You sound . . . as if you aren't at all convinced that the *Golden Bough* and *Northanger Abbey* could furnish me with inspiration. I assure you that it is possible to draw poisoned water from the clearest of wells."[51]

It was not the controversial claims of the author or the press but the unlikely enthusiasm of Sir Terence Rattigan that grabbed headlines for Orton and ensured the life of his play. Rattigan's first play, *First Episode,* had been produced when he was twenty-two; by the age of twenty-five he was earning £25,000 a year in royalties. *French Without Tears* (1936) and *While the Sun Shines* (1943) each ran on the West End for more than 1,000 performances. As the author of *O Mistress Mine* (1944), *The Winslow Boy* (1946), *The Deep Blue Sea* (1952), *Separate Tables* (1955) the name Rattigan became synonymous with the well-made play. It was Orton's technical maturity—the extraordinary assurance in his manipulation of characters, his powers of dramatic organization—that impressed Rattigan. "I wouldn't have liked *Sloane* if I hadn't seen its classic construction," Rattigan says. "I saw the classical roots. The critics did not. They saw it as part of a movement. But Orton understood that a play, if it's any good, has to have its basis in structure. What was going to happen to Mr. Sloane? It's no more than telling a story. And there's no theatre without story and never has been."

Rattigan escorted Vivien Leigh, a frequent star in his plays, to see Orton's in the first week of its run. "I fell wildly in love with *Entertaining Mr. Sloane,*" Rattigan says. "Vivien saw it as a funny, rather camp play. I went much further than that. I saw style—a style, well, that could be compared with the Restoration comedies. I saw Congreve in it. I saw Wilde. To me, in some ways, it was better than Wilde because it had more bite. I was delighted by Orton's feeling for words.

Albee and Coward have a certain kind of verbal felicity that usually isn't meant to express character. They are still in a naturalistic tradition of dialogue. Joe had something richer. Orton was way beyond a naturalistic tradition and yet you could read it as if it were perfectly naturalistic. Vivien said to me, 'If you feel so strongly about the play, you ought to write to the author.' I said all right if she'd write to Madge Ryan, whose performance she'd loved."

Orton was delighted with his first fan letter:

14th May 1964

Dear Joe Orton,

I don't think you've written a masterpiece—and you wouldn't want me to say that you had—but I do think you have written the most exciting and stimulating first play (is it?) that I've seen in thirty (odd) years' playgoing.

I think you *will* write a masterpiece before the decade is out—provided, always, that you don't try to. But your gift of dialogue is such that whatever you write will henceforth provide pleasure, not only to me, but to many hundreds of thousands of others.

Sincerest congratulations,

Terence Rattigan

P.S. But of course you will write that masterpiece.
P.P.S. And *this* one should give you a great success in the West End—whither, I trust, it is bound.

Rattigan spoke to Donald Albery about his enthusiasm for the play, but Albery had not yet decided whether to bring it into the West End. Notices were mixed, and although box-office receipts had risen from £250 for the first week to £439 for the third and last week at the Arts Theatre, the show had lost money. Then Rattigan himself ensured *Entertaining Mr. Sloane*'s destination by investing £3,000 in a West End transfer. "I told Donald I'd go half and half with him," Rattigan recalls. "I said: 'I don't think we're going to make any money out of this, but this talent has to be nurtured. Quite nice notices. Four weeks. Then, that's it. There are so many plays like it. *Sloane* mustn't die at the Arts.'" Although he appreciated Rattigan's generosity, Orton was embarrassed by it—the first of many writers' enthusiasms for his work that he couldn't repay with mutual admiration:

It never fails to amaze me how kind and generous people like Bill Naughton and Lord Willis are to me. I wouldn't have supposed it, judging from the things they write, that I'd appeal to them. I've never liked anything either of them have written. It's like Rattigan's eulogies: I can't return them with any degree of conviction. I'd like to think I'd be as nice to somebody if I admired their writing. But who could it be? "God," Kenneth Halliwell says.

[March 14, 1967]

"Orton thought it very funny that I, of all people, should have thought his play so good," Rattigan says with a smile, remembering their first meeting at the swank Ivy Restaurant, where Orton arrived in black leather without the required tie and ended being photographed with Rattigan's borrowed orange and yellow MCC tie draped around his neck. "To my alarm," says Rattigan, "they plastered outside the Wyndham's Theatre that passage from my letter. People who came to see my plays were not likely to go and enjoy Joe's. In a way, I wasn't Orton's best sponsor. I'm a very unfashionable figure still, and I was then wildly unfashionable critically. My sponsorship rather put critics off, I think. They're not very quick at seeing something good straight off. It takes two or three plays before they realize. With Orton, it took perhaps a bit longer. When he died, they'd cottoned on to the fact that they'd lost possibly their best."

On June 29, Orton became a West End playwright. His jubilation is recorded in the scrapbook, which suddenly explodes into a two-page collage to record the event. Surrounding the colorful letters that spell out MR. SLOANE (inside the "o" is pasted "even the men will blush") was a series of fantastic headlines dominated by NEVER SO MUCH! SO QUICK! IN ITS 46TH CONSECUTIVE YEAR. ALONE IN ITS GREATNESS. FIRST WEEK GROSS $128,450! IT HAD TO HAPPEN. Orton composed his own marquee, studding the page with adjectives—"gorgeous," "exciting," "sensational," "wow," "London's most gayest," "KING SIZE horrors!", "kinky boots." The only review interspersed between Orton's fantasy of triumph and the announcement of the transfer was W. A. Darlington's second try at coming to terms with the play. Under the headline:

3 REPULSIVE
FOLK WELL
ACTED

Darlington, while still finding the characters "shameless and repulsive in the extreme," added, "I have to pay the author's skill the compliment of admitting that I sat through it last night a second time on its transference to Wyndham's and was held throughout."

Orton's glee spilled over to other pages. The Wyndham's program is framed by a series of cut-out comments: "Audience reaction horrible—it laughed"; "I'm broadminded—but this time you've gone too far"; "This is a disturbing and terrible thing." Three days after its opening on the West End, the scrapbook had more to boast. *Entertaining Mr. Sloane* tied with Bill Naughton's *Alfie* in *Variety*'s London Critics' Poll for the best new British play; and Orton came two votes behind Charles Wood (*Cockade*) for the most promising playwright of the year. All the news was good. After a decade of dreaming of breaking into print, Orton found the text of *Entertaining Mr. Sloane* was to be published three times: as a book, as part of Penguin's New English Dramatists anthology series, and as the August play of the month in *Plays and Players*. Orton, who had been surviving on £3 a week until his first royalty check, found his weekly earnings to be as much as £239. The play was sold to Paris in August, and the next year to Spain, the United States, Israel, and Australia. It would also be made into a film and a television play. Orton had arrived in the style of his comedy—with a vengeance.

The fact that Orton mixed ideas and entertainment confused some critics, who labored under the false and infuriating notion that art and commerce are necessarily antagonistic. Orton came up against this bias in the first extended piece of criticism about *Entertaining Mr. Sloane,* written by John Russell Taylor in his grudging introduction to the play in Penguin's *New Dramatists 8*: "Living theatre needs the good commercial dramatist as much as the original artist." Orton was furious at such critical stupidity. "Are they different, then?" he wrote Peggy Ramsay, quoting Taylor's distinction between commercial success and art, and asking to withdraw the play from the volume.

> *Hamlet* was written by a commercial dramatist. So was *Volpone* and *The School for Scandal* and *The Importance of Being Earnest* and *The Cherry Orchard* and *Our Betters*. Two ex-commercial successes of the last thirty years are about to be revived by our noncommercial theatre: *A Cuckoo in the Nest* and *Hay Fever*. *Thark* is also mooted. I've no ambition to bolster up the commercial theatre, but if my plays go on the West End I don't expect this to be used as a sneer by people who judge artistic success by commercial failure. There is no intrinsic merit in a flop. . . .[52]

"There are good plays and bad plays," Orton said again. "With *Sloane*—people were always saying 'Oh it's just a commercial play.' It infuriated me because it wasn't; there isn't such a thing. It was a good play or a bad play."[53] Almost as soon as *Entertaining Mr. Sloane* settled into its West End run, there were people eager to proclaim it a bad play. The public outcry was precipitated by Peter Cadbury, the chairman of Keith Prowse Ltd., London's largest ticket bureau, who, while announcing to his stockholders a £98,000 increase in ticket sales over 1963, took the opportunity to blast plays that were "unsuitable and unacceptable to a large part of the public" and that "reflect the lowest forms of human life. . . ." In an editorial entitled "Killing the Goose," on August 22, *The Times* praised Mr. Cadbury for "rushing in where others who think as he does fear to tread," but disagreed with Cadbury's suggestion of stricter control over theatrical content. "That," *The Times* said, "would be worse than the disease he purports to have diagnosed."

The ads took advantage of the furore. "The persecution and assassination of *Entertaining Mr. Sloane* is still taking place. . . . WARNING: This play is not suitable for the narrow minded." Orton relished the scandal which proved the comic truth of his play: that the culture hid its violence behind a show of propriety. The scrapbook is filled with cuttings from the outspoken and the outraged. Above them are bannered: AUNT EDNA ROCKS WEST END, FILTHY TRADITIONS, VIOLENT ART. West End impresario Emile Littler joined forces with Cadbury to denounce *Entertaining Mr. Sloane* as "absolutely filthy," and went still further by condemning the Royal Shakespeare Company's brilliant season of *Marat/Sade, Endgame, The Birthday Party*, and *'Afore Night Come* as a "programme of dirt." Littler's accusations were especially piquant to Orton since Littler was currently producing (and had helped to write) *The Right Honourable Gentleman*, a play about Sir Charles Dilke and the sexual scandal that ruined his political career.

Orton had found the society's nerve. He was not the first English satirist but arguably the best playwright to engage in a war of attrition against a public whose flagging robustness extended to its threadbare theatrical vocabulary about plays, where "vulgarity," "sensation," and "grotesque" were used as pejorative terms when, in fact, they are the essence of great comedy. *Entertaining Mr. Sloane* defied critical categories. "I don't think the four characters are 'vile.' Do you?" Orton wrote Glenn Loney about the American critics' response to the Broadway production of *Entertaining Mr. Sloane*. "Has New York never heard of Total Theatre? That is what *Sloane* is. You accept it. Don't bother whether it's a comedy or a tragedy or a farce or a drama—it's all of those, and, perhaps, none. . . ."[54]

Orton was against violence for its own sake. "I hope that the violence in my plays is not of an inconsequential nature. . . . I'm always horrified by violence in some things, especially American films and novels. . . . I watched an American TV series called 'The Invaders' and the violence in that seems to me totally gratuitous. I mean, it was necessary for the old man in *Sloane* to be beaten up on the purely pragmatic grounds of the plot, and I couldn't have had the play working otherwise. In the same way, to go back to the old cliché about Shakespeare, you can't have certain scenes in *King Lear* without having Gloucester's eyes put out. . . ."[55]

Orton thought of himself as a realist, not a cynic. *Entertaining Mr. Sloane* is more than an exploration of English hypocrisy and the cosy landscape of woollies, bickies, and garden gnomes. Orton made a deliberate spectacle of human animality, and of the need to deny and transcend the body. Man's urge for self-aggrandizement and self-perpetuation, like that of any other animal, requires killing; there is a need to impose—either literally or symbolically—a sense of suffering and death on others in order to ensure a sense of personal victory. In *Entertaining Mr. Sloane*, the family live a lie and need the lie to sustain a sense of their well-being. The Dadda, with his knowledge of Sloane's murder and his determination to turn him in, threatens all the other lives. His murder allows life to flow more plentifully to the others. In this sense he is a sacrificial victim, functioning along the ritual lines Orton claimed to have studied in *The Golden Bough,* where sacrifice encouraged a good harvest. Sloane, Kath, and Ed make a bargain that fortifies their magical sense of power over life and death. Everything is renewed, all failure forgotten. Each sidesteps the threat of annihilation. Sloane wins his freedom and a guarantee of the good life. Ed and Kath, once terrified of abandonment, have multiplied their power and pleasure by sharing Sloane. Ed's business acumen is validated ("Put it down to my skill at the conference table," he swaggers to Kath). And Kath, with Sloane's baby inside her, has symbolically defeated death and grown "bigger" as the curtain comes down with her relaxing victoriously on the sofa.

ORTON'S COMEDY teased the society with its own evil and tested what it held sacred. The youthfulness of his writing inevitably forced a confrontation between generations. "This confrontation between generations of depraved youth and age valiantly upholding decency and moral standards—is in one sense peculiarly modern," wrote Hilary Spurling, whose essays on Orton were among the most perceptive during his lifetime. "But it is also an ancient dispute. . . . If the public sometimes seems disproportionately excited—as it did with Orton or with Con-

greve, Wycherley, even Farquhar—it is because the outcry is directed
. . . at the modish trappings (in Orton's case, vice, crime, ever more
rarefied brands of kinkiness) rather than the essential and more deeply
offensive truthfulness which they conceal."[56]

Orton's battles with the public were not always comic. He was
fiercely threatened by institutions and the irrational control they
wielded in the name of authority. "Accept your condition without tears
and without abusing those placed in authority," barks the inspecting
psychiatrist, Dr. Rance, in *What the Butler Saw*. Orton went to the
American Embassy to get a visa to attend the Broadway rehearsal of
Entertaining Mr. Sloane in 1965, and found himself in a double bind
as preposterous as any Dr. Rance could invent. "The Eagle on the
American Embassy building in Grosvenor Square is made of black
metal," he wrote. "From a small distance it looks like a bat or a vulture
about to sink upon its prey." Orton wanted to stay in the United States
six weeks. His request was denied. It was not Joe Orton Playwright who
stood before the Embassy officials but Joe Orton Jailbird and Menace
to Private Property. To contain his fury, Orton wrote down his negotiations with officialdom weeks before he finally won his case. The narrative was never published, but it shows Orton beset and suffocated by
the very categories *Entertaining Mr. Sloane* wanted to subvert:

> . . . He hunched himself over my passport, my visa application form
> and my Memorandum of Conviction. His eyes darted from one to
> the other. Finally, he looked up, sat back, a bewildered expression
> on his face.
>
> "What's all this about?" he said.
>
> I didn't know how to answer. I said nothing. He sat up in his
> chair, stiff and upright. His eyes narrowed.
>
> "Can you explain what this—" he pointed to the Memorandum,
> "—whole thing was about?"
>
> "It was a joke."
>
> This wasn't true. The outrages against a middle-brow reading
> public were serious enough. They'd occupied my time and energies
> for close on five years before I was caught. They could never be
> justified. Or explained.
>
> "A joke!" he screeched the word quietly. "The—er—authorities
> don't seem to have regarded it as a joke."
>
> "No," I said.
>
> He sighed. "I may as well tell you, Mr. Orton, that your visa will
> be automatically refused. That is the law. Your actions, you see,
> resulted in the damaging of other people's property. And that
> counts as moral turpitude." He paused to let the full weight of

his words sink in. "However, you can apply for a temporary waiver of ineligibility. In order to do this you must convince a consular officer that you are a deserving case. Do you wish to make an application?"

"Yes," I said.

He fiddled with a drawer in his desk and produced a sheaf of papers, looked through them.

"I'm a policeman," he said, "and I must warn you that I have ways of checking your statements. If you make any false ones that will be another reason why we shouldn't issue a temporary waiver of ineligibility."

"Yes," I said. I'd been through this before. I knew that the thing to do was to be docile and polite. I didn't think he had the power to beat me up. But, you never know. "I wouldn't make false statements," I said. . . .

"Are you a homosexual?" he asked, suddenly and rather surprisingly from the context.

"No," I said.

He lapsed into silence. . . . "Would you mind seeing a doctor?" he spat out the words as though to check any further revelations.

"Why?"

He spread his hands. "You force me to be blunt. You may have a psychopathic personality. This—" (waving his hands to the papers on his desk) "—is a very, very disturbing case."

"I don't mind seeing a doctor," I said.

"Good. Now I want you to fill in this form." He handed me a form. "When do you want to go to New York City?"

"On the second of September. The director wants me to discuss the play with him before rehearsals begin."

I dropped the name Alan Schneider, along with *Who's Afraid of Virginia Woolf?* I didn't think he'd heard of either. He certainly hadn't heard of *Entertaining Mr. Sloane.* Just as well, I suppose.

"I can't have your waiver of ineligibility ready for the second of September," he said. "We'll try for the twentieth, shall we?"

"Yes," I said.

"You go out there and fill in that form. I've a lot of paperwork to do." . . .

I waited in the entrance hall. I spread the form out and studied it. It was worse than I'd expected. "Name any clubs or organizations to which you have belonged since reaching the age of sixteen." "What is your itinerary?" "Name the addresses of your residences since reaching the age of sixteen. With length of stay in each." "Have you ever travelled through a Communist country?" That was the easiest. I completed the form and waited.

Then the man at the first desk rang through and said I was ready. I went past the secretaries and found the man at his desk. He didn't say anything. I gave him the form.

"You've never belonged to any club. Never joined anything?"

"No," I said.

He looked at me with fresh eyes, his tones were cold and disbelieving.

"Not even the Boy Scouts?" A pink flush appeared on his cheeks.

"No."

He stood up and eased himself past me. "Let's go talk to the doctor. . . ."

. . . While I waited to see the doctor I studied the sheet of paper. It was a typewritten document with the arms of the United States on top.

It said:

"This office regrets to inform you that it is unable to issue you a visa because you have been found ineligible under the following section of the Immigration and Nationality Act, as amended: (Only the checked items apply to your case):"

There were two sections.

(i) "Section 212 (a) (15) which prohibits the issuance of a visa to anyone likely to become a public charge."

This wasn't checked.

(ii) "Section 101 (a) (15) which prohibits the issuance of a temporary visitor's visa to applicants who fail to establish they are non-immigrants under the terms of the law."

This wasn't checked.

The rest of the paper was blank. And then I saw a check. There was no explanation beside it, just the figures "212 (a) (9)" written in longhand. Nothing else.

. . . I went into a comfortably furnished room and shut the door. A tall, elderly man sprang to his feet. He said he was the doctor and asked me to sit down. . . .

It escaped his notice, though not mine, that he sat on the couch while I sat at the desk.

"Now, young man," he said in a quiet reassuring voice, "tell me what 'all this' is about."

I went over the same ground. . . . "It was a joke," I said. "I don't do it anymore."

"It—um—uh," he gave a little squeal of laughter, though not humourous, "doesn't sound funny to me."

"It was reported in the *Daily Mirror*," I said. "And *Reader's Digest*."

I wasn't particularly proud of this. It was more something to say.

The doctor nodded, his eyes held a wary expression. "It was in the press?"

"Yes."

"Hmmm." There was a silence. I could hear the women and children talking in the hall. Neither of us said a word, the doctor shook his head, his mind seemed to be concentrating on something that was worrying him. "You got six months in an institution for this?" he said.

"Yes."

"There must've been something else?" He leaned forward, his neck sticking from his shirt. "Wha—What?"

"I used to write false blurbs," I said. "On the inside of the book jackets. The writing I did was exactly the same as the writing I do now. I used to type quite long pieces. Many people borrowed the book from the library on the strength of my blurbs. And returned them with complaints when the published story didn't live up to mine." He wasn't listening. I stopped and began again. "It was a more limited public than my present one. But the standard of writing was the same."

A muffled groan escaped his lips. "It's still going on?" He half rose from the couch. I thought he was about to call for help.

"No, no!" I shouted, anxious not to alarm him. "I'm talking about my plays."

"I don't know what they want me to do with this case," he seemed desperate. "Have you received any treatment?"

"Only in Brixton. I was on remand for medical and mental reports."

"You saw a psychiatrist in prison?" He clutched at this straw.

"Yes."

"How often?"

"Once. For about ten minutes."

"What happened to you then?"

"I was sent back to the cells. I was in solitary confinement for twenty-three hours a day."

He brushed aside a foreign country's attempts to rehabilitate me with a curt gesture and strode into the outer office.

"I want the report of the prison psychiatrist on this young man's case," he said to the secretary. "Will you see to that for me?"

"Yes," she said.

"I'll see you again perhaps some other time then, young man," said the doctor, re-entering the room. He couldn't conceal his relief. "Good morning to you."

After signing another form authorising them to check my records I left the building. I couldn't hope to get to the United States on

my own. I needed help. So I went to tell my agent what had happened. I caught a seventy-three bus. Behind me two women were
discussing [the BBC television program] "Dr. Who and the Daleks."

"Very far-fetched," the first woman said. "I like something you
can believe in."

"Yes," said the second. After a long pause she said, "You know
where you are with human beings, don't you."

When Orton finally arrived in New York in September, he was
delighted by the city and his production. "I find New York a very old
fashioned city," he wrote Peggy Ramsay. "It's like time-travelling back
to the thirties. It has an old world charm."[57] Orton explored Manhattan,
sometimes with a young Cypriot waiter he'd picked up and with whom
he was photographed grinning boyishly on top of the Empire State
Building. At night, he was often in the company of his director. Alan
Schneider was the high-roller of American avant-garde theatre and a
notoriously spiky personality. His production of *Who's Afraid of Virginia Woolf?* was one of the major American successes of the sixties.
With it he became the most influential, if not always the most subtle,
interpreter of the best of contemporary theatre. Schneider's productions
introduced the American public to Edward Albee, Edward Bond,
Harold Pinter, and Samuel Beckett; Orton was impressed by him and
respectful of the line of important writers to which his name was now
added.

Orton had himself photographed under the behemoth marquee of
the Lyceum Theatre. Grinning in long shot and dwarfed by the tower-
ing billboards spelling out in gargantuan red letters the name of the
play and the director, Orton, like his billing, was barely visible. "Sheila
[Hancock as Kath] is delicious. Oh, I wish London could see it," Orton
wrote to Peggy Ramsay, excitedly assessing the first Broadway previews.
". . . It's curious how *Sloane* changes. It was a terrifically German
play in Germany. And now it has a smoothness which is oddly American. I know you'll shudder with horror when I say that it's slick here.
But I mean it as a compliment. I mean *Virginia Woolf* was too, I think.
In a way, I suppose, the London production (gimcrack as it was) was
typically English. Will the French one be French and the Israeli one
Jewish? A play to suit all tastes perhaps?"[58]

The only real worry Orton admitted to his agent was George
Turner, the actor playing the Dadda. "I don't like the old man," Orton
wrote to Peggy Ramsay. "He's played as a spinsterish, malicious recluse.
I was shocked at first. But, as it's so much geared to the whole production I can't ask for it to be changed. In fact it couldn't be changed

because it's basic to Alan's production. However, it does worry me. But it achieves one thing—the old man is never a sympathetic character which means that no one will mind him being murdered."[59] Schneider always had difficulty with the capriciousness of the murder; and by exaggerating the Dadda's ugliness, the production somewhat sidestepped Sloane's amorality. It made the death "rational." In the same way, Schneider cut Sloane's recounting of his crime—"The air round Twickenham was like wine"—because, according to Dudley Sutton, who was again playing Sloane, Schneider "couldn't elicit 'excuses,' meanings from me. My concern wasn't the meaning. My concern was the rhythm. That speech should be delivered like a machine gun." Sutton objected to "Actor's Studio fiddle-faddle," and saw Sloane as a "survivor who's not analytic. As long as he's got a bed, books, the car, he can happily lay about the house and get well fed." Sutton argued a lot with Schneider. "I picked up this trick from Brendan Behan, an old drinking mate of mine," Sutton explains. "If you've got something to say and you want somebody to listen, you've got to attribute your idea to somebody else. Behan used to say, 'As Théophile Fuckin' Gautier once wrote,' and then say what he wanted. I used to say to Schneider: 'There's a very old expression in the Irish Theatre. "Never mind the fuckin' acting, lets get on with the fuckin' play." ' "

Orton's only serious disagreement with Schneider was about staging the Dadda's murder. "He wanted to bring the curtain down before the murder," Orton wrote to Michael Codron. "I said 'NO!' " But Orton's buoyancy about Schneider's production still echoed through his letter to Codron:

> . . . The first previews are over. Very well received on the whole. We had a packed house for Saturday night. Can't tell whether it will run, though. Better not be too optimistic. The usual comments in the intervals—"Very weird," "Well, *I'm* not impressed," and even "This reminds me of *A Taste of Honey*." But the applause is genuine enough. The second act makes them stumble. Give you two guesses why. And some of them resent it being called a comedy. Alan and I have asked Slade Brown to take the "comedy" off the bills. . . .
>
> Lee [Montague as Ed] is wonderful. Beautiful. Don't forget he's the author's casting. But Sheila is the pride of the faggots. They treat her like Judy Garland or Dietrich. Irritates me. But she's marvellous. I don't think she's better than Lee, just more camp. We've told her to tone down some of the camp. It's better when she's in control of it. But, all the same, she is terrific. Edward Albee saw it last night. He likes it very much. What more could

you want. An anonymous silly old queen in the interval last night
was shrieking, "Marvellous, but of course, it won't run!"[60]

Entertaining Mr. Sloane had two weeks of previews. At first, audiences were small; but word of mouth built quickly so that the second
week was sold out. "We've been having fabulous houses," Orton wrote
Halliwell. "Full almost every night. Last two nights it's poured with a
tropical downpour just before the performance and angry patrons who
hadn't booked have been turned away. I said it might be better if we
didn't have the critics. Word of mouth is doing so well. . . . Tennessee
Williams has been to see it twice. And, so I'm told, is wild over it.
Says it's the funniest play he's ever seen. . . . June Havoc came last
night. I met her at interval. With a blonde wig on (her not me). Peter
Shaffer saw it the other night, said he didn't recognize the play from
London. He said that over here he realised what a very brilliant play
it was—talked about elegance and wit, etc. . . . And the only cuts I've
allowed are minor. . . . Just shows actually how much damage Dromgoole did. And (while I think of it) I've been wondering how much
damage [Peter] Wood did. But there I know you'll say I told you so."[61]

Orton expected the play to be more disturbing to an American
audience than Schneider did. "I'm not hopeful of success," he wrote
Halliwell after the first week's previews. "But then we never were, were
we."[62] He reported the audience's bitter resentment of Eddie. "Schneider won't face up to the extent of their resentment," Orton told Halliwell. "They laugh exaggeratedly with Kath and even Sloane in order
to assert their heterosexuality. Schneider will only go as far as saying
that they're horrified of laughing with Eddie in the first act. He says
they don't know what Eddie is. But I told him that they will when the
reviews come out. But as Eddie is being played right the audience are
very worried that this attractive masculine man should be a power and
a threat to them (they identify with Kath—Sheila gets rounds of ap-
plause on some of her lines—but it's only that they want to show their
solidarity). Last night when she said 'It's murder' to Sloane in the third
act someone nearby said 'Atta girl!'—of course they imagine that is the
point where the action turns and the tide runs in her favour ending up
with her winning. Imagine their disbelief when Eddie wins! . . . People are loving or hating it. . . ."[63] But by the end of the previews,
Orton's studied detachment about the show had given way to excitement. "Think of me on Tuesday night and, even more about two
o'clock Wednesday morning," he wrote Halliwell. "Such a pity if the
critics do damn it. It really is good. Thanks to Alan."[64]

The play opened on October 12 to a star-studded first-night audi-

ence. At curtain time two of New York's then most influential daily
critics—Walter Kerr and Richard Watts—were not in their seats.
Schneider waited fifteen minutes. "I'm saying to the PA, 'For Chrissake
let's go up! Let's go up.' He said, 'We can't go up. We haven't got the
Tribune or the *Post.*'" At twenty minutes past curtain time, Schneider
walked down the aisle to explain the situation to Howard Taubman,
then critic of *The New York Times* and by virtue of his paper the most
important of daily reviewers. Taubman was nervous and glancing at
his watch. But Schneider's gesture of politeness was a tactical error. No
critic likes to think that another is more important than he, especially
the critic of *The New York Times,* whose outrageous sense of importance is sustained by the equally outrageous hit/flop economic system
in which American theatre seems doomed to continue. Theatre protocol
forbids any other critic being seated in front of the *Times* critic.
Schneider approached Taubman unaware of this pecking order. After
hearing the reason for the delay, Taubman, unsmiling, replied: "Am I
my brother's keeper?" Finally, twenty-five minutes late (confirming the
publicity wisecrack that the hardest thing about dealing with critics
is to get them to go to the theatre), Kerr and Watts sauntered into
the Lyceum and the curtain went up. "Never an auspicious way to
begin," Schneider says. "Especially for a comedy."

The reviews were blistering; and, typically, somewhat incoherent.
"I thought it was merely a smelly spectacle," wrote John McClain, a
writer who had been promoted from shipping news to drama critic in
William Randolph Hearst's right-wing New York *Journal American.*
"We are right back at the Boston Tea Party, standing on the dock
throwing homosexuals into the drink as fast as they are unloaded, and if
this is [England's] best play of any year they are in serious trouble. . . ."
The *World Telegram and Sun* claimed that the play "had the sprightly
charm of a medieval cesspool." But the most damaging attack came from
Howard Taubman. "Whether it is in earnest or not," he began, *"Entertaining Mr. Sloane* is a singularly unattractive play. If it means to
be drama it is forced and incredible. If it seeks to be comedy, it is too
broad. If it aims to be caricature, it succeeds all too well. . . ."

Schneider had driven Orton and Dudley Sutton to the loading dock
at the back entrance of *The New York Times* to get an early edition
of Taubman's review. Sutton sat in the car and read the notice out loud.
Schneider was in tears; Orton was dazed. "He walked around all night,"
Schneider remembers. The next day he left for London. *Entertaining
Mr. Sloane,* with only a handful of positive reviews, closed after thirteen
performances.

Taubman kept beating *Entertaining Mr. Sloane* even after he'd helped to kill it. In a Sunday *Times* essay after the play had closed, he indicted the play for the characters' lack of nobility, dramatizing in his smug and vicious moralizing the same lust to appear good that Orton dramatized on stage:

> In itself *Entertaining Mr. Sloane* is too insignificant to merit further belaboring. . . . Like so many other young playwrights Joe Orton is outraged by the corruption and hypocrisy he finds all around him. He is prepared to cry out mercilessly that protestations of honor and virtue are an obscene sham. . . . Okay. A perfectly valid job for the playwright in any era. The Greeks did it superbly more than 2,000 years ago. William Shakespeare, Ben Jonson and friends in good Queen Bess's time relentlessly held up the mirror to nature. . . .
>
> But how does Mr. Orton go about it? Like so many of his modish tribe, he chooses the easy, supercilious, repellent way. He uses characters so lost in honor and decency, so sunk in dirt and degradation, that his point is vitiated almost before he has begun. . . .
>
> The handling of Kath is an object lesson in how to demean a play, with the director and performer guilty of complicity. . . . Such a performance might bring a smirk to the lips of a theatregoer of debased tastes. It might secretly delight those epicenes who look upon the public humiliation of women as grand sport. But it is repugnant to anyone who believes that even a foil in black comedy deserves something juster than nasty, vulgar patronizing. . . .[65]

"Thanks for Taubman's second front," Orton wrote to Glenn Loney. "I liked it better than the initial offensive. He's been forced to take the play seriously. When he says lines like 'In itself *E.M.S.* is too insignificant to merit further belaboring,' the Lady doth protest too much. I'm glad they hate it. And I agree wholeheartedly with Judith Malina and Julian Beck. If critics adored one's work one would have to watch out. . . . I get a kick out of lines like 'Ben Jonson and his friends in good Queen Bess's time.' You see, there you have the reason why he can't understand the play. One of my characters would say a line like that—seriously, as seriously as Taubman says it. And *I* would think it was funny that the character says it. . . ."[66]

The week after Taubman's salvo in the Sunday *Times*, Schneider waded into the ruckus. "What is it about the gnat of *Mr. Sloane* that strains him so profoundly?" Schneider asked. He pointed out that Taubman's overheated idiom—referring to Kath as "a simpering idiot" —had gone well beyond the bounds of reasoned debate. "I shudder to think what Mr. Taubman might say about the evils of two other somewhat more serious examples of this genre, *The Killing of Sister*

George and John Osborne's *A Patriot for Me.*" Listing a number of impressive plays he had directed that had been maligned as "meaningless aberrations on our chaste body theatric"—*Waiting for Godot, Who's Afraid of Virginia Woolf?, Endgame, Happy Days, The Dumbwaiter*—Schneider added, "While I am certain that neither *Sloane*'s author nor its director has any illusions about the play's claim to eminence in this pantheon of depravity, I have not the slightest doubt of its ultimate vitality and durability in the history of contemporary drama, its relevance to our behavior and value patterns; as well as its dramatic virtues, relative say, to a much more praised recent British import *The Right Honourable Gentleman* which Mr. Taubman recommends as an evening for adults—while reviling *Sloane* as fit only for degenerates and debased women haters."

But Schneider's reply to Taubman rankled Orton in underrating his theatrical intentions.

> I pasted the clipping very neatly into my cuttings book—which will eventually go to Boston University, USA for their "Joe Orton Collection" (*sic*) [Orton wrote to Schneider's assistant, who had sent him the article]. Well, at least, they wanted a collection *before* the recent disgraceful goings on at West 45th Street. I thought Alan's letter to the *Times* good. On the whole. Though one or two passages brought out my paranoia. The one I'd like someone to explain is: "I shudder to think what Mr. Taubman might say about the evils of two other *somewhat more serious* examples of this genre, *The Killing of Sister George* and John Osborne's *A Patriot for Me.*" End quote. Now—(as I roll up my sleeves)—I haven't seen *A P. for Me.* And I've no doubt at all that J. O. will have treated homosexuality in a "serious" manner. But I have seen *Sister George* and it is a very, very little little piece about lesbians—or at least we're given to understand that it's about lesbians—I couldn't find much evidence of any more lesbianic a relationship than most women have with their mothers. So what does Alan mean? (By the way—do read this letter in the spirit in which it's written, not in a rage or anything like that. I find it difficult to smile in print.) No, but seriously, *Sister G.* is light-weight. . . . That's the way it's being played. That is why it's having a success with the middle-brow, middle-class audiences. It is not serious at all. Not nearly as serious as *Sloane*. Which isn't "serious" in the obvious sense, but "serious" as a piece of writing. I take my writing very, very seriously. It is the only way to write. . . .[67]

Orton signed his letter "Joe—a serious writer." *Entertaining Mr. Sloane* was the first fruit of a decade of hard work; but in public, he hid the seriousness and the pain of his search for a style. "I'd written several plays that were all more or less failures," he told the BBC in 1964, speaking as the West End's newest success. "Even in those, I could still write dialogue. A play isn't just writing dialogue, it's something very strange. I don't know what it is. Maugham said that being a playwright was nothing to be proud of because you could be a moron and still be a playwright. It's just a knack, like walking on a high wire. You can be an absolute thick and walk on a high wire. It's nothing to do with intellect or intelligence. Just something that you have. If you've got the knack and the ability to write dialogue, then there's no reason why you shouldn't write a play."[68]

Ultimately the literary fireworks of *Entertaining Mr. Sloane*'s naturalistic dialogue showed up the play's essential scenic tameness. The piece did not use the stage with full playfulness—a fact Orton recognized. "The new full length play [*Loot*]," Orton told the BBC, "is, I think, an advance. But of course you can't tell until you've written it. But I think it's an advance."[69] In his subsequent plays, Orton would work more boldly with theatrical artifice. In them, his dazzling capacity to manipulate words would be matched with an equally startling talent for constructing hilarious stage images. *Entertaining Mr. Sloane* toyed with farce, but the cut and thrust of the play's third act had a potential for mayhem that never made the transition from language to movement.

"I feel, looking back on everything now from a distance—six months and three thousand miles," Orton wrote in 1966, about the Broadway version of *Sloane,* "that perhaps everything was too broad. But given a brilliant comic—viz: Sheila [Hancock], in the lead, it's difficult to see how else it could've gone. I still stick to my statement—did I make it, I wonder?—that the New York production was better than London. If we'd had that production—plus Sheila we'd 've run a year in London. Of course the only place I've ever seen my play is still in Germany. Did I tell you that I'd been to Berlin where it was perhaps a shade better than Hamburg. There were thirty-eight curtain calls and every one deserved. . . ."[70]

5

SCANDALOUS SURVIVAL

One does not kill by anger but by laughter. Come let us kill the Spirit of Gravity.

—Friedrich Nietzsche, *Thus Spake Zarathustra*

THE TRANSITION between *Entertaining Mr. Sloane* and *Loot* was *The Good and Faithful Servant*, completed in June 1964 and aired by Rediffusion Television in April 1967. In this poignant and bitter one-act play, Buchanan—a commissionaire—is retiring after fifty years of service. He has lost an arm on the job. Like the company's gifts of a clock and a toaster, his body is on the verge of breakdown. When he visits a lady friend on the evening of his retirement, she is shocked at the sight of a whole man:

EDITH. Your arms! Where has the extra one come from?
BUCHANAN. It's false.
EDITH. Thank God for that. I like to know where I stand in relation to the number of limbs a man has.

Orton concentrates his irony on the slavish belief in industrial routine. At Buchanan's first get-together of ex-employees in the company's recreation centre, he talks to another old man—an exchange that maps the bleak horizon of their lives:

OLD MAN. I was almost mentioned in a well-known sporting periodical once.
BUCHANAN. I never got as far as that.

Later, Buchanan reminds the Old Man: "I worked here. I was on the main entrance. . . ." But Buchanan's life and his presence amount to nothing. "Nobody knows me," he says to himself. "They've never seen me before." In the foreground, the shrewish director of activities, Mrs. Vealfoy, claps her hands and forces them into recreation: "We're going to run through all the songs with 'Happy' in them. . . ." Buchanan registers his gradual disenchantment by finally smashing his retirement gifts with a hammer. At the finale, as his new wife Edith chats to him about a vacation, Buchanan sits silently in bed, tearfully aware of his wasted life. He dies as she gossips about a forthcoming company dance, concluding: "We have so much to be thankful for. . . ."

Despite *The Good and Faithful Servant*'s seething disgust, the blast of its irony was muted by the naturalistic format. Melodrama has a comforting predictability and is too tame for comic devastation. A survivor, Orton was compelled to exhibit his mastery of the dead world that *The Good and Faithful Servant* documented in a style as extreme as his own success. The threat of anonymity, the suffocating memory of his upbringing and literary failures, were symbolic deaths from which Orton now drew power for life. With success, he embarked on a play whose manic laughter registered the weirdness of his scandalous survival.

Loot is about scandalous survivors: Fay, the predatory nurse with designs on McLeavy's money; Hal and Dennis, lovers and robbers; and the psychopathic Detective Truscott, pursuing his omnipotent fantasies first in crime solving and then in larceny. "I fancy myself as a ghoul," Hal says in a line cut from the first draft of *Loot*, after tipping his mother's corpse out of her coffin to bury stolen money. The joke defines a strange and indifferent universe, literally "touching the dead" and showing death as capricious as life.

Written between June and October 1964, *Loot* was originally titled *Funeral Games* and subtitled "A Farce." "If you don't like *Funeral Games* as a title, do you like Comedy of Horrors better," Orton wrote Michael Codron on October 15, the day before he delivered the play to his producer. ". . . It has a nice play on Chamber of Horrors and Comedy of Errors. Or is it too high for the public? . . . I prefer *Funeral Games* myself." *Loot*, the genial title Kenneth Halliwell pinned to the play, had the whiff of a thirties whodunit—apt enough for the plot, but not for the lacerating moral spirit or the humor.

In farce, Orton could marry terror and elation in his highly stylized theatrical idiom. Violating social and familial pieties, farce's pandemonium created the panic Orton wanted in laughter. In tragedy, character is fate; in farce, where characterization is minimized and action emphasized, mischief is fate. Orton understood the kinship between tragedy and farce. And he made the most of it in *Loot*. "*Sloane* took a comedic view of things, *Loot* takes a farcical view of things normally treated as tragic," he said in his first public statement about the play. "Farce is higher than comedy in that it is very close to tragedy. You've only got to play some of Shakespeare's tragedies plain and they are nearly farcical. All gradations of theatre between tragedy and farce —light comedy, drama—are a load of rubbish."[1]

Orton's classic view of farce was not the traditional English equivalent of Parisian boulevard farce: the crude bedroom capering of the Whitehall farces or the frothy, well-plotted Ben Travers Aldwych escapades. In the hands of contemporary practitioners, farce had dwindled to a bourgeois fun machine. In *Loot* Orton returned farce to its age-old scope and ferocity, adapting the genre to his own free-wheeling outspokenness. "I am a great admirer of Ben Travers," Orton said, discussing farce in *Plays and Players*. "But the boundaries he set to present-day farce are really too narrow. As I understood it, farce originally was very close to tragedy, and differed only in the *treatment* of its themes— themes like rape, bastardy, prostitution. But you can't have a farce about rape any longer. French farce got as far as adultery, but by Ben Travers's time it was only *suspected* adultery, which turned out to have been innocuous after all. A lot of farces today are still based on the preconceptions of a century ago, particularly the preconceptions about sex. But we must now accept that, for instance, people *do* have sexual relations outside marriage: a thirties farce is acceptable because it is distanced by its period, but a modern farce which merely nurses the old, outworn assumptions is cushioning people against reality. And this, of course, is just what the commercial theatre usually does. In theory there is no subject which could *not* be treated farcically—just as the Greeks were prepared to treat any subject farcically. But in practice farce has become very restricted indeed. . . . My feeling is that the dramatist must have the right to change formal gear at any time. There's supposed to be a healthy shock, for instance, at those moments in *Loot* when an audience suddenly *stops* laughing. So if *Loot* is played as no more than farcical, it won't work."[2]

The Good and Faithful Servant took aim at corporate paternalism. *Loot* was a more ferocious attack on this faith in authority. Mischievously, Orton raised the issue of faith directly in Detective Truscott's final exit speech in *Loot's* first draft. It was part of the formula of detective fiction that *Loot* parodied. That formula, as W. H. Auden brilliantly observes, requires "an innocence which is discovered to contain guilt; then a suspicion of being the guilty one; and finally a real innocence from which the guilty other has been expelled, a cure effected, not by me or my neighbours, but by the miraculous intervention of a genius from outside who removes the guilt by giving knowledge of guilt."[3] Truscott of the Yard, of course, inverts every expectation of the detective, and through him Orton sends up the daydream of a return to innocence. In the original version, the guilty remain free, having bribed Truscott into silence. True to detective form, Truscott pauses with a valise of stolen money in hand to pronounce the prerequisite hymn to moral harmony:

> TRUSCOTT. . . . Goodwill has been established where there was none before; our lives have been enriched; we have taken a positive attitude and affirmed something. I don't want to bring religion into this, but . . . I do think it proves, in a roundabout way, the abiding validity of the ethical system upon which this country is founded.

In *Loot* Orton's laughter found new strength by tilting against death, the Church, the English police, and the idea of English justice. "One *must* shake the audience out of its expectations," he said. "They need not so much shocking, as *surprising* out of their rut."[4]

Orton pushed the laughter until it exposed taboo areas behind public attitudes. The words "sick" and "filth," so often levelled at Orton's work, contain a fear of infection. The taboo's aim is prohibition of "infection," an inhibition of thought that demands conformity but provides no insight. "Whenever one dares not question any further or when it does not occur to one to do so, one is dealing with a taboo."[5] The taboo represents society against the individual; and Orton's laughter was the revenge of the individual against a smothering consensus. Between the extremes of McLeavy's beleaguered passivity and Detective Truscott's megalomania, *Loot* dramatized the danger of taboos that keep knowledge at a low level. "I ignore stories which bring officialdom into disrepute," explains McLeavy, who assumes much to his cost that to overlook chaos is to create order. Where McLeavy is the quintessential victim ruled by taboos, Truscott is a bully who exploits the taboos about English justice for his own power. In his interrogation, Truscott continually places others in the childlike position of being forbidden to answer questions, the same role into which those who obey taboos are put by society. When McLeavy is arrested, he finally protests about Truscott's abuse of power and asks to see a higher authority. "You can see whoever you like, providing you convince me first that you're justified in seeing them."

Sporting with a corpse and a coffin is chilling business, but Orton used it to tap a reservoir of deep and unexplored public feeling. In acting out his own oedipal resentments, he systematically examined the irrational associations that surround the ritual of death. "If you're absolutely practical—and I hope I am—a coffin is only a box," Orton said, responding to the charge of offensiveness for staging *Loot*'s hijinks around a coffin. "One calls it a coffin and once you've called it a coffin it immediately has all sorts of associations."[6] *Loot* poses questions about the attitudes surrounding the taboo, and then shocks its audience with the detachment of its practical solutions. "As for the taboo ingredients of *Loot*," Orton explained sensibly, "I have a great reverence for death, but no particular feeling for the little dust of a corpse. And the family is strongly Roman Catholic for the traditional farcical reason that they must be respectable and believable—and there are no equivalent outward trappings in a Protestant household to establish the air of religious respectability."[7]

Orton's previous plays had delighted in exposing sexual prudery. *Loot* went a step further, unmasking the most profound twentieth-century prudery: death. The detective story was the prototype of the thriller/horror saga, which found its most popular expression in the sixties fad for psychopathic slaughter typified by the James Bond stories. The deaths that people paid to see and that entertained them on TV were violent, spectacular, and gruesomely attractive. This phenomenon, which Geoffrey Gorer aptly dubbed "the pornography of death,"[8] paid no attention to authentic grief and mourning. The cosmetic idea of death succeeded at the box office and catered to the social prudery. Natural death replaced sex as society's unmentionable, and entertainments avoided it.

Loot revels in the "impropriety" of natural death. The play revolves around a corpse, which is stripped naked and then stashed in the cupboard. The Lord Chamberlain, whose job then was "to prevent public offence being given," found this exceedingly offensive:

> I am desired by the Lord Chamberlain [wrote the Comptroller to the producers on December 31, 1964] to inform you that he will only consider granting a license for the above named play if certain scenes are rewritten so that:
> 1. The corpse is obviously a dummy.
> 2. The corpse remains fully clothed throughout the play and is not undressed, even behind a screen, at any time; and the accompanying dialogue is adjusted accordingly.
> 3. The false eye business is removed.

"Anything is legal with a corpse," argues McLeavy, a statement to which Truscott and, evidently, the Lord Chamberlain took exception

as defenders of "the rights of the dead." The Lord Chamberlain's in-
structions were an irony fit for the play's debate: the viscera of the
dead were to be protected by authority, while the work of a living
writer was being eviscerated. This same refusal to acknowledge death
was crucial to the play's joke about the embalmer's art. Mrs. McLeavy has
been, as Fay says, "scientifically preserved." She is "good for centuries,"
Hal reminds Dennis, who is worried about the bodily juices rotting the
cash in the coffin. Hal is implored by Fay to take a last look at his
mother: "You'll never see her again." Hal is quick to notice the absurdity of the remark. There is hardly anything left of his mother in the
corpse.

In the ritual of burial, the dead are staged as if they are alive. Mrs.
McLeavy not only "looks as if she might speak"; but, dressed in her
WVS uniform, she looks as if she might walk, too. So Orton tests the
prudery about clothing the dead by having the corpse undressed. "Bury
her naked? My own Mum?" says Hal, combing his hair in the mirror
during this crisis of conscience. "It's a Freudian nightmare." Mrs.
McLeavy is dressed to meet her Maker; by stripping her, the dream is
defiled. Mrs. McLeavy would never greet her husband, let alone God,
in the raw. The body is "corrupted," old, ugly, and shameful; something, even in death, to be denied. While they denude the corpse, Hal
dreams of building a temple to the living flesh in a three-star brothel:

> HAL. . . . I'd advertise "By Appointment." Like jam. . . . I'd have a
> French bird, a Dutch bird, a Belgian bird, an Italian bird—
>
> FAY *hands a pair of false teeth across the screen.*
>
> —and a bird that spoke fluent Spanish and performed the dances
> of her native country to perfection. (*He clicks the teeth like
> castanets.*) I'd call it the Consummatum Est. And it'd be the
> most famous house of ill-fame in the whole of England.

At the finale, when Truscott discovers the body and asks McLeavy
if his wife wanted to be buried in the nude, mention of the word
"nude" sends the old man into a fury. He asks Truscott to leave the
house: "I can't allow you to insult the memory of my late wife." Mc-
Leavy's sentimentality invests dead matter with human feeling. When
he first hears of the funeral parlor being robbed, McLeavy asks: "Human remains weren't outraged?" In the original version, Orton spelled
out the detachment in Dennis's reply: "Nothing human was touched."
By mingling the diabolic and the delightful, Orton shows up the unwit-
ting irrationality of "normal" behavior. When McLeavy discovers his

son's crime, he is scandalized. Hal reminds him of his own peculiar behavior: "You had her filleted without a qualm. Who could have affection for a half-empty woman." McLeavy groans in anguish, a despair which is always hilariously self-referring:

> HAL. You've lost nothing. You began the day with a dead wife. You end it with a dead wife.
>
> MCLEAVY. Oh, wicked, wicked. *(Wildly.)* These hairs—*(Points.)*—they're grey. You made them so. I'd be a redhead today had you been an accountant.
>
> TRUSCOTT *(removing his pipe from his mouth)*. We really can't accept such unlikely explanation for the colour of your hair, sir. . . .

Initially, Hal hides the corpse in the wardrobe. He is forced to unlock the door by Fay, who soon turns the discovery to her own financial advantage and gets a percentage of the loot. In the original version, the corpse fell out of the wardrobe at Fay's feet. After this was disallowed by the Lord Chamberlain, Orton conjured in the minds of his audience a much more offensive stage picture.

> HAL *gives her the key. She opens the wardrobe, looks in, closes the door and screams.*
>
> FAY. . . . This is unforgivable. I shall speak to your father. *(Pause.)* She's standing on her head.

Mrs. McLeavy is meant to be "at rest"; not—as she grotesquely appears —at play. To Orton, once life had left the body, the corpse was an irrelevance. The image made the point which Hal underlined in the original by disputing his father's sanctimonious dismay: "The position of the body in space can't affect you."

"This is a house of mourning," Fay reminds Hal, insisting on ritual protocol as he shouts down the hall for his father to stop ogling the wreath from The Friends of Bingo. In the confusion of events, Mr. McLeavy, who begins the day planning "to keep his wife's memory green" by planting a rose garden that "will put Paradise to shame," has completely forgotten the sacredness of her memory by the end of it. Having held his tongue, flabbergasted, at the news that Mrs. McLeavy made over her will to Fay, he can't contain himself when Fay claims that in her dying breath Mrs. McLeavy accused her husband of murder. "Complete extinction has done nothing to silence her slanderous tongue," he says, having spent most of the play hiding a lifetime's residual anger behind platitudes. For all the pretense to decorum, Mrs.

McLeavy is never mourned. "Grief is a delicate emotion," Fay says in one blue-pencilled line. "Any kind of physical activity dispels it." Laughter engineers a detachment from grief and anxiety, and Orton's play dramatizes this. "Your sense of detachment is terrifying, lad," Truscott tells Hal. "Most people would at least flinch upon seeing their mother's eyes and teeth handed around like nuts at Christmas." *Loot* mocked life for its meaninglessness—a fact to which Orton was as much resigned in life as in art. After Elsie Orton's funeral, Orton brought back a set of her well-polished false teeth to London and presented them to the cast of *Loot*:

> I'd taken my mother's false teeth down to the theatre. I said to Kenneth Cranham [who played Hal], "Here, I thought you'd like the originals." He said, "What?"'''Teeth," I said. "Whose?" he said. "My mum's," I said. He looked very sick. "You see," I said. "It's obvious that you're not thinking of the events of the play in terms of reality if a thing affects you like that." Simon Ward [who played Dennis] shook like jelly when I gave them to him. . . .
>
> [January 4, 1967]

". . . Mr. Orton feels that too many writers for the theatre become obsessed with dialogue," *The Stage* reported in 1966, after *Loot* was successfully moored in the West End. " 'A plot gives you something to fall back upon and gives rise to lines itself!' "[9] By then Orton was speaking from eighteen months' painful experience. A good proportion of the brilliant epigrams and exchanges of the final text were embedded in the hodgepodge of the original. But the script Orton submitted to Michael Codron in October 1964 was all wild talk and tame action.

Originally Fay dominated the machinations; and Truscott, the sleuth whom Irving Wardle in *The Times* a decade later would call "as great a comic character as the English stage has produced since the war," had only eight lines in the first act. Orton had not fully explored his characters, and there was not sufficient leeway for comic complication. Dennis, for instance, has no real relation to or passion for Fay in the original. He doesn't compete for Fay's affection as he does in the final version where, by acquiring the loot, he can make himself a more attractive proposition to her than can McLeavy. The pace of farce is hellbent; and, however preposterous, the structure must dramatize necessity. The questions of McLeavy's fate and Fay's avaricious designs on him, which keep an audience guessing throughout the final version of the play, were settled straightforwardly in Act 1 of the first draft. Fay tells McLeavy she is going to marry him: "This is what I'm offering you. The chance to be pointed out as the contented husband of a practising Christian." The jokes spelled out the greed that Orton would later let the actors play rather than say (Fay: ". . . If hearts and souls are one, bank accounts must follow. That's logic"). Having maneuvered McLeavy to his knees for a proposal of marriage in Act 1, the finale merely wraps up an inevitable conclusion. In the first draft, McLeavy suggests a trade-off with Dennis; but not having prepared the audience for a switch in the plot, the last-minute idea rings false. McLeavy's comic comeuppance is to marry a self-confessed murderess and agonize over when and how he will become Fay's victim number eight: "Does Heaven reserve no crumb of comfort for the off-white of soul," he says, in the penultimate laugh of the first-draft finale. "It's a punishment fit for Judas." By the final draft, Orton had galvanized the situation brilliantly. McLeavy is caught in a web of terrifying complications. After McLeavy has lied to Truscott about the whereabouts of the stolen money to protect his son, Hal double-crosses his father. He suggests to Truscott that he'd be happy to testify against his father. So, instead of threatening to frame McLeavy to protect his larceny (as Truscott does in the first version), Orton now lets Truscott actually arrest him without explanation:

> MCLEAVY. I'm innocent. (*A little unsure of himself, the beginnings of panic.*) Doesn't that mean anything to you?
> TRUSCOTT. You know the drill, Meadows. Empty his pockets and book him.
>
> MCLEAVY *is dragged away by* MEADOWS.
>
> MCLEAVY. I'm innocent! I'm innocent! (*At the door, pause, a last wail.*) Oh, what a terrible thing to happen to a man who's been kissed by the Pope.
>
> MEADOWS *goes off with* MCLEAVY.

"JOE ORTON tells me the play is finished and I shall have it in my hot sticky hands at the end of the week," Codron wrote to Kenneth Williams on October 12, 1964. It was Williams whom Orton had in mind for Truscott, the play's best invention but also its biggest problem. Codron, who had produced Williams in three revues and one play, engineered a meeting between the two men while Orton was in the middle of writing *Loot*. "At the time, Kenneth was balancing the actor/cabaret turn personas," Codron says. "He wasn't committed to not being a serious actor. Joe fell completely under his spell."

Williams was surprising to meet—a complicated, touching man who bore no apparent relation to the haughty buffoon of the "Carry On" films or the whining camp voice from the radio programs " 'Round the Horne" and "Beyond Our Ken." His actual speech was clipped, animated, and vivid. But in recounting his stories, Williams's voice would slip easily into the wide range of delicious postures that had made him one of England's most popular comedians, sprouting plummy and pinched vowels as it swooped from posh to dead common. Williams made the act of speaking funny. There was something dangerous in the unpredictable gusto of his conversation. He spared no one—not even himself—in making a comic point. This approach was not the only thing Williams shared with Orton. Williams's own baroque powers of conversation had the same shape and satiric intention in the delivery that *Loot* was developing in its dialogue. Orton and Williams were immediately simpatico. "At the end of the meeting," Codron recalls, "Joe said, 'I'm writing something at the moment. I'll write it for you.'"

Orton and Williams were a good audience for each other. "We did get on very well. He was a great *activator*. He had tremendous energy," Williams says. "At the end of our meeting, Joe told me I'd influenced him. 'Having met you I want to make this detective more like you.'" Orton had never seen Williams on stage and didn't know his very special theatrical abilities. But the first draft of *Loot* bore the imprint of their meeting. "He did suddenly get fired with the idea of writing a zonking great part for me," Williams says. "Instead of finishing his play and starting something else with me in mind, he dovetailed the two. As a result, Fay, the nurse, who begins as the prime mover of the plot and should go on being the prime mover, ceases to be. She almost becomes an appendage. I remember during the production Geraldine McEwan, who played Fay, said to me, 'This character's extraordinary. She's a resolute woman who comes into this household determined to run everything; and should—according to the logic of the first act— succeed in doing so. But she doesn't. She begins marvellously and then peters out.' I never had the courage to say what I felt to be the truth of the situation. I did really feel that Joe had overbalanced the original intention."

"When the play arrived, I could not see Truscott and Ken at all," Codron recalls. "It needed a lugubriousness and dopiness. Ken is a bright person. I thought the play was good and could be made better; but I thought, 'This is obviously not Ken's play. Ken must turn it down.' But he didn't." Whatever his supposed qualms, Codron was very excited about getting Williams to sign for the play. A week after

receiving the script, he was writing Williams to inform him that Peter
Wood had been asked to direct what was now to be called *Loot,* and
requesting in "sweet reasonableness" for Williams "to stay in the play
for the length of a normal pregnancy as you yourself said very percep-
tively I thought. . . ."

As originally conceived, Truscott was more a literary lampoon than
a satire on English justice. Orton intended both. But the nature of
Williams's outrageousness lent itself to broad parody, so Orton steered
the role that way:

> TRUSCOTT. . . . You have before you a man who is quite a personage
> in his way—Truscott of the Yard. (*He takes out his pipe and
> begins to fill it slowly, in silence.*) Have you never heard of
> Truscott? The man who tracked down the limbless girl killer?
> Or was that sensation before your time?
> HAL. Who could kill a limbless girl?
> TRUSCOTT. She was the killer.
> HAL. How did she manage it if she was limbless?
> TRUSCOTT. That is a question I'm not prepared to answer to any-
> one outside the profession. . . .

The detective, as Auden points out, "must be either the official
representative of the ethical or the exceptional individual who is in a
state of grace."[10] The appealing fantasy behind detective fiction is the
restoration of a state of innocence. Orton reversed these expectations.
Truscott is a representative of a corrupt society, in which psychopathic
ruthlessness substitutes for a "state of grace." Truscott's genius is for
illogic, not logic. Unlike Sherlock Holmes with his passion for the answer or Inspector French of Scotland Yard with his devotion to duty,
Truscott has only one pure motive: his commitment to his legend.

Loot was rushed into production more on the impetus of Orton's
reputation than on the accomplishment of his script. By December,
Codron had collected an all-star cast, including Duncan Macrae, Geraldine McEwan, Ian McShane, and Williams, and planned a six-week
tour before returning to London for a West End run. Peter Wood, who
had originally given Orton the ending to *Entertaining Mr. Sloane* and
had been slated to direct it, was signed to direct *Loot.* Wood, however,
was commuting between London and New York, directing Ibsen's *The
Master Builder* at the National and Jean Kerr's situation comedy *Poor
Richard* on Broadway.

While *Loot* was hurt by the absence of a director to help reshape
it before rehearsals began in January 1965, Orton found inspiration for

his rewrites in the character of the real Detective Sergeant Harold Challenor, whose outrageous methods of detection captured more headlines than criminals. Challenor was the subject of the first police inquiry into their own ranks under the 1964 Police Act. "Orton was obsessed with Challenor," Williams remembers. "He never stopped reading the reports and giggling uncontrollably. He said, 'This man's mad.' " The conclusion was shared by a psychiatrist giving evidence at the inquiry, who found the London detective "quite mad indeed."

A former male nurse, with the thick neck, cropped hair, and ridged eyebrows of a prizefighter, Challenor had been commended seventeen times for his work on the Metropolitan Police. But his concern for law and order had turned into a mania, which led him to plant evidence on law-abiding citizens. He made every situation into a spectacle of his own heroism and omnipotence. Once, according to his wife, he "walked home seventeen miles through a storm and his clothes had dried on him. His feet were bleeding. He said he'd done it to keep fit." Challenor also told her: "If anyone tells you I am going to have a nervous breakdown, you are not to take notice."[11]

The Times headlines implied method in Challenor's madness: SGT CHALLENOR WORKED 102 HOURS IN ONE WEEK . . . NOVEL CRIME FIGHTING METHODS SUCCEED. But the story that emerged was much more unsavory. Challenor had picked out a demonstrator protesting the Greek royal visit in 1963 and arrested him, saying, "You're fucking nicked, my old beauty." On the way to the police station, riding in the police tender, the demonstrator told the inquiry, "Challenor was leaping about. A girl's voice shouted, 'Will you give us a lift?' And Challenor leaned out and shouted, 'Yes! Round the bleeding chops!' " Later, according to the demonstrator, he'd been beaten seven times on his way to the "charge room." Challenor produced a brick from his desk, saying, "We have got to stop them throwing bricks at royalty." He showed it to the demonstrator. "There you are, my old beauty," he said. "For carrying an offensive weapon, you can get two years." Another Challenor victim, whose conviction of seven years' imprisonment for demanding money with menaces and possessing an offensive weapon was finally quashed, testified that Challenor had planted an iron bar on him in his jail cell and fabricated the charge. He testified that Challenor, looming large in his dark blue raincoat, came into the cell saying, "Hello my little darling, hello my little darling. I don't want you. I want your pals." When no names were forthcoming, Challenor threw down the iron bar. The prisoner refused to pick it up. Challenor threatened him with it and then punched him in the face.[12]

In February 1965 Challenor was finally suspended from the police force. "I think it's very unhealthy for a society to love the police the way the English do," Orton said. "When you have that kind of affection for authority, you begin to have the makings of a police state. I think wariness of the police is a much healthier attitude."[13] As a homosexual Orton had been entrapped by police, so he told friends; and, once in custody, had been propositioned by them. This gave another dimension of anger to *Loot*'s satire. "Obviously you've got to have police; they're a necessary evil," Orton said. "I've no objection to them tracking down murderers and bank robbers, clearly you can't have people behaving in a completely anarchic way. I believe, though, that they interfere far too much with private morals—whether people are having it off in the backs of cars or smoking marijuana, or doing the interesting little things that one does. . . ."[14]

In the final version of the play, Orton appended an epigram from George Bernard Shaw's *Misalliance*. "Anarchism," says Lord Summerhays, "is a game at which the Police can beat you. . . ." Challenor was living confirmation of Orton's fantasy. Gradually Truscott assumed Challenor's salient characteristics. "You're fucking nicked, my old beauty," was grafted verbatim into Truscott's dialogue as he nabs McLeavy. Truscott continues: "You've found to your cost that the standards of British justice are high."

Initially Truscott lacked Challenor's psychopathic unpredictability, which makes him dangerous and disturbing as well as funny. *Loot*'s original violence was ludicrous violence; and pain was generalized, so that its implications were easily dismissed. The terrifying frivolity of the characters veered in the first draft toward silliness. Truscott's transformation from buffoon to bully was slow to evolve. In the first of many revised endings, Truscott sends Dennis, Fay, and Hal to jail and keeps the money for himself, wheeling it offstage in a pram which holds a gramophone playing "Land of Hope and Glory": "Your guilt shall be purged. Society has weighed you in her balance and found that she has been short measured. To Judgement! To Retribution! To Justice!"

The extravagant ending was an attempt to unite Orton's comic statement with his star's persona. Kenneth Williams became the scapegoat for *Loot*'s literary inadequacies. The burden of the play's success or failure fell on his bony shoulders. Williams, like Duncan Macrae, who played McLeavy, was a celebrated theatrical exotic cast in a role that demanded a veneer of normality. His stage presence was alert, glittering, hungry to please, tinged unmistakably by hysteria. Truscott, however, was unnerving because he vacillated between the articulate and the oafish. "My wife is a woman," he says, in a joke stolen from Wycherley's *The Country Wife*. Nothing about a Kenneth Williams performance was believably dim or menacing. Physically, he was slim; emotionally, despite the comic caterwauling, he was vulnerable. No amount of rewriting could disguise his personality or mobilize these qualities to serve the sinister side of the character. Williams sensed this from the beginning of rehearsal. His diaries recount his mounting anxiety as Truscott (and *Loot*) underwent major literary surgery.

6 January 65

With Joe. We discussed *Loot*. He said he wanted to add another character as an assistant to Truscott [Meadows] and try to find a third act ending. So, we're back at the old trial and error game with three weeks left to rehearse—no definite script. This play has been around since last October and now this sort of activity! I spoke against change unless it was something that altered the structure and it was concrete. I objected to a character being added. . . .

15 January

Rehearsal at Duke of York's. Spent all day plotting Act III. It was laborious and involved all rewriting. The script is now so altered that practically no one has a proper copy. Our books are full of amendments and erasures. Lunched with Wood. I felt as though I was in a maze of despair. . . .

21 January

My relationship with Wood is getting very strained. Today, when he asked me to alter dialogue I'd already learned once more—I refused. I dislike doing this as I'm well-aware that defiance of authority is a bad example to the cast. There are occasions on which he forces one into rebellion simply because what he's doing is wasteful and futile. Again and again he makes the point about logic and reasonableness whereas the level on which this play will succeed is not that at all. The cast still don't know the lines well enough to use them. We are still mainly preoccupied with business, geography. There's a curious tiredness creeping in, too—despite the fact that there's no real hard work. Just loads of talk.

26 January

No one seems to get a real improvement on the scenes nor is the dialogue really flowing. It breaks and dries. Left at 6—totally depressed. Moreover, I'm now worried about the play—it seems a random collection of bits with no sense of wholeness.

28 January

I can't see any sense of construction in the piece, perhaps it's just a lack of an audience. Perhaps—oh this is the worst period of all— waiting to see if the thing will be able to fly. . . .

"THE PLAY is a disaster," Orton wrote Halliwell from Cambridge after the opening. "There were hardly any laughs for Truscott. The audience seemed to take the most extraordinary lines with dead seriousness. Can't you ring me? It's all so dreadful. I've already had two rows of nerve-wracking proportions. I've said to Wood that I'm not a commercial writer and perhaps he understands now why it's impossible that I should ever be a 'National humourist.' "[15] Still, Orton put on a brave public face. "I think *Loot* should be a success,"[16] Orton rashly told the press in the first week of tryouts at Cambridge, where the show had sold out. But in his scrapbook he had pasted a cartoon of a scowling bear with arms akimbo and a large welt on its head, captioned: DO YOU FEEL LIKE A BEAR WITH A SORE HEAD? The Cambridge reviews weren't bad, they were disastrous. "A particularly nauseating article," began the Cambridge *Review*, ". . . an evening of very British rubbish." The Cambridge *News* reported that the "audience laughed more at the actors' skills than at the script and some of them found it difficult to laugh much at all." Two weeks later the same Cambridge critic put not too fine a point on his reaction to *Loot:* "a very bad play—shapeless and without style, inexcusably vulgar and even boring." "Horrendous" was Codron's one-word professional assessment of *Loot*'s debut. "Kenneth, having decided he couldn't be himself, was playing Truscott like Himmler. He decided to disguise himself like a little Gestapo in this extraordinary mackintosh. Nothing happened." Orton's lines, the critics observed, were amusing from moment to moment; but they didn't seem to lead anywhere.

The problem was not only in the play's structure but in the entire production, which groped for a style to deal with such a new and dangerous game. "I made the mistake of thinking *Loot* far too much of a Restoration or early-eighteenth-century play in modern times," Wood says. "I tried to do the play with a kind of cod formality as if it were *Way of the World* or something. Joe quite liked the idea; or at least, he never made any objection to it. It was a mistake not to have plumped for absolute realism. I was kind of afraid of the play. There was something about the body of the late Mrs. McLeavy which could disassociate the audience. I tried to find a style which would allow the body to be thrown about and be totally accepted."

"Unless *Loot* is directed and acted perfectly seriously, the play will fail. As it failed in its original touring version," Orton wrote later in his notes for the American production of 1968. "A director who imagines that the only object is to get a laugh is not for me."[17] But in 1965, with his reputation on the line and a successful West End director stressing the artifice and the jokes, Orton kept his peace and paid the consequences. Every directorial device deflected attention from the macabre reality of the events and the characters. Desmond Heeley's set was a startling and streamlined art nouveau edifice, painted wedding-cake white, which vied at every moment with the dialogue for the audience's attention. Like spectres, the actors stalked about this glossy environment dressed in black. "We did it in black and white as a sort of Pop Art set," Wood explains. "I was thinking of things like Tom and Jerry cartoons where, no matter how hard they hit the cat over the head, it remains funny because the essential violence has been stylized to the point where it's essentially acceptable."

Wood's first reaction to the barrage of hostility that greeted the play was to increase *Loot*'s formality. At one point, he introduced a metronome that ticked away behind the footlights. "What's that for?" Williams demanded, angry at being made still more like a puppet than a person. "Wood said, 'This play is essentially stylistic. I wanted the dialogue delivered in a stylistic fashion.' " At Cambridge, the performances were turned out to the audience rather than toward each other. The effect was to make *Loot* more like a cabaret than a farce ensemble. The panic of finding a style and an audience response sent each performer scurrying into his special successful mannerisms. The actors had been dissatisfied and confused in rehearsals, and Cambridge gave credence to their fears.

"*Loot* is a serious play," Orton stressed in his production notes for the Americans. ". . . Ideally, it should be nearer *The Homecoming* than 'I Love Lucy.' Don't think I'm a snob about 'I Love Lucy.' I've watched it often. I think it's very funny. But it is purely aimed at making an audience laugh. And that isn't the prime aim of *Loot*. . . . It's most important to get the subtext of the play right. The play shouldn't be one long giggle—there should be depths. It can never work as a rival to *Barefoot in the Park*."[18] But in the beginning, this distinction was not clear in Orton's mind. Instead of the curtain coming up on a house of mourning, where laughter should become unsettling in the ritualized context, the audience met Truscott pushing a pram with a gramophone as he reconnoitered with his police sidekick, Meadows, for a little burlesque cross-talk about their mission. Both were dressed as tramps. "Were you issued a barrel organ?" Truscott asks, in a joke whose silliness tells an audience not to take him too seriously. Meadows says no and asks, "I wonder, sir, if I should change my boots? These are regulation issue and as such are well-known to suspected persons."

Having established their motive for the audience (and killed any surprise for Truscott's entrance into the McLeavy household), they set to work with Truscott's gramophone playing "Abide with Me" as the semi-detached housefront is rolled out to reveal McLeavy sitting beside the coffin. The end of Act 1, which in the final version has the horrific and hilarious image of Truscott puzzling with his magnifying glass over Mrs. McLeavy's false eye, had at Cambridge a burlesque and completely conciliatory tone. Orton's anger at the abuse of police authority was reduced to a sight gag. As Mrs. McLeavy is carted off for burial, Truscott is seen outside the house climbing the drainpipe. Meadows enters and approaches. "As Meadows draws near to Truscott," the stage directions read, "he salutes smartly. Truscott returns the salute, clinging with one hand to the drainpipe."

"I do my best work rewriting," Orton said in 1967. *Loot* was proof of this boast. "What I usually do is cut because I find cutting is the real thing. An awful lot of plays could be made so much more brilliant by cutting only there isn't anything to cut. If you haven't got a story and a plot, you can't cut."[19] After the Cambridge fiasco, it was clear that *Loot* needed more plot, sharper dialogue, and a new production concept. Wood began to strip away the formality and attack the script naturalistically. Orton was sent back to London to rewrite. "The burden of my song to Joe was this—the play needs to reach in action the same anarchic conclusions of the dialogue," Wood says. "I wanted the whole play to rebound on an innocent person. Originally, it didn't." On February 9, Codron and Wood presented the cast with the first pages of Orton's staggering series of rewrites. The original play had run to only eighty-nine pages. Before the end of their six-week engagement, the actors would learn and insert in their scripts 133 pages of new and rewritten material. Kenneth Williams, who from the outset disagreed with Wood's correct instinct about the need for logical complication in the farce, was livid:

9 February 65

Codron and Wood arrive. They brought with them the rewrites. I thought they were lousy and said so. At least see the show as it stands now that we've gained a bit of confidence and say that you want changes. . . . So, the rewrites apparently are essential, and we start all over again. I think there's going to be an endless round ahead of putting patches on a leaking hulk that will never be right because of a basic flaw: the play begins about Fay and her story is never developed beyond Act I. . . . After the show, went to see Noel Willman and Peggy Ramsay. He said I was at my best in the play when I appeared to be emotionally involved. This is a good clue to what I've been missing. (The Challenor bit—"I'll have you, you

young bugger, etc. . . .") Every time you get that kind of involvement in the performance—the whole play works.

The cast began a schizophrenic régime of rehearsing the rewritten
play in the afternoon while performing the beleaguered original version at night. "It was the most painful period of my life," Kenneth
Williams says. "I felt again and again as an actor that we simply weren't
gaining the audience's confidence. We never did establish confidence
for the simple reason that we were in a terrible quandary ourselves wondering which version was the right one. We were tentative, which is
death for Orton. You must take the stage with enormous conviction
and panache." But panic had set in amongst the cast, as Williams's diary
reports about the two days following Orton's first batch of rewrites:

> *10 February*
> Unconfident performance. One laugh for loss of another. . . . And
> it had the effect of taking away the character of Truscott. Before—
> with two interrogations—I had a chance of establishing the char-
> acter. Now, with both of them split—I have completely lost it.
> Script in rags. Cast is utterly demoralized. I shouldn't have set foot
> near this rotten mess.

> *11 February*
> . . . Wood talks to the cast about the evil of negative thinking.
> That's a lot of help! . . . Laurence Olivier came round and said,
> "You haven't got a play here, that's your trouble. . . ."

Williams wasn't the only one worried about Orton's rewrites. Peggy
Ramsay, who'd seen the play at Cambridge and Brighton, wrote to
Michael Codron on February 10 to lodge a protest while admitting that
the Brighton performance "was very much slicker and more professional . . . this play is already better than *Sloane* at any time. . . ."
Wood's attempts to tighten the plot's logic led inevitably to the sacrifice of mischief for motivation. *Loot*, Peggy Ramsay thought, was "beginning, very slightly, to lose Joe's personal and unique voice."

The reviews were not getting better, either. "As a farce, *Loot* isn't
strong enough," wrote the critic from *Isis*, when the company reached
Oxford. "The climaxes misfire and the jokes—if so they are—are mis-
timed. . . ." While Williams was skeptical about the rewrites which
came into the script almost daily, he shared the company's admiration
for the stamina and calibre of Orton's work under pressure. "Joe admired Wilde for the great pains he took with his work. He used to
quote me Wilde's dictum: 'Talent is the infinite capacity for taking

pains.' He took pains. Polish. Reconstruct. Give you another edition. Another page. Every word polished painstakingly until the whole structure *glitters*. His application, his industry, and his *consistent* diligence—astonished me in that period of three editions of the play. . . . By the third week, he'd got that weak thing, that awful weak giddiness when the pressure's been too much. You start to laugh. That awful laugh at no joke. That laugh that comes from nothing. . . ."

At Oxford, the hysteria mounted. "Everyone on the verge of a nervous breakdown," Orton wrote wearily to Halliwell, enclosing a damning review from the Oxford *Mail* which he felt was justified. "Kenneth Williams disasterous [*sic*]—just all his old performances from 'Beyond Our Ken.' And then he wonders why he isn't getting laughs. 'ow many 'usbands 'ave you 'ad? (ugh). . . . We've now a rebellious company on our hands plus a temperamental star. . . . I wouldn't have believed when I wrote the play that it could be so difficult. . . . I try to keep very very calm. . . . Do try and hang on doing something if you get too fed up without me. I'll be back as soon as humanly possible. I'm not just gallivanting about down here. It's the most depressing few weeks I've ever lived through."[20] After a playful tussle with Ian McShane, Orton ended up with a black eye, bruised and embarrassed. The cast started to display their exhausted frustration. Williams was angry at everybody; Duncan Macrae was coming offstage muttering to himself; even the equable Geraldine McEwan, who told the press "I can only work when I'm happy,"[21] finally cracked:

16 February

I [Kenneth Williams] said in front of the company and Wood that the rewrites were all a mistake and our only chance was to go back to what we started with. P. Wood said no. So on we go to utter failure. . . . I rang Codron and asked him to come down as quickly as possible. He refused saying P. Wood asked him not to come down and a load of crap about "I must obey my director" (we'd already had P. Wood saying I must obey my manager). Utterly spurious of course. He thinks I'm exaggerating and all is alright. Geraldine came off shouting: "I CAN'T GO ON WITH THIS ANYMORE! I CAN'T GO ON." And crying. I obviously can't come into London with material like this.

18 February

Show went like suet pudding. Playing this stuff is like trying to catch bath water in your hand. It keeps slipping through your fingers. Geraldine now shaking and ill. Tonight at the hotel, David Battley (Meadows) started crying uncontrollably and left the room.

22 February
We died in the second half and never got them back again. An
inquest afterwards with P. Wood, Joe Orton, and Codron. Poor
Joe just looked beaten into the ground; and Wood did go on at him.
"You've got to write more. More rewrites." The boy's got nothing
more to write.

"Last night was appalling," Orton wrote to Halliwell in desperation over Geraldine McEwan's hysterics. "She had to be taken home
and given sedation. The stage manager has collapsed with some form
of food poisoning. Wood is now saying, 'Perhaps we ought to take it
off and bring it back much later and not risk the big commercial stakes.
Bring it back at the Royal Court. It's coterie entertainment, and perhaps it shouldn't be forced on a public like this one.' I keep up a
constant moan about, 'I'm not a commercial playwright. I never said
I was.' Last night he took McShane and me out to dinner and I suddenly found myself being subjected to a lot of psychological chat—
'Of course the trouble with you is that you can't communicate. It's
your great fault as a person and as a writer.' Etc.... Wood says that a
line like 'With your intimate knowledge of rare drugs' is private humour. Not funny with a wide audience. I don't agree. He said John
Whiting always condemned that kind of humour. So I said, 'Well he
never wrote a fucking decent play in his life. And *The Devils* has
longeurs compared to which *Loot*'s are brilliant high-spots.' I said to
Ian afterwards that 'Wood wants something I have and resents that
I have it.' I don't at the moment know what it is.... Everybody here
is behaving like the most ridiculous caricatures of Hollywood theat-
ricals...."[22]

Loot was still wordy, still too clumsily plotted; but under Wood's
guidance, Orton had achieved a lot in the month of rehearsing. A farce
structure, with its twists of plot and reversal of expectation, had been
imposed on the material. The original first act, which rambled to thirty
pages of character exposition, had been successfully telescoped to
fifteen. Dennis now lusted after Fay, and the triangle took on erotic
complication. Fay, once the front-runner in the farce, fell back to third
lead behind Truscott and McLeavy, opening up new possibilities for
action. Having reconceived Fay's role, Orton always emphasized to
producers this shift in the play's balance. "She must be kept in her
place," he wrote about the American production. "(Always a difficult
thing for the Americans to do with their women.) . . . But she isn't to
be allowed to swamp the play. It isn't a play about Fay. . . . She should
ideally be under thirty. I want the erotic idea behind a girl in her late

twenties and boys in their teens. She isn't a mother substitute. None of your Tennessee Williams' drag queens."[23] The rewrites emphasized the erotic idea; and the triangle allowed Orton to have fun with the stereotypes of "the homosexual," which was always part of the play's intended mischief. In the early versions, Orton pushed the sexual point too bluntly. He had Hal, panicked by the sight of the law, urging Dennis: "Go on, act normal." To which Dennis replied: "What's that?" But the trio's sexual involvement made comment unnecessary. "I don't want there to be anything queer or camp or odd about the relationship of Hal and Dennis," Orton wrote in the American production notes. "Americans see homosexuality in terms of fag and drag. This isn't my vision of the universal brotherhood. They must be perfectly ordinary boys who happen to be fucking each other. Nothing could be more natural. I won't have the Great American Queen brought into it." The *ménage à trois* gave *Loot* new areas of innuendo and stage business:

> DENNIS. We've never involved a woman in anything unsavoury before.
>
> *He takes the lid off the coffin.* FAY *piles money into his arms.* HAL *does the same.*
>
> (*To* FAY.) Half of this money is mine. Will you marry me?
> HAL. We're splitting the money three ways now, baby. You'll have thirty-four thousand.
> DENNIS (*to* FAY). Is that enough?
> FAY. You've a slight lead on Mr. McLeavy at the moment.
>
> *She kisses him.* DENNIS *trembles and drops the money back into the coffin.*
>
> HAL (*angry*). Hurry up! What's the matter with you?
> DENNIS. My hands are trembling. It's excitement at the prospect of becoming engaged.
> HAL. You're too easily aroused. That's your trouble.

Orton was learning to write action, and his jokes were becoming more economic and specific in service of the play's momentum. The rewrites show him struggling to reveal character through gesture. He'd already found some marvellous routines to indicate Truscott's disturbing megalomania. "I conduct my cases under an assumed voice and I am a master of disguise," Truscott boasts to Hal, doffing his trilby. "You see—a complete transformation." The detective pastiche was no longer tentative and generalized, but precise and subtle. Orton puckishly allowed Truscott to judge Fay's confession of seven counts of manslaughter the way critics would assess Orton's own symbolic slaughter: "Your style is simple and direct. It's a theme which less skillfully handled could have given offence." Truscott no sooner meets Fay than he exposes her as the murderer of her first husband. "My methods of deduction can be learned by anyone with a keen eye and a quick brain," he says. "When I shook your hand I felt a roughness on one of your wedding rings. A roughness I associate with powder burns and salt. The two together spell a gun and sea air. When found on a wedding ring only one solution is possible. . . ." This not only sent up the detective's unerring "logic" but built a much richer sense of Fay's past. It also enacted the wit of an epigram buried in *Loot*'s repartee: "The process by which the Police arrive at the solution of a mystery, is in itself a mystery."

"The nearer we got to London," Orton said of *Loot*, "the better it went. It's a London play."[24] Orton's work was good; but the show, lumbered with the beautiful but ill-conceived set, was still not good enough. Orton became embattled and belligerent over the production. The strain caught up with him. A misunderstood remark of "no comment" by Peggy Ramsay, after seeing the play at Golders Green, produced a furious letter on February 28 from Orton that spelled out his view of the play and his future if it failed:

> What have you got to be upset about? *Loot* is in far better shape than when we sold it to Michael. I wanted to write a farce. The nearer I come to it the unhappier you are. I have not turned "an interesting failure" into a second-rate farce; I've turned a failed farce into a successful farce. There are a dozen writers who can turn out interesting failures. Phoney intellectuals think there's a merit in it. *Eh?* is what used to be called a mess not a farce.
>
> I know what my authentic voice is better than anyone else. It is vulgar and offensive in the extreme to middle-class susceptibilities.
>
> I've already told Michael that I'm doing nothing else to the play until I get an assurance that we're going to the West End. If *Loot* folds through no fault of its own, I'll wash my hands of writing. Don't imagine that failure will stimulate me. It never has done yet.
>
> That you hated *Sloane* I can forgive. Dromgoole's production, plus the acting, left a lot to be desired. But if you dislike *Loot* as well, perhaps it is the essential me as a writer you dislike. And we both of us better think seriously of parting company.

Despite the threats, Orton continued with rewrites and Peggy Ramsay. But the pressure mounted. At Bournemouth in the first week of March, Codron's more conservative co-producer, Donald Albery, took exception to the direction of some of Orton's pungent rewrites. Albery was not the only one who was not amused. On March 3 *The Times* reported that in Bournemouth two dozen old ladies stormed out of the massive Pavilion Theatre on opening night in protest "to dialogue which uses the word brothel and which satirizes sex, patriotism, death and the law." Orton referred to this segment of the audience as "The Bump and Trot Brigade"—a phrase referring to the thump of the seats as the spectators made for the lobby. Orton liked to wander through the lobby at intermission and retail overheard fragments of conversations to the actors after the show. " 'Well, my dear, I was at the Thompsons' only yesterday at their barbecue and they warned me it was filth. And like a fool I rejected their advice,' " Williams recalls Orton telling him. It became their sport. "In the hotel I heard people discussing *Loot*," Williams says. "One woman said to the man, 'It was a good job you didn't come. The play was disgusting absolutely filthy.' 'What was it about?' 'Oh—it's about Jesus, do you see . . . being a queer.' There was no reference to Jesus being homosexual, not one reference. People did say the most extraordinary things. Presumably they must have come away very angry."

They were angrier in Manchester, where police were stationed in the wings after the Watch Committee disallowed Truscott's query about Dennis's illegitimate children:

> TRUSCOTT. . . . Where does he engender these unwanted children? There are no open spaces. The police patrol regularly. It should be next to impossible to commit the smallest act of indecency, let alone beget a child. Where does he do it?
> HAL. On crowded dance floors during the rumba.

Confident about the play's improvements, Codron promised Peggy Ramsay "we shall not regard sneeringly what the Manchester papers say about *Loot*. . . ."[25] There was no way to overlook the message in their reception—DAZZLING AT TIMES BUT EASY TO FORGET (*Daily Mail*); EXPERIMENT IN FUN FAILS TO AMUSE (*Daily Telegraph*). Only the Manchester *Evening News* went to the other extreme, calling *Loot* "the funniest thing to have hit Manchester since 'Beyond the Fringe.' " The round of rewriting continued. "Manchester was terribly depressing," Wood remembers. "Nobody laughed. Joe and I would get together in his hotel room and work through the morning and then insert the lines in the afternoon." But after the Manchester notices, desperation set in. "I took Joe Orton to supper," Williams noted in his diary on March 11. "The boy admitted he was punch drunk with rewrites."

Suddenly people began maneuvering for safety in case of disaster. Codron wrote to Orton on March 12 asking for a guarantee of right of first refusal on his next play. "I feel strongly that if I do manage to get a West End theatre for *Loot,* with or without the help of Donald Albery, and despite all the jeremiahs advising me not to bring it in, I shall be inevitably risking more capital than has been spent so far," Codron said. Dissension also erupted between Codron and Wood over the director's apparent absence from a Manchester performance. "I said to the cast, 'Oh well, I'm going off to watch the Hallé Orchestra,' because Joe's rewrites were in the second half," Wood explains. "It was a joke. What I did was go upstairs and sit in the circle. There I sat through the first half roaring with laughter because nobody else was. I came backstage afterwards and Joe was very pleased. 'Well,' he said, 'there's one person in Manchester for whom the play is a masterpiece.' I never dared say it was me." But after the performance, Wood took Kenneth Williams and Geraldine McEwan to dinner and, according to Codron, "at this meal, allegedly asked both the stars to support him in his pleas to me for the production not to be brought to London."

At Wimbledon, Williams noted in his diary on March 15, "Codron told us there was no theatre. The Phoenix would rather be dark than have us." Wimbledon was *Loot*'s last stop before the West End, and the Phoenix's refusal was the production's final humiliation. The theatre was the white elephant of Emile Littler's empire, which even Codron had to admit "nobody wanted to play." Codron cast about for other theatres and other directors. Patrick Dromgoole was asked to doctor the production but demurred. *Loot* wheezed to a flat and inevitable end. "Geraldine confided to me in the dressing room that she will not come into town with it," Williams wrote on March 19. The next day, the production's last, Williams wrote:

> Wood turned up for the matinee after ignoring us for a week! . . . Michael Codron met the cast afterwards. If the company were keen, he could put it in the Lyric Hammersmith. But the company all said no. So the play died tonight after 56 performances of about three editions.

Loot was a dead horse, but it continued to be flogged. Two days after the show closed, the London *Evening News* ran a vicious, ranting article. "Personally I thought it was one of the most revolting things I had ever seen," wrote a reporter who was not a drama critic, ". . . the management pasted over the bills at Wimbledon: 'This show is unsuitable for children'. . . . It would have been better if Michael Codron had displayed some new ones: 'THIS PLAY IS UNSUITABLE.' " The notice was the final nail in *Loot*'s coffin. The play became a legendary failure. "It was an appalling flop," Williams says. "A great . . . big . . . flop." Orton's reputation and his energy had been seriously diminished. "After *Loot* folded on tour," he said, understating the blow, "there was a long period when I didn't do anything at all."[26]

"I HARDLY DARE MENTION *Loot*. Is anything happening?" Orton wrote to Peggy Ramsay on June 29, 1965, from Morocco, where he had gone with Halliwell for the first extended vacation of his life. "I know I'm greedy. Most writers with a play going on Broadway and a director of [Alan Schneider's] calibre producing would be content for the time being. But I do have a feeling that poor *Loot* is being left out in the cold—moan, moan, isn't it, from me." But away from London, his sense of urgency about *Loot* and the weight of its failure were lightened by the benevolence of sunshine and new sensations. "I'm feeling fine," he reported to Peggy Ramsay. "So tired though. I need two cups of very black coffee in the morning just to wake me up. Much more relaxing than Bournemouth."

In England, *Loot* was stalled; and in America, after *Entertaining Mr. Sloane*'s disastrous reception on Broadway, the prospects of relaunching *Loot* were stone cold. For the rest of 1965, Orton busied himself with a TV play, his version of *The Bacchae*—a fun palace revolution set in a Butlin's holiday resort and called *The Erpingham Camp*. Orton had first explored the notion as a film treatment for Lindsay Anderson, developing it into a Brechtian epic complete (in early drafts) with illustrative banners such as SCENE 5: AN EXAMPLE OF THE ACTIVE LIFE OF THE CHURCH. ERPINGHAM PREPARES HIMSELF TO MEET THE PEOPLE. THEOLOGY DISCUSSED. THE PADRE PROVES THAT CHRISTIANITY IS ESSENTIAL TO GOOD HEALTH. Orton submitted the play on October 24, 1965, still planning, as he wrote to Glenn Loney, "to spend the winter writing a stage play."[27] But worries about *Loot*'s fate and the March shooting schedule for *The Erpingham Camp* prevented him from getting down to work.

In January 1966, Oscar Lewenstein bravely picked up *Loot*'s option. "I'm at the present on tenterhooks over *Loot*," Orton wrote to Loney in March. "I had a meeting with Oscar Lewenstein and we put the first wheels in motion. We're flying high among the stars at the moment. We'll be down to earth again soon."[28]

Orton had made plans to leave for a three-month holiday in Morocco on April 12, the day after *Loot* was to open in The Century Theatre production at Manchester's University Theatre, under Braham Murray's direction. "If I go away on the twelfth, with the fate of the play still undecided—I'm staying away," Orton wrote Peggy Ramsay on March 12, telling her to warn his producers. Orton's hectoring couldn't hurry Lewenstein and Michael White (who had joined forces with Lewenstein as co-producer) into a production. They were interested in watching how the play did in Manchester. Murray, who as an Oxford *wunderkind* had directed *Hang Down Your Head and Die* on the West End, had pestered Peggy Ramsay; and with no one else committed to the play by the new year, she had let him have it. "I honestly don't know whether he can be entrusted with it," she wrote Orton. "We can't make any second mistake in the production of this play and we must be QUITE sure."[29] Murray was no mistake. His production would be *Loot*'s new lease on life.

Murray understood the passion behind both *Loot* and Orton: "That final image of *Loot* with Fay flanked by the two fellahs saying, 'Let's keep up appearances'—that was what Joe was about," Murray says. "He was trying to work out this central relationship of men to women. It was terribly Marlowe. Men in a mess. Truscott is the old conscience, the old morality; that conscience is dead in our time. It lingers and has become corrupt. Joe knew that the whole sexual thing was going to have to be redefined. He knew that in the violence and sex, especially in the sorts of relationship which had been regarded as being wrong and perverted, there was an immense power to be harnessed for good. In order to liberate the positive side of all those drives, you had to explore the deepest resources of your own nature. He knew that if he could go right into it and face it all himself, then he would climb into the light." Orton's experience in television with *The Erpingham Camp* gave him more faith in a naturalistic attack on *Loot*'s rewrites. "I'm very pleased with *The Erpingham Camp*," Orton wrote to Glenn Loney after the shooting. "It's been directed and acted absolutely *real*. With astonishing results. H. Pinter says it's like *The Battleship Potemkin*. I won't go as far as this, but it's very good. . . ."[30] In the *Loot* revisions, Orton built up the reality of the relationships, and the horror. "Joe's main objection to Peter Wood's version," says Murray, who worked with Orton on the revisions, "was that it overlooked the black side of the play. There was no horror. Wood made sure that a coffin didn't look like a coffin."

Murray opted for a naturalistic environment. "The style of the set . . . the tone . . . is right,"[31] Orton wrote to Michael White. Orton cut 621 lines from Wood's version, compressing the action and allowing the characters to react more immediately to each other's demands rather than be sidetracked by their own verbal felicity. And for the Manchester production, Orton made Truscott's interrogation of Hal more specific and alarming. Instead of "standing over Hal" when Truscott says "in any other political system I'd have you on the floor in tears," Orton gave brutal impact to the line by adding "shouting, knocking Hal to the floor." Orton now wanted Truscott "beating, knocking and punching him. Hal screams with pain." After McLeavy is dragged off to jail, Orton intensified the predatory evil of his characters in short, quick strokes:

> DENNIS. What will you charge him with, Inspector?
> TRUSCOTT. Oh, anything will do.
> FAY. Can an accidental death be arranged?
> TRUSCOTT. Anything can be arranged in prison.
> HAL. Except pregnancy.

Orton gave Fay a sly, curt coda to resolve the plot point. "We'll bury your father with your mother," she says. "That will be nice for him, won't it?" Fay's consideration coats the poisonous truth that McLeavy is as good as dead.

At last the play was finding the right balance between fun and pain, frivolity and fury. "I'd like to get married. It's the only thing I haven't tried," Dennis tells Hal in the Wood version of *Loot*. Hal's reply has no comic reverberation: "Put her out of your mind, baby, and concentrate on the job at hand." In Manchester, the line was recast to ricochet off the idea of Dennis's heterosexual fling. Hal says: "I don't like your living for kicks, baby. Put these neurotic ideas out of your mind and concentrate on the problems of everyday life." Instead of Hal dishing Fay with a lacklustre: "She's not your sort. She's religious," Orton made the revised line dance: "She's three parts Papal nuncio."

But it was McLeavy who benefited most from the confidence of Orton's rewrites. McLeavy's credulous worry about human remains being desecrated; his bewilderment ("It's going to take me a long time to believe she's dead. She was such an active sort of person") were added in Manchester. Orton also underlined McLeavy's faith in authority. "I hope he finds what he's looking for," McLeavy now said to Fay about Truscott. "I'd like to be of assistance to authority." With a clear understanding of how he wanted his play to rebound on McLeavy,

Orton showed him kowtowing to law and order even as it oppressed him. His deference to the police also gave Truscott energy for new outrageousness:

> TRUSCOTT. . . . . I'm going to have this place turned upside down.
>
> MCLEAVY. Oh, dear, what a nuisance. And in a house of mourning, too. . . .
>
> TRUSCOTT. There's no cause for alarm. It's a mere formality. You're quite safe. (*He smiles. To* MCLEAVY.) There's no one more touchy than your hardened criminal. (*He puts his pipe away.*) I'll be back in ten minutes. And then, I'm afraid, a lot of damage will be done to your property. You'll be paying repair bills for months to come. One unfortunate suspect recently had the roof taken off his house.
>
> MCLEAVY. Isn't there anything I can do to prevent this appalling assault upon my privacy?
>
> TRUSCOTT. Well, sir, if you can suggest a possible hiding-place for the money.
>
> MCLEAVY *hangs his head.*
>
> MCLEAVY (*almost in a whisper*). I can't, Inspector.
>
> TRUSCOTT. Very well. You must take the consequences of your ignorance.

Murray managed to get the Lord Chamberlain to reinstate most of the cuts imposed on the touring version. But when the play reopened in Manchester on April 11, the police were in the stalls just in case. To Orton's delight, *Loot* got a hearty welcome from the *Daily Telegraph*, which, besides finding it "very funny" and the plotting "as fast and frivolous as Feydeau's," commented that "it seems a pity that Joe Orton's *Loot* was withdrawn during its preliminary tour."[32] With a surge of renewed hope for his play, Orton dashed off last-minute casting suggestions to Michael White before leaving for Morocco:

> The way it's played at Manchester does leave me wide open to accusations of a "message" ending. Quite wrong . . . Fay. The way it's being played at Manchester—as a real woman, a real nurse, is right. . . . It is the third part in the play. I don't want any of these "monsters." I want a real woman. Not a man in drag. And this is about the most difficult thing to achieve in the West End Theatre. So please Vivien Merchant or the girl in Manchester. . . . The boys in Manchester are poor . . . clean as a whistle sexually. . . . One can't imagine them having each other or Fay or anyone. . . . The

director. This is up to you. I'm not good on directors. Get somebody
straightforward if possible. Somebody who'll know his onions. I'm
dead against anyone too arty. I think it's a good 75% casting. De-
pending on what you think after you've seen Manchester I wouldn't
violently object to Braham Murray. But then, on directors, I'm a
blank. . . .³³

Orton's buoyant conviction about the prospects of *Loot*'s revival
evaporated almost as soon as he and Halliwell settled into their apartment on the Rue de Menchamps in Tangier. Instead of bringing news
of production plans, Peggy Ramsay's letters brought more exasperation.
"I'm certainly *not* rewriting *Loot*," he wrote to her on May 8, after the
Evening News had printed a squib about Orton being in Tangier to
rewrite his play. "Didn't they read the Manchester notice in *The Daily
Telegraph*? . . . Has anything at all happened with regard to that ill-
fated play during the last month? I forget it for long periods of time
here and then suddenly remember it and want to ring you." Orton
was eager for every scrap of news about the play's progress. The Royal
Court, with William Gaskill taking over artistic control from George
Devine, had shown renewed interest; and now, it was rumored the
National were nibbling. "If the National want *Loot*," he wrote to Peggy
Ramsay on May 12, "move Heaven and Earth to see they do it. I'm tired
of the dallyings of the commercial theatre. I'd be delighted to let them
have it on any terms. As long as everybody stops *talking* and puts it
on!!" He enclosed a scowling photograph of himself "merely to indicate my state of mind when I remember that another six months option
is running out and that *still* nothing appears to be being done about
the play which so many people one hears are interested in (foul, foul
grammar, but I'm doped to the eyes). . . ." In a postscript, he pleaded,
"Has any progress been made at all?"

Peggy Ramsay counselled Orton not to panic, assuring him that
"*Loot* will go on some way or another." But by June, the news from
London had gone from bad to worse. "You say you hope I'm not frantic about the play and that if we have to wait a month or three months
it would be worth it for a good production. I absolutely agree," he
wrote on June 10. "But November—the latest date to be mentioned
is six months off. Oscar by then will have had an option for nearly a year!
It will be *two* years since I wrote it. Even so I wouldn't be worried if
it was put on this year. I'm starting to really panic at the idea of delay-
ing it any longer than November. It must go on *this year*!!! . . . I've
just been reading the *Times* crit of [John Osborne's] *A Bond Hon-*

oured and it seems to me that the kind of thing I ushered in in *Sloane* and do in *Loot* is provoking a lot of hostile press. Which is why *Loot* *must must* go on within the next six months. Or we'll run the risk of having them jeering 'old hat' when it does appear out of sheer spleen." In her reply, Peggy Ramsay reported the devastating news that the Royal Court, who had been stringing Orton along, enthusiastic about his work in general but ambivalent about *Loot*, would probably drop the play.

The news sent Orton into a fury. " 'When sorrows come they come not single spies, but in battalions.' I felt like Richard III receiving the messengers," Orton wrote to Peggy Ramsay on June 18, in a zestful, vitriolic attack on the English theatre scene:

> I think it's disgusting with so much utter shit put on in both the commercial and subsidized theatres that a play like *Loot* should have this difficulty. I'd understand it after Wimbledon, but not after a really pretty average Rep production which succeeded in attracting such a glowing notice in *The Telegraph.* . . .
>
> I'm sick, sick, sick of the theatre. . . .
>
> I think you'd better warn Oscar [Lewenstein] that if the *Loot* option runs out in January with no sign of the play being put on I shan't renew the option. I shall throw the play on the fire. And I shan't write a third stage play. I shall earn my living on TV.
>
> I'm really quite capable of carrying out this. I've always admired Congreve who, after the absolute failure of *Way of the World* just stopped writing. And Rimbaud who turned his back on the literary world after writing a few volumes of poems.
>
> Of course, I know you're doing your best. All the foregoing isn't including you. As they say "I've every confidence in your abilities." Certainly at the moment it's "JOE CONTRA MUNDEM."

Orton was so angry, he forgot to sign the letter, but added a typical postscript: "A millionaire out here has gone dotty about me. He keeps smacking my arse and groping my cock and saying 'You're an attractive little bugger.' So perhaps I shall be able to give up writing after all!!!"

By mid-July, when he was back in London, Orton's angry threats to Lewenstein had mellowed into regret. "Could we meet perhaps and talk some more about *Loot*," he wrote Lewenstein. "It's getting a very old baby, isn't it? I'm about to write a new TV play [*Funeral Games*]. I don't want to be stuck in that medium for ever and ever."[34] In fact, he didn't have to wait long for a London production. On August 19,

The Times announced that *Loot* would reopen at the Jeanetta Cochrane Theatre under the direction of Charles Marowitz.

"It was a sort of Off–West End theatre," explains Marowitz, who had set up a London extension of Edinburgh's Traverse Theatre at the Cochrane. "This meant the play could be tried out in a London setting for only about £2,000; and Lewenstein and White could give *Loot* a London production without risking much capital." Marowitz was an energetic and abrasive American expatriate who had settled in England in 1958 and hammered out a name for himself as a drama critic and experimental director. He was smart, tireless, and equipped with a hustler's nose for publicity. He enjoyed controversy and took a New York street kid's delight in making enemies of the Establishment. His literary instincts were excellent, although many felt them more secure than his directing talent. But if London had an avant garde in the mid-sixties, a large part of it resided then as it does now in him. Marowitz was committed to the new: not only to mounting the best of European and American theatre but to developing and exploring experimental performing techniques. *Loot* had the potential for both West End and avant-garde success. Marowitz saw in Orton another feather in his cap as Big Chief of the English fringe. But whatever his ambitions, Marowitz had a clear and correct understanding of Orton's literary uniqueness. "Orton, like Wilde, was a master of artificial diction," he wrote in *The New York Times,* "and, unlike Wilde, a master craftsman as well."

As Marowitz tells it, he found *Loot* very funny but overwritten; he asked to work from the original script: "The interesting thing is that our production was very much like the original script that had been departed from in the Wood production." In fact, Orton, always suspicious of directorial tampering and now sure of his text, never showed Marowitz the shabby original version that bore only a faint resemblance to the final *Loot*. He gave Marowitz, instead, a retyped copy of the Manchester script. "Any Orton script is like a monkey wrench immersed in suds," Marowitz wrote in *Confessions of a Counterfeit Critic.* "In order to reach the hard metal underneath, you have to wash away quite a lot of lather."[35] This half-truth reflects the limitation of Marowitz's production. Marowitz and Orton had different ideas of just how plausible the play's action should be. "Joe's idea of *Loot*'s plausibility was straighter and more serious than mine. He'd sometimes talk about the play in Chekhovian terms. It's not a serious play in Chekhovian terms. To Joe, it was in places. He was always saying to me: 'We must make this absolutely truthful as it would happen in life.' It was

a very peculiar argument because in principle I agreed that *Loot* had
to be played straight, realistic; but it couldn't be as it happens in life
because nothing in that play happens as it happens in life. You've got
to get the style of the play and make that style truthful."

Marowitz believed in the laughter but not in the comic truth of
Orton's tale. "*Loot* had all the prolixity of a splendid liar improvising
a massive falsehood," he said. But Orton insisted on the truthfulness
of his metaphor ("Most people think it's a fantasy," he said, on receiving the *Evening Standard* Award for *Loot*, "but Scotland Yard know
it's true"). He laughed at Marowitz's disbelief in his view of humanity:

> I went to the Criterion . . . Marowitz was there. I told him of the
> man who'd written to *Penthouse* Magazine. "He said he'd decided
> to see whether spanking wouldn't improve his marriage," I said. "And
> he'd talked it over with his wife. He said, 'We'd decided that I
> would spank her should occasion arise, but that there must be a
> genuine occasion. Next day she came to me with a gleam in her
> eye holding up one of my best shirts which she'd scorched while
> ironing.' So," I said to Marowitz, "he belted her. And, apparently
> the sex was marvellous. And now they do it all the time. Only it
> comes expensive on shirts." "What a morbid mind this character
> has," Marowitz said, addressing everybody present. "What about
> the other one," Kenneth Cranham [who played Hal] said, "where
> she takes his thin pyjamas down and whips him savagely on the bare
> buttocks?" "Oh yes," I said to Marowitz, "only he found that it
> hurt him. And now he wants to stop. Only his wife has developed a
> taste for it. And she won't let him fuck her without first having her
> have his bottom spanked." Marowitz snickered to himself and said
> I'd made it all up.   [January 5, 1967]

Marowitz became a figure of fun to Orton and the cast. "Just a line
to let you know I'm having a total experience (as Charles M might
say) . . ." Orton wrote in a postcard to the inimitable Michael Bates,
who brought a new dimension of square-jawed oafishness and terror to
Truscott. Knowing Marowitz's reputation for experiment, Bates had
insisted on a clause in his contract that he would not improvise ("I'm
not wasting my rehearsal time trying to be a chair or a wastepaper
basket"). Bates's Truscott was marvellous. "He was just a brainless
idiot," he explains. "I borrowed quite a lot from the sergeant majors
I knew in the Army—the bellowing and frozen smiles. But I had great
respect for them. . . ." Upright, religious, patriotic, Bates was the an-
tithesis of Orton in his private life; but as a great farce actor, he was

sympathetic to Orton's theatrical instincts. "Joe's ideas were often better than the director's. He felt *Loot* should be very real. He would have liked the play more real. He was right. If you've got something extraordinary, you've got to make it believable. He was very practical, and I liked him a great deal."

What seemed extraordinary to the cast when they began rehearsals was not Orton's madness but Marowitz's method. "The first day we rehearsed," Simon Ward says, "Charles took Kenneth Cranham and me aside. He sent everybody else out of the room. He sat on one side of the table, and we sat on the other. Marowitz said: 'What do you think these boys do together?' I thought to myself: I don't believe it. This is nonsense. 'I don't know, Charles. I don't think there's any buggery,' I said. 'I think it's probably mutual masturbation,' Ken Cranham said. Marowitz said: 'I think that's right. Now who do you think initiates?' Kenneth and I were kicking each other under the table. We couldn't believe this was happening. 'Which one of you is the active and which one of you is the passive?' Marowitz asked. 'Oh, I probably initiate,' Kenneth said, who played Hal. Marowitz said: 'Right. That's how we're gonna play it. Dennis doesn't do anything.' When we came to do it, the first thing Dennis says to Hal is an active command—'Lock the door!' It's absolutely the other way around! Marowitz put us into this emotional straightjacket. He wanted the relationship to be clear-cut: one of them a doer, the other a receiver. He couldn't even accept that, like life, people aren't one thing or another. God, his stupidity! He thought Hal's entrance wasn't funny enough and because Hal has a line that indicates he reads comics, Marowitz at first had Hal coming on in a Batman costume! In general, Charles never really understood the joke of the play. He didn't understand the lines. I didn't think he could move people around the stage; and when I read the notices of the play, I didn't believe it was the same one I was in."

Orton had asked Lewenstein for a "straightforward" director; and Marowitz was certainly head-on. Orton wanted success, so he kept out of Marowitz's way, although sometimes his guarded face betrayed itself. "Joe had a muscle in his forehead which would throb when something was getting at him," Marowitz remembers. "It was a kind of clenching in the forehead that was very visible, as if a hand was on his skull and squeezing it tight. It was a signal. . . ." Orton kept his critical opinions about the production to himself before the opening. After *Loot*'s success, he spoke his mind about Marowitz, even when suggesting that he mount the play in New York: ". . . God knows I'm not a fan of his. I think a lot of the direction in *Loot* is atrocious. But on the principle of Better the Devil you know than the Devil you don't, I'd think about it. With a stronger cast his direction wouldn't stick out so much. And it is a success in London!! Remember that."[36]

Marowitz and Orton had streamlined and restructured the Manchester script to good effect. With Marowitz, Orton found two large comic bits of business that clinched the play in a way Orton had never before been able to manage. It was Orton's prankster's notion to have Mrs. McLeavy's glass eye drop out of the cadaver onto the floor and for Truscott literally to stumble over it. But how to deliver the ghoulish surprise. In the original, when Hal and Fay pick up the corpse, the stage direction coyly indicates, "something falls from it and rolls away." When Fay asks what it is, Hal says, "Nothing." His chagrin is kept to himself, and so is the joke. Later, after Truscott picks the eye up and pockets it, he produces it at the end of the second act:

> TRUSCOTT. . . . Could you explain to me what this object is?
> MCLEAVY (*looking*). It's a marble.
> TRUSCOTT. No, sir. Not a marble. (*He regards* MCLEAVY *calmly.*) It looks suspiciously to me like an eye.
> MCLEAVY. An eye?
> TRUSCOTT. Yes. (*Pause.*) The question that I want answered is, to whom does it legally belong?
>
> MCLEAVY *looks dumbfounded.*
>
> CURTAIN

In later rewrites, Orton had merely embellished the joke, but never found a way of properly orchestrating it into the mayhem. "I'm not sure it's an eye," McLeavy offers in the Manchester script. "I think it's a marble that has been trod on." To which Truscott replies: "It's an eye, sir. The make is clearly marked: J & S Frazer, Eyemakers to the Profession." The jokes were getting better but, theatrically, the situation was still static. Orton's growth as a craftsman can be measured in how within a year this information was vividly recast for Marowitz's production. The eye's disappearance becomes farce business, a shared anxiety for actors and audience that is captured in word and gesture:

> HAL. Something dropped out? We couldn't find it?
> FAY. Yes.
> HAL. I know what it was.
> FAY. What?
> HAL. One of her eyes!

They drop to their knees. They search. TRUSCOTT *enters. They stand.*

Orton had put panic into his prank and set up the joke for a much larger payoff. It comes unexpectedly at the end of the first act, after Truscott's belligerent interrogation of Dennis—who claims Truscott is not from the Metropolitan Water Board but a policeman who kicked him when he was remanded on suspicion of bank robbery. Truscott grabs Dennis by the collar and shakes him: "If I ever hear you accuse the police of using violence on a prisoner in custody again, I'll take you down to the station and beat the eyes out of your head."

No sooner is Dennis out of the room than Truscott gradually discovers what the audience clearly knows already is an eye out of Mrs. McLeavy's head. While the transposition of Truscott and Dennis's exchange had been made in Manchester, Marowitz cut away swatches of dialogue to leave to the last moment Truscott's elaborate and masterful double take of the eye. "At rehearsals of *Loot,* Orton took greatest interest in the black devices: the corpse, the coffin, the dead woman's clothes, the glass eye," Marowitz wrote later in *The New York Times.* "He was childishly delighted with the protracted business that had been devised with the glass eye at the end of the first act."[37] Marowitz and Michael Bates worked out an elaborate pantomime, with Bates providing the stage eye from a tiger his father had shot in India. It was a hilarious comeuppance. The rest of the cast watched from the wings as Bates, squinting above his brush moustache, caught sight of something on the ground, casually felt the buttons of his coat, then his fly, then picked it up, sniffed it, put it to his ear and rattled it, then took his magnifying glass from his pocket, and blinking first as if to get it in focus, stared hard at the object, giving "a brief exclamation of horror and surprise" as the curtain came down on Act 1.

"NEAR THE END," the *Daily Telegraph* critic had written in the Manchester review of *Loot,* "Mr. Orton seems to waver as if he were losing confidence." The observation was accurate. The script had huffed and puffed to its finish. Orton couldn't spring the final trap on McLeavy with the ease the satire required. Too often *Loot's* sport with the law turned into loquacity:

FAY. You must prove me guilty. That is the law.
TRUSCOTT. You know nothing of the law. I know nothing of the law.
That makes us equal in the sight of the law.

FAY. I'm innocent until proven guilty. This is a free country. The
law is impartial.
TRUSCOTT. Who's been filling your head with that rubbish? The law
isn't impartial. Don't think for a minute it is.

Now Orton, at Marowitz's insistence, cut the last two sentences, elimi-
nating the hint of lecture and maximizing the laughter. Truscott's
avenging spirit was fully drawn and focused in Marowitz's production.
Whatever judgment Orton made on justice had to be conveyed in the
action. In earlier drafts, Orton's voice kept stepping out of character
to make a point. Now he trusted his metaphor to speak his meaning.
One vestige of the early scripts that Orton had retained until the London production was Truscott's *bon mot* about justice: "Justice is a
whore so old that she uses her sword to prevent the masses getting near
enough to sniff her skirts." Too much of a mouthful, the idea was
translated into action by the final draft. At the finale McLeavy finds
himself handcuffed on a trumped-up charge and stymied by Truscott's
fast talk:

MCLEAVY. You can't do this. I've always been a law-abiding citizen.
The police are for the protection of ordinary people.
TRUSCOTT. I don't know where you pick up these slogans, sir. You
must read them on the hoardings.
MCLEAVY. I want to see someone in authority.
TRUSCOTT. I am in authority. You can see me.

McLeavy starts to panic and ends up being dragged offstage screaming: "I'm innocent! I'm innocent! Oh, what a terrible thing to happen
to a man who's been kissed by the Pope!" Originally, Orton had Mc-
Leavy exiting with a ludicrous curse: "You'll be sorry you were born.
I'm asking the Fathers to bring Bell, Book and Candle. You'll probably disappear in a puff of smoke." Now McLeavy ends not as a belli-
cose figure of fun, but as a beleaguered Irishman who is the victim of
his own ignorance. Prior to the London version, the best reversal Orton could spring on McLeavy was to have him collapse into a chair in
exhausted frustration after Truscott's routine about authority, only
to have Truscott slap handcuffs on him for "trying to escape." But the
stage picture was too small, the moment too static, for the moral outrage the ending demanded. As Orton finally wrote it for Marowitz,
McLeavy's disintegration and his struggle to assert his innocence raised
the scene to something large, active, and memorable.

Once Orton had put the play on the right theatrical track, *Loot* coasted smoothly, delightfully to its conclusion. By the time it reached London, Orton had brusquely accounted for McLeavy's future in prison; established Truscott's police locker as the safest place to stash the stolen money; and worked out the final living arrangements of the other three in twenty-one lines. It was a bravura bit of plotting.

In the course of rewriting, Orton had tried every theatrical combination to end the play. But each ending limited the play's meaning instead of opening it up. Now, finally in control of his method, Orton played on the obsession in all farce with shattering appearances at the finale. The unmasked once again adopt their personas to go out into the world:

> HAL (*pause, to* DENNIS). You can kip here, baby. Plenty of room now. Bring your bags over tonight.
>
> FAY *looks up.*
>
> FAY (*sharply*). When Dennis and I are married we'd have to move out.
> HAL. Why?
> FAY. People would talk. We must keep up appearances.
>
> *She returns to her prayers, her lips move silently.* DENNIS *and* HAL *at either side of the coffin.*

CURTAIN

Loot OPENED AT THE Jeanetta Cochrane Theatre on September 27, 1966. It was a sluggish production with a drab set in which, as Orton wrote, "a lot of lines are muffed" as a result of "having inexperienced actors in the parts. In general the tone of the London production is OK. . . . If we replaced Fay, McLeavy and (possibly) Dennis by more experienced actors (not necessarily better—just more experienced in comedy) the play would be a lot better."[38] Orton's dazzling writing, however, triumphed over every limitation. By the end of the week, Orton saw the play described by Alan Brien in the *Sunday Telegraph* as "the most genuinely quick witted, pungent and sprightly entertainment by a new young British playwright for a decade." It was clear that *Loot*, as Ronald Bryden wrote in *The Observer*, "establishes Orton's niche in English drama." Bryden proceeded to dub Orton the "Oscar Wilde of Welfare State gentility." Orton also found himself compared with Ben Jonson, George Bernard Shaw, and Lewis Carroll. He didn't

demur, taking a stunned delight in his reviews and sharing the critics'
enthusiasm for his play and his talent. "I have a lot of vices," he told
the *Evening Standard,* "but false modesty is not one of them. The best
thing about *Loot* is the quality of the writing."[39]

The battle for his play had been won. "Rare, darling?" Peggy Ramsay says of *Loot*'s rebirth on the West End. "It's almost impossible."
Nonetheless on November 1, *Loot* transferred to the Criterion Theatre,
"with huge success" according to *The Guardian.* Orton now had a telephone, a television, and a rack full of long-playing records. Otherwise
the trappings of his life with Halliwell did not change with *Loot*'s sudden acclaim. What did change was Orton's confidence. The play's reception set his imagination racing and emboldened his sense of fun.
By December, he had managed to finish the first half of *What the
Butler Saw,* his last full-length play. He'd also begun his diary—the
first since adolescence—an indication of the new eventfulness of his
life and his confidence in his future.

Loot struggled at the box office. Orton and Halliwell made frequent
excursions to the "Cri," as they called it, with Halliwell affecting a
walking stick with a silver knob and Orton anxiously checking the
house receipts:

> Went to the Criterion tonight. Gloom, gloom. The takings have
> dropped by about 300 pounds. We clearly aren't going to have a
> long run. About another month and we'll be off. This may be be-
> cause there are no names in the cast. Much of the play's lack of
> success must be put down to the theme and the undoubted fact
> that the general public are, where plays are concerned, ignorant shits.
>
> [February 18, 1967]

Orton relished the sparky backstage banter. Halliwell managed to
make friends with the cast and enjoyed some of the residual glory of
Loot's success. The camaraderie was new to both of them. The actors
played up to Orton's sense of humor, and he recorded many of their
stories in his diary: Simon Ward's mysterious letters and phone calls
from an illiterate Scotsman who wanted to produce him in James Bald-
win's homosexual novel *Giovanni's Room* ("Of course, laddie, we'll
have extensive rehearsals. In depth"); a conversation, overheard by
Sheila Ballantine, between women on a bus: "One woman said, 'There's
a lot of blue about lately.' After a pause the other woman said, 'Yes. And
there's a lot of green about too.' There was another pause and the first
woman said, 'And there's a lot of red. Have you noticed?' " Orton also

had much to recount to the cast about the ludicrous spinoffs of success. There was the film producer who'd asked him to script the life of Alfie Hinds, the infamous ex-convict who escaped from jail to prove his innocence. " 'Your attitude to authority in *Loot* is exactly Alfie Hinds's. You see,' he said, 'in a way it's similar to *Loot*—an ordinary man fighting the might of the law. And winning.' 'Except that in *Loot* he doesn't win,' I said. 'Ah well,' the producer said, looking a bit put out, 'We couldn't expect you to write *Loot* all over again.' "

But there were also more substantial things for Orton to celebrate with the cast: the publication of the play, the proposed option of *Loot* by David Merrick for Broadway and its production in a dozen countries within the year; and most important, *Loot*'s selection as the winner of the *Evening Standard* Award for the Best Play of 1966. Whereas nothing seemed to go right for Wood's production, nothing seemed to go wrong for Marowitz's. Orton was in a weird, thrilling, slightly unnerving state of grace, whose magic even his producer couldn't resist mocking:

> I walked to Duke Street and called on Michael White. He had the original of the caricature of the cast in *Loot* on his wall. He said, "I was going to give it to you." I said, "But, of course, you're too mean." He said, "Yes. And, in any case, you're too spoilt as it is." We talked of the play. He showed me a review in *Queen* Magazine that I hadn't seen. The takings went up again last night. Good news which brought smiles to everybody's face. . . .
>
> [January 5, 1967]

Orton had known since December that he was the winner of the *Evening Standard* prize. Its public announcement on January 11, 1967, came none too soon for the flagging box office at the Criterion. ("Perhaps," Orton wrote Peggy Ramsay, "you ought to arrange for me to appear nude at the Victoria Palace to give the show a boost."[40]) On the morning of the award ceremony, Orton rang Michael White, who told him, "If the award doesn't bring some people in we're sunk."

The *Evening Standard*'s first edition came out at 10:30 a.m. A banner front-page headline announced: SCANDAL! BUT LOOT HAS IT. "There was no runner up," Orton wrote in his diary, thrilled with the "splendid" headline. "It was four to one. Penelope Mortimer thought *Loot* simply nasty. The four men over-ruled her, though." The editorial, under the headline GLOWING THEATRE, praised the vitality of the contemporary English stage ("probably not since the Elizabethans has it displayed so much richness, colour, depth and imagination"). It was an important day for Orton, representing not only the culmination of *Loot*'s tortuous history but also the public acknowledgment of his hard-won literary skill. He tried to work on *What the Butler Saw*, but found it "too difficult to concentrate." He was taking Peggy Ramsay to the luncheon ceremony. He set off for her office at noon, dressed for his moment of vindictive triumph in Halliwell's striped suit, a gaudy wide-flowered tie, and a high-collared striped shirt.

I arrived at Peggy's office. There were three letters for me. . . . One was from the editor of *Plays and Players* telling me that the critics, in their annual poll, had voted *Loot* the best play of 1966. So I've got a bonus.

Peggy and I decided to walk to Bury Street to Quaglino's where the luncheon was held. . . . When we arrived at Quaglino's Sheila Ballantine was just going in. We greeted each other in a conspiratorial whisper. It was so grand inside. I left my coat and Peggy and I appeared at the top of a staircase. The Toastmaster, in a sort of hunting pink coat, asked our names. We gave them and he boomed them out over the crowd below. It was like a thirties film of *Lady Windermere's Fan*. . . .

Quite crowded. Bill Gaskill came up. Very bright-eyed. "Loved *Loot*," he said. "I'm so glad," I said. "It's always nice to convert somebody." Spoke to Oscar for a while. Peggy saying how brave he was to have taken up an option. True in a way, I suppose. Though she has a convenient lapse of memory about the period (ten days before rehearsals were due to begin) when Oscar, dissatisfied with the casting, asked me if I wanted to cancel the production. "If we cancel," I said, "when will we remount it?" "I can't guarantee when we'll do that," Oscar said. This is the play's last chance, I thought. If it comes to grief now plus the original tour, the dubiety as to *Loot* will harden into certainty. Everyone will be sure that the play is no good. "It must go on," I said. "With this cast. I must let the London critics see the play. After that I'll shut up about *Loot* and write another play." All this, naturally, wasn't mentioned, or even thought of, probably, except by me. . . .

The lunch was announced. On the board it said "Mr. and Mrs. Orton." Peggy laughed. "I'll be your wife for the afternoon," she said. All I could think of was how embarrassing if, as I'd originally planned, I'd taken Kenneth.

In the doorway of the dining room I spotted Michael Codron. Dark-suited and a little po-faced. Though as this is natural with him I thought it was nature not the occasion. "Congratulations Joe," he said. "You can imagine what I must be feeling." "No, I can't," I said. "I haven't got that strong an imagination." All done with a merry sort of twinkle, but it had the effect of a knee in the groin. . . .

After the coffee the Toastmaster announced that the meal had ended. Rather surprisingly I thought. The lights for the television cameras came on. And the business of speeches began. And then, after Frank Marcus had made a long speech about me ["I'm giving you the award on behalf of the Metropolitan Water Board, The Metropolitan Police and the Church of Rome," he said. ". . . Don't let them make you respectable"], I went up on the platform. I was nervous. Drinking the wine hadn't helped much. I didn't say much. I said, as near as I can remember, "In the early days we used to give complimentary tickets to various organizations. We sent a few to Scotland Yard. And the police loved the play so much that they rang up asking for more tickets. Everyone else thinks the play is a fantasy. Of course the police know that it's true." And then I said that I hoped to get another award in about two years. Robert Morley, later on, said that it was no good having one. You had to have two for bookends.

A lot of funny speeches. One wonderful one from Frankie Howerd. Only I can't remember what it was now. . . .

And then the Toastmaster said that was all. The lights were switched out and people started going home. It was over.

I was on the front of the *Evening Standard* receiving the award. I'm very happy. Pleased though that I've almost finished the first draft of *What the Butler Saw*. It'd be difficult to have to begin a play from scratch. . . .

Orton brought the statuette back to Noel Road. He and Halliwell invited a few people from the building to watch the ceremony on television. Mr. and Mrs. Corden, from the basement flat, who had served as models for characters in other plays, were there. So was Miss Boynes, the old lady who lived beneath them, for whom Orton fetched the Sunday papers. These people were Orton's ad hoc family—a strange, sad group he gathered around him to bask in the afterglow of his triumph:

We had a sandwich or two. I showed Mrs. Corden the menu for lunch. "How lovely," she said. "It looks like a skilled printing job to me. But, of course, the actual luncheon isn't as good as Mr. Corden's firm's annual get-together's dinner. It was at the Savoy. And we had a sweet which was like straw. I have never, in the whole of my life, tasted anything so scruptious. That is the only word to describe it. Scrumptious," she said, saying the word twice and hoping that nobody would notice she'd made a mistake the first time. . . .

Mr. Corden, after examining the award statuette suddenly said, "Under the green baize bottom is a bolt which bolts the actual

object to the marble plinth. If you were to strip the baize away
you'd see the workmanship beneath." Like turning round the
Rokeby Venus to see how the frame was made.

Excerpts from *Loot* were to be shown on the ITV program "Acco-
lade." During the rehearsals the previous week Orton had worried that
Charles Dyer's *Staircase* would be given more time than *Loot*. "I don't
trust the television company not to slant the programme to give the
impression that *Staircase* is at least equal with *Loot*."[41] His instinctive
paranoia proved accurate:

> The programme called "Accolade" was a disappointment. The ex-
> cerpt from *Loot* was good. The set seemed to have more style on film
> than in reality. The performances were excellent. Then we had a long
> excerpt from *Staircase*. For no good reason. It wasn't a runner up.
> As had been suggested (by inference) in the *TV Times*. The real
> blow fell when . . . we came to the luncheon. But, by this time, the
> programme was over. When Frank Marcus announced me as award
> winner the sound was off. I appeared briefly with the sound still off
> and the captions and credits coming over my face. Then the sound
> came on for the other winners. The whole had the effect of the man
> with the bladder hitting the Emperor on the head as he rode in
> triumph. Just to take him down a peg and remind him that he
> wasn't a god. . . . Went to bed very disgruntled. [January 11, 1967]

Whatever the momentary blow to Orton's ego, balm came quickly
at the box office. Four days after the *Evening Standard* Award,
Michael White's business manager, Mark Linford, pulled Orton aside.
"Joe, come and see something," he said. "It's what you've been waiting
for." No botched spectacle of the playwright's triumph was as important
or thrilling as this:

> The stalls were packed. He took me upstairs to the circle. The
> circle was packed. And in the gallery they were standing. "I hope it
> builds from this," I said. "It mustn't be just tonight. It must go on.
> We're not out of the wood yet." "We've not lost a single customer
> since the award," Mark said. "No one has complained since Wednes-
> day. Now they've been told they can enjoy it they do."
>   [January 15, 1967]

Orton, who felt *Loot* was a young person's play, gave orders to the
box office to refund money to any elderly people who were outraged
by it. He had other ways of dealing with younger, irate customers. One

man wrote to the management after leaving *Loot* in the interval: "As Christians, we were naturally dismayed to see the Roman Catholic Church abused, but even were I not a Christian I should have been ashamed to take my mother and sister to hear the accompanying filth. I am in consequence writing to the Lord Chamberlain, suggesting that the play should be reviewed yet again, and at the least severely edited." The letter was passed to Orton. Edna Welthorpe replied on April 14, 1967:

> Please let me say at once that I am conscious of a great feeling of uneasiness at writing to you. I must write, however, to tell you that you are not alone in disliking the play *Loot*. I myself consider it to be the most loathsome play on in London at the present moment. "Bestial" is how I described it to an acquaintance the other day. When I tell you that in the second act (which you had the good fortune to miss), there was a discussion upon the raping of children with Mars bars with other filthy details of a sexual and psychopathic nature I'm sure you'll pardon my writing.
>
> Please, please, as a fellow Christian, let me applaud your design in writing to the Lord Chamberlain. I myself have written several letters to the papers (none alas published) and am trying to contact my M.P. at the moment. I took an elderly aunt of mine to see the play recently and really I had to go round to the manager afterwards and demand an apology. This truly horrible play shouldn't contaminate our streets.
>
> It was most wrong of me to write to you, I'm sure. Your letter was passed to me for filing. I do hope you will respect my confidence in this. It has received the most respectful attention here. Naturally, I cannot express any opinion but my own. And that you have fully.
>
> I am trying, in a solo capacity, to arrange a meeting with the Lord Chamberlain to protest against plays in general and this travesty of the free society *Loot* in particular. I wonder if you'd like to be included in our mission?

Edna was never in higher spirits. She was stirring up trouble in public as well as in private. When the novelist David Benedictus objected to *Loot* winning the *Plays and Players* Award, Edna thrashed *Loot* in the magazine, calling it "a piece of indecent tomfoolery." Above Edna's letter was one by Donald H. Hartley, Orton's other pseudonym, praising his work and calling Benedictus's credentials into question: "Really, if every pip-squeak circus pony were to give awards for the Horse of the Year, goodness knows where we should be!"

But the play didn't need Orton's pranks to generate publicity. Both

Orton and *Loot* received an incredible boost when, after intensive competitive bidding, news of a film sale for a reported £100,000 to the producers Bernard Delfont and Arthur Lewis hit the newspapers on March 1. According to *The Times*, "it was one of the highest amounts ever paid for a straight play." "Absolutely ridiculous," Orton wrote in his diary about the figure. "I suppose they've added the amount I'd get if the play ran for two years on Broadway."[42] In his hometown, the Leicester *Mercury* ran Orton's picture under the headline: EX-PRISONER SELLS PLAY FOR £100,000. "It's better than carting around great loads of brick or sweeping up the cutting room floor of some Leicester factory,"[43] Orton bitterly told the *Mercury* reporter, not denying the rumored sales figure.

Orton was now "a name"—someone to be reckoned with. The avidity of the film producers was an indication of his new power. Orton learned about the movie sale when he and Halliwell visited Peggy Ramsay at her apartment to watch his guest appearance on "Call My Bluff"—Orton's first celebrity outing where, along with Eva Gabor, Kenneth Williams, and Maxine Audley on the quiz show, he came across (he thought) like "a young Robert Mitchum."[44] Orton had expected to find Peggy Ramsay alone. Instead, he and Halliwell were greeted by Oscar Lewenstein and Arthur Lewis, who had just shelled out option money for the film rights of *Loot*:

> This afternoon he [Arthur Lewis] rang Peggy and asked if he could buy the option. Peggy said that if he came round with a cheque for £20,000 he could have it. He rushed round. Oscar then said to Peggy, "See what happens if you ask for 25." So she did. He signed a cheque for £18,000 with another £7,000 when the contract is signed. When the man had gone . . . Oscar said, "Only this afternoon I was saying to Michael White 'I expect about £5,000 is all we'll get for *Loot* now.'" Remarkable the man must be. Especially as *Loot* is quite unsuitable for filming.

Loot would be a dismal failure on the screen—and on Broadway, as Orton also predicted, where it would flop after twenty-three performances. "I *curse* Michael White from the bottom of my pitiless soul for getting some sucker to agree to an on Broadway production," he wrote to Peggy Ramsay on May 30, after the David Merrick negotiations had fallen through and Harold Orenstein had been found. "It will flop in a fortnight. I was looking forward to The Establishment or Cherry Lane. White suddenly is energetic at the time when his usual lethargy would've been most welcome. Still, it's Kismet (Ah, the exotic east is in my blood!). We can but trust in the will of Allah and insist that we take Michael Bates and Kenneth Cranham to Broadway." But Orton dismissed *Loot*'s certain Broadway failure with the insouciance of a man secure in his own success. "Who cares what the Americans do—as long as they pay plenty of cash they can play *Loot* in the middle of Times Square," he wrote in his diary on May 26, 1967. "Reputations are made in London, only money is made in New York."

Loot BROUGHT ORTON'S CRAFT to its maturity. Confident, independent, and successful, Orton was growing free of the fear that had weighed down his early prose and forced it to revel in all that was dark, inferior, and culpable in others. He was no longer oppressed in the same way by guilt and inferiority; and his plays, which were projections of these fears, took on an expansive good humor. There was a hint of forgiveness in his high spirits. Even Orton's handwriting changed from its cramped, adolescent jaggedness to an open, fluid, authoritative hand. The ten months between October 1966, when *Loot* made its London debut, and August 1967, when he died, would be Orton's most fecund literary period. He wrote his ghoulish capriccio about the Church and Christian charity, *Funeral Games*; the film script *Up Against It*; the major revisions on *Ruffian* and *Erpingham Camp*, published as they were produced under the title *Crimes of Passion*; and his farce masterpiece, *What the Butler Saw*. Almost his entire oeuvre was either written or rewritten in the comic voice he'd acquired through *Loot*. Orton's was a unique voice whose echoes invoked descriptive comparisons to Wilde and Firbank; but it was now also indubitably his own.

In theatrical terms, Orton's comic voice made new dramatic demands on the contemporary actor, special demands that turned the act of speaking itself into a startling contest. The actor's competition with Orton's language (whose quality of wit seems always to be above the class of the characters) became part of the play's tension and fun. "There's a performing technique to Orton," Kenneth Williams says. "You've got to breathe. If you're going to say lines like 'The Vatican would never grant an annulment. Not unless he'd produced a hybrid,' you've got to gather it up, otherwise it's lost. If you're going to stop in the middle, the whole impact is destroyed. This is in the tradition of classic English comic writing. It goes for Wilde, the same construction, the same intake of breath. It occurs also in Coward. Shaw uses the construction again and again. In *Saint Joan*, the Inquisitor says: 'It's not enough to be simple. It's not enough even to be what simple people call good. The simplicity of a darkened mind is no better than the simplicity of a beast. . . .' The accumulated momentum is deadly, going right to its conclusion. He is speaking to a simple country girl, but he replies in language of total authority. The same is true of Orton. It could be Truscott, or Erpingham, or Rance in *What the Butler Saw*. Orton's dialogue has impact; and to get the full thrilling clout of it, the dialogue *must flow*."

The liberties Orton took with language and plot were built on a disciplined vision that his productions had yet to match. "It suggests," Ronald Bryden concluded in his review of *Loot*, "that the British theatre will need to find an Orton style, as it has done for Pinter, Wilde and Coward."[45]

6

THE FREAKS' ROLL CALL

To be able to recognize the freak, you have to have some conception of the whole man. . . .

—Flannery O'Connor, *Mystery and Manners*

HOW CAN YOU AVOID tormenting men if one has decided to make them gods?"[1] Orton copied Camus's question into his notebook and used farce to torment the godlike vanity of his characters:

ERPINGHAM. I shall confiscate your luggage. What is your chalet number?

DR. RANCE. My brief is infinite. I'd have sway over a rabbit hutch if the inmates were mentally disturbed.

TRUSCOTT. How dare you involve me in a situation for which no memo has been issued.

Each character has his kingdom—whether holiday camp, psychiatric ward, or police squad. Each is a freak of power and propriety. The elegance of Orton's comic syntax aspires to perfection, while the characters who speak it are unabashedly imperfect. They speak a language of reason but live a life of chaos. "People think I write fantasy, but I don't," Orton said. "Some things may be distorted in the way painters distort and alter things, but they're realistic figures."[2] The distortion captures the lopsided spirituality of an unbelieving age which, by making man its ultimate concern, has twisted and isolated him.

Farce, Eric Bentley has said, "is the theatre of the surrealist body."[3] Farce glories in fracturing form and sporting with man's obsession with unity. Orton extends farce beyond the bedroom. The chaos of confused identities and the riot of bodies galvanized by human need expose the flimsiness of reason with which man creates his patchwork of coherence. "I've learned to accept the irrational in every day life," quips Mc-Corquodale in *Funeral Games*. Behind the carapace of normality, human beings are driven by unreasoning desires and defenses that can turn them from the respectable to the rampaging. Orton wrote this into his plays. He also found it in his life:

When I left the theatre I took the Piccadilly line to Holloway Road and popped into a little pissoir—just four pissers. It was dark because somebody had taken the bulb away. There were three figures pissing. I had a piss and, as my eyes became used to the gloom, I saw that only one of the figures was worth having—a labouring type, big, with cropped hair and, as far as I could see, wearing jeans and a dark coat. Another man entered and the man next to the labourer moved away, not out of the place altogether, but back against the wall. The new man had a pee and left the place and, before the man against the wall could return to his place, I nipped in there sharpish and stood next to the labourer. I put my hand down and felt his cock, he immediately started to play with mine. The youngish man with fair hair, standing back against the wall went into the vacant place. I unbuttoned the top of my jeans and unloosened my belt in order to allow the labourer free rein with my balls. The man next to me began to feel my bum. At this point a fifth man entered. Nobody moved. It was dark. Just a little light spilled into the place from the street, not enough to see immediately. The man next to me moved back to allow the fifth man to piss. But the fifth man very quickly flashed his cock and the man next to me returned to my side, lifting up my coat, and shoving his hand down the back of my trousers. The fifth man kept puffing on a cigarette and, by the glowing end, watching. A sixth man came into the pissoir. As it was so dark nobody bothered to move. After an interval (during which the fifth man watched me feel the labourer, the labourer stroked my cock and the man beside me pulled my jeans down even further), I noticed that the sixth man was kneeling down beside the youngish man with fair hair and sucking his cock. A seventh man came in, but by now nobody cared. The number of people in the place was so large that detection was impossible. And anyway as soon became apparent when the seventh man stuck his head down on a level with my fly, he wanted a cock in his mouth too. For some moments nothing happened. Then the eighth man, bearded and stocky, came in. He pushed the sixth man roughly away from the fair-haired man and quickly sucked the fair-haired man off. The man beside me had pulled my jeans down over my buttocks and was trying to push his prick between my legs. The fair-haired man, having been sucked off, hastily left the place. The bearded man came over and nudged away the seventh man from me, and, opening wide my fly, began sucking like a maniac. The labourer, getting very excited by my feeling his cock with both hands, suddenly glued his mouth to mine. The little pissoir under the bridge had become the scene of a frenzied saturnalia. No more than two feet away the citizens of Holloway moved about their ordinary business. I came, squirting come into the bearded man's mouth and quickly pulled up my jeans. As I was about to leave I heard the bearded man hissing quietly, "I suck people off! Who wants his cock sucked?" When I left the labourer was shoving his cock into the man's mouth to keep him quiet. I caught the bus home.   [March 4, 1967]

"You can't be rational in an irrational world. It isn't rational," says Dr. Rance in *What the Butler Saw*. Orton tested reason more elegantly in his plays than in his life. "I'm a great believer in the absolute logic of *Alice in Wonderland*," he said in the program note for *Loot*. "It's the kind of logic I put into my plays." Orton studied Feydeau, who went so far as to number his characters and their position on the stage as he made up the ground plans for his comedies. When Oscar Lewenstein spotted an inconsistency in *What the Butler Saw*, Orton patched it up, reminding him, "The mathematical precision of the play is unimpaired." Orton boasted about *Loot*'s logic: after all, the ability to deploy it had been hard won.

Funeral Games was the transitional play between *Loot* and *What the Butler Saw* in which Orton tried to solidify the stylistic advances of language and logic in *Loot*. Written in five drafts between July and mid-November 1966, *Funeral Games* dealt with Charity as part of an ITV series on "The Seven Deadly Virtues." There was a new tone and texture to the play's laughter. "In the garden of her detached ranch-type dwelling the vision of the Lord came upon me," Pringle says, extolling The Lady of the Wand ("a woman of great humility and private fortune"), and explaining the decision to seek revenge on his wife, Tessa, for her suspected adultery:

> I was swept up and the springs of my heart were opened. I made a vow. Taking my cue from Holy Writ. "My wife must be punished." The words I spoke weren't rejected or pooh-poohed. I was hoisted high on the shoulders of two priestly personalities. (*Tears roll down his cheeks.*) The Lady of the Wand shook out the glorious strands of her golden hair. There were loud hosannas. Palm branches. I was

girt in white. The grounds of that Surrey mansion were ablaze with ecumenical spirit until the small hours. My commandment was repeated like a catechism: "Thou shalt not suffer an adultress to live."

The cadences of Pringle's speech swell his sense of control and bolster the illusion of reason. Bitterness has vanished from Orton's laughter, to be replaced by a buoyant sense of philosophical detachment. Tessa, who befriends the ancient and ailing defrocked priest McCorquodale, holds up one of his watercolors. "It was my intention to represent—in a symbolic fashion—the Christian Church," McCorquodale explains. Tessa scrutinizes the canvas: "A bird of prey carrying an olive branch. You've put the matter in a nutshell."

The freak, repellent in life, is made compelling in *Funeral Games* by laughter, which matches the caprice of nature with the caprice of language, whose purpose is to lure the characters away from panic. Orton magnifies the monstrousness of his characters and their baroque prose. "Take my dying curse. You diabolic crumb from the table of the damned!" McCorquodale shouts at Pringle, slapping him in the face for committing adultery with Mrs. McCorquodale (Val) and forcing McCorquodale to murder her. Pringle retorts: "I'll teach you to strike a man of admitted charity." The men of God throttle each other.

Pringle is a religious charlatan. "Sit down," he commands Caulfield, the man he hires to snoop on Tessa. "Or kneel if you prefer. I want you to behave naturally." Pringle's sect is called "The Brotherhood" ("We've a house of contemplation, in the Arcade. Pay us a visit. . . . We hang about on street corners"). A self-styled god, Pringle is also The Word: "Copies of my brochure *Blessings Abound* are still available. It'd be as well to purchase one. It gives the background to my teaching." Orton's delight and disgust with his characters is built into their outrageousness, allowing him to startle his audience with the unforeseen. McCorquodale, who has buried his wife in the cellar under a ton of smokeless coal, confesses his crime within minutes of meeting Caulfield:

CAULFIELD. You're a murderer?
MCCORQUODALE. These "with it" expressions aren't familiar to me.
CAULFIELD. Wasn't it a happy marriage?
MCCORQUODALE. We bickered occasionally over the nature of God. Nothing more serious.

Orton tried to rev up his plotting to create the sharp, brief juxtapositions which the grotesque requires. In Part 1, Pringle is hell-bent on revenge. "You can't kill your wife. What about the sixth commandment?" Caulfield reasons with him. Pringle replies, "If she can break the seventh, I can break the sixth." He pulls out a gun; and, invoking the humble and the meek's thirst for blood, exits firing it. In the next scene, Pringle confronts Tessa ("You'll soon be burning in some low, hot nook of Satan!"). Tessa, whose visits to McCorquodale are an act of charity, can't believe that Pringle has murder on his mind. "You must be mistaken," she tells Caulfield. "We celebrate our wooden wedding in a fortnight." But Pringle means business and is about to shoot Tessa through the heart when Caulfield crowns Pringle with a bottle. Sobered ("You're still alive? I've broken my vow. I'm unworthy of the name of Christian"), Pringle is advised by Caulfield to forgive his wife:

> PRINGLE. I won't tolerate forgiveness. It's a thing of the past.
> CAULFIELD. Love thy neighbour.
> PRINGLE. The man who said that was crucified by his.

In a few brief exchanges they reach a compromise that gives the plot another sharp turn. Instead of murdering his wife, Pringle will just say he's killed her. Tessa agrees to stay with McCorquodale as his "wife." "This'll be worth a million in publicity. Make a bit of a splash in the weekend Press," Pringle says, already imagining the headlines in The Brotherhood's newspaper and savoring his righteous glory. " 'Vengeance Is Mine,' says 'No Nonsense Parson.' These human interest stories can increase a congregation a thousandfold." Having ruthlessly negotiated the "death" pact, Pringle exits with a blessing: "Trust in the Lord. We shall meet in the glory of the Infinite Morning."

But in Part 2 reports of the "murder" turn Pringle into a star. Gifts are lavished on him—a ring "from a fervent admirer of Western Civilization"; a silver-backed clothes brush from a woman journalist who "wanted the privilege of kissing hands that'd taken human life." Orton's outrageousness is the theatrical equivalent of a shout: startling the English public with an idea it ordinarily won't accept—man's appetite for blood. In the morning mail, Pringle receives a letter from a reporter accusing him of *not* having murdered his wife. Pringle contemplates legal action for defamation of character. "For saying you're innocent?" says Caulfield. "You'd never get away with it. There must be hundreds of innocent people in the country." Caulfield, who knows he can find a dead body in McCorquodale's cellar, is sent in search of "proof." "You don't need a complete body," he tells Pringle. "An arm would do. (*Pause.*) Or a head."

The "surrealist body"—the illusion of the torso freed from rational content or expectation by the momentum of farce—now becomes part of the fun. Unaware of the corpse, Tessa prepares tea for Caulfield and McCorquodale as Caulfield emerges from the cellar, "his hands and face . . . smeared with coaldust." The refined and the atrocious are juxtaposed. As Tessa puts the tea cake on a doily, Caulfield is laying down a meat cleaver, carrying "a human hand, severed above the wrist, wrapped in sacking." Caulfield grumbles to McCorquodale: "I couldn't get her head off. It must be glued on." McCorquodale replies: "She was always a headstrong woman." The grotesque is the violent extreme of farce's capriciousness; and Orton instinctively pursues the genre's cruelty, gloating over the anarchy of his imagery:

> TESSA (*to* CAULFIELD, *over her shoulder*). Do you want to wash your hands before tea?
> CAULFIELD. Yes.
>
> TESSA *picks up a teapot and goes out.*
> CAULFIELD *goes to the sink. He washes the hand and his own.*

Caulfield hides the hand in Tessa's cake tin while they have tea. Orton's dialogue draws out the comedy of the hand, and its final horrific discovery. During the meal, Tessa notices Val's watch on Caulfield's wrist and becomes suspicious when Caulfield explains he found it "in the street." Val, Orton implies, was once Tessa's lover, and Tessa takes the watch with the intention of going to the police. "Val had a lot of friends in the Police," Tessa says. "She used to sing songs in praise of Authority at her concerts." As Tessa clears away the dishes, she and Caulfield are suddenly at loggerheads over the cake tin. He is adamant; she is indignant:

> CAULFIELD. Don't open that tin.
> TESSA. Why not?
> CAULFIELD. I bought a plastic hand from a Novelty shop. I put it into your cake tin.
>
> TESSA *turns from wrapping up the cake.*
>
> TESSA. That was very silly of you. Neville down the road is in trouble of that sort. His little playmate had a convulsion. Her mother is putting it into the papers. (*She lifts the tin.*) I'm glad you had the sense to tell me.
>
> *She takes off the lid and looks in. She gives a shriek of horror.*
>
> (*Gasping with fright.*) It's real. . . . (*Trembling.*) I can spot plastic fingers a mile off.

The grotesque sidesteps every normal response, allowing a variety of moods and emotions to exist at the same moment. Tessa demands to know Val's whereabouts:

> MCCORQUODALE. She was taken up to Heaven. In a fiery chariot. Driven by an angel.
> TESSA. What nonsense. Valerie would never accept a lift from a stranger. . . .

In the next line we suddenly glimpse the pathetic. Tessa goes into the cellar "to gauge the full extent" of McCorquodale's crimes. McCorquodale knows what she'll find and has no choice but to tie her up:

> MCCORQUODALE (*pause, wearily*). In the closet you'll find a rope. . . . I bought it a month ago. I intended hanging myself.
> CAULFIELD. What stopped you?
> MCCORQUODALE. The weather turned nice.

The logic in *Funeral Games* is more tortuous than in *Loot*. Tessa knows of Val's murder; but if she reports the crime, her "murder" will be exposed as a fraud. Caulfield now counsels Pringle actually to kill Tessa in order to break the impasse:

> PRINGLE. I've already killed her once. I couldn't do it again. I'd be a murderer.
> CAULFIELD. You are a murderer. In the eyes of the world. I'm only asking you to live up to your public image.
> PRINGLE. That's a terrible thing to ask a man to do.
> CAULFIELD (*pause*). Unless you kill your wife she'll accuse you of not being her murderer.

"Truth must win," Tessa proclaims, cutting herself free of her fetters with a dagger McCorquodale once used for "circumcising the faithful." "Otherwise life is impossible." She is about to set off for the police when she discovers Caulfield and Pringle at the threshold of McCorquodale's room. McCorquodale recognizes Pringle as his arch-enemy, the "ecclesiastical poltroon" who seduced Valerie and banished him from the religious order. He vows revenge: "I'll see every soul in Christendom knows that the blood on your hands is a fraud." They attack one another, the mayhem being aggravated by their reasoning. McCorquodale wants Tessa alive because she is proof of Pringle's innocence. Pringle wants Tessa dead because her existence belies his image as a holy murderer. Tessa tries to call McCorquodale off:

TESSA. You mustn't cause trouble. I shall deny that I'm alive.
MCCORQUODALE. I'll kill you, then.

He grabs her, and holds the sword to her breast.

TESSA. You can't destroy me. I'm the evidence.
PRINGLE. You can't expose his guilt without establishing my innocence.

With the characters hamstrung by their own logic, Orton again twists the situation:

CAULFIELD *takes the gun from* PRINGLE's *coat and fires.* TESSA, PRINGLE *and* MCCORQUODALE *scatter. Pause.*

TESSA (*running behind sofa*). Who's he after?
PRINGLE. You.

. . . TESSA *throws the meat cleaver at* CAULFIELD. *It crashes among the medicine bottles, and drops down beside* MCCORQUODALE.

Caulfield finally catches Tessa, shoves a gun against her head, and pulls the trigger—the chamber is empty. Crying in relief, Tessa exclaims: "Somebody is going to pay for Val's death." But justice in Orton's monstrous world is never done. Once Pringle's seduction of Val is made public, Tessa realizes she's been twice betrayed. "Stealing my husband and concealing the fact that she had one of her own. It's scandalous behaviour." Truth, justice, and Val are immediately forgotten. "She tempted the Lord," Tessa explains, referring to Pringle. "It would be blasphemous to raise a hand in her defence."

The ending fizzles out, with Orton unable to bring off in imagery the dizzying confusions and final resolution that, a few months later in *What the Butler Saw,* he would accomplish with such aplomb. McCorquodale is reinstated into The Brotherhood and given the title of Bishop Bonnyface. Tessa remains with the new Bishop. Caulfield asks to be put "on to God's payroll," and threatens blackmail. "We're children of Light. Not criminals," Pringle rebukes him before putting Caulfield on the "priestly path." "Tangle with the Prince of Peace and you'll find a knife in your back." Pringle too gets his happy end, claiming Val as his adulterous wife and proudly taking credit for her murder as the police cart him off to jail.

Orton's freaks make a mockery of Christianity, but his comedy is Christ-haunted. "Christ!" McCorquodale prays, in a line too solemn to survive Orton's editing. "Let me die tonight. Don't tease me. I've laughed long enough. I'm out of breath and tears roll down my cheeks."

Laughter becomes Orton's search-and-destroy mission. "I've screeched at Heaven and received no reply," McCorquodale says in one draft. "If only I could find someone who'd been kissed or kicked by God. I wouldn't feel so bad. But, and you can quote me, I've seen neither hide nor hair of anything supernatural in a lifetime spent behind some of the best altars in the country." Like the artists who carved gargoyles on a Gothic cathedral, Orton used the grotesque to summon the totality of life, a living hell as well as an intimation of heaven. "God is as likely to be found among the tripes as in the heart," he wrote in his notes. "He created both after all." Orton's outrageousness always challenged the moral whoopee about man's goodness, teasing the public into accepting a much more complex view of human nature. "Orton understood that his irreligiousness was entirely religious," Kenneth Williams says.

"I think the Christian religion is a terrible mistake," Orton himself said. "In the beginning at the time of the Roman Empire, it had meaning because Christians were probably rebels against a dreary, boring Establishment."[4] The Church had long been the Establishment; to Orton, faith was now frozen in cliché-ridden postures and threadbare ceremonies. Pringle explains The Brotherhood's Christmas: "We call that the Festival of the Renewal of the Spirit. . . . We have a cot with a baby in it outside the church. I dare say you're surprised by the unusualness of the conception?" In real life, Orton found Christmas "a hateful time." The tepid celebrations depressed him. "Drunken people behaving in a foolish way," he wrote after a trip to the West End on December 23, 1966. "Singing and shouting. What for I'd like to know. They've nothing to celebrate." Material impoverishment was as disturbing as the spectacle of spiritual impoverishment:

> Kenneth said when he went out he saw an old woman in Mark's and Spencer's. She was very poor. And she'd bought herself a packet of jam tarts and half a chicken. Obviously she could afford nothing else. How awful to be trying to celebrate when you're old and lonely. I wish there was something to be done. We're not taking any notice of Christmas. [December 24, 1966]

But religious hypocrisy fascinated Orton too much for him to pass over Christmas Day without comment. He saw power and public manipulation where others saw piety. "Usual messages from the heads of the Establishment," he noted. "The Queen from Windsor, The Pope from Rome: Pilate and Caiphas celebrating the birth of Christ."

"LET US GO TO PRISON," Pringle says at the finale of *Funeral Games*, as Orton lampoons the faith of the faithless in resurrection. "Some angel will release us from our place of confinement." Orton himself was no longer the prisoner of his environment. He was no longer confined to the blinkered anonymity of a bedsitter existence. John Orton had become Joe Orton—a new man whose transformation even Orton's family accepted with amazed respect. "Note how I started this letter," his sister Leonie wrote to him early in 1967, "with your new name."[5] Finally in control of his life and his talent, Orton had turned the threats of his past into promise. In the last year Orton's laughter took on a special richness that signalled his new sense of freedom. At the end of *What the Butler Saw*, the characters climb out of the chaos, up the rope ladder, into the blazing light. In private Orton was less ironic about the change of direction in his own life. "I'm going up, up, up," he wrote to Glenn Loney.[6]

In the sixteen weeks between December 1966 and April 1967, Orton's career took a miraculous leap forward. *Loot* won the *Evening Standard* Award, was slated for Broadway, and sold to the movies; *Entertaining Mr. Sloane*, after being scuttled by ITV, was rescheduled for production; *The Good and Faithful Servant* went into rehearsal with Donald Pleasence; *What the Butler Saw* was through its first draft; *The Erpingham Camp* was revised for the *Crimes of Passion* double bill at the Royal Court; and most unexpectedly, Orton had been contacted by The Beatles about writing the screenplay for their next movie. Nothing, not even his mother's death on December 26, seemed to impair Orton's fecundity. The plots of old, failed novels (some of them partly Halliwell's invention) were being recycled by Orton into new commercial products. Orton was free to be himself; and he had found a way of making that self acceptable to the world. He was throwing off the dead weight of his past.

Halliwell on the contrary was increasingly lumbered by his. He could only watch the small miracle of Orton's success and his transformation with seething envy and fear. *His* manuscripts gathered dust in the drawer; *his* mother's death was a fact from which he'd never really recovered. While Orton gallivanted around London seeing agents, producers, reporters, Halliwell stayed at home, his suffering excluding him from life and simultaneously draining it from him. He could never forgive Orton his happiness; failure seemed life's corroboration of his worthlessness. Halliwell was suddenly Orton's answering service and, when Orton required it, his sounding board. He found himself oppressed by the very subjects Orton mined for his laughter— sexuality, isolation, pride, rage, control. Once, hallucinating on hashish,

Orton saw himself as a little boy being beaten by a teacher, and the teacher was Halliwell. Every nagging demand, every petty contradiction conveyed the anger and unhappiness Halliwell tried hard to bridle. Orton began to look upon him in the way a successful graduate often views an old tutor, with an affectionate nostalgia tinged with disdain.

Halliwell struggled to establish something for himself in the midst of Orton's windfall. In early January 1967 Orton and Halliwell carried five of Halliwell's collages to Anno Domini, the antique store then on the King's Road whose proprietor, having seen a screen done by Halliwell at Peggy Ramsay's apartment, was interested in selling his work. To Orton, who was eager for Halliwell to find some outlet for his talent and an interest outside their relationship, it was an exercise at once hopeful and desperate:

The shop smelt of damp. It had natural coloured hessian on the walls. Freddie Bartman got up when we entered. He was a youngish, middle-aged man with glasses. "What have we here," he said, with a certain eagerness as Kenneth placed the first of the pictures against the wall. It was a macabre Venus made of bits of fingers and mouths on a background that looked like a crumbling tube station wall. "Well!" said Freddie, looking impressed. "You've certainly got something here." The next picture seemed to be of eggs bursting over a suburban landscape. A negress, cut from a book of African art, lifted up her hands and screamed. Freddie examined it and went on to the three I had brought: a hideous youth sitting in the foreground with a nightmare scene going on behind, a cadaverous monk and a wraith-like nun standing either side of a small picture which was captioned "Rosencrantz was Jesus CHRIST?" and lastly, a bull made of human hair leaping around in a sandpit and charging [with] three human eyes. Freddie turned the pictures around and said, "I think they'd have to be dolled up a bit. Don't you?" He looked beadily around for confirmation. "I think they ought to be mounted nicely. Don't you?" "They should be framed," I said. "Oh yes," he said. "They'd want nicely framing." . . . "Let me show you my intentions," Frieddie said, leading the way to the cellar.

"I'd put them in this room," he showed us into an underground cavern. "I'd take those mirrors down," he'd led us into another room, musty and evil-smelling. "I'd make a show of it for you." . . . "You want a nice framer," I heard him saying to Kenneth. "I'll look out for one. Let me know. And what are you thinking of asking for them?" Kenneth looked vague. "Let's leave that till they're framed and ready," I said, emerging from the lavatory. "Right you are," said Freddie. "We'll leave it to fate then, shall we?" He promised to ring Kenneth with the name of a picture

framer. Kenneth said he'd have fifteen framed to start with. "Just
to start with," Freddie cackled to himself. "After all," he said, "we
don't know whether they're going to bite, do we?"

[January 6, 1967]

Every tentative step Halliwell made in the world was shadowed by
the heavy knowledge of the sudden discrepancy in their situations.
Orton was big-time; and Halliwell's efforts were woefully small-time.
Where Orton's plays were accessible and well publicized, Halliwell's
collages would be shunted into the basement of an undistinguished
shop. While Orton's work found enthusiastic backers, Halliwell had to
invest his own money in mounting his "productions." Orton, who had
found a public, understood the horror of public indifference and feared
it for Halliwell. "Whether anybody will come is the problem," he
wrote on February 13, when he and Halliwell delivered the framed
pictures to Anno Domini. By the end of March, Halliwell's pictures
were finally on display. But, fearing prosecution, Bartman refused to
hang two of them. "The two pictures are a nude Venus and a picture
called COSY COUPLES—several sections of young men cut from physical
culture magazines juxtaposed with large flowers and distant views of
houses," Orton wrote. "Freddie B. is a nervous twit. Like all the middle-
classes. Too nervous to live. He was even timid of using Kenneth's
poster which makes use of Steinberg drawings. 'As though,' Kenneth
said, with some truth, 'anybody will go and see the pictures stuck away
at the wrong end of the King's Road.' "⁷ Not many people did see the
exhibit, which would become for Halliwell yet another sour memory
in a lifetime of bitterness.

There was no good news in Halliwell's life. For Orton, there seemed
to be very little bad. On January 12—the day after Orton's triumph at
the *Evening Standard* Award had been spoiled by the TV program
about it—he was contacted by Walter Shenson, who had produced
A Hard Day's Night and *Help,* to rewrite a new Beatles script. Shenson
wanted to send Orton the script with a view to working on it. In one
telephone call, Orton was being offered the keys to Celebrity City.
"I was very impressed by this, but I put on a nonchalant manner,"
Orton noted. " 'Well, I'm frightfully up to my eyes in it at the moment,'
I said. 'I'm writing my third play.' 'I'd certainly love to have you take
a look at this draft,' he said. 'I've discussed it with the boys. I mean I
mentioned your name to them. They didn't react too much, I must say.
But I think I can persuade them to have you.' By this time I was feeling
foolish and not at all nonchalant. 'Yes,' I said. 'Please send the script
over and I'll read it.' "

Orton read The Beatles script and the first draft of *What the Butler
Saw* on the same day. "Pleased, but still a lot of work to be done,"[8] was
his verdict on the new farce. His usual procedure was to put away a
play for a few months to get new ideas and objectivity about the work.
The Beatles script would be a relaxing change of pace, and fit neatly
into his timetable for *What the Butler Saw*. Inevitably a screenplay for
The Beatles was a challenge too alluring to decline:

> Liked the idea. Basically it is that there aren't four young men.
> Just four aspects of one man. Sounds very dreary, but as I thought
> about it I realised what wonderful opportunities it would give me.
> The end in the present script is the girl advancing on the four to
> accept a proposal of marriage from one of them (which, the script
> coyly says, we shall never know). Already have the idea that the end
> should be a church with four bridegrooms and one bride. *The
> Homecoming* in fact, but alibied in such a way that no one would
> object. Lots of opportunities for sexual ambiguities—a woman's
> bedroom, at night, her husband outside, and four men inside. I also
> would like to incorporate a lot of material from the first novel
> Kenneth and I ever wrote called *The Silver Bucket*. In it a young
> girl is expelled from her native village for an unnamed offence.
> Already see how it could be one boy expelled from some great in-
> dustrial metropolis accompanied by a ceremony of mammoth pro-
> portions. Could be funny. As long as I wasn't expected to write a
> naturalistic script. . . . Basically The Beatles are getting fed up with
> the Dick Lester type of direction. They want dialogue to speak.
> Also they're tired of actors like Leo McKern stealing scenes. Diffi-
> cult this as I don't think any of The Beatles can act in any accepted
> sense. As Marilyn Monroe couldn't.   [January 15, 1967]

Orton met Shenson for lunch the next day. ("I gave away a few of
my ideas. Enough to whet his appetite. . . . Over lunch he said that
one of the ideas for a new Beatles' film was *The Three Musketeers*.
'Oh, no,' I said. 'That's been done to death.' 'Brigitte Bardot wanted
to play Lady de-Winter,' he said. 'She's been done to death as well,'
I said. 'Oh, heh, heh, heh, boy!' he said. 'You certainly are quick.' ")
By the end of the day, Orton had a title for his original script: *Up
Against It,* and had written the first two pages. "Miss Drumgoole and
Father Brodie have come to life as interesting characters. Which should
delight the Beatles," he wrote. "I'm not bothering to write characters
for them. I shall just do all my box of tricks—Sloane and Hal on them.
After all if I repeat myself in this film it doesn't matter. Nobody who
sees the film will have seen *Sloane* or *Loot*." The next morning Shenson
was on the phone to Orton saying that The Beatles' manager, Brian

Epstein, was "delighted" he'd do the film. Orton felt the first seductive strokes of the movie rubdown, the slap and tickle of famous names and big paydays:

> "You'll be hearing either from Brian or Paul McCartney. So don't be surprised if a Beatle rings you up." "What an experience," I said. "I shall feel as nervous as I would if St. Michael, or God was on the line." "Oh, there's not any need to be worried, Joe," Shenson said. "I can say, from my heart, that the boys are very respectful of talent. I mean, most respectful of anyone they feel has talent. I can really say that, Joe."   [January 17, 1967]

Movies are a dubious adventure for most writers because they regard their work as part of the culture's permanent intellectual diet and end up being treated like flavor of the month. Orton was fascinated by power and the large public. An inveterate tease, he fancied the challenge. His instinct was to woo The Beatles coyly. After Orton waited a week for The Call, it finally came at dinnertime on January 23. "Epstein's adviser rang while I was eating a meal of mashed potatoes, tinned salmon and beetroot," Orton noted. "He asked if I could 'meet the boys' on Wednesday. Said I'd ring him back tomorrow to confirm."

Orton arrived promptly the next day at Epstein's office to be faced with the screenwriter's first debilitating hazard: waiting. "After about five minutes or so a youngish man with a hair-style which was way out in 1958, short, college-boy came up and said, '. . . I'm Brian Epstein's personal assistant,' " Orton wrote in his diary on January 24.

> It crossed my mind to wonder why the English have never got around to finding a perfectly respectable word for "boy-friend." "I'm afraid there's been a most awful mix-up. And all the boys' appointments have been put up an hour and a half." I was a bit chilly in my manner after that. "Do you want me to come back at six?" I said. "Well, no. Couldn't we make another appointment?" "What guarantee is there that you won't break that?" I said. "I think you better find yourself a different writer." This said with indifferent success, though the effect was startling. He asked me to wait a minute and went away to return with Brian Epstein himself. Somehow I'd expected something like Michael Codron. I'd imagined Epstein to be florid, Jewish, dark-haired and overbearing. Instead I was face to face with a mousey-haired, slight young man. Washed-out in a way. He had a suburban accent. I went into his office. "Could you meet Paul and me for dinner tonight?" he said. "We do want to have the pleasure of talking to you." "I've a theatre engagement tonight," I replied, by now sulky and unhelpful.

"Could I send the car to fetch you after the show?" I didn't much relish this flim-flammery, left almost tripping over the carpet and crashing into the secretary who gave a squeal of surprise as I hurtled past her. This I never mention when re-telling the story. I always end on a note of hurt dignity.

Orton's first glimpse of The Beatles' world caught the ludicrous contradiction in these cultural supermen: playing rebel and living posh.

Arrived in Belgravia at ten minutes to eight. . . . I found Chapel Street easily. I didn't want to get there too early so I walked around for a while and came back through a nearby mews. When I got back to the house it was nearly eight o'clock. I rang the bell and an old man entered. He seemed surprised to see me. "Is this Brian Epstein's house?" I said. "Yes, sir," he said, and led the way to the hall. I suddenly realised that the man was the butler. I've never seen one before. . . . He took me into a room and said in a loud voice "Mr. Orton." Everybody looked up and stood to their feet. I was introduced to one or two people. And Paul McCartney. He was just as the photographs. Only he'd grown a moustache. His hair was shorter too. He was playing the latest Beatles record "Penny Lane." I liked it very much. Then he played the other side —Strawberry something. I didn't like this as much. We talked intermittently. Before we went out to dinner we'd agreed to throw out the idea of setting the film in the thirties. We went down to dinner. The trusted old retainer—looking too much like a butler to be good casting—busied himself in the corner. "The only thing I get from the theatre," Paul M. said, "is a sore arse." He said *Loot* was the only play he hadn't wanted to leave before the end. "I'd've liked a bit more," he said. We talked of the theatre. I said that compared with the pop-scene the theatre was square. "The theatre started going downhill when Queen Victoria knighted Henry Irving," I said. "Too fucking respectable." We talked of drugs, of mushrooms which give hallucinations—like L.S.D. "The drug not the money," I said. We talked of tattoos. And after one or two veiled references, marijuana. I said I'd smoked it in Morocco. The atmosphere relaxed a little. Dinner ended and we went upstairs again. We watched a programme on TV; it had phrases in it like "the in crowd" and "swinging London." There was a little scratching at the door. I thought it was the old retainer, but someone got up to open the door and about five very young and pretty boys trouped in. I rather hoped this was the evening's entertainment. It wasn't, though. It was a pop group called The Easybeats. I'd seen them on TV. I liked them very much then. . . . A French photographer arrived. . . . He'd taken a set of new photographs of The Beatles. They wanted one to use on the record sleeve. Excellent photographs. The four Beatles look different in their moustaches. Like anarchists in the early years of the century. After a while . . . I talked to the leading Easybeat. Feeling slightly like an Edwardian masher with a Gaiety girl. And then I came over tired and decided to go home. I had a last word with Paul M. "Well," I said, "I'd like to do the film. There's only one thing we've got to fix up." "You mean the bread?" "Yes." We smiled and parted. I got a cab home. Told Kenneth all about it. Then he got up to make a cup of tea. And we talked a little more. And went to sleep.   [January 24, 1967]

Orton looked upon *Up Against It* as a lark. His instruction to Peggy Ramsay reflected his insouciance:

"We should ask 15,000 pounds," I said, "and then if they beat us down, remember no lower than 10,000. After all whether I do it or not is a matter of indifference to me." Peggy agreed. She said she'd ask 15 and try to get 12 and a percentage. "If they won't pay us 10 they can fuck themselves," I said. "Of course, darling," Peggy said.   [January 25, 1967]

While the contract was being negotiated (£5,000 for the first draft, with the right to buy the script back if unacceptable to The Beatles), Orton blithely continued writing. He had rummaged through discarded manuscripts and found that *Head to Toe* gave him the bare bones of action, which he could beef up with his new epigrammatic style. "Might have been designed with The Beatles in mind," he wrote after rereading the novel, pleased to discover amidst the comic peregrinations and convoluted prose four male characters embroiled in political assassination, guerrilla warfare, and transvestite capering. "In any case," he concluded on January 29, "I shall enjoy writing the film."

Orton didn't waste time. By February 11, when he was summoned to Shenson's palatial flat for one final pep talk before the contract was signed, the first draft of the script was almost completed. Shenson, sitting behind a cigar in a room that up to 1917 had been part of the Russian Embassy, "was most concerned to impress me that 'the boys' shouldn't be made to do anything in the film that would reflect badly on them," Orton wrote, getting his first dose of the screenwriter's second debilitating hazard: the commercial compromise. "'You see,' he said, 'the kids will all imitate whatever the boys do.' I hadn't the heart to tell him that the boys, in my script, have been caught in-flagrante, become involved in dubious political activity, dressed as women, committed murder, been put in prison and committed adultery. And the script isn't finished yet. I thought it best to say nothing of my plans for The Beatles until he had a chance of reading the script. We parted at five o'clock amicably. With the contract, according to him, as good as signed. And, on my part, the film almost written."

Orton's plans for The Beatles were more dangerous and murky than The Beatles' plans for themselves. "We were the first working-class heroes in England to ever get anywhere without changing their accents," John Lennon explained in 1972 during a postmortem on The Beatles in *The National Observer*. "Changing the life style and the appearance of youth throughout the world didn't just happen—we set out to do it; we knew what we were doing." Orton's laughter, as he half-suspected, would turn out to be too hard-edged and wild for their image. Orton used The Beatles to deliver a barrage of startling comic ideas at odds with their benign personas. The two main characters in *Up Against It*, Ian McTurk and Christopher Low, are run out of town for their purported outrages against the living (McTurk's adultery) and the dead (Low's blowing up the town's Memorial to the Fallen). Orton's dialogue conjures up the wicked and faithless world McTurk and Low encounter, where there are no "basic human values":

LOW. I'm hungry and thirsty. I need help.
MRS. O'SCULLIAN. I'm not interested in your private life.

COATES. . . . If you're rich it doesn't matter whether you disgust people or not. In fact I'll go as far as to say that the poor prefer the rich to be disgusting.

THE MAYOR. Like most men in positions of trust I was engaged in illegal activities. . . .

The script teased the cosy, lustless screen rendition of romance. "Anything worth doing, is worth doing in public," McTurk observes. In their outrageousness, the characters are always commenting on the absurdity of the courtly romantic setting. "I must go," Rowena says to McTurk, shafting him yet again in the last minutes of the film. "Love seems out of place in a garden in the moonlight." McTurk finds solace in the arms of a second woman who has unsuccessfully pursued him throughout the film. "My heart is broken," he tells Patricia Drumgoole, about to propose marriage as Orton lampoons the romantic equation of suffering with satisfaction. "But everything else is in working order." After their adventures, the characters are more pragmatic about life.

The marriage takes place—a happy ending in which romantic propa-
ganda is puckishly inverted so the bride can have three bridegrooms.
"Just the happy quartette," coos the photographer snapping the new
marriage of Love, Money, and Lust on the steps of the church. The
third husband is a rebel leader who sees marriage as a radical act.
"Getting married and having children is the most rebellious thing a
man can do," says Jack Ramsay. "It shows a disregard for the conventional bourgeois status-quo and a fine, careless anarchic sense of the
absurd." Marriage, which institutionalizes the sexual scarcity romance
promotes, gives way in the film's final image to a vision of sexual
abundance:

> *Int. hotel bedroom. Morning. The sun streams into the room.*
> MISS DRUMGOOLE *is in bed with* RAMSAY, MCTURK *and* LOW.

> MISS DRUMGOOLE. It's a wonderful dream! I hope we have a happy
> married life!

> *The young men kiss her. There is a struggle.* MISS DRUMGOOLE
> *squeals with delight and disappears under the coverlet with her
> husbands.*

> ### THE END

"Oscar Lewenstein read *Up Against It* and liked it very much,"
Orton wrote on February 25, a day after he'd handed in his first draft.
"He thought it had a poetic quality. This is because I used all the
romantic clichés—moonlight, roses, unrequited love and the Cinderella
figure of the poor girl who loves him and is finally rewarded by his love
in the last reel. O.L. said he liked least the scenes in the Albert Hall
(with the shooting of the woman Prime Minister Lillian Corbett). This
clearly because of the parody of the Kennedy assassination he doesn't
think that Epstein, The Beatles or W. Shenson will opt for it."

It was panic, not poetry, that the script emphasized. Orton also
parodied the Sydney Street Siege. A mêlée erupts after McTurk, Low,
and Ramsay—enlisted as urban guerrillas—refuse to allow the Archbishop of Canterbury, who leads a procession of Lillian Corbett's
mourners, into the cathedral. The Archbishop turns out to be a woman.
"I'm Princess of The Church," she says. "Let me pass. I've some hard
praying to do." Upheaval is elevated to anarchist apocalypse in Orton's
battle scene where McTurk, Low, and Ramsay run their ambulance
into an enemy truck and start a chain reaction of destruction from
which no one emerges victorious.

Amid flames, explosions, and wreckage, "men with stretchers" rescue the by now shocked, injured, and well-nigh senseless McTurk, Ramsay, and Low. They are "placed on stretchers and wrapped in blankets with the other victims of various disasters." The dead and injured are reloaded into a larger fleet of ambulances; but once again the ambulances are destroyed, and "hundreds of men with stretchers attempt to put the injured, the dying, the sick, unhappy army of victims into some sort of shape." Nothing can diminish the panorama of suffering. Every heroic gesture turns into fiasco. Orton even produces the final abyss from which no one escapes:

> . . . Shots are fired and the stretcher bearers collapse as badly injured as their patients. More stretcher bearers pick up the stretcher bearers. They're hit in their turn and collapse. The victims and the helpers struggle together in the mud of the battlefield. An army of ambulances moves away from the camp. . . . At this point, with a loud roar, the earth caves in and the ambulances, full of suffering humanity, crash into the hole which has opened up in the treacherous subsoil.

Havoc is Orton's metaphor for history: a tableau of viciousness in which to be saved from one disaster is only to be eligible for still greater violence and danger. Low, McTurk, and Ramsay take their lives into their own hands. "Seeing what has happened before, they decline to be helped and fight off the stretcher bearers." The victims become victimizers in a struggle to cling to life and remain intact. A priest appears at this spectacle of carnage:

> Shouts and screams from the injured. Blood pouring from bleeding wounds. On the edge of a gaping hole amid the carnage. Onto the scene steps Father Brodie, holding high the cross upon which our Lord died, accompanied by nuns and choir boys singing a hymn to the glory of immortal god.

The immensity of the contradiction floors the rebels. Low, "struck dumb, kneels." McTurk, overcome by despair, "bursts into tears and sits sobbing." But Ramsay "shrieks with maniacal laughter and begins to leap about in a kind of glee." Orton would choose the last course; his grotesque laughter rejected the impotence of despair.

"I've just got McTurk in prison," Orton wrote on February 6, "and, realise, of course, the whole script is about schizophrenia." Like Orton, the characters teeter between optimism and disenchantment, rebellion and acceptance, male and female roles. "Back! Back to the women! Our only hope!" pleads one character, grabbing the steering wheel of a car as McTurk and Low try to change allegiance from the all-female government troops to the male rebels. The driver replies: "No! The men! We must go on!"

Originally the split personality was crudely staged by having Mc-Turk divided into four players who answer to the same name. But in his rewrite for Oscar Lewenstein, Orton wrote separate characters: McTurk the nihilist; Low the activist; and Jack Ramsay the outrageous renegade, whose tactics are "the smear, the lie, and in extreme cases, the truth." The characters inhabit a weird, dissociated landscape with its own special menacing sense of insecurity. (The production plans called for a "Max Ernst modernity," in which "some sets have false perspectives and colour is used as a weapon."[9])

Up Against It flaunted Orton's new vitality, transforming the murderous into the marvellous. But Halliwell had no way to turn dread into delight. He was becoming increasingly petrified by the awful fears that Orton remade into public pleasure. Kenneth Williams remembers dropping in on Orton and Halliwell in mid-February and finding only Halliwell at home. "I was depressed. When I got to the flat, Halliwell answered the door. He hadn't got his toupee on and this great boiled egg came to the door, and said in a prissy voice, 'Yes.' And I said, 'Hello.' 'Joe isn't here,' Halliwell said. I said, 'Well, I'll come and see you.' Halliwell answered, 'But Joe's not here, you don't want to see me.' (Halliwell's terrible inferiority always came to the surface. He always believed he was only wanted because of Joe.) 'Nonsense,' I said. 'I'd love to see you. And I can smell something cooking.' 'Oh, it's a bit of haddock I'm cooking for him,' Halliwell said. 'Oh, I love haddock,' I said, and walked in. 'Well, there's only enough for two,' he said. 'Nonsense,' I said, 'split the two bits in half, and put an egg on top. We'll all have it!' I sensed Halliwell's inwardness and his desire not to talk, but I made him talk. I told him, 'It's rubbish, you answering the door like that. I like you very much.' "

Halliwell had lived with self-loathing too long to believe anyone could like him. His identity was under such siege that every encounter was a potential danger. The slightest abrasion could send him into a fury. At the end of February, with *Up Against It* completed, Orton and Halliwell planned a holiday in Libya for which they needed visas. Even here, Halliwell was forced to struggle for validation:

Kenneth and I made a trip to South Kensington to apply for visas to Libya. The man at the Consular section looked at my application and said, "One pound please." I gave him a pound and he asked me to call back on Monday. When Kenneth gave in his form and his passport, the man looked at him oddly and said, "Will you call tomorrow morning?" . . . We went away. Kenneth making a great fuss. "I always knew we shouldn't try to go to a country with visas! I don't intend going where I'm not wanted! . . ." [February 23, 1967]

Halliwell's instinct was always to retreat, rejecting the source of pain before it could reject him. Orton disarmed the world while Halliwell's fear antagonized it. The threat of being invalidated on any level was so great that Orton had to telephone the Libyan Embassy for him the following day. "Kenneth . . . is in such a rage that it isn't possible to get him to do anything," Orton reported in his diary. "He has to go and see the consul tomorrow. 'I can't get the photographs changed in time,' Kenneth said. 'It's just impossible.' 'Wait and see if that's what they want. They may just wish to check that you're not your own brother,' I said."[10] But the question of identity was no laughing matter to Halliwell. Any situation that rekindled his fears of being "nobody" was always terrifying. Halliwell went to the Embassy "very unwilling and with a long face." He returned "wreathed in smiles."[11] The Embassy had only wanted to assure themselves that Halliwell, whose passport listed his job as "free-lance writer," would write nothing about Libya. The Embassy's inefficiency over their visas filled him with a familiar foreboding:

"I had a dream last night," Kenneth said, in a mournful voice, "that we went to get our tickets and the plane was full." "I wonder you don't start chewing laurel leaves like the Delphic oracle," I said. [February 26, 1967]

Halliwell and Orton left for Libya on March 2. The preceding week had been especially exciting for Orton, and Halliwell longed for his exclusive company away from the punishing glitter of success. Peggy Ramsay and Oscar Lewenstein had both read *Up Against It* and been fulsome in their praise. Lewenstein, who as a director of Woodfall Productions had been associated with *Tom Jones, A Taste of Honey, The Loneliness of the Long Distance Runner,* and many other high-quality productions in the short-lived British cinema renaissance, thought *Up Against It* "probably the best first draft of a screenplay I have ever read."[12] Two days before their departure *Loot* was sold to the movies, and the newspapers were ballyhooing the sales price on the day that Orton and Halliwell left the country. "Joe Orton slipped out of the country to make a temporary home in a simple, second-class hotel in Libya," the *Evening News* reported. "He is there not as a refugee from the £100,000 which Bernard Delfont and Arthur Lewis have paid for the screen rights to *Loot*, but to work on an original film script. . . ."

A legend was being concocted around Orton. But Halliwell was never mentioned, never photographed, never seen. Orton's publicity exacerbated Halliwell's own terror of invisibility; and the one person whose presence had given Halliwell's life cohesion was fast becoming unreal to him. Halliwell, who sought so many "magical" solutions to his problems, looked on the holiday as an important rapprochement. But what was undertaken in hope would end in fiasco—the beginning of their end.

> . . . At London Airport, K.H. came over rather stuffy, looking at the main entrance hall, crowded with people, he said, "What extraordinary people to be at London Airport at this time in the morning." When he went into the departure lounge he said, with relief, "I see we've a better lot of people in here. Those out there were only visitors. They really shouldn't allow that kind of riff-raff in the airport at all." When I pointed out that his remarks were pretty amazing considering the circumstances, he said, "I don't want a lot of people about in the airport I'm leaving from. It's spoiling everything." He then went to the duty free tobacconist's and bought a hundred Sobranie cigarettes. He sat next to a Pakistani and his wife and opened the cigarette carton. A customs official appeared at his side. "Excuse me, sir," he said. "Did you buy those cigarettes here?" Kenneth said he did. "Then you're not supposed to break the seal, sir. You are infringing the regulations. I must ask you not to smoke them or they'll be confiscated." Kenneth looked furious and embarrassed. "Dreadful petty officials," he muttered as the man went away. . . .

After a disastrous time in Tripoli trying to find a hotel room, they were taken to a ship:

> "A ship!" Kenneth gave a cry of alarm. "We'll find ourselves in Saudi Arabia branded as slaves." "Ship very good hotel," the taxi-driver said. "Hot and cold in all rooms." He drove at a rapid rate onto a quay, stopped with a jerk, flung open the doors of the taxi and welcomed us to the T.S.S. *Carina* billed (on the side of the ship) as Libya's "only floating hotel." We paid the taxi driver and climbed the companionway.
>
> The *Carina* was a second or third class ex-German cruise ship. It was moored to a wharf. The town was around the ship in a half-

circle. Inside the ship we found our way to the reception desk. I asked for two single rooms. "We have no single rooms," the manager said (he was fat, Greek or Levantine, he had dark glasses and kept them on always, even at night). "We have only double room." "How much?" I said. "Eightpound ten," he said. "For two?" He gave a smile and a shrug, "I'm sorry, for one." "Eight pounds ten a week?" I said. "A night." "I'll take a double room," I said. The manager called a young boy to attention. The boy was fair-haired and plain in a pretty uniform. "Take the gentlemen to 112," he said. The boy, who didn't understand, or even care, what the manager said immediately disappeared down a stairway. We waited for ten minutes until he returned. . . . The page boy had parked Kenneth and I outside a cabin and left us after discovering that the cabin was already let. It took another half-an-hour as the manager, the page and the steward, separately and together, opened the door with a pass-key and stared in at two suitcases on the floor. After a long while they went away and left us alone in a tiny corridor outside a door marked, in fading, scratchy paint "Herren." "Oh my God!" Kenneth said, rounding upon me savagely, "look what a mess you've got us into now! Dumped on a ship in the middle of some wretched Fascist state! I'm going to faint!" I found myself saying, "Pull yourself together! There's no need to behave badly." "I warned you what it would be like. No travel agency does Libya. I'm not surprised," Kenneth said. "This is probably a brothel!" Even this would've been interesting but, as though to prove him wrong, a plum-faced matron was seen shepherding three young children down the corridor to the loo. "This way, sir," the manager said at my elbow, "there's been a mistake." Behind me Kenneth said, "What's going to happen if they're full here? We shall be sleeping in the open." "Don't be ridiculous," I said. "I shall go to the British Consul." "He's probably an Arab!" Kenneth said. "That'll land us in a worse mess than ever."

The fat manager opened the door of cabin 115 (also outside a door marked "Herren") and showed us what we were getting for £8.10 a night. . . . It was a cabin with two bunks, both already made up for the night, the sheets were spotless, the blanket obviously freshly laundered. The whole area of the cabin would've been a generous linen cupboard. "The room also includes a shower," said the manager rather proudly attempting to fling open the door of the shower and finding that it needed a little effort to do so. The shower was in the lavatory and so, as I later discovered, it wasn't possible to use the lavatory after a shower because the shower saturated the lavatory pan and reduced the toilet paper to pulp. The manager went away leaving us alone.

"We could stay at the Hilton for this price!" Kenneth screamed with rage. "I'd rather not discuss it," I said. "We must make the best of it." . . . [Later that day, we] strolled along an embankment into the city. Cars roared past. . . . A few depressed and aged Libyans were seen at intervals under trees. It was altogether like a balmy night in Hull or Birkenhead. . . . We walked back to the ship.

On board the evening was just beginning. Large numbers of English, American and German middle-class men and women (all the women seemed to be the same dyed blonde hag) were laughing in loud raucous tones. A few middle-class Libyans were strolling about. "Wog bourgeoisie is even worse than the home product," I said, rather wishing Kenneth was in a better mood to appreciate the remark. "Shut up!" Kenneth said, pushing crossly past a gaggle of excited young women. "I'm in no mood to appreciate your remarks." We went to our cabin. I took a shower, Kenneth took his clothes off and then discovered that the curtains didn't fit properly over the windows. The window gave onto the deck and anyone strolling by could see right into the cabin. Whilst I was having a shower Kenneth discovered that it wasn't possible to open the windows more than an inch and that the ship had central heating. We were being suffocated in our cabin. "Go and have a shower," I said. "It's supposed to be good for the nerves." "Fuck the shower!" Kenneth said. He hung a bath towel over the window to hide us from the world. "I must have a drink of water," he said. He then filled a glass of water from the washbasin and put an Alka Seltzer tablet into it, though as I pointed out Alka Seltzer wasn't sold as a protective against typhoid. "It makes the water taste better, though," Kenneth said. We both sat on our bunks sipping Alka Seltzer and listening to the bumping from the upper deck and the shrieking, laughing people pushing into the lavatories just outside our paper-thin door. "Sleep will be impossible tonight," Kenneth said. "We might snatch an hour or two," I said. "What've they all come here for, I wonder?" The answer wasn't long in coming for a band, in the "ballroom" just down the corridor suddenly struck up "South of the Border" and the dancing began.

Until half-past two the next morning the band played a selection of dance tunes from the early forties. . . . "It's as though they're still fighting the desert war," I said. "I wouldn't be surprised if Rommel suddenly appeared on deck." I dropped off into a kind of delirium at two o'clock and woke up to hear an American woman saying, "I'm going to the little girls," a lot of laughter and a man's voice saying, "Me for the little boys." More laughter. More hysterical conversation from drunken gay oilmen and their drunken gay wives. Almost everything they said seemed to be in inverted commas. At the end of a hush which fell upon the ship at three o'clock, a steward knocked on the cabin next door and said, "Your five o'clock call sir." Kenneth and I engaged in desultory conversation until seven when we got up and dressed. . . . We went to the travel agency at nine. . . . With a feeling of relief I booked two seats [to London]. The travel agent looked at our tickets. "You came only yesterday?" he said, in surprise. "Yes," Kenneth said. "The hotels are full." The man nodded. "The hotels are always full," he said. . . .

On the way home, in the airport bus, I sat in front of a black lower-middle-class Noel Coward. He was with his fiancée and kept up a constant stream of dated badinage interspersed with outmoded forms of Imperialist thought like "I fight with my hands," "To use a knife is cowardly," "I never swear in front of women," "I always wear a tie at functions," and even "The r.a.f. is the finest body of men in the world." This mixed with the kind of facetious chatter that would be howled down in the fourth form. "The depressing thing about a lot of coloured people," Kenneth said, "is their pathetic imitation of everything that is bad in the white races." "Did you hear his remarks on Communism?" I said, suddenly remembering a stretch of dialogue I'd forgotten. "He said, 'We should shoot the bastards. They are ruining the economic trade of the world.'" "What was he like?" Kenneth said. "Oh, about thirty-five, bespectacled," I said. "I thought he was about seventeen," Kenneth said. The taxi drew up at the flat and we both stumbled out— home again after a day trip to Tripoli.   [March 1–2, 1967]

"I didn't see a cock the whole time—except my own and that glimpsed only briefly in a cracked mirror,"[13] Orton wrote to Kenneth Williams shortly after their return. But to Halliwell there had been nothing funny about the trip. It was one more dismal disappointment, which sent him into a deep depression. Almost at once his body started to plague him: first mysterious spots on his legs, then heart palpitations, then pains in his chest. Orton saw no problems with the trip. "I hated it and came back," he explained to Peter Willes, who was aghast at the waste of £200; "you can do that when you're rich."[14] Orton could turn every threat into promise; his success could redeem the past. What to Halliwell was a miserable failure only enhanced Orton's celebrity and *Loot*. "The publicity has been good for the play," he wrote in his diary. "The House Manager tells me that the matinee was up and the evening performance sold out except for a few seats."[15]

THE FATAL PATTERN accelerated. "Kenneth v. depressed. I was feeling merry," Orton wrote in his diary on March 10. "I'd finished cutting *Entertaining Mr. Sloane* for Rediffusion and now have no work to do.

I'm quite free. The BBC wrote asking me to do a play for their Wednesday play series. I shan't though. I don't want to do anything this year except perhaps the second draft of *Up Against It* and the recension of *What the Butler Saw*. If I've time on my hands at the end of the year I'd like to amuse myself by writing a bit of rubbish under an assumed name: in the nature of a joke play."

Up Against It fizzled out quickly as a Beatles project. Orton suspected this on March 7 after Shenson found the first half of the script "fascinating" and promised to speak to Epstein in L.A. about it. "He suggested Antonioni to direct. Rubbish!" Orton could get no reply from The Beatles or Epstein about the movie. The problem, Orton and Peggy Ramsay guessed, was with Epstein. "An amateur and a fool," Orton fumed toward the end of March. "He isn't equipped to judge the quality of a script. Probably he will never say 'yes,' equally hasn't the courage to say 'no.' A thoroughly weak, flaccid type."

Orton was too involved in his own work to empathize with Halliwell's complaints. "Kenneth has a pain in his chest when he doesn't take his tablets. He told me this morning," Orton wrote in the diary on March 22. " 'They don't last eight hours,' he said. 'When the effect wears off the pain returns.' I hope there's nothing seriously wrong. 'You must go to a specialist if it doesn't get better,' I said." Squabbles started to dominate their life. "Kenneth H. and I went for a long trot and argued most of the way—traffic and heat aggravating the argument into a fever pitch. The argument was about Ivan the Terrible. At one point Kenneth said, 'You know I'm taking these tablets. They calm me down. And you're working overtime to override the effect of the tablets, aren't you?' When we got home we had a cup of tea and it was smiles until bedtime" (March 23). "Constant rowing over small things," Orton reported on March 31 about their walk to Hampstead Heath.

Their mutual dissatisfaction had begun to show:

> Kenneth has decided that what is wrong with him isn't his heart but his liver. He isn't eating. Just sipping milk every few hours. Most tiresome. I got my own lunch. There was nothing in the cupboard but spaghetti. I had spaghetti and cheese and tomatoes. As Kenneth has decided to go on a hunger strike I shall now get all my meals. This doesn't particularly worry me, except that it means we're starting to live quite separate lives. [April 2, 1967]

On April 4, Orton learned that *Up Against It* was being returned— "No explanation of why. No criticism of the script. And apparently, Brian Epstein has no comment to make either. Fuck them." On April 10, the *Evening Standard* reported "the shock to Joe Orton's pride."

But two days later, Oscar Lewenstein turned Orton's disappointment to advantage by buying the script for £10,000 and 10 percent of the producer's profits. Orton's almost magical resilience inevitably sank Halliwell into even deeper depression. Unable to compete, he instinctively tried to punish and control Orton:

> Long argument with Kenneth the gist of which was "Tell me what you want for lunch and I'll get it." "I'll have eggs and bacon." "You can't because the shops are shut." He then began to argue over suitcases. "I don't think we should buy new ones." Since, as I pointed out to him, he was the one who suggested we bought new ones in the first place this rather surprised me. "Are you going to wear your blue suit for the summer?" he said. "No," I said. "Then why did you have it altered?" he said. "If you hadn't had them altered I could've worn them." "But if you could wear them," I said, "they wouldn't've fitted me. That's why I had them altered." "And now they don't fit me," he said. "No," I said. "But if they'd've fitted you they wouldn't've fitted me. And as they didn't fit me I had them altered. And now I've had them altered they don't fit you."   [April 11, 1967]

The knots into which Halliwell tried to twist Orton were the same painful tactics of psychic control that Orton was making fun of in *What the Butler Saw*. The inspecting psychiatrist jams the mind of Geraldine Barclay, a secretary who has come for a job and finds herself certified insane:

> RANCE. . . . Who was the first man in your life?
> GERALDINE. My father.
> RANCE. Did he assault you?
> GERALDINE. No!
> RANCE (*to* DR. PRENTICE). She may mean "Yes" when she says "No."
>   It's elementary feminine psychology. . . .

The struggle between license and control, identity and invisibility, consciousness and "self-consciousness" is at the core of the play's desperation—a mirror image of Orton's own struggle with Halliwell's neurotic problems. The sexual and psychological exploitation satirized by *What the Butler Saw* not only dominated their lives, but also the public imagination:

> Saw a poster for a film called *Libido Means Lust*. It said, "What happens when a sadistic sex-maniac falls in love!" On the way home I noticed a crit of *The Diary of a Madman* which is being

presented, for four weeks, at the Duchess with [Nicol] Williamson.
I thought how fashionable madness is at the moment. The film
Marat/Sade is just out. Of course it's the perennial fascination of
watching lunatics. Four hundred years ago they'd have gone to
Bedlam for the afternoon. Now a director and actors re-create a
madhouse in a theatre. Let's look at mad people. At queer people.
They have only to look in the mirrors. Kenneth H. said, "In *What
the Butler Saw* you're writing about madness." "Yes," I said, "but
there isn't a lunatic in sight—just doctors and nurses."

[March 14, 1967]

"I hope I can keep up sufficient frenzy to the end of the play,"
Orton had written in his diary on December 24, 1966, when he was
already halfway through *What the Butler Saw*. To simulate the schizophrenic experience, his plot required the kind of accelerating momentum in which at a certain speed personality starts to disintegrate.
It also needed the double-binding exchanges that create suffocating
psychic static. Orton typed up a long single-spaced list of exclamations
and ripostes, which he distributed among his characters whenever a
situation called for a putdown or comic jolt:

The most interesting love/hate patterns it has ever been my privi-
lege to witness.
You revolting fur-covered bitch!
And let me tell you, there is a great deal of very good chastity in
the world.
Sometimes your phraseology appals me.
You're talking like a shop-girl again!
In a pathologically elevated mood.
A word not in current use except in the vernacular.
Every sacred cow pastures in England.
Do you mind keeping your tasteless comments to yourself?
Keep the word, destroy the meaning, that has always been the
English way.
Screaming Jesus!
You shoulder-length prick!
He likes women—you know strip clubs, menstruation, mothers-in-
law.

He experimented with longer jokes in the same way, developing
them first in a list (and sometimes in the voice of his character), then
finding a place for the best of them when the plot warranted. Many of
the epigrams and laugh lines never made it into the play; but they were
kept on file to be used in future work:

I once delivered a girl child whose body was covered with sexual openings—like a Marine's dream.

Greek paederasty was a noble ideal. I hope one day to see it prac-tised in this country alongside the Christian virtues of Love Thy Neighbour and turn the other cheek.

In an age of declining faith, sir, surely it's enough for the young to hold spiritual convictions. It's an act of pedantry to ask that they should be the right ones.

"Hard at work on *What the Butler Saw*," Orton noted on Decem-ber 28, 1966. "I wrote a scene where Geraldine disguises herself as an Indian nurse. Cut it though after laughing a lot. Held up the action. And whenever anything makes me roar with laughter it's a sure sign it must be cut out."

While working on his own farce, Orton paid close attention to productions of classical farces, making sure that he steered clear of the failures he saw in others. Sardou's *Let's Get A Divorce* left him cold. "Lots of running about, but not a single funny line. A third act that was a joke (unintentional). There wasn't a single situation of any interest. Sardou should be left where he belongs, gathering dust on the shelf of the commercial theatre."[16] The exhilaration and impact of Orton's jokes created an illusion of tumult, but for the jokes to register the actors had to stand still to be heard. Orton was making new de-mands on farce and was conscious of the delicate issue of pace. "Last night I heard *Occupe-Toi d'Amélie* on the wireless," he wrote on December 27. "Surprisingly good. Better, by far, than that nauseating production of *A Flea in Her Ear* at the National. It has speed and managed to capture the style. At the National they gabbled the lines. Everything was taken at breakneck pace with the result that it seemed to drag. Of course the advantage of sound radio was that no idiot designer got in the way. In *A Flea in Her Ear* the sets and costumes appeared to be fantasies of a demented pervert."

Farce made the most of what Orton, quoting Shakespeare, called the theatre's "two hour traffic." He preferred the vividness and astonish-ment of the stage to the long-winded "two day traffic" of the novel. Orton saw a chance for action and surprise missed in *Rosencrantz and Guildenstern Are Dead*. He admired Tom Stoppard's "wonderful idea . . . how I wish I'd stumbled on it." But the play disappointed him because it never seized its potential for action. "It should've been about the futility of students—always talking, talking, talking and never doing anything. Great events, murders, adulteries, dreadful revenge happening all around them and they just talk. This is what the play should have been about but wasn't."[17]

What the Butler Saw attempted in its own way what Orton felt Stoppard had not. Torture, nymphomania, transvestism, incest, blackmail, bribery parade across the stage while psychoanalytic prattle twists experience into meanings all its own. "The ugly shadow of anti-Christ stalks this house," deduces Dr. Rance, hot on the trail of his case study. "Having discovered her Father/Lover in Dr. Prentice the patient replaces him in a psychological reshuffle by the archetypal Father-figure—the Devil himself. . . ."

Orton fed his characters into farce's fun machine and made them bleed. Their pursuit of identity turns gradually from the ridiculous to the murderous. Drunk, numb, bruised, and bloody, they are disturbing figures who transform the landscape of farce from daydream to nightmare. Even the play's title, with its evocation of Edwardian pier entertainments, spoofs boulevard titillation while offering a much more unsettling spectacle to its paying customers. This reversal was the kind of mischief Orton relished. When Oscar Lewenstein later suggested teaming with Binkie Beaumont to mount *What the Butler Saw* in the West End at the Haymarket—the bastion of escapist bourgeois entertainment—Orton was delighted.

> "That'd be wonderful," I said. "It'd be sort of a joke even putting *What the Butler Saw* on at the Haymarket—Theatre of Perfection." We discussed the set. "It should be beautiful. Nothing extraordinary. A lovely set. When the curtain goes up one should feel that we're right back in the old theatre of reassurance—roses, french windows, middle-class characters. . . ."   [July 27, 1967]

"Why are there so many doors?" asks Dr. Rance, when he first stalks through the garden into Dr. Prentice's clinic. "Was the house designed by a lunatic?" Orton draws attention to the trappings of conventional farce, then turns it to his own more serious ends. Dr. Prentice's clinic, which begins as the setting for his botched seduction of the prospective secretary, Geraldine Barclay, ends as a hothouse of Freudian hyperbole and priapic pandemonium. "Civilizations have been formed and maintained on theories which refuse to obey facts," explains Dr. Rance, rationalizing Miss Barclay's semi-nude presence in the clinic and Prentice's ludicrous tall-tale of being attacked by her. "As far as I'm concerned this child was unnaturally assaulted by her own father. I shall base my future actions upon that assumption." *What the Butler Saw* satirizes analytic omniscience while making panic look like reason.

"You know what psychiatrists are like," Orton told the *Evening News* on June 9, 1967. "They take everything you say so seriously. Everybody is a little like psychiatrists today. They've got this enormous wish to explain everything. Religion—especially Christianity—tries to show things following a logical progression. And for all we know the whole thing may turn out to be some vast joke. There's all sorts of things that can't be explained. I don't know what we're all doing here. It all seems very ridiculous but I presume there must be a purpose."

Orton's writing gave him a sense of order and direction. Meanwhile, like a character in an Orton farce, Halliwell had been slowly going out of control and seeking medical help which gave him psychoanalytic answers, but no cure:

Kenneth Halliwell had been to a new doctor. The doctor examined him and said he hadn't got appendicitis. He said it was nervousness and has given him tranquillizers. "It's because your mother died when you were eleven and it was a traumatic experience. You are imagining this appendicitis out of guilt," he said. "Whatever are you guilty about?" I said. "I don't know," Kenneth said.

[April 14, 1967]

What the Butler Saw is a celebration of the neurotic patterns brilliantly illuminated by Orton on stage but dismissed by him offstage with Halliwell. Between the lines of Orton's dialogue runs the real-life terror, which could not be laughed away. "I don't want drugs," wails Mrs. Prentice, lurching for the whiskey bottle on Prentice's desk. "I want account taken of my sexual nature." Ignored and mocked by an indifferent husband, Mrs. Prentice dabbles in nymphomania and lesbianism:

MRS. PRENTICE. Whose fault is it if our marriage is on the rocks? You're selfish and inconsiderate. Don't push me too far. (*With a toss of her head.*) I might sleep with someone else.
PRENTICE. Who?
MRS. PRENTICE. An Indian student.
PRENTICE. You don't know any.
MRS. PRENTICE. New Delhi is full of them.

If Prentice hasn't lived up to his wife's expectations, neither has she to his. Sexual inadequacy is the visible sign of a deeper one. Dr. Prentice and his wife refuse to see the part each plays in the other's problems. Instructing Geraldine to lie on the couch and think of her favorite work of fiction, Dr. Prentice explains: "My wife is a nymphomaniac and consequently, like the Holy Grail, she's ardently sought after by young men. I married her for her money and, upon discovering her penniless, I attempted to throttle her. She escaped my murderous fury and I've had to live with her malice ever since." Prentice, like Orton, is a victim of his own casual pragmatism.

In *What the Butler Saw*, the air is full of legitimate demands that are never heard. As needs go unheeded, the demands become more irrational, the actions more outrageous:

> RANCE. . . . Were you molested by your father?
> GERALDINE (*with a scream of horror*). No, no, no!
>
> DR. RANCE *straightens up and faces* DR. PRENTICE.
>
> RANCE. The vehemence of her denials is proof positive of guilt. It's a text-book case! A man beyond innocence, a girl aching for experience. The beauty, confusion and urgency of their passion driving them on. They embark on a reckless love-affair. He finds it difficult to reconcile his guilty secret with his spiritual convictions. It preys on his mind. Sexual activity ceases. She, who basked in his love, feels anxiety at its loss. She seeks advice from her priest. The Church, true to Her ancient traditions, counsels chastity. The result—madness.

Geraldine, who has been straitjacketed, sedated, and shorn of most of her hair by Dr. Rance in an ecstasy of analytic prognosis wants her clothes and her identity back. So does Nick, the blackmailing pageboy who has seduced and been photographed *in flagrante delicto* with Mrs. Prentice in the linen cupboard of the Station Hotel (Mrs. Prentice: "When I gave myself to you the contract didn't include cinematic rights"). Prentice wants to salvage his reputation; and in the frantic confusion, even Dr. Rance wants confirmation of his role. "Let me cure your neurosis," he begs Geraldine. "It's all I want out of life." Totally self-absorbed and driven by the impetus of their own needs, nobody listens:

> NICK. Have you given a thought to my predicament?
> PRENTICE. No. I'm obsessed by my own.

Dr. Rance is conceived as an "inspector"—the inquiring and fault-finding eye to whom everyone looks for confirmation. To Rance, life is a casebook. Under Rance's gaze, everyone in *What the Butler Saw*—even Mrs. Prentice, who is in league with him against her husband's apparent malpractice—is reduced by his engulfing presence to the terri-

ble status of nonentity. Rance tells Nick "sternly": "I am a representative of order, you of chaos. Unless that fact is faced I can never
hope to cure you."

Rance scrambles everyone else's picture of the world:

> PRENTICE. Your interpretation of my behaviour is misplaced and
> erroneous. If anyone borders on lunacy it's you yourself!
> RANCE. Bearing in mind your abnormality that is a normal reaction.
> The sane appear as strange to the mad as the mad to the sane.
> Remain where you are. I shall give you a capsule.

Fearing Rance's judgment, Prentice is never free to be himself. He
exists in a perpetual state of "petrified" self-consciousness. He struggles
to keep his fictions in line; from the first lie about Geraldine's state of
undress, Prentice weaves a network of falsehoods in order not "to give
himself away." But this spirals into increasingly mad behavior, which
takes Prentice ever further from the truth and from himself. Having
colluded with Rance's assumption that the nude girl was not Geraldine
Barclay ("She's taken my secretary's name as her 'nom de folie' "), he has
then to continue the tall-tale by claiming that Miss Barclay was sighted
downstairs. When Rance demands to know what she was doing there,
Prentice, thinking fast, answers: "She's making white golliwogs for sale
in colour-prejudice trouble-spots"—an answer that from Rance's viewpoint has madness written all over it. "These hellish white homuncules
must be put out of their misery," Rance commands. "I order you to
destroy them before their baleful influence can make itself felt. . . .
The man's a second Frankenstein."

Prentice forgets everything but the manic needs of the moment. All
his energy is exhausted in defensive maneuvers that enslave him in
impersonations intended to protect him from the judgment of others.
Instead of allaying insecurity, his defenses compound it. Prentice tries
to hide Geraldine's dress and underwear from Mrs. Prentice when she
bursts into his office after her night at the Station Hotel, dressed in a
fur coat and very little else:

> MRS. PRENTICE (*in a surprised tone*). What are you doing with that
> dress?
> PRENTICE (*pause*). It's an old one of yours.
> MRS. PRENTICE. Have you taken up transvestism? I'd no idea our
> marriage teetered on the edge of fashion. . . . Give me the dress,
> I shall wear it.
> PRENTICE (*reluctant*). May I have the one you're wearing in ex-
> change?

MRS. PRENTICE (*putting the glass down*). I'm not wearing a dress.

She slips off her fur coat. Under it she is dressed only in a slip.
DR. PRENTICE *cannot conceal his surprise.*

If he can get Miss Barclay clothed, Prentice can get her out of the
clinic and resume "being himself." But he is labelled a transvestite
when he asks again politely to borrow one of his wife's dresses. "I find
your sudden craving for women's clothing a dull and, on the whole, a
rather distasteful subject." Orton relishes Prentice's anxiety. Prentice
again tries to shift Geraldine's underwear, dress, and shoes from sight.
He never quite succeeds, and is always forced to disguise his actions in
preposterous contortions when somebody catches him at it. Farce becomes a paradigm of neurotic defensiveness. Orton choreographs every
move, using fear as the dynamo to drive his fun machine:

> . . . *He* [DR. PRENTICE] *shakes out* GERALDINE's *underclothes, sees
> her shoes and stockings and picks them up.* MRS. PRENTICE *enters
> from the hall.* DR. PRENTICE *swings round, turns his back on her
> and walks away, bent double in an effort to conceal the clothing.*

MRS. PRENTICE (*alarmed by this strange conduct*). What's the matter?
(*She approaches.*) Are you in pain?
PRENTICE (*his back to her, strangled*). Yes. Get me a glass of water.

> MRS. PRENTICE *hurries into the dispensary,* DR. PRENTICE *stares
> about him in desperation. He sees a tall vase of roses. He removes
> the roses and stuffs the underclothing and one shoe into the vase.
> The second shoe won't go in. He pauses, perplexed. He is about
> to replace the roses when* MRS. PRENTICE *enters carrying a glass of
> water.* DR. PRENTICE *conceals the shoe under his coat.* MRS. PREN-
> TICE *stares. He is holding the roses. He gives a feeble smile and
> presents them to her with a flourish.* MRS. PRENTICE *is surprised
> and angry.*

MRS. PRENTICE. Put them back at once!

> The shoe slips and DR. PRENTICE, *in an effort to retain it,
> doubles up.*

Should I call a doctor?
PRENTICE. No. I'll be all right.
MRS. PRENTICE (*offering him the glass*). Here. Drink this.

> DR. PRENTICE *backs away, still holding the roses and the shoe.*

PRENTICE. I wonder if you'd get another glass? That one is quite the wrong shape.

MRS. PRENTICE (*puzzled*). The wrong shape?

PRENTICE. Yes.

MRS. PRENTICE *stares hard at him, then goes into the dispensary. DR. PRENTICE tries to replace the roses in the vase. They won't go in. He picks up a pair of scissors from his desk and cuts the stalks down to within an inch or so of the heads. He puts the roses in the vase and wraps the stalks in his handkerchief and puts it into his pocket. He looks for somewhere to conceal the second shoe. He gets on his knees and shoves the shoe between the space on top of the books on the lower shelf of the bookcase. MRS. PRENTICE enters carrying another glass. She stops and stares.*

MRS. PRENTICE. What are you doing now?

PRENTICE (*lifting his hands*). Praying.

Later, Mrs. Prentice discovers the hidden shoe. She reports what she's found and seen to Dr. Rance. From her viewpoint, she's telling the truth. Rance confronts Prentice. "Are you in the habit of wearing women's footwear?" In hysterical desperation, the impersonation takes over Prentice. He answers: "My private life is my own. Society must not be too harsh in its judgements." Once begun, each falsehood compounds the need to continue the lie or face even greater humiliation. The confusion of identities is not just the traditional change of clothes, but an upheaval of consciousness where the dizzying maneuvers and counteractions become a stage picture of the mind in retreat:

GERALDINE. We must tell the truth!

PRENTICE. That's a thoroughly defeatist attitude. (*He bundles her behind the curtain.*)

In *What the Butler Saw*, Orton's laughter dramatized the predicament it revenged: the process by which identity is discounted. Geraldine Barclay, like Halliwell, is a "secretary" who has lost her identity. From Geraldine's point of view (as from Halliwell's, who voiced the paranoid idea to his doctor), her identity is literally stolen from her. Both Prentice and Rance refuse to admit her existence. She is cancelled out and becomes literally a nonentity—"a non-existent *thing.*"

Prentice, of course, knows the truth, but for practical reasons cannot tell it. In the same way, Orton knew how much Halliwell had done for him but would never acknowledge him in public. "Halliwell claimed

that he influenced Orton and helped him in a very basic way," Dr.
Ismay said. *"But nobody knew."* Like Halliwell, whose talents by Orton's admission were real but "hidden," Geraldine's real self is maneuvered into a position of invisibility. On stage Orton turns the
anxiety of being discounted into a painfully funny and haunting situation. Geraldine can't be seen or make herself seen by the others. Despite
the fact that Geraldine Barclay is flesh and blood under Rance's nose,
his conviction that she is someone else of no particular importance
makes it impossible for him to take her into account. "Identity," R. D.
Laing reminds us, "requires the existence of another by whom one is
known. . . ."[18] Geraldine, like Halliwell, is hidden from view by forces
outside her control. No one claims to know her.

Prentice sees a way to escape. He asks Nick to undress. "I want
you to impersonate my secretary. Her name is Geraldine Barclay. It
will solve all our problems if you agree to my request." Nick, who has
returned Mrs. Prentice's wig and dress along with the compromising
negatives of their caper, becomes Geraldine Barclay. And Geraldine,
already with her hair cropped short by Dr. Rance, vanishes into the
personality and clothes of Nicholas Beckett. Nick and Geraldine speak
and act like their opposite sex. When these identities are threatened,
the characters split again and proliferate. Geraldine becomes Gerald
Barclay. Nicholas Beckett, dressed in the drugged Sergeant Match's
policeman's outfit, impersonates his brother on the police force in order
to arrest himself and so be extricated from the proceedings. Orton
makes a spectacle of their chaotic nonentity. Having engineered the
hallucinatory effect, Orton unleashes its fragmentation on Mrs. Prentice:

> NICK *hurries into the hall.* DR. PRENTICE *hurries into the dispen-
> sary.* MRS. PRENTICE *enters from the ward.* NICK *re-enters from the
> hall wearing only underpants and the helmet. Upon seeing him*
> MRS. PRENTICE *shrieks and backs away.* NICK *runs into the garden.*
>
> MRS. PRENTICE (*at the desk, weakly*). Oh, this place is like a mad-
> house!
>
> DR. RANCE *enters from the ward.* MRS. PRENTICE *turns upon him,
> wildly.*
>
> You must help me, doctor! I keep seeing naked men.
> RANCE (*pause*). When did these delusions start?
> MRS. PRENTICE. They're not delusions. They're real.
> RANCE (*with a bray of laughter*). Everyone who suffers from hallu-
> cinations imagines they are real. . . .

Like the others, Mrs. Prentice finds herself on the verge of collapse. Her experience is continually invalidated by Dr. Rance's explanations. After a flurry of half-naked bodies clutching wounded limbs and scraps of clothes has again bolted across her path scurrying for safety, Mrs. Prentice throws herself hysterically into the arms of Dr. Rance as he re-enters the room: "Doctor, doctor! The world is full of naked men running in all directions." And so it is.

The momentum, which Orton could never quite master in *Loot*, builds masterfully in *What the Butler Saw*. Tumult is created not only by a brilliant traffic plan but by the brilliant play of language whose reversals send each character rebounding from scene to scene in crazed pursuit of reality. The combined velocity catches all the characters in its slipstream:

> GERALDINE. I'm not a patient. I'm telling the truth!
> RANCE. It's much too late to tell the truth.

As *What the Butler Saw* speeds up, reality for the characters becomes more frantic and violent. Hysteria threatens and shrinks their world. They are at first confused, then numb, and finally pushed by panic to the brink of insanity. The centrifugal force of events impels the characters to cling to their defenses. This, in turn, creates the hilarious and hideous spectacle of people literally being "driven out of their mind." Act 1 ends with Sergeant Match discovering Geraldine, dressed in Nick's pageboy gear, cringing behind the curtain: "I want a word with you, my lad." The terror of being denied is raised to a new pitch— and the stage direction reads: "A siren begins to wail."

Act 2 begins with Geraldine happy to be arrested and confessing what has happened. Since she's dressed as a boy, her account of Prentice's attack is immediately misconstrued by Sergeant Match as a homosexual act. Prentice refers to Geraldine as "she"; but Geraldine, who can only be arrested as Nicholas Beckett, must stick to her male disguise:

> RANCE . . . (*He advances on* GERALDINE). Do you think of yourself as a girl?
> GERALDINE. No.
> RANCE. Why not?
> GERALDINE. I'm a boy.
> RANCE (*kindly*). Do you have the evidence about you?
> GERALDINE (*her eyes flashing an appeal to* DR. PRENTICE). I must be a boy. I like girls.

DR. RANCE *stops and wrinkles his brow, puzzled.*

RANCE (*aside, to* DR. PRENTICE). I can't quite follow the reasoning there.

PRENTICE. Many men imagine that a preference for women is, *ipso facto,* a proof of virility.

RANCE (*nodding, sagely*). Someone should really write a book on these folk-myths. (*To* GERALDINE.) Take your trousers down. I'll tell you which sex you belong to.

GERALDINE (*backing away*). I'd rather not know!

RANCE. You wish to remain in ignorance?

GERALDINE. Yes.

RANCE. I can't encourage you in such a self-indulgent attitude. You must face facts like the rest of us.

Geraldine's predicament displaces in laughter the schizoid bind of the homosexual from which Orton tried to extricate himself. Geraldine is defined by other people's definitions of her sexuality. She is forced to live up to their unreal expectations. The situation is a recipe for madness that Orton had been trying to clarify since 1961 in the novel *Head to Toe.* Where *Entertaining Mr. Sloane* aspired, in Orton's words, "to break down all sexual compartments,"[19] the wit in *What the Butler Saw* bombards conventional sexual attitudes, while its situations dramatize society's compulsion to categorize. Under the onslaught of Rance's labels, Geraldine quickly becomes mystified about herself and loses a sense of her physical identity:

GERALDINE, *unable to stand the ordeal any longer, cries out to* DR. PRENTICE *in anguish.*

GERALDINE. I can't go on, doctor! I must tell the truth. (*To* DR. RANCE.) I'm not a boy! I'm a girl!

RANCE (*to* DR. PRENTICE). Excellent. A confession at last. He wishes to believe he's a girl in order to minimize the feelings of guilt after homosexual intercourse.

GERALDINE (*wild-eyed, desperate*). I pretended to be a boy. I did it to help Dr. Prentice.

RANCE. How does it help a man if a girl pretends to be a boy?

GERALDINE. Wives are angry if they find their husbands have undressed and seduced a girl.

RANCE. But boys are fair game? I doubt whether your very personal view of Society would go unchallenged.

Provoked beyond endurance, GERALDINE *flings herself into* DR. RANCE's *arms and cries hysterically.*

GERALDINE. Undress me then, doctor! Do whatever you like only prove that I'm a girl.

In the confusion, the characters no longer feel real. They lose a sense of being in their bodies. Nick and Geraldine can no longer recognize each other's gender:

NICK. Why is he wearing my uniform?
PRENTICE. He isn't a boy. He's a girl.
GERALDINE. Why is she wearing my shoes?
PRENTICE. She isn't a girl. She's a boy. (*Pouring whisky.*) Oh, if I live to be ninety, I'll never again attempt sexual intercourse.

The characters are not only disguised, they feel disembodied. In this wild game of hide-and-seek, people appear to each other as phantoms:

NICK *supports himself on the desk and stares at the sobbing* MRS. PRENTICE.

NICK (*to* GERALDINE). Is she mad?
GERALDINE. She thinks she is. She imagines you're a figment of her imagination.
NICK (*to* MRS. PRENTICE, *nodding to* GERALDINE). She can see me. Doesn't that prove I'm real?
MRS. PRENTICE. No. She's mad.
NICK. If you think I'm a phantom of your subconscious you must be mad.
MRS. PRENTICE (*with a hysterical shriek*). I am mad!

Caught in the web of mistaken identities, the characters function frantically but at an increasing distance from themselves. Their grip on reality is paralyzed. "What have you done with Geraldine Barclay?" Rance asks Prentice, suspecting he's killed her and condemning him as "a transvestite, fetishist, bi-sexual murderer," displaying "considerable deviation overlap." Geraldine feebly replies: "I'm here." The timbre of her voice indicates her uncertainty. No one in the play is certain of being *here*. Nick: "If the pain is real I must be real." Mrs. Prentice: "Is this blood real?" Dr. Prentice: "I've been too long among the mad to know what sanity is." Since their inner world has been tortured into such insecurity, the characters grope for validation from the outside world, whose messenger is its official inspector, Dr. Rance. However, he refuses "to get involved in metaphysical speculation" about Nick's or anybody else's identity. But to the characters, the establishing of their reality is now a matter of psychic life or death. Each attempts to escape the terror of nonentity, which draws them deeper into it.

HALLIWELL was caught in the very psychic dilemma Orton dramatized in *What the Butler Saw*. Like the characters of the play, Halliwell found himself stalemated. No matter how hard he tried, he couldn't get anywhere. His future would be the result of the present, the present was the result of the past, and the past was unalterable. As the TV producer at Peter Willes's party told him, he was a "middle-aged nonentity." Orton had been part of Halliwell's defense, but Orton's success and growing independence threatened all that. Without him, any sense of direction or purpose was lost. When they were still writing together, Halliwell too had tried to find a form for his anger and turn his murderous instincts into fiction. Donelly in *The Boy Hairdresser* dreams of a peace from pain, and of one last laugh on the emptiness in himself and the society that helped to create it. "He lacked the courage to die and the courage to live. He wanted a sign. Any excuse, O Lord, any excuse." Donelly finds his excuse when his friend is murdered. "Suicide," Donelly thinks to himself, "is an insult to the body; it is self-hatred, which dries up energy and makes it infertile. He would be fixed forever in a dead and withered sterility. And when time ceases, will there be nothing to know but the follies and discontentments of the past?" Halliwell's life hadn't changed substantially since that self-portrait was written in 1960. "His aloneness," as they had written of Donelly, "was vast about him." Murder was the perverse solution Halliwell had predicted for himself in fantasy. And, as it was for Donelly, murder seemed to be Halliwell's only way of making his presence felt, of proving to the world and Orton and himself that he could act. That he mattered.

Annihilation as a desperate remedy for impending chaos is also tested in *What the Butler Saw* when Prentice pulls a gun on Rance and threatens murder. Each declares the other mad, each desperately trying to force life to submit to his view of it:

> PRENTICE (*waving his gun*). Stay where you are, doctor! Your conduct today has been a model of official irresponsibility and bloody-mindedness. I'm going to certify you.
> RANCE (*quietly, with dignity*). No, I am going to certify you.
> PRENTICE. I have the weapon. You have the choice. What is it to be? Either madness or death?

RANCE. Neither of your alternatives would enable me to continue to be employed by Her Majesty's Government.

PRENTICE. That isn't true. The higher reaches of the civil service are recruited entirely from corpses or madmen. Press the alarm!

DR. RANCE goes to the wall and presses the alarm. A siren wails. Metal grilles fall over each of the doors. The lights go out. The siren wails to a stop. The room is lit only by the glare of a bloody sunset shining through the trees in the garden.

An overloading of the circuit! We're trapped.

The bars are a stunning image of emotional stalemate. They clang down with an impressive thud, and the sound makes the metaphor both terrifying and funny. The infernal glare of the "bloody sunset" surrounds the characters' frantic groping to get free. Orton added this visual evocation of a living hell in July 1967, when life with Halliwell was becoming intolerable. The tantrums, the abuse, the threats of death, the whole melodramatic performance of depression were Halliwell's pleas for pity and affection. Orton remained unmoved. (Rance: "Lunatics are melodramatic. The subtleties of drama are wasted on them.") The trap into which Rance and Prentice fall had snared Orton and Halliwell. Fearing engulfment, their identities vied for autonomy. The situation, as Orton knew, was as painful as it was ludicrous.

The cage is *What the Butler Saw*'s crucial image. The farceur, as Eric Bentley says, "sees man as hardly higher than the apes."[20] Behind the bars in *What the Butler Saw*, the characters scurry for safety. Rance disarms Prentice ("I'll have you in a jacket within an hour. It's a hat trick!"), and proceeds to reminisce about how he "once put a whole family into a communal strait-jacket." With the human zoo whimpering behind him, Rance depicts himself as the Frank Buck of the insane: "It was my own family, you see. I've a picture of the scene at home. My foot placed squarely on my father's head. I sent it to Sigmund Freud and had a charming postcard in reply."

When the cage descends in *What the Butler Saw*, all the boundaries and personalities have broken down. But then the nightmare of disorder is transformed instantly into a fairy tale of harmony. All the characters—even the statue of Sir Winston Churchill—are made whole. Geraldine reports the loss of her "lucky elephant charm" to Rance. Nick produces a similar charm. "Oh, my heart is beating like a wild thing!" exclaims Mrs. Prentice, fitting the two pieces of jewelry together, and showing Nick and Geraldine that it makes a brooch—the very piece of jewelry she broke in half and gave to the illegitimate twins she was

forced to abandon after being raped as a chambermaid in the Station
Hotel after the war. "It was impossible for me to keep them—I was
by then engaged to be married to a promising young psychiatrist." Mrs.
Prentice's hilarious revelation is topped by Dr. Prentice, who tells them
the inscriptions on the brooch, and claims paternity:

> PRENTICE. . . . I haven't seen it since I pressed it into the hand
> of a chambermaid whom I debauched shortly before my marriage.
> MRS. PRENTICE (*with a cry of recognition*). I understand now why
> you suggested that we spend our wedding night in a linen cup-
> board!
> PRENTICE. I wished to re-create a moment that was very precious to
> me. If you'd given in to my request our marriage would never
> have foundered.
> MRS. PRENTICE. From this time on we'll never make love except in a
> linen cupboard. It's the least I can do after the years of suffering
> I've caused you!

"The ending works as 'all is forgiven'—just as in the later Shakespeare plays," Orton wrote, after rereading the play on July 16, 1967.
The situation also echoes the baby left in the handbag at Victoria Station cloakroom in *The Importance of Being Earnest*. While working
out the elaborate plot points for Orton's happy ending, the audience
momentarily forgets the implications of this harmony. Rance brings it
into focus. He is "wild with delight": not at the spectacle of human
happiness, but at the thought that his theory has been proved right. "If
you are this child's father . . . she *is* the victim of an incestuous assault!"
Up to this point, Rance's analysis has been a fiction that twists every
scrap of information into a narrative fit for the best-selling book he
wants to write ("A beautiful but neurotic girl has influenced the doctor
to sacrifice a white virgin to propitiate the dark gods of unreason . . .").
But fiction turns out to be fact. Mrs. Prentice has also been attacked by
Nick. So Rance has a bonus of double incest for his book. He can hardly
contain himself. Joyously, he embraces his case studies. "Double incest
is even more likely to produce a best-seller than murder—and this is
as it should be for love *must* bring greater joy than violence."

Dr. and Mrs. Prentice's suffering and outrageousness have their
roots in sexual guilt; in fact, the whole farce is based on covering up
sexual guilt. Now the characters are magically redeemed from it. The
scene builds to an exhilarating image of unity and guiltless transcend-
ence. "Everyone embraces one another," reads the stage direction. And
then, "in a great blaze of glory," the rope ladder drops through the skylight. The beleaguered *deus ex machina*, Sergeant Match—wearing his

torn leopard-skin dress, and bleeding—clambers down. "We're approaching what our racier novelists term 'the climax,' " says Dr. Rance (a clever pun on the Greek for "ladder").

At the finale, the phallus of Sir Winston Churchill is discovered and unveiled. The comic orgy creates new fertility, and Sergeant Match holds up a symbol of fertility, "a section from a larger than life-sized bronze statue." The penis, symbol of comedy's disruptive freedom and unrelenting sexual mischief, is waved by Match over the proceedings like a magic wand. In what is perhaps the purest expression of the antic spirit in modern theatre, the play conjures a kind of halo around Match, whose leopard-skin dress signifies Dionysus and who clutches in his hand the emblem of polymorphous perversity. "The dying sunlight from the garden and the blaze from above gild Sergeant Match as he holds high the nation's heritage." (Although there was no Lord Chamberlain to censor the play in 1969, Orton's phallic fun was edited out by Sir Ralph Richardson, who turned the missing part of Sir Winston Churchill into a cigar. What was intended as one final outlandish image of triumphant stage anarchy became merely a giggle. The change found its way into the published script, and the phallus was not restored until Lindsay Anderson's production in 1975.)

"Let us put our clothes on and face the world." The play's last command is given by Prentice, the man responsible for getting the characters undressed. The line was reassigned to Sir Ralph Richardson; and so, in the published text, Rance has the last word. But this spoils the symmetry of Orton's farce. Having brought one cover-up to a close, Prentice initiates another by getting Match to agree to keep these "remarkable peccadilloes" out of the paper. "I'm glad you don't despise tradition," Prentice tells Match.

Prentice has learned no moral lesson. Life is returned to "normal," and the cycle of social hypocrisy begins once again. The clothes, which throughout the play are an active part of this social disguise, are once more picked up by the characters. Soon they will impose on each a style and sexual role that farce, as a celebration of formlessness, has momentarily broken down. Clothes are part of the magical invulnerability they all seek, extensions of the psychic armor they will adopt to keep their cravings and confusions hidden from the public and themselves. This yearning to transcend the body and its demands is as brutalizing as it is profound. And the final stage picture makes the contradiction brilliantly clear: "They pick up their clothes and weary, bleeding, drugged and drunk, climb the rope ladder into the blazing light."

IN THE FIRST PRODUCTION of *What the Butler Saw*, which opened post-humously at the Queen's Theatre in London on March 5, 1969, the cage scene was the most confusing moment of an inept production. Where Orton had called for bars over "each window," the West End director, Robert Chetwyn, lowered iron bars like a curtain across the proscenium. The bars had to be cranked down. Instead of descending with a shocking clatter, they creaked (like the rest of the production) into place. H. M. Tennent's all-star cast of Coral Browne, Julia Foster, Stanley Baxter, and Sir Ralph Richardson had to perform the last fifteen minutes of the play separated from the audience by an iron grid. The effect was puzzling and disastrous. At the back of Hutchinson Scott's set was a revolving door leading to the dispensary, inexplicable in a doctor's office. On the side, the all-important second door leading to the hall was almost out of sight-line, and meant that the actors had to make their entrances in profile. Sir Ralph Richardson as Rance handled this problem by not coming through the hall door even when the script called for it. "He came through the swing door," Coral Browne recalls, "which confused an audience and made it seem like he'd come from outer space."

Sir Ralph, an august and lovably eccentric actor, was totally lost in the whirlwind of Orton's language. He had memorized the script, as was his custom, by writing it out on large music sheets, which he put on a music stand. "He learned it in rhythm and turned over each page as if it were a musical score," Coral Browne explains. "Sometimes it was difficult for him to learn because he had no idea of what the words meant. He couldn't get 'nymphomaniac' right because I don't think he'd heard of one of those. He would refer to it as 'nymphromaniac.' When he had one of those long speeches with words like 'transvestite' or 'nymphomaniac,' he was hopelessly at sea. He'd learned the rhythm of Orton but not all the words. And when he'd dry, he'd continue on saying 'Di-da-di-da-di-da-di-da.' Nobody in the audience seemed to take any notice."

Peggy Ramsay was sent to Brighton to assess the production a week before its opening in the West End, and her verdict was depressing. She compared it to the first production of *Loot*, "all prose and face-pulling. . . . The actors aren't enjoying or expanding or feeling any zest in their parts whatsoever; most particularly Sir Ralph. Sir Ralph just seemed quite frozen in Act One. . . . In Act Two, he is much better but then nobody in the cast is enjoying the play, which never flows, and which doesn't seem to have any fun about it. To me it simply struck a chill."

In Brighton, Sir Ralph found himself vociferously attacked for being in the play at all. "There were old ladies in the audience not merely tearing up their programmes, but jumping up and down on them out of sheer hatred," Stanley Baxter, who played Dr. Prentice, remembers. "Even the house manager had to leave town." Richardson answered every one of his letters of complaint by hand. "Ralph got terribly, terribly depressed. He'd turned down the play a few times before finally accepting it, and he thought he'd made a terrible mistake taking part in what he came to regard as a dirty play." Sir Ralph's delivery reflected his apprehension, as Hilary Spurling so aptly observed: "Orton used English as she is actually spoke. But not, of course, as she is spoke at H. M. Tennent's. The discrepancy is most glaring in Sir Ralph Richardson's extraordinary chanting—as though the text had been delivered to him in the form of church responses: a protective mannerism adopted, presumably, on the grounds that any close scrutiny of the meaning of these lines might well reveal disturbing implications."[21]

Orton had discussed with Oscar Lewenstein the choice of Richardson as the manic, sharp-tongued Dr. Rance, and commented:

> I'm not sure. Although I admire Richardson I'd say he was a good ten years too old for the part. And he isn't particularly noted for his comic acting. I'd like Alastair Sim. Oscar wasn't too keen. Both Kenneth and I thought Oscar misguided in suggesting Richardson. But I didn't feel inclined to argue till later.[22]   [July 27, 1967]

Richardson, and the rest of the star-studded cast, added an aura of respectability to Orton. "Watching these actors is like watching cook and nanny—butler too for that matter—floundering with a vague sense of impropriety in what they dimly take to be some nursery naughtiness on the part of the young master," Hilary Spurling wrote. "Their bland, ponderous gamboling is especially bizarre with, in this case, a young master so slippy on his feet, and one whose 'naughtiness' is rather more outrageous than this fond cast envisage. So that, while they appear to feel the whole thing is plainly beneath them, it is also, for the most part, plainly quite beyond them."

While the English muted the text, the Americans mutilated it. They cut the play's central images of death and rebirth: the cage, the blood, the penis, and the rope ladder. Orton destroyed the boulevard safety of farce, only to have the Americans restore it in a campy, sloppy Off Broadway production which the critics characterized as "enchanting," "sunny," "disarming," and "friendly." As is typical of the American commercial theatre, Orton had been devoured without being digested.

The production was a commercial success and an artistic disaster. *What the Butler Saw* was voted Best Foreign Play of the Year in the *Village Voice* "Obie" Awards.

"IT'S NO GOOD making a show of affronting the middle-classes and then being surprised if your enemies retaliate in a nasty way," Orton wrote in March 1967. "That's what enemies do."[23] Two years later, on the opening night of *What the Butler Saw* in the West End, Orton's enemies retaliated. At the beginning of the second act, someone in the gallery screamed at Sir Ralph Richardson: "Give back your knighthood!" Shouts of "Filth!", "Rubbish!", "Find another play!", "Take it off!" bombarded the actors as they struggled bravely through the lines. "At first I thought it was a drunk or someone mentally deranged. Then it became clear that it was militant hate that had been organized. An actor can feel it in his pores," says Stanley Baxter. "It's the first time it ever happened to me. The first time for Sir Ralph, too. It was a battle royal. The anger really came through at the curtain calls. The gallery wanted to jump on the stage and kill us all. The occasion had the exhilaration of a fight. The auditorium was divided. The gods hating us and the rest on our side. But the gods made enough noise to destroy it. We tried to get the good lines in between the barracking. But, of course, the first night audience in that atmosphere got no idea of what the second act was all about."

DEAD PLAYWRIGHT BOOED BY GALLERY bannered *The Sun*. The history of theatre is the history of first nights, and no first night in the sixties was more volcanic than that of *What the Butler Saw*. The production and the premiere were a shambles. Critics mistook the flaws in the production for limitations in the script, and Orton's best work became the most grossly misunderstood and underrated. "The misjudgment of *What the Butler Saw* was truly reprehensible," Charles Marowitz wrote in *Confessions of a Counterfeit Critic*. Harold Hobson, who would later, in *The Sunday Times*, describe *What the Butler Saw* as "a wholly unacceptable exploitation of sexual perversion,"[24] smugly ignored the play in his initial review, using the space instead to portray Orton as the Devil's theatrical henchman. "Gradually," he wrote elsewhere, in *The Christian Science Monitor*, "Orton's terrible obsession with perversion, which is regarded as having brought his life to an end and choked his very high talent, poisons the atmosphere of the play. And what should have been a piece of gaily irresponsible nonsense becomes impregnated with evil."[25] Only Frank Marcus of the *Sunday Telegraph* appreciated Orton's achievement. Under the headline A CLASSIC IS

BORN, he wrote: *"What the Butler Saw* will live to be accepted as a comedy classic of English literature."²⁶ Not until Lindsay Anderson's brilliant revival of *What the Butler Saw* at the Royal Court in 1975 would the play's reputation be firmly established.

"I'D LIKE TO WRITE a play as good as *The Importance of Being Earnest*," Orton had said in 1966, when asked about his "ultimate aims." "I admire Wilde's work but not his life, it was an appalling life. Unlike Wilde, I think you should put your genius into your work, not into your life."²⁷ On stage, monstrous dreams were conquered by climbing out of the chaos. In life, Orton never made it because his genius *did* go into his work, and Halliwell, the man who made it all possible, was neglected.

"How did you kill your wife? In the authorized version," Caulfield asks Pringle in an early draft of *Funeral Games*. Pringle replies, "I hit her with a hammer." Orton had imagined his ending not only in fiction but in life. On June 27, 1967—the day Halliwell first took aim at Orton's head—he had gone to a suburb of Tangier to visit the home of one of his boyfriends:

> The house was lit by oil lamps . . . on the wall there was a telephone and in the second bedroom was an extension. The bedroom with the telephone extension belonged to the brother. . . . Larbi suddenly produced a gun and pointed it at me. I held up my hands. "I kill you," Larbi shouted wildly. We all laughed as he pulled the trigger. I had the feeling that no writer with an eye for the ironic could resist having the playwright of promise falling dead beside the telephone extension.

But later in that afternoon, in the midst of a quarrel with Halliwell, Orton would survive the eery foreshadowing of his death:

> Kenneth anxious to sell his share of the boy said, "Yes, he's very good in bed, and he'll do anything." "How do you know?" I said. "You've asked him to do so little." Kenneth said, "Oh all boys will do anything." "They won't," I said. "There's lots of things they won't do." It was very irritating to be told by someone who likes being masturbated that the boys "will do anything." "You said yourself that he wouldn't take it. It was your excuse for having him in the first place." Kenneth became violently angry shortly after this and attacked me, hitting me about the head and knocking my pen from my hand. . . . I got back to the flat about 9:45. Kenneth

was lying in his bed in a towel dressing gown, looking tight-lipped. I realised that it was no good speaking to him, the "sore" would come sooner or later. I'd just settled down for the night when the door opened and Kenneth entered. I was selfish, I couldn't bear not to be the centre of attention, I was continually sneering at him for only wishing to be masturbated while I was "virile" in fucking boys. "I saw you in Nigel's car," he said, "and I've never seen you at a distance before. I thought what a long-nosed ponce." The holiday had been too perfect. I was determined to spoil it somehow. "And when we get back to London," he said, "we're finished. This is the end!" I had heard this so often. "I wonder you didn't add 'I'm going back to Mother!'" I said wearily. "That's the kind of line which makes your plays ultimately worthless," he said. It went on and on until I put the light out. He slammed the door and went to bed.

SIX WEEKS LATER, Orton was dead.

DOUGLAS ORTON identified his brother; Peggy Ramsay identified Halliwell. "It was extraordinary to see Kenneth," she said. "They do it so exquisitely. Spotlit. He looked like a Roman emperor—relaxed, noble, serene. I looked hard and felt nothing."

"IS THIS THE 2:30 or the 2:45?" asked the attendant, when the first of Orton's funeral party arrived at the West Chapel of Golders Green Crematorium on August 18. Peter Willes arranged the service, and the aura of sanctimonious fiasco that Orton so relished in life went with him to the grave. None of the two dozen mourners stood as the coffin, draped in maroon, was carried into the red brick chapel and down the aisle to the tape-recorded music of The Beatles' "A Day in the Life":

> I read the news today oh boy
> About a lucky man who made the grade . . .

The song was Orton's favorite. But the psychedelic references had been spliced out, and the sound was barely audible. Harold Pinter read Marion Lochhead's "Nox Est Perpetua."[28] Donald Pleasence read his own poem, "Hilarium Memoriam J.O.," which began:

> *Some met together when he died*
> *Not in the name of any god*
> *But in his name*
> *Whom they lost to the coffin,*
> *The box which caused him endless mirth,*
> *His lesson—which he could not read again*
> *Hilarity in death.*

Orton's coffin was propped on a conveyor belt in front of the small bronze crematorium door. It was a surreal scene, made all the more macabre by being totally cosmetic. The door was merely a theatrical exit, since the coffin was removed and cremated elsewhere after the service. At the conclusion of the reading, the conveyor rollers began to turn and Orton's coffin lurched slowly toward the door, which opened by remote control to receive it. The service was over in fifteen minutes. A professionally lugubrious attendant walked across the black and white marble altar floor and opened the doors to the Arcade. There, beside a small iron stand on which a handwritten card read "Floral Tributes for Mr. Joe Orton," seventy wreaths were spread out on the flagstones.

Halliwell had been cremated at Enfield in Middlesex the previous day. Only Peggy Ramsay and three Halliwell relatives attended his funeral. One of them suggested that Halliwell's ashes be mixed with Orton's. Peggy Ramsay asked Douglas Orton. "Well," he said, agreeing, "as long as nobody hears about it in Leicester."

The ashes were mixed and scattered in the Golders Green "Garden of Remembrance." Their deaths confirmed the vision of Orton's comedy, that reality is the ultimate outrage. Their epitaph was Orton's plays: a heritage of laughter created out of a lifetime's hunger for revenge.

NOTES

CHRONOLOGY OF PLAYS AND FILMS

PUBLISHED WORKS BY JOE ORTON

INDEX

NOTES

1 JOKERS ARE WILD

1. See Harold Hobson, *The Christian Science Monitor*, March 19, 1969; Benedict Nightingale, *New Statesman*, July 18, 1975.
2. Peggy Ramsay to Halliwell, September 28, 1966.
3. As quoted in Charles Marowitz, "Entertaining Mr. Orton," *The Guardian*, September 19, 1966.
4. Halliwell to Kathleen O'Brien, August 3, 1950.
5. Diary, March 9, 1966.
6. Halliwell to Peggy Ramsay, May 6, 1967.
7. J. R. Ackerley, *My Father and Myself* (London: Bodley Head, 1968), p. 140.
8. Interview with Alan Brien, BBC Radio, July 14, 1964; transmitted July 28, 1964.
9. "This is a story of an eruption, an explosion, an outburst . . . of inspiration," Orton wrote to Lindsay Anderson in August 1964 in an outline of what would become *The Erpingham Camp*. "A representative group of sturdy, honest English folk, respectably pleasuring themselves at an August Holiday Camp, find themselves subjected to the influence of an intense, demonic leader. Their conventional habits—which anyway are more skin-deep than is generally supposed—are cast aside; they feel liberation; they abandon themselves under the tutelage of Don [Dionysus] to impulse. . . . Propriety, in the person of the dubious Manager of the Camp, rashly attempts to intrude and to veto. But the forces of impulse are too strong; and catastrophe can be the only result. . . ."
10. Although Pentheus, "the man of suffering," persecuted Dionysus, he was also, as his name reveals, doomed from the beginning to Dionysiac suffering. The leopard-skin dress on Sergeant Match is intended to evoke this. Dionysus had a half-female character symbolized by his long robes and almost hermaphroditic body. According to Karl Kerenyi in *The Gods of the Greeks* (London: Thames and Hudson, 1971), pp. 268–9, "When last heard from, Dionysos and his triumphal procession had conquered India—even more exotic animals appearing in his train, which even in earlier times had included great beasts of prey— lions, leopards, panthers—all of them tamed by wine."
11. Diary, July 23, 1967.
12. Nietzsche, *Thus Spake Zarathustra* (London: Penguin Books, 1961), p. 219.
13. Orton, *Head to Toe* (1961) (London: Anthony Blond, 1971), p. 149.
14. Diary, July 12, 1967.

15. Orton, *Funeral Games* and *The Good and Faithful Servant* (London: Methuen, 1970), p. viii.
16. Interview with Giles Gordon, *Transatlantic Review*, no. 24 (Spring 1967), p. 96.
17. Diary, June 28, 1967.
18. "Orton Murder—Hammer Attack Frenzy," *Evening News*, September 4, 1967.
19. Listed as the title of the diaries in the Coroner's Report; but the title page was not returned with the diaries to the Estate after the inquest.

2 SOMEBODY FROM NOWHERE

1. R. B. Pugh, ed., *The Victoria History of the Counties of England* (University of Leicester Institute of Historical Research, 1958), p. 302.
2. Jack Simmons, *Leicester: Past and Present,* Volume 2: *The Modern City, 1860–1974* (London: Eyre Methuen, 1974), p. 138.
3. Interview with Barry Hanson, Royal Court programme for *Crimes of Passion,* June 6–17, 1967.
4. Pugh, ed., *The Victoria History of the Counties of England,* p. 302
5. *Evening Standard,* May 7, 1964.
6. Halliwell to Kathleen O'Brien, August 12, 1950.
7. Diary, December 28, 1966.
8. Adolescent Diary, May 3, 1950.
9. As quoted in Patricia Johnson, "Money and Mr. Orton," *Evening News,* June 9, 1967.
10. Orton to Peggy Ramsay, June 10, 1966.
11. As quoted in the Leicester *Mercury,* June 22, 1964.
12. Adolescent Diary, April 3, 1949.
13. Reprinted in the Leicester *Mercury,* August 10, 1967.
14. Interview with Barry Hanson.
15. Interview with Alan Brien, BBC Radio, July 14, 1964; transmitted July 28, 1964.
16. As quoted in the Leicester *Mercury,* June 4, 1964.
17. Adolescent Diary, February 19, 1950.
18. Adolescent Diary, March 12, 1950.
19. Adolescent Diary, April 2, 1950.
20. Adolescent Diary, April 6, 1950.
21. Adolescent Diary, May 21, 1950.
22. Interview with Barry Hanson.
23. *Ibid.*
24. *Ibid.*
25. Adolescent Diary, July 2, 1950.
26. Adolescent Diary, July 5, 1950.
27. Interview with Barry Hanson.
28. *Ibid.*
29. *Ibid.*
30. *Ibid.*
31. Adolescent Diary, February 23, 1950.

3 UNNATURAL PRACTICES

1. Interview with Giles Gordon, *Transatlantic Review,* no. 24 (Spring 1967), p. 99.
2. *Ibid.,* p. 98.
3. Halliwell's statement to the police, April 28, 1962.

4. Interview with Giles Gordon.
5. As quoted in the Hackney *Gazette*, May 18, 1962.
6. As quoted in the Islington *Gazette*, May 18, 1962.
7. *Ibid.*
8. As quoted in Patricia Johnson, "Money and Mr. Orton," *Evening News*, June 9, 1967.
9. Orton's statement to the police, April 28, 1962.
10. Alexander Connell, "A Successful Prosecution," *Library Association Record*, May 1963, p. 102.
11. Statement of Detective Sergeant Henry Hermitage, G Division, May 2, 1962.
12. Interview with Barry Hanson, Royal Court programme for *Crimes of Passion*, June 6–17, 1976.
13. Rupert Croft-Cooke, *The Caves of Hercules* (London: W. H. Allen, 1974), p. 82.
14. As quoted in the *North London Press*, May 8, 1962.
15. Interview with Barry Hanson.
16. Halliwell to the Cordens, May 21, 1962.
17. Interview with Barry Hanson.
18. Orton to the Cordens, July 29, 1962.
19. Halliwell to the Cordens, September 5, 1962.
20. Orton to the Cordens, July 29, 1962.
21. Halliwell to the Cordens, May 21, 1962.
22. Orton to the Cordens, July 29, 1962.
23. Orton to the Cordens, August 14, 1962.
24. The Cordens were a constant source of amusement, even inspiration, to Orton. In his diary, February 27, 1967, he writes: "Mr. Corden tried to explain to me, on the stairs, how I should fiddle the income tax. 'You want to ring for a taxi. Go to the West End. Note carefully the fare and, when you come home, double it. And if anybody says anything, you swear blind that you came home by taxi when, in reality, you came home by bus. Oh, there are many little fiddles that the ordinary person simply will not take the trouble to learn.' 'That's quite right,' Mrs. Corden called up the stairs, 'Mr. Corden was in accounting.' She climbed the stairs and stood breathless telling me how he was in a firm of accountants. (He was a Commissionaire.)" Orton couldn't resist teasing the Cordens and wrote to them in one letter from prison: "I'm writing to you using the complete works of Shakespeare as a writing block. I'm sure you'll understand."
25. Halliwell attended the Wirral Grammar School from 1937 to 1943. He obtained a School Certificate in 1941 in English Language, English Literature, History, German, Greek, Latin, Mathematics, and Physics. He took his Higher School Certificate in Ancient History (Good), Greek (Pass), and Latin (Pass), with subsidiary German (Pass), in 1942.
26. Halliwell to Kathleen O'Brien, January 3, 1951.
27. *Ibid.*
28. Interview with Barry Hanson.
29. Halliwell to Miss C. Brown, March 12, 1953.
30. Interview with Barry Hanson.
31. Halliwell to Miss C. Brown, June 8, 1953.
32. As quoted in the *Evening Standard*, October 3, 1966.
33. Interview with Barry Hanson.
34. As quoted in "What Prison Did for This Playwright," *Daily Mail*, June 22, 1965.

35. Interview with Barry Hanson.
36. Halliwell to Charles Monteith, September 22, 1959.
37. Halliwell to Charles Monteith, May 22, 1959.
38. Diary, March 25, 1967.
39. Interview with Alan Brien, BBC Radio, July 14, 1964; transmitted July 28, 1964.
40. Interview with Barry Hanson.
41. Charles Monteith to Orton and Halliwell, November 30, 1955.
42. Charles Monteith to Orton and Halliwell, May 27, 1957.
43. Orton to Charles Monteith, June 2, 1957.
44. Halliwell to Charles Monteith, July 15, 1959.
45. As quoted in Paul Radin, *The Trickster* (London: Routledge, Kegan & Paul, 1958), p. 185.
46. Diary, July 27, 1967.
47. Diary, March 13, 1967.
48. Orton to Kenneth Williams, June 6, 1967.
49. As quoted in *The Letters of Oscar Wilde*, edited by Rupert Hart-Davis (London: Hart-Davis, 1962), p. 341.
50. *Daily Telegraph*, May 15, 1964.
51. Interview with Barry Hanson.
52. Orton to Kenneth Williams, April 3, 1966.
53. Diary, March 10, 1967.
54. Diary, January 29, 1967.
55. Orton's statement to the police, April 28, 1962.
56. As quoted in the *Daily Sketch*, November 30, 1966.
57. As quoted in the *Evening Standard*, October 3, 1966.
58. As quoted in the *Leicester Mercury*, June 4, 1964.
59. "The Bitter Bit: Joe Orton Introduces *Entertaining Mr. Sloane*," with Simon Trussler, *Plays and Players*, August 1964.

4 MONSTROUS FUN

1. See Martin Esslin's introduction to *New Radio Drama* (London: BBC, 1966), p. 7.
2. Orton to John Tydeman, November 6, 1963.
3. *Ibid.*
4. Orton to John Tydeman, December 23, 1963.
5. Orton to Peggy Ramsay, May 16, 1966.
6. Interview with Alan Brien, BBC Radio, July 14, 1964; transmitted July 28, 1964.
7. Orton to Glenn Loney, March 12, 1966.
8. Orton to Glenn Loney, March 25, 1966.
9. Diary, July 11, 1966.
10. Harold Pinter to Orton, March 15, 1966. Pinter wrote another long, undated letter explaining his criticism of *Loot*, in which he observes: "*Ruffian, Sloane* (which production I detested) and *Erpingham* (which production I liked) seem to me to preserve a remarkable balance in themselves—they're many-layered shifting things. The great distinction and joy of your best writing is that (within a beautifully organized rhythmic structure) it possesses an inner resonance of shifting references *and* at the same time a sustained sense of dramatic momentum from one sentence to the next. (I don't apologise for that sentence!) . . ."

11. As quoted in James Fox, "The Life and Death of Joe Orton," *The Sunday Times Magazine*, November 22, 1970.

12. Harold Pinter, as quoted in Martin Esslin, *The Peopled Wound* (London: Methuen, 1970), pp. 58–9: "The world is full of surprises. A door can open at any moment and someone will come in. We'd love to know who it is, we'd love to know exactly what he has on his mind and why he comes in, but how often do we know what someone has on his mind or who this somebody is. . . ?" See also the comment on Orton in Kathleen Tynan, "In Search of Harold Pinter," *Evening Standard*, April 26, 1968.

13. Diary, June 24, 1967.

14. Eric Bentley, *The Life of the Drama* (New York: Atheneum, 1964), pp. 219–56.

15. As quoted in the *Radio Times*, August 29, 1964.

16. *The Observer*, September 1964.

17. *The Listener*, September 10, 1964.

18. As quoted in the *Daily Mail*, June 22, 1965.

19. As quoted in Charles Marowitz, "Entertaining Mr. Orton," *The Guardian*, September 19, 1966.

20. *Ibid.*

21. As quoted in Patricia Johnson, "Money and Mr. Orton," *Evening News*, June 9, 1967.

22. In *The Ruffian on the Stair* Wilson haunts Joyce as he himself is haunted. Likewise, Sloane tries to spook Kemp into silence about his previous murder; *Loot* keeps the mother's corpse on stage and her invisible presence feeds the frenzy; and in *What the Butler Saw* Geraldine Barclay is visible but unseen by the others, who hunt for her and even seem like apparitions to each other in the mayhem.

23. Interview with Barry Hanson, Royal Court programme for *Crimes of Passion*, June 6–17, 1967.

24. Including Alan Ayckbourn, Robert Bolt, Edward Bond, Howard Brenton, Christopher Hampton, David Hare, Frank Marcus, David Mercer, John Mortimer, Peter Nichols, Steven Poliakoff, and David Rudkin.

25. *The Times*, September 3, 1970.

26. As quoted in *Harper's and Queen*, May 1973.

27. As quoted in *Plays and Players*, August 1964.

28. Interview with Alan Brien.

29. Diary, February 5, 1967.

30. As quoted in *Plays and Players*, August 1964.

31. John Russell Taylor, *The Second Wave* (London: Methuen, 1971), p. 140.

32. Interview with Alan Brien.

33. Orton to Peggy Ramsay, May 26, 1967.

34. Orton to Peter Gill, May 22, 1967.

35. Interview with Alan Brien.

36. Orton to Alan Schneider, September 14, 1965.

37. As quoted in Peter Burton, "I'm Not a Political Animal Says Joe Orton," *The Stage*, October 6, 1966.

38. Bernard Levin, *The Pendulum Years* (London: Cape, 1970), p. 49.

39. Interview with Giles Gordon, *Transatlantic Review*, no. 24 (Spring 1967).

40. H. Montgomery Hyde, *The Other Love* (London: Heinemann, 1970), p. 252.

41. As quoted in *Plays and Players*, August 1964.

42. *Ibid.*
43. *Ibid.*
44. Interview with Barry Hanson.
45. Orton to Michael Codron, undated (1964).
46. Orton to Alan Schneider, production note.
47. As quoted in *Plays and Players*, August 1964.
48. Orton to Peggy Ramsay, November 16, 1965.
49. *Daily Telegraph*, May 7, 1964.
50. As quoted in Glenn Loney, "What Joe Orton Saw," *After Dark*, September 1970.
51. Orton to Glenn Loney, March 25, 1966.
52. Orton to Peggy Ramsay, October 17, 1964.
53. Interview with Giles Gordon.
54. Orton to Glenn Loney, October 10, 1965.
55. Interview with Barry Hanson. For another vitriolic response to *Entertaining Mr. Sloane* and Orton, see Pamela Hansford Johnson's *On Iniquity* (London: Macmillan, 1967), in which Orton is named along with Edward Bond, John Whiting, and David Rudkin as a corrupting force in society; and her parody of the play's plot in her novel *Cork Street, Next to the Hatters* (London: Macmillan, 1965).
56. Hilary Spurling, "Early Death," *Spectator*, August 18, 1967.
57. Orton to Peggy Ramsay, September 27, 1965.
58. *Ibid.*
59. *Ibid.*
60. Orton to Michael Codron, undated (October 1965).
61. Orton to Halliwell, October 9, 1965.
62. Orton to Halliwell, October 2, 1965.
63. *Ibid.*
64. Orton to Halliwell, October 9, 1965.
65. *The New York Times*, October 13, 1965.
66. Orton to Glenn Loney, October 26, 1965.
67. Orton to Joy Small, November 4, 1965.
68. Interview with Alan Brien.
69. *Ibid.*
70. Orton to Glenn Loney, March 25, 1966.

5 SCANDALOUS SURVIVAL

1. As quoted in "Farcical Tragedy," *Southern Weekly News and Brighton Gazette*, February 5, 1965.
2. As quoted in Simon Trussler, "Farce," *Plays and Players*, June 1966.
3. W. H. Auden, *The Dyer's Hand and Other Essays* (London: Faber & Faber, 1963), p. 158.
4. As quoted in *Plays and Players*, June 1966.
5. Alexander and Margarette Mitscherlich, *The Inability to Mourn* (New York: Grove Press, 1975), p. 91.
6. Interview with Giles Gordon, *Transatlantic Review*, no. 24 (Spring 1967).
7. As quoted in *Plays and Players*, June 1966.
8. Geoffrey Gorer, *Death, Grief and Mourning in Great Britain* (London: Cresset Press, 1965), pp. 169–75.
9. As quoted in *The Stage*, October 6, 1966.

10. Auden, *The Dyer's Hand*, p. 154.
11. As quoted in *The Times*, October 7, 1964.
12. *The Times*, November 12, 1964.
13. As quoted in Charles Marowitz, "Entertaining Mr. Orton," *The Guardian*, September 19, 1966.
14. Interview with Barry Hanson, Royal Court programme for *Crimes of Passion*, June 6–17, 1967.
15. Orton to Halliwell, undated (February 1965).
16. "Farcical Tragedy."
17. Orton to Michael White, July 14, 1967.
18. *Ibid.*
19. Interview with Giles Gordon.
20. Orton to Halliwell, undated (February 1965).
21. As quoted in the Manchester *Evening News*, March 13, 1965.
22. Orton to Halliwell, February 19, 1965.
23. Orton to Michael White, July 14, 1967.
24. As quoted in "Joy Through Strength," *The Observer*, March 28, 1965.
25. Michael Codron to Peggy Ramsay, March 8, 1965.
26. Interview with Barry Hanson.
27. Orton to Glenn Loney, March 25, 1966.
28. *Ibid.*
29. Peggy Ramsay to Orton, undated (July 1965).
30. Orton to Glenn Loney, March 25, 1966.
31. Orton to Michael White, July 14, 1967.
32. *Daily Telegraph*, April 12, 1966.
33. Orton to Michael White, April 11, 1966.
34. Orton to Oscar Lewenstein, undated (July 1966).
35. Charles Marowitz, *Confessions of a Counterfeit Critic* (London: Eyre Methuen, 1973), p. 157.
36. Orton to Michael White, July 14, 1967.
37. Charles Marowitz, "Farewell, Joe Orton," *The New York Times*, April 7, 1968.
38. Orton to Michael White, July 14, 1967.
39. As quoted in the *Evening Standard*, January 12, 1967.
40. Orton to Peggy Ramsay, May 28, 1967.
41. Diary, January 4, 1967.
42. Diary, March 11, 1967.
43. As quoted in the Leicester *Mercury*, March 2, 1967.
44. Diary, February 24, 1967.
45. *The Observer*, October 2, 1966.

6 THE FREAKS' ROLL CALL

1. Albert Camus, *The Rebel* (1951) (London: Hamish Hamilton, 1953; Penguin Books, 1962), p. 62.
2. Interview with Barry Hanson, Royal Court programme for *Crimes of Passion*, June 6–17, 1967.
3. Eric Bentley, *The Life of the Drama* (New York: Atheneum, 1964), p. 252.
4. Interview with Barry Hanson.
5. Leonie Orton Barnett to Orton, March 31, 1967.
6. Orton to Glenn Loney, undated (1967).

7. Diary, March 25, 1967.

8. Diary, January 15, 1967.

9. Orton to Oscar Lewenstein, production note, undated (1967).

10. Diary, February 23, 1967.

11. Diary, February 24, 1967.

12. Oscar Lewenstein to Richard Lester, May 10, 1967.

13. Orton to Kenneth Williams, March 4, 1967.

14. Diary, March 4, 1967.

15. *Ibid.*

16. Diary, March 31, 1967.

17. Diary, April 9, 1967.

18. R. D. Laing, *The Divided Self* (London: Tavistock Publications, 1960; Penguin Books, 1965), p. 139.

19. Interview with Giles Gordon, *Transatlantic Review*, no. 24 (Spring 1967).

20. Bentley, *The Life of the Drama*, p. 250. Orton wrote in his diary on March 18, 1967: "Long walk through Regents Park. . . . Sat in the blazing light and noticed how hideous the bright sunshine made everyone (including myself) appear. Like blanched and unsavoury apes."

21. Hilary Spurling, "The Young Master," *Spectator*, March 14, 1969.

22. Lewenstein contradicts the diary entry. "Joe suggested two people for Dr. Rance —one of them was Richardson and the other was Alastair Sim. I remember Joe telling me how he had seen Richardson in I think it was "Blandings Castle," a series on TV, and how much he admired him in it. He may have had second thoughts but he didn't tell me. Clearly I would not have allowed someone to be cast that I knew he did not approve."

23. Diary, March 11, 1967.

24. *The Sunday Times,* July 20, 1975.

25. *The Christian Science Monitor,* March 19, 1969.

26. *Sunday Telegraph,* March 9, 1969.

27. As quoted in the *Evening Standard,* January 12, 1967.

28. "Nox Est Perpetua" by Marion Lochhead:

> *Perpetual night and endless sleep*
> *Will us, and all our loving, keep.*
> *The roman poet, long ago,*
> *Saw all light end in shadow, so.*
>
> *A little light, a fragile flame*
> *Before the quenching darkness came.*
> *In endless night love, scorched by hate,*
> *Must lie, not stir of dawn to wait.*
>
> *Perpetual night and endless sleep*
> *May these not long for, who must keep*
> *A weary vigil, wakeful lie*
> *To watch themselves and others die.*

CHRONOLOGY OF PLAYS AND FILMS

PLAYS

The Ruffian on the Stair (1963)

   London. First broadcast on the BBC Third Programme, August 31, 1964; directed by John Tydeman. First stage production without decor by the English Stage Company at the Royal Court Theatre on August 21, 1966; directed by Peter Gill. First staged with *The Erpingham Camp* as *Crimes of Passion* by the English Stage Company at the Royal Court Theatre, June 6–17, 1967; directed by Peter Gill, designed by Deirdre Clancy.

   New York. First presented at the Columbia University School of the Arts, 1968–9; directed by William Garry. Produced with *The Erpingham Camp* as *Crimes of Passion* by Henry Fownes, Frank Bessell, Bruce Hoover, Leonard Mulhern, and George Thorn at the Astor Place Theatre, October 26, 1969; directed by Michael Kahn, designed by William Ritman.

Entertaining Mr. Sloane (1963)

   London. Produced by Michael Codron and Donald Albery at the New Arts Theatre Club, May 6, 1964. Transferred to Wyndham's Theatre, June 29, 1964, and to Queen's Theatre, October 5, 1964; directed by Patrick Dromgoole, designed by Timothy O'Brien.

   Germany. Première at the Deutsches Schauspielhaus in the Theater im-Zimmer, Hamburg, November 2, 1964; directed by Hans Lietzau, designed by Karl Groning.

   New York. Produced by Slade Brown, Tanya Chasman, and E. A. Gilbert at the Lyceum Theatre, October 12, 1965; directed by Alan Schneider, designed by William Ritman.

The Good and Faithful Servant (1964)

   London. First produced by Rediffusion Television on April 6, 1967; directed by James Ormerod. First staged at the King's Head, Islington, March 17–28, 1971; directed by Frederick Proud.

Loot (1964–6)

    London. Produced by Michael Codron and Donald Albery. First presented at the Arts Theatre, Cambridge, February 1, 1965; directed by Peter Wood, designed by Desmond Heeley. Closed in Wimbledon March 20, 1965. Produced at the University Theatre, Manchester, April 11–23, 1965; directed by Braham Murray. Finally produced by Oscar Lewenstein and Michael White with the London Traverse Theatre Company at the Jeanetta Cochrane Theatre, September 27, 1966; directed by Charles Marowitz, designed by Tony Carruthers. Transferred to the Criterion Theatre, November 1, 1966.

    Germany. Premiered at the Deutsches Schauspielhaus in the Theatersaal de Unileverhauses, Hamburg, February 15, 1966; directed by Hansgunther Heyme.

    New York. Produced by Losal Productions, Inc.; by arrangement with Oscar Lewenstein and Michael White, at the Biltmore Theatre, March 18, 1968; directed by Derek Goldby, designed by William Ritman.

The Erpingham Camp (1965)

    London. Produced (in an early version) by Rediffusion Television, June 27, 1966; directed by James Ormerod. First staged with *The Ruffian on the Stair* as *Crimes of Passion* by the English Stage Company at the Royal Court Theatre, June 6–17, 1967; directed by Peter Gill, designed by Deirdre Clancy.

    New York. Produced with *The Ruffian on the Stair* as *Crimes of Passion* by Henry Fownes, Frank Bessell, Bruce Hoover, Leonard Mulhern, and George Thorn at the Astor Place Theatre, October 26, 1969; directed by Michael Kahn, designed by William Ritman.

Funeral Games (1966)

    London. First presented by Yorkshire Television on August 25, 1968; directed by James Ormerod.

What the Butler Saw (1967)

    London. Produced by Lewenstein-Delfont Productions Ltd. and H. M. Tennent Ltd. at the Queen's Theatre, March 5, 1969; directed by Robert Chetwyn, designed by Hutchinson Scott.

    New York. Produced by Charles Woodward and Michael Kasdan at the McAlpin Rooftop Theatre, May 4, 1970; directed by Joseph Hardy, designed by William Ritman.

FILMS

Entertaining Mr. Sloane. Directed by Douglas Hickox; screenplay by Clive Exton. Starring Beryl Reid, Harry Andrews, Peter McEnery, Alan Webb. Produced by Douglas Kentish. Distributed by EMI (1969).

Loot. Directed by Silvio Narizzano; screenplay by Alan Simpson and Ray Galton. Starring Richard Attenborough, Lee Remick, Hywel Bennett, Milo O'Shea. An Arthur Lewis Production for British Lion (1970).

PUBLISHED WORKS
BY JOE ORTON

The Ruffian on the Stair (radio version) in *New Radio Drama:* London, BBC, 1966.

Entertaining Mr. Sloane: London, Hamish Hamilton, 1964; New York, Grove Press, 1964. New edition (with introduction by John Lahr), Eyre Methuen, 1973.

Loot: London, Methuen, 1967; New York, Grove Press, 1967.

Crimes of Passion (containing the revised *The Ruffian on the Stair* and *The Erpingham Camp,* as well as author's notes on changes for the Lord Chamberlain): London, Methuen, 1967.

Funeral Games and *The Good and Faithful Servant* (with an introduction by Peter Willes) : London, Methuen, 1970.

Until She Screams (sketch for *Oh! Calcutta!*): New York, *Evergreen,* no. 78 (May 1970).

What the Butler Saw (with an introductory essay by John Lahr): New York, Grove Press, 1970; London, Methuen, 1969.

Head to Toe: London, Anthony Blond, 1971; Panther paperback edition, 1971.

Orton: The Complete Plays (with an introductory essay by John Lahr): London, Eyre Methuen, 1976; New York, Grove Press, 1977.

INDEX

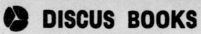

DISCUS BOOKS

DISTINGUISHED NON-FICTION

THEATER, FILM AND TELEVISION

ACTORS TALK ABOUT ACTING Lewis Funke and John Booth, Eds.	15062	1.95
ANTONIN ARTAUD Bettina L. Knapp	12062	1.65
A BOOK ON THE OPEN THEATER Robert Pasoli	12047	1.65
THE CONCISE ENCYCLOPEDIC GUIDE TO SHAKESPEARE Michael Martin and Richard Harrier, Eds.	16832	2.65
THE DISNEY VERSION Richard Schnickel	08953	1.25
EDWARD ALBEE: A PLAYWRIGHT IN PROTEST Michael E. Rutenberg	11916	1.65
THE EMPTY SPACE Peter Brook	32763	1.95
EXPERIMENTAL THEATER James Roose-Evans	11981	1.65
FOUR CENTURIES OF SHAKESPEARIAN CRITICISM Frank Kermode, Ed.	20131	1.95
GUERILLA STREET THEATRE Henry Lesnick, Ed.	15198	2.45
THE HOLLYWOOD SCREENWRITERS Richard Corliss	12450	1.95
IN SEARCH OF LIGHT: THE BROADCASTS OF **EDWARD R. MURROW** Edward Bliss, Ed.	19372	1.95
INTERVIEWS WITH FILM DIRECTORS Andrew Sarris	21568	1.95
MOVIES FOR KIDS Edith Zornow and Ruth Goldstein	17012	1.65
PICTURE Lillian Ross	08839	1.25
THE LIVING THEATRE Pierre Biner	17640	1.65
PUBLIC DOMAIN Richard Schechner	12104	1.65
RADICAL THEATRE NOTEBOOK Arthur Sainer	22442	2.65
SOMETHING WONDERFUL RIGHT AWAY Jeffrey Sweet	37119	2.95
TO DANCE Valery Panov	47233	3.95

GENERAL NON-FICTION

ADDING A DIMENSION Isaac Asimov	36871	1.50
A TESTAMENT Frank Lloyd Wright	12039	1.65
AMBIGUOUS AFRICA Georges Balandier	25288	2.25
THE AMERICAN CHALLENGE J. J. Servan Schreiber	11965	1.65
AMERICA THE RAPED Gene Marine	09373	1.25
ARE YOU RUNNING WITH ME, JESUS? Malcolm Boyd	09993	1.25
THE AWAKENING OF INTELLIGENCE J. Krishnamurti	45674	3.50
THE BIOGRAPHY OF ALICE B. TOKLAS Linda Simon	39073	2.95
THE BOOK OF IMAGINARY BEINGS Jorge Luis Borges	11080	1.45
BUILDING THE EARTH Pierre de Chardin	08938	1.25
CHEYENNE AUTUMN Mari Sandoz	39255	2.25
THE CHILD IN THE FAMILY Maria Montessori	28118	1.50
THE CHILDREN'S REPUBLIC Edward Mobius	21337	1.50
CHINA: SCIENCE WALKS ON TWO LEGS Science for the People	20123	1.75
CLASSICS REVISITED Kenneth Rexroth	08920	1.25

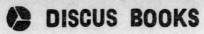

DISCUS BOOKS

DISTINGUISHED NON-FICTION

DISCUS BOOKS

DISTINGUISHED NON-FICTION

MOZART Marcia Davenport	45534	3.50
NATURE OF POLITICS M. Curtis	12401	1.95
THE NEW GROUP THERAPIES Hendrick M. Ruitenbeek	27995	1.95
NOTES OF A PROCESSED BROTHER Donald Reeves	14175	1.95
OF TIME AND SPACE AND OTHER THINGS Isaac Asimov	24166	1.50
DELMORE SCHWARTZ James Atlas	41038	2.95
THE RISE AND FALL OF LIN PIAO Japp Van Ginneken	32656	2.50
POLITICS AND THE NOVEL Irving Howe	11932	1.65
THE POWER TACTICS OF JESUS CHRIST AND OTHER ESSAYS Jay Haley	11924	1.65
PRICK UP YOUR EARS John Lahr	48629	3.50
PRISONERS OF PSYCHIATRY Bruce Ennis	19299	1.65
THE LIFE OF EZRA POUND Noel Stock	20909	2.65
THE QUIET CRISIS Stewart Udall	24406	1.75
RADICAL SOAP OPERA David Zane Mairowitz	28308	2.45
THE ROMAN WAY Edith Hamilton	33993	1.95
SHAHHAT: AN EGYPTIAN Richard Critchfield	48405	3.50
SHOULD TREES HAVE STANDING? Christopher Stone	25569	1.50
STUDIES ON HYSTERIA Freud and Breuer	16923	1.95
THE TALES OF RABBI NACHMAN Martin Buber	11106	1.45
TERROR OUT OF ZION J. Bowyer Bell	39396	2.95
THINKING ABOUT THE UNTHINKABLE Herman Kahn	12013	1.65
THINKING IS CHILD'S PLAY Evelyn Sharp	29611	1.75
THOMAS WOODROW WILSON Freud and Bullitt	08680	1.25
THREE NEGRO CLASSICS Introduction by John Hope Franklin	49452	2.75
THREE ESSAYS ON THE THEORY OF SEXUALITY Sigmund Freud	29116	1.95
TOO STRONG FOR FANTASY Marcia Davenport	45195	3.50
TOWARDS A VISUAL CULTURE Caleb Gattegno	11940	1.65
THE WAR BUSINESS George Thayer	09308	1.25
WHEN THIS YOU SEE, REMEMBER ME: GERTRUDE STEIN IN PERSON W. G. Rogers	15610	1.65
WILHELM REICH: A PERSONAL BIOGRAPHY I. O. Reich	12138	1.65
WOMEN'S ROLE IN CONTEMPORARY SOCIETY	12641	2.45
WRITERS ON THE LEFT Daniel Aaron	12187	1.65